Penguin Books
Everest South West Face

Christian Bonington was born in London in 1934. 'Since 1962,' he writes, 'I have devoted my life to adventure and mountaineering as a freelance writer, photographer and lecturer.' He has a remarkable number of mountaineering achievements to his name, including the first ascent of the Old Man of Hoy and the Central Pillar of Frêney, Mont Blanc, the first ascents of Annapurna II (26,041 ft), Nuptse in Nepal (25,850 ft), and the Central Tower of Paine in South Patagonia. He was leader of the successful first ascent of the South West Face of Everest in 1975 and his book *Everest: the Hard Way* is an account of this expedition. He is also the author of *I Chose to Climb* and *Annapurna South Face*.

Chris Bonington is married, with two children, and lives in Cheshire. He was awarded the C.B.E. in 1976.

D0809876

Chris Bonington

EVEREST
SOUTH WEST
FACE

Penguin Books

Penguin Books Ltd, Harmondsworth,
Middlesex, England
Penguin Books, 625 Madison Avenue, New York,
New York 10022, U.S.A.
Penguin Books Australia Ltd, Ringwood,
Victoria, Australia
Penguin Books Canada Ltd, 2801 John Street,
Markham, Ontario, Canada L3R 1B4
Penguin Books (N.Z.) Ltd, 182–190 Wairau Road,
Auckland 10, New Zealand

First published in Great Britain by Hodder and Stoughton 1973

First published in the United States with the title *The
Ultimate Challenge: The Hardest Way up the Highest
Mountain in the World* by Stein and Day/Publishers 1973

Published in Penguin Books 1975
Reprinted 1976, 1977
Copyright © Christian Bonington, 1973
All rights reserved

Made and printed in Great Britain by
Hazell Watson & Viney Ltd, Aylesbury, Bucks
Set in Linotype Juliana

In memory of TONY TIGHE

CONTENTS

ILLUSTRATIONS

PLATES

ACKNOWLEDGEMENTS

Doug Scott: Plates 6, 7, 9–12, 14, 15
Chris Bonington: Plates 1–5, 8
Nick Estcourt: Plate 13

LINE DRAWINGS

FOREWORD

by Lord Hunt of Llanvair Waterdine, C.B.E., D.S.O.

It is a truism that success can be perceived in different ways. Some achievements in the field of adventure have, unfortunately, been marred by the controversies to which they have given rise, either during or after the event; conversely, there have been great enterprises where the goal has not been reached but which, nevertheless, have captured the public imagination and been acclaimed as triumphs.

Scott's journey in 1912–13, failing in its purpose to be the first to reach the South Pole, failing in the struggle to return, is one such example. The disappearance of Mallory and Irving not far below the summit of Everest in 1924, is another. There is no doubt that tragedy or injury enhances the impact of such adventures in the public mind; the French first ascent of Annapurna, successful in the evident sense of reaching its objective, was the more sensational for the suffering through frostbite of Herzog and Lachenal on their way down the mountain. Other examples can be found in pioneering journeys on the oceans or in the air. Heroism and tragedy inherent in these stories have so fired the minds of people everywhere that they have lived on to inspire succeeding generations.

Bonington's story is of a different order. Here was a team of Britishers and Sherpas who were forced to a halt on the great South West Face of Everest by winter, cold and wind and who returned unscathed to tell the tale. True, tragedy did occur in the Khumbu Ice Fall, but this sad episode falls outside the context of the Expedition itself.

Many mountaineers can match the sentiments of Chris Bonington and his team mates, which he expressed to me in a letter, written doubtless in circumstances of extreme duress, from Camp 4 at 24,600 feet:

By the time you get this you will know whether we have succeeded or failed. Being realistic I think the latter in strictly material terms is the most likely, but in terms of effort, human relationship and self-sacrifice I feel our attempt on the South West Face has been well worth while . . .
I don't think anyone has succeeded in contending with the elements over such a period of time, at such altitude, on previous expeditions . . . We're still in good spirits, whatever the outcome.

I was much moved by this letter, both for the simple ring of sincerity it contains and because it evoked similar feelings which I have experienced on turning back after nearly reaching the top of a high mountain.

But what I find intriguing, and heartening, is that the accolade of achievement should have been accorded spontaneously to this group of splendid young men, by a wider public without comparable experience. It is greatly to the credit of the news media that the story should have been portrayed in such a way as to enable people to discern and accept a truer meaning to success than that of reaching the top of the world by the most difficult way. The combination of individual skill, courage and endurance with the cohesion which enabled this party to strive in unity and harmony against all the odds, only to prove the impossible, has come loud and clear through television, sound radio and newspaper reporting of the 1972 Everest expedition.

But it is in no sense to underrate the quality of the various news media to suggest that only through the genuine account of someone who lived through those testing weeks high on the mountain face last winter, can the listener or reader gauge the true measure of these men. No one who has experienced the appalling conditions prevailing at high altitude in the Himalayan winter can doubt that Bonington's team was stopped in their tracks at the ultimate limit of human achievement imposed, for the time being, by natural forces.

In a world as conditioned as our western civilization by material values, sporting records and tangible rewards, it is good to be made aware that more important than all these things is the spirit which moves individual people and the strength of moving together.

This is one of the great stories of our time.

18 March 1973   JOHN HUNT

THE GRENADIERS
OF NEPAL

Some talk of Walt Bonatti, of Dougal and of Don,
of Smith and Joe or Patey, and even Bonington,
They are the game's great hard men, the short ones and the tall,
but I could write screeds on the heroic deeds of the Sherpas of Nepal.

Up in the Sola Khumbu, south west of Everest,
there lives a brand of hillman, the strongest and the best.
I've climbed with famous Tigers and many a budding star,
but they're not as tough, made from the same stuff, as the man from
    Namche Bazar.

You think you are a hard man, as strong as strong could be,
you'll carry more than he can, but listen here to me,
he'll take your load twice over and when he sees you drop,
he'll pick up you and your rucksac too and go till you're both at the
    top.

You've risked your life there's no doubt, on an overhanging wall,
but have you tried your axe out on a great big bad ice-fall?
You'll take a chance a few times making sure the route goes through,
but certainly not fifty days on the trot like the Sherpas have to do.

You think maybe you're special, maybe you're just naïve,
for at a certain threshold you'll find it difficult to breathe,
So now you're sucking oxygen, what's so special about that?
I know a man won't take air from a can, he's from the village of Ghat.

Some talk of Ed or Tilman, I couldn't name the lot,
there's many a great hillman whose name I have forgot,
But of all the unsung heroes who's the bravest of them all?
I've tried to explain, but I'll say it again – the Sherpas of Nepal.

DAVE BATHGATE

1

BEGINNINGS

The gully stretched endlessly in front of me; six steps, a rest, breathless in the snow – then another six steps. Aware of Ang Pema just behind me, determined not to let him overtake, not to weaken, I looked up and the top seemed to get no closer; concentrated on the snow in front of my nose. Ten steps this time; I succeeded in making eight, and then lay panting against the snow. My heart was beating so hard that I thought it would burst; time and distance slipped by slowly. The top was just above – just ten, slow steps – and suddenly, after two months' effort, with the same magnificent view, a new world opened out before me. It was 1961 and I was on Nuptse, the third peak of Everest. We had been climbing its South Face, and this day was our fulfilment – we were going for the summit.

My first impression was one of boundless space, of a sea of brown, rolling hills flecked by the occasional snow-cap, reaching to a distant horizon. There was no haze, each distant undulation was etched sharp in the cold, thin air. In a way this view is even more striking than that of Everest, just the other side of the deep gorge described by the Western Cwm. Its summit is a mere three thousand feet above where we were standing that day – less than the height of Snowdon – a squat, black pyramid, veined with snow and ice, towering above the void of the Western Cwm. And we turned right, Ang Pema and I, to follow the ridge of Nuptse to its highest point, 25,850 feet. The summit, a corniced snow-cap, left just enough room to sit down. I collapsed, thankful that our own struggle was over, uncomfortably aware that I had reached my own limit, that those extra three thousand feet to the summit of

Everest would be beyond my capabilities without the use of oxygen.

From the summit of Nuptse we had a unique view of the South West Face of Everest, but that day I'm afraid I cannot claim to have formed an immediate ambition to tackle it. We had been too close to our limits on this 25,850-foot mountain to entertain thoughts of technical climbing at even greater heights. In 1961 we weren't ready for the South West Face of Everest. And so we turned away from the summit of Nuptse and, strangely, the memory that clung in my mind was not that of the squat pyramid of Everest but of those boundless arid hills of the Tibetan plateau which seemed to stretch for ever to the very edge of the world.

Everest, however, exerted its own special magnetism on others, even after it had been climbed by John Hunt's party in 1953. The Swiss, who had made two valiant attempts in the spring of 1952 and the autumn of 1953, returned in 1955, both to repeat the South Col route up Everest and make the first ascent of Lhotse. The Indians and the Chinese attempted the mountain in 1960; the Indians admitted failure in the face of high winds, whilst the Chinese claimed success on the pre-war North Face route. The Indians made a further attempt in 1962 but were once again defeated. Then in 1963 came the massive American Everest expedition, with a budget of $405,263, and twenty team members. They repeated the South Col route, and then Tom Hornbein and Willi Unsoeld, in what was almost a mini expedition within the expedition, climbed the West Ridge to traverse the mountain and come back down by the South Col.

This was an outstanding achievement since they made their build-up with a comparatively small group of Sherpas and support climbers, and had a top camp at only 27,250 feet, giving them a long and arduous summit-push, up completely unknown ground. It was unlikely that they could have retreated back down it, had they failed to make the summit. In 1965 the Indians returned once more and this time were luckier with the weather, putting no less than nine climbers on the summit by the South Col route. It was around this time that climbers began to think of the South West Face of Everest. It was an obvious challenge – the highest face on the highest mountain in the world.

Though at this stage big wall climbing in the Himalayas had barely started, the South Face of Nuptse was probably the biggest and most difficult face that had been climbed up to this point in time. Most of the difficulties were concentrated in its lower parts, on an ice ridge that pierced the lower defences of the wall, reaching a height of approximately 21,000 feet. Above this, the Face opened out into a series of snow arêtes, slopes and gullies that led to the summit. We had used about 8,000 feet of fixed rope, but nowhere had the angle been steep enough to necessitate Jumars – which was just as well, for in those days we had never even heard of them. On the one short vertical rock section, we had made a rough rope ladder.

The first time I had heard the South West Face of Everest mentioned as a possible objective was in the summer of 1965. I was climbing with John Harlin, the American climber who swept through the European climbing scene in the early sixties. He was one of the most colourful and controversial figures of the post-war years. With the physique of a Tarzan, far-flying ambition and imagination, an overpowering personality and tremendous determination as a climber, in the course of a few years he put up several routes that represented a definite step forward in Alpine techniques. In effect, he was bringing to Europe the climbing techniques developed on the sheer granite walls of Yosemite by a small group of Californian climbers and then adapting them to Alpine conditions. We were planning to tackle the Eiger Direct that summer, and did a number of training climbs together. John was always full of far-fetched schemes, some of which remained castles in the air, but others surprisingly came off. At one stage we were planning a two-man assault on a series of peaks down the line of the Rockies and Andes, using a light plane to get from climbing area to climbing area. The project was to last eighteen months, and would have included a dozen first ascents. He also talked of the South West Face of Everest, dreaming of an international expedition. We never got further than dreams, however, and neither of us got down to any detailed planning, or even had any real concept of just what such a project could entail.

I backed out of the Eiger Direct project that autumn, worried about the prospects of a winter attempt on the Face, of which I, personally, had no experience. I was also dubious about the practicality of John's plans. At this stage he wanted to make an Alpine-style single push up the wall, without using any fixed ropes. This was something that I felt was probably impractical under winter conditions.

Anyway I came back into the climb on a more professional level when I was asked to go out as photographer for the *Daily Telegraph Magazine*. Becoming more involved in the actual climbing than I had originally intended, I ended going about three-quarters of the way up the Face. The climb changed from a *blitzkrieg* push to a drawn-out siege, using fixed ropes, and snow-holes for camps. In fact, the climbing was very similar to Himalayan climbing, without the problems of altitude, but with cold that was probably more extreme than in the Himalayas and technical difficulty that was considerably greater.

It was on the Eiger Direct that I came to know Dougal Haston; we'd met in passing in Chamonix and Leysin, but somehow both of us had been reserved, regarding each other, no doubt, as potential competitors. On the Eiger Direct, however, we spent a certain amount of time together, sharing snow-holes and doing some climbing on the Face. Dougal is single-minded and even then knew exactly what he wanted to do in life – to climb to the limit – and knowing this, he was very easy to work and climb with. There was no manoeuvring for position on a climb to get the best pitch, or to avoid some of the harder or more dangerous work. He just took everything as it came.

Tragically, John Harlin was killed in the final stages of the climb; we had lost a good friend and mountaineering lost one of its most colourful and imaginative innovators. Had he lived, he would undoubtedly have gone on to many other exploits, one of which could have been the South West Face of Everest.

But he had kindled an interest in Dougal and myself. We both got frostbite on the final day of the climb, Dougal fighting his way out of the Wall in a storm, and myself sitting on the summit waiting for him to arrive.

We spent a few weeks in the London Hospital under the care of Mike Ward, who was doctor on the 1953 Everest expedition and has become an expert in mountain illnesses and injuries. Part of our treatment was to be immured in a hyperbaric oxygen-tank for hours on end. This entailed being shut into a cylinder shaped like a space capsule, into which was pumped pure oxygen. You couldn't take anything into the cylinder with you because of the danger of static electricity igniting skin or clothing and sending you up in a puff of smoke, and so you just lay there for hours on end. The thoughts of both of us turned to Everest – but at this time neither of us had any experience of large scale organizing. I had been on two Himalayan expeditions, to Annapurna II and Nuptse, but at this stage taking on the overall responsibility of leading an expedition was too much for me. I just could not see myself in this role. And so we needed a leader, and who better than Mike Ward. He had been to Everest, had the right contacts with the mountaineering establishment and yet seemed forward-looking and modern in his approach. We asked him whether he would like to lead such an expedition and he expressed interest – but there were other problems. The Nepalese Government had just banned mountaineering in Nepal. This was mainly due to the increased tension on the Nepalese–Tibetan frontier created by the Indo–Chinese war. The fact that there was no immediate chance of going to Everest and, even more I suspect, the fact that none of us at this stage was fully committed to the idea of organizing such an expedition, meant that it simply faded away, one of those projects that never really got off the ground.

But others were thinking of Everest's South West Face in a much more determined way. The Japanese were planning to go to Everest at the first available opportunity, to attempt the Face. They already had a great deal of experience in the Himalayas; in most years the number of Japanese expeditions to Nepal is equal to the sum of all the other expeditions from different nations. In addition, an increasing number of Japanese climbers had been coming to Europe to extend their knowledge and experience of high-standard technical climbing.

2

THE JAPANESE
EVEREST
EXPEDITION

1969–70

Nepal opened its frontiers to climbers once again in 1969, and that very same spring, a small Japanese team went to Everest to make a reconnaissance of the South West Face. The party included Naomi Uemura who was to be involved in the subsequent international expedition. They climbed the Ice Fall, taking ten days to do it, and had a close look at the Face to reassure themselves that it was feasible. The following autumn they came out with a larger party to make a reconnaissance in force. This time the party numbered twelve, led by H. Mihashita, and once again Uemura was a member. Their aims were to get as high as possible on the Face, and to gain experience of altitude for a full-scale attempt in the spring of 1970. The team gathered at Lukla, the air strip four days' march from Everest, on 4 September, having been flown in by chartered plane. They established Base Camp on 16 September, and by 28 September had climbed the Ice Fall and established Camp 2 at the foot of the Face. It took them a further fortnight, until 15 October, to establish Camp 3, just below a rock buttress on the lower slopes of the South West Face, at a height of 23,000 feet. The Face had a good covering of snow, and they were not unduly troubled by wind. They succeeded in establishing Camp 4 in the middle of the gully at a height of 24,600 feet, where there was just enough snow to carve out platforms for their tents. However, they determined to bring out alloy platforms for their spring attempt. Above Camp 4, the great Central Gully runs up towards the Rock Band, dividing after about 800 feet, with the left-hand prong of the Y running up towards the left-hand end of the Rock Band, where a deep-cut gully leads up towards the West Ridge. A narrower chimney seems to go up to the left-hand end of a snowfield that stretches across the upper part of the Face, to another gully at the right-hand end, which in turn leads up towards the south summit of Everest. The right-hand fork runs up towards a long snow ramp which leads across the bottom of the Rock Band to its right-hand edge.

The Japanese chose the left-hand fork, and climbed over hard wind-packed snow to establish Camp 5 at a height of 25,600 feet on 29 October. Once again, there was just enough snow to carve out a tent platform. M. Konishi and Uemura moved into the camp and on 31 October reached a point just below the Rock Band. On the following day, two other members of the team, Nakajima and Satoh, reached the same point and forced another pitch. They had now fulfilled their objective, being confident that a route could be made through the Rock Band with sufficient build-up of supplies at their top camp. They had been extremely successful, and had probably been fortunate with the weather, in that they were barely troubled by the high winds that seem to dog most post-monsoon attempts on Everest, or other mountains of over 26,000 feet. It must be noted, however, that to reach the foot of the Rock Band, at a height of approximately 26,000 feet, without any intention of getting higher, is considerably easier than pushing on above, for the real problem is sustaining an extended line of communications to supply climbers out in front for the final push.

Uemura stayed on at Khumjung throughout the winter, making arrangements for the spring attempt, and getting the full benefit of staying for a long period of time at the same altitude as the Sherpas. Living at a height of around 11,000 feet, you undoubtedly gain a great deal of benefit from fast acclimatization, while living much higher than that is probably a mistake. Hillary led an expedition in 1961 which wintered at 19,000 feet before attempting Makalu without oxygen. In this case, the climbers were very definitely badly run down after their long stay at altitude.

The Japanese spring expedition was a massive affair. It numbered thirty-nine Japanese, of whom nine were representatives of the media, and had a grand total of seventy-seven Sherpas, twenty-six being designated as high-altitude Sherpas for work above

Camp 2, in the Western Cwm. The leader was Saburo Matsukata, a man of seventy years of age. He led the expedition from Base Camp and some of the problems that occurred later on in the expedition might well have arisen from this cause. They set out with a dual objective, to climb Everest by the South Col route as well as attempt the South West Face. To make the mountain still more crowded, the Japanese skiing expedition also planned to reach the South Col to make a ski descent from as high on Everest as possible.

The expedition moved into Base Camp in mid-March, after an acclimatization period, and started work on the Ice Fall on 24 March. It took ten days to make a route through the Ice Fall and, on 4 April, Camp 1 was set up at the mouth of the Western Cwm. The expedition was dogged by ill-fortune however. On 5 April, six Sherpas of the Japanese skiing expedition were killed in the Ice Fall, and then, on 9 April, another Sherpa of the Everest expedition was killed. The entire expedition, and particularly the Sherpas, were badly shaken by these two accidents. I was on the South Face of Annapurna at the time, and several of our Sherpas had relatives amongst the casualties. Not surprisingly, they were deeply shocked by the accident; the impact on the Sherpas with the Japanese expedition must have been even greater.

The leader of the Japanese expedition, S. Matsukata, only reached Base Camp on 11 April, after these crises had occurred. One cannot help wondering just how effective was his control over events during the course of the expedition.

In spite of the accidents in the Ice Fall, the Japanese succeeded in maintaining the momentum of the expedition, and established Camp 2 at the foot of the South West Face. This becomes in effect an advanced base camp for any expedition attempting Everest, whether it be by the South West Face, the West Ridge or the South Col. Ironically the common route up through the Ice Fall is by far the most serious and dangerous part of any climb on Everest from the south. It is like playing Russian roulette and, however careful an expedition is in making the route, it cannot avoid a certain element of objective danger. The risk of an accident occurring increases statistically with the number of people going through an ice fall. In the case of the two Japanese expeditions, there must have been around 150 people going through the Ice Fall at one time or another and, of course, the Ice Fall Sherpas make the trip daily throughout an expedition to keep the Advanced Base and high camps stocked.

The Japanese had decided to tackle the South East Ridge (the original route climbed in 1953) as well as the South West Face. This would give them a more guaranteed chance of success and might serve as a good descent line for the Face assault team should they succeed.

The team now divided into two distinct parties, with the Face team even having a separate Advanced Base Camp, slightly closer to the Face itself than that of the South East Ridge team. They only nominated the members of each at this point, however, and the split was done by the leadership of the expedition. The selection was not well received by all members.

In his official report on the expedition, Hiromi Ohtsuka stated, 'It would have been better if the grouping of the members were decided beforehand according to their own wishes, although it was necessary to observe the condition, aptitude and intention of every member.'

The selection was announced on 17 April. Nine members of the team led by M. Konishi, leader of the autumn reconnaissance, were selected for the Face, and sixteen members were chosen for the South East Ridge. What immediately becomes evident is that the South East Ridge had priority in Sherpa strength for the initial route-making and build-up on the Lhotse Face. In addition, Uemura, who had been to the high point on the South West Face in the autumn and was probably the best acclimatized member of the entire team, having spent all winter in Sola Khumbu, was apportioned to the South East Ridge.

The expedition had fallen into the trap of having split objectives and was concentrating on the almost certain success of repeating the South East Ridge to get the first Japanese on the summit of Everest. In doing so they were prejudicing their chance of success on the greatest challenge of all, the South West Face.

The South East Ridge team had their share of set-backs. On 21 April they had their own expedition's second fatality, and the seventh of the two expeditions on Everest at the time. Narita had a sudden heart attack while eating his evening meal at Camp 1, and died before even his companions sitting beside him could do anything about it. The entire team was badly shocked by the tragedy. Ohtsuka writes:

Every member hearing the news was in a state of great shock, Narita being one of the strongest and youngest [aged twenty-eight] members of the expedition, it was unbelievable as to how such a thing could have happened. We remember him that afternoon waving to us with a smile and therefore his death seemed to be a dream.

Although he was not in good condition at the time of establishing base camp he recovered completely by going down to Lobuje to take some rest for a week. He resumed his work with other members at this stage. Was it because he wasn't acclimatized? I was quite concerned over this question. But our doctors judge this accident may have no relation with the high-altitude sickness, though this is not certified.

Narita's death put back their schedule still further, for all the members of the team went back to Camp 1 for a farewell ceremony, and eleven went all the way down to Tukura, one day's march below Base Camp, where they cremated the body.

But the climb went on. By 28 April they had reached the South Col on the South East Ridge route, though on the South West Face progress was lagging. Ropes had only just been fixed up to the site of Camp 3, at a height of 23,000 feet. During this period the situation was discussed at Advanced Base and, because of the way the expedition was slipping behind schedule and the growing amount of sickness in the team, it was decided to put off the South West Face assault, and concentrate all efforts on the South East Ridge.

Four days later, on 1 May, Hiromi Ohtsuka, no doubt pressured by the South West Face team, changed his mind once again, and formulated a new compromise plan to allow both teams a chance of reaching the summit. The outline of the plan read:

(1) Both the South West Face and the South East Ridge projects will be carried out.

(2) Face Camp 4 (8,000 m.) will be established just below the Rock Band in the South West Face by 12 May.

(3) The summit assault from the South East Ridge will be carried out twice on 11 and 12 May.

(4) Matsuura and Uemura were assigned for the first summit-assaulting members. The second assaulting team would consist of a member and one Sherpa.

(5) 350 kilograms worth of equipment and food will be carried up by Doi, Kamiyama and sixteen Sherpas to Camp 5 of South Col.

The South West Face team still had a low priority. Progress on the South East Ridge was now swift, however, and on 11 May, Matsuura and Uemura reached the summit of Everest on a perfect, windless day. The following day, Hirabayashi and the Sherpa, Chotare, also reached the summit.

Things were not going so well, however, on the South West Face where Camp 4 was established on 6 May, using duraluminium frame platforms. On 8 May, Konishi and Yoshikawa reached a height of 25,600 feet (7,800 m.), once again taking the left-hand route explored by the autumn reconnaissance team. Two days later on 10 May, Kano and Sagano with two Sherpas pushed the route out higher. There was much less snow than there had been in the autumn; instead, there were broken rocks of an unpleasant slatey nature. They were forced to take off their crampons and left their ice pegs behind, at a height of about 26,000 feet (7,900 m.). It was pure rock-climbing from here, and conditions were ideal – windless and comparatively warm. They reached an altitude of 26,400 feet (8,050 m.), just below the Rock Band, at the point where a comparatively easy-looking ramp stretched left towards the crest of the West Ridge. A narrow chimney forked right, through the Rock Band, to arrive on a broad snow ledge that stretched back, right to a gully that would have led to the south summit. It would have given difficult climbing, but they were confident that they could climb it and, having reached this point, the pair dropped back down towards Advanced Base Camp for a rest. On the way down, just below Camp 3, Kano was injured by a falling stone. That same afternoon Nakajima, at Camp 4, was also hit by a stone. Hiromi Ohtsuka, who seemed the effective leader of the expedition, being up at

Advanced Base, decided to call off the attempt on the South West Face, on the grounds that the stonefall was too dangerous, and that in the time available before the arrival of the monsoon they would be unable to force the Rock Band and put in a summit assault. He therefore resolved to concentrate the teams' effort on making two more assaults on the South East Ridge. This also enabled their single lady member, Miss Watnabe, to establish a world feminine height record, in reaching the South Col. They ran out of good weather however, and on 20 May the expedition was called off.

Might the expedition have been successful if they had concentrated from the start on the South West Face? One cannot help feeling that this might well have been the case. In the circumstances, the leadership of the expedition seems to have concentrated on getting to the top of Everest by any means and, consequently, gave the more exacting objective a lower priority. The stonefall, which was quoted as one reason for calling off the expedition, does not seem to have been much worse than that which either the Germans or ourselves experienced in 1972. Hiromi Ohtsuka was aware of these problems and in his summing up of the expedition states:

As deputy leader of the expedition, I would like to state some of the characteristic problems of the expedition and the possibility of the South West Face.

(1) Our expedition was a large force consisting of 39 members, including nine reporters and cameramen. At the Base Camp the members came close to 120, including the Sherpas and local Sherpas. There were more than 60 members living together even at Camp 1 and higher. A 39-member expedition is too large to work as a cohesive unit. One leader should not have more than 12 to work with otherwise there will be a lack of common bond among the members. Furthermore, the pleasures of mountaineering will be stifled.

(2) Our expedition consisted of two distinct groups which had the same objective to acquire the summit of Mt Everest but with a different route and different tactics. This scheme has made the expedition into such a large size. The necessity of such a big expedition should be considered with restraint in the future. I want to pay tribute to the American expedition which scaled the summit

both from the South East Ridge and the West Ridge. I have come to know how hard it is to keep close co-ordination between the two teams with different tactics. If there is a need to set up an expedition with a similar set-up as ours, it is necessary to set up two distinct ones beforehand, under the powerful organization committee of the expedition. And there are reasons to believe that even such an organizational set-up has its own set-backs.

But the Japanese came away with the belief that success on the South West Face was possible, with the right kind of expedition. Subsequent expeditions to the South West Face might well have been advised to study and act on Ohtsuka's advice.

3
THE INTERNATIONAL
EVEREST
EXPEDITION

Spring 1971

The international Everest expedition was next in what had become a long queue for Everest. I first became involved in the venture in April 1969 when I received a letter from Jimmy Roberts, a retired Lieutenant Colonel in the Gurkhas who now runs a trekking business in Nepal, telling me he was going to attempt the South West Face and asking my advice on equipment. He was joint leader with Norman Dyhrenfurth.

At the time I was organizing an expedition to the South Face of Annapurna, for the spring of 1970. I already knew Jimmy well, having been with him on Annapurna II in 1960 when he was leader of a combined services expedition. It had been my first Himalayan expedition and I had been very impressed by his style of leadership. Though dogged by ill-health, and unable to go above 16,000 feet on the mountain, his sound judgement, planning, and incisive leadership had been instrumental in ensuring our success. I couldn't help being tempted by the possibility of going to Everest in 1971 and therefore asked in my reply whether there was any chance of joining the expedition. I had a letter back a couple of weeks later, not only welcoming me aboard but suggesting I should take over the climbing leadership. A few weeks later Norman Dyhrenfurth was on his way to Europe from the States, and he broke his journey at London Airport. He has a flashing smile, the looks of a film star specializing in rugged but slightly glamorous adventure, yet at the same time he was obviously a man of considerable warmth and sincerity. His record, both in Himalayan experience and as an organizer and fundraiser, was impressive.

He had been to the Everest massif three times – twice to climb

Everest (1952 and 1963) and once to make an attempt on Lhotse (1955). He had also climbed Dhaulagiri in 1960. Like John Hunt, he had carried loads high and distinguished himself as a tactful and diplomatic leader. There was also no doubt that he and Roberts were well matched. Dyhrenfurth, with his resourcefulness in getting financial support, his skill in public relations and his ability at handling the press, was the ideal front man, while Roberts, with his Army background and his great rapport with the Sherpas, was perfectly suited for the job of dealing with the vast logistical back-up to the expedition.

I felt honoured by the trust that Norman and Jimmy had placed in me, but I was able to spare little thought for the expedition itself. My own attempt on Annapurna now filled my horizon. Although I had twice been to the Himalayas, I had never before led an expedition or undertaken such a gigantic responsibility of organization. Besides, in 1969 it seemed doubtful whether the international expedition would ever take place, since the Japanese who were making the first attempt might well have been successful. Already, that autumn, there were disagreements over the composition of the team and the goals of the expedition. This was partially caused by the way the expedition had evolved and mutated over a period of years, changing both in form, composition and objective.

It had started off as a small group of people who happened to come from different countries but knew each other well; they had decided to go on an expedition together. The co-founders were John Amatt, who came from Wilmslow in Cheshire, and Lief Patterson, a Norwegian. They had met in Norway in 1965 when they were members of teams attempting first ascents on the gigantic Trolltind Wall, one of the most impressive rock walls in Europe. They met again in Peru in 1966 and discussed the possibility of forming an expedition. Patterson was already planning a trip to Antarctica and so they decided on this as a venue. The fact that it was to be international in character was almost coincidental. But then the Antarctica project fell through and they looked round for other objectives and decided on the Rupal Face of Nanga Parbat. At this stage the team numbered six, none of whom had climbed before in the Himalayas. Amatt therefore came up with the idea of inviting Jimmy Roberts to be their leader, to give them the benefit of his considerable Himalayan experience. This also fell through, however, since the Germans had succeeded in getting permission to attempt the Rupal Face in 1970. They therefore decided to go for the South West Face of Everest. It was a big step from Antarctica, particularly for a comparatively inexperienced team.

It was at this stage that Norman Dyhrenfurth became involved in the expedition. He had been thinking of an international expedition to Everest completely independently – in fact had had the idea from way back in 1952 before the mountain had even been climbed. He wrote to Jimmy, who had been his transport officer on the American Everest expedition, inviting him to join him. At this stage Dyhrenfurth's expedition was no more than an idea, while Jimmy had an expedition, albeit a comparatively inexperienced one with little expertise at fund-raising or large-scale organization. And so Jimmy welcomed the suggestion and proposed that he and Norman should join forces as joint leaders.

The merger made the expedition feasible on practical grounds, since it seemed doubtful whether the original group could possibly have gathered the necessary funds or have coped with the mammoth task of organizing a major expedition, the members of which were scattered all over the world. Norman Dyhrenfurth plunged into the task with enthusiasm, however, broadening the scope of the expedition to include climbers from all the Alpine nations and from Japan. It now became truly international, but this also brought many problems.

It was at this stage that I came into the enterprise. Norman proved himself a brilliant co-ordinator, keeping everyone informed with a series of long and detailed newsletters. Inevitably, however, he had to make many of the decisions himself, some of which were dictated by sheer economic necessity. The trouble with having embarked on an international expedition was that no one national body could be expected to take responsibility for the expedition in the way, for instance, that the Mount Everest Foundation had taken my own Annapurna South Face expedition under its wing. This meant that Norman Dyhrenfurth became financially responsible for the expedition, which began to escalate in cost almost with the speed of the Concorde project.

The team now began to expand very quickly. He invited Michel and Yvette Vaucher from Switzerland, Pierre Mazeaud from France, Wolfgang Axt and Leo Schlömmer from Austria, Toni Hiebeler from Germany. They were all well-known, accomplished mountaineers with impressive records behind them. And yet I was getting increasingly worried about the way the expedition was going. Appreciating Norman's need to increase the numbers participating in the expedition to bring in further finance, I was impressed by the fullness and frequency of his newsletters. What worried me was whether I was going to be able to control a group of climbers of this calibre, all of whom would presumably want their turn out in front, and all of whom would have come with dreams – or the determination – of being in the summit party. My own authority would be tenuous, and I could even end up in an uncomfortable position as go-between for the expedition leadership and climbing members.

During the course of the Annapurna expedition, I experienced quite enough problems even in guiding a group of people most of whom I knew very well, and all of whom spoke the same language. Moreover, they had a strong vested interest in getting on together, both in the sense of wanting to maintain long-standing friendships and needing to work together on future climbing ventures. In addition, I was desperately tired, both from the experience of organizing and leading an expedition, and the actual climbing itself. It was while on Annapurna that I decided to withdraw from the international expedition.

I broke the news to Jimmy Roberts on my return to Kathmandu. Having already recommended Dougal Haston as a possible member, I now suggested Don Whillans as my replacement. On getting back to England, I began to have some doubts about the step I had taken. Could I afford to turn back from such a considerable mountaineering challenge? Jimmy Roberts came to see me in August to ask my advice about equipment for the expedition, and with this level of involvement I could not resist the temptation to ask whether I could come back on board. Both Jimmy and Norman very kindly welcomed me back, but once in the team again, things seemed, if anything, blacker.

At that point, the expedition was resting on very shaky financial foundations, and the team, although studded with well-known names, seemed to lack cohesion. In a way I envied Don and Dougal, who had no worries about the financial side of the project, since all they had to do was to go along and climb. I, on the other hand, was inevitably to be involved in fund-raising and working for the media. But what would happen if the expedition ended up with a gigantic debt? I should certainly have felt obliged to shoulder my share of it, yet could have ill-afforded to do so. My serious doubts about the outcome of the expedition, and my own role within it, forced me out once again. I did have one more chance of going back in, when the B.B.C. asked me to go out as their reporter, but I had crystallized my own doubts about the venture and therefore resolved to stay out.

By February 1971 the expedition was ready to set out for Nepal. Just getting it organized had been a magnificent achievement by Norman Dyhrenfurth. The team was well equipped, had the most sophisticated oxygen system, developed by Dr Duane Blume, ever to be used in the Himalayas, and the project was financially viable, largely as a result of the participation of the B.B.C. The team had also had some further additions on the climbing side, with Carlo Mauri from Italy, Uemura and Ito from Japan, both of whom had been members of the previous year's Japanese Everest expedition, and Harsh Bahuguna from India. The team on setting out from Europe numbered twenty-two, back up by a large media team of eight, of whom several were experienced climbers.

Before I had pulled out of the expedition I had expressed some doubt about the size of the party, stressing that I felt twelve to be the maximum number of climbers I could cope with on the South West Face. In addition, of course, I wanted a strong Sherpa force to perform the task of load carrying. Norman therefore suggested having a secondary objective, but rather than merely repeat the South Col route, he was more ambitious, planning to go for the true West Ridge of Everest. This had been attempted in 1963 during his American Everest Expedition, but Hornbein and Unsoeld who made the West Ridge route had strayed on to the North Face to avoid some of the difficulties of the ridge line. At the time Norman's decision to attempt two routes seemed the only practical course, though with hindsight one can see that this was one of the most serious, fundamental mistakes of the expedition. The team was weaker in numbers than that of the Japanese in 1970 yet was tackling a more ambitious secondary objective. The international expedition had fifty-five Sherpas compared to the seventy-five that the Japanese had had. This number was to prove barely sufficient to sustain a single assault on the mountain.

But in mid-February 1971 when the team assembled in Kathmandu chances of success seemed good. The entire team walked out to Base Camp from Kathmandu in preference to flying to Lukla, the air strip that is only four days' easy walk from the Everest Base Camp. In this way they were able to acclimatize at a steady rate, and, perhaps equally important, get to know each other. They also paused at Pheriche, just short of Base Camp, for further acclimatization. So far everything seemed to be going well; morale was high and there was a fine spirit of camaraderie within the team. Friendships were fast forming, many of which were to last through the well-publicized differences that were to occur later on.

Dougal Haston, though, was slightly perturbed by the light-hearted way in which the majority seemed to treat the venture; he had the feeling that many saw the trip as a holiday and were little aware of the grim discomfort and effort that inevitably form a major part of any Himalayan expedition. There were also some heated discussions on the route to be taken on the South West Face; the American contingent, particularly Colliver and Peterson, who were full of the big wall-climbing ethic cultivated in Yosemite, were talking blithely of forcing a route straight up the centre of the Rock Band.

Norman Dyhrenfurth believed in a democratic form of leadership and wanted to give everyone the maximum satisfaction in their role on the expedition. There had been some complaints on the previous year's Japanese expedition that the two teams to tackle the South West Face and the South Col route had been selected without consulting the members. Dyhrenfurth allowed the team to make their own choice. Below is the form it took.

South West Face	West Ridge
Evans (U.S.A.), Co-ordinator	Axt (Austria), Co-ordinator
Colliver (U.S.A.)	Bahuguna (India)
Ito (Japan)	Teigland (Norway)
Uemura (Japan)	Eliassen (Norway)
Haston (U.K.)	Vaucher (Switz.)
Whillans (U.K.)	Mme Vaucher (Switz.)
Schlömmer (Austria)	Mauri (Italy)
Hiebeler (W. Germany)	Isles (U.S.A.)
Peterson (U.S.A.)	Mazeaud (France)
	Steele (U.K.)

The title of Co-ordinator given to John Evans and Wolfgang Axt is indicative of the problems that Dyhrenfurth was going to meet in controlling the members of the team. With such a large number of talented climbers, all of whom had established a personal reputation in their own country, it seemed inadvisable to appoint any one of them as leader over the others.

Dyhrenfurth planned to work mainly between Base and Advanced Base, in a co-ordinating role, while Roberts stayed in Base, keeping the Sherpas and porters moving systematically up the mountain to supply those in front. It was decided that the Sherpas would be divided into two equal groups, working independently of one another, their deployment being decided by their respective co-ordinators working with Roberts.

The expedition's Base Camp was established on 23 March, and the team immediately started work on the Ice Fall, which was especially dangerous that season. It was a fortnight before they had managed to force their way through this maze of tottering séracs. At this stage everyone was working well together. Each day two parties would go up into the Ice Fall, while back at Base Camp the others either rested or worked on the gear and food. The latter was to prove a considerable problem. Wolfgang Axt had been given the unenviable job of organizing the food. He is a health fanatic and the diet reflected his beliefs. There were huge quantities of pumpernickel and various other health foods which the other climbers found to be totally inedible at altitude. A more serious factor was that the food had not been pre-packed in ration packs. This had to be done at Base Camp, and since the packages were not sealed it was inevitable that as the food found its way up the mountain, the most attractive items were pirated. As a result, by the time it reached the front climbers, they were left the remnants that no one else fancied.

Once the Ice Fall had been forced, the route was quickly pushed out to Camp 2, and the lead climbers of the two parties started work on their respective routes. It was already becoming uncomfortably evident that there were barely enough Sherpas to support these two efforts. On the American Everest expedition the climbers had taken an active part in load-carrying, particularly in the early part of the venture; on this expedition, however, there was a strong school of thought amongst the climbers that they should do as little carrying as possible, saving their strength for the summit bid. There was also growing friction between the two teams, the West Ridge team feeling that the Face team were getting priority of Sherpas for their build-up. In addition, the approach to the West Ridge from the Western Cwm was proving to be more difficult than it had been in 1963. Even in the Face team, there was some trouble. Schlömmer felt that Don Whillans and Dougal Haston, who were pushing out the route towards Camp 3, were hogging the lead, and complained accordingly.

In spite of these problems that were beginning to show themselves, it is just possible that the expedition could have succeeded on at least one of the routes without a major rift, had they been spared an appalling accident followed by an unusually savage and prolonged storm. Wolfgang Axt and Harsh Bahuguna had been working out in front trying to establish Camp 4 on the West Ridge. They had been working at altitude for some time and both were getting tired; the weather was beginning to deteriorate and so they decided to return to Advanced Base Camp. In an inquiry held afterwards, Axt described to Norman Dyhrenfurth what happened next:

We were not roped during the descent, there was no need, there were no difficulties at all. Since I knew Michel [Vaucher] and Odd [Eliassen] had placed fixed ropes on all the steeper sections, I left my climbing rope and my harness and Karabiner at the new camp. At

first Harsh went ahead. Around 2 p.m. the weather turned bad. Soon
we were caught in a raging storm. When we reached the long rope-
traverse I took over the lead and got across it hand over hand. It was
very long and tiring as hell. At the far end I waited for Harsh to
follow. Voice communication was impossible, the storm was much
too strong. I waited for a long time, perhaps as much as an hour. My
hands and feet lost all feeling. Then I saw Harsh tied into a fixed
rope with a harness and Karabiner, groping his way round the last
corner of the steep ice-slope that separated us. He waved with one
hand. Everything seemed O.K., no indication of any serious difficulty.
I was really worried about frostbite so I went down. Just before I got
to the camp I heard his screams and alerted everybody. I couldn't
have gone up as I was completely done in.

When he was asked why he did not stay with Bahuguna:

I had no idea how bad things were with him, and besides what
could I have done without a rope or Karabiner? Harsh had taken his
gear but I would have had to go back hand over hand over that long
traverse. I simply didn't have enough strength in me for that and
my hands and feet felt like blocks of ice.

Immediately, a rescue party set out and reached Harsh some
hours later when it was already beginning to get dark. The conditions were savage, with the wind and snow gusting across the
slope. Harsh was semi-conscious, hanging by his harness on the
fixed rope, his anorak and upper clothing pulled up exposing his
body to the storm. Vaucher and Eliassen tried to lower him
straight down to easier ground, since it was impossible to get him
back across the traverse. Unfortunately they ran out of rope
before he reached the bottom of the slope. He was lying, helpless
on the slope, suspended by the rope. Whillans, with considerable
courage, cramponed, unroped, across to him. Harsh was now
unconscious, very close to death. Even if they had managed to get
him down, it is unlikely he could have survived the journey
back to Camp 2. There was nothing Don could do to get him
down so he had to make the agonizing decision to abandon a man
who still had a spark of life left in him.

The storm did not abate and the party at Camp 2 were trapped
there for a further ten days. They were unable to recover Harsh's
body till the end of the storm and it was left hanging there, a

grim reminder of the tragedy. In the enforced idleness of days spent in sleeping bags, the members of the team had ample opportunity to brood over Harsh's death. Food was short; everything became covered in spindrift, with gear and sleeping bags getting progressively damper.

During the storm Mazeaud and Mauri had come up with the suggestion that they should abandon the West Ridge, which was obviously going to extend the limited resources of the expedition too much, and instead go for the South Col. Dyhrenfurth was unhappy about the suggestion, but against his better judgement agreed that there should be a vote amongst the West Ridge team. Peter Steele and Eliassen voted for abandoning the alternative route altogether and going for the Face, while the rest of the team voted for the South Col route, and Dyhrenfurth endorsed this decision.

The first task once the storm ended was the grim one of taking down Harsh Bahuguna's body. Several members of the team also were forced back to Base Camp, weakened by sickness. The remnants of the two parties started work on their respective routes. After a few days, however, it became increasingly obvious that there simply weren't enough Sherpas to support two separate attempts; indeed, there were barely sufficient for the Face. Jimmy Roberts strongly recommended that the South Col route should be abandoned; Norman Dyhrenfurth, having agreed to let the 'Latins' have their way, was unhappy about going back on his word but soon realized that he had little choice in the matter. Fair to the last, he held another vote, even allowing the Sherpas to have their say. The Sherpas voted overwhelmingly in favour of the Face route, preferring a straightforward line, protected all the way by fixed ropes, to the much longer way by the South Col.

Mazeaud, Mauri and the Vauchers were furious, suspecting intrigue. They retired to Base Camp and Yvette Vaucher even pelted the unfortunate Dyhrenfurth with snowballs. After a series of savage arguments the four decided to withdraw from the expedition. Hiebeler also was forced to withdraw for reasons of health rather than protest. Several more members of the team were knocked out by illness and never really recovered. Peter Steele, the doctor, was kept hard at work with a whole series of ailments, the most serious of which was a virus infection, a rare type of glandular fever, which attacked almost every member of the expedition. Dyhrenfurth was struck down and was so ill that he had to return to Europe, leaving Jimmy Roberts in charge. John Evans, the Face Co-ordinator, was also affected. Only Whillans, Haston, Ito, Uemura, Schlömmer, Axt and Peterson remained untouched.

Don Whillans was the obvious choice as successor to John Evans as climbing leader and he now took over. They returned to the Face at the end of April. Don and Dougal went out in the lead, supported by Uemura, Ito and the Sherpas. They quickly established Camp 4, using the platform left by the Japanese, on which they pitched Whillans Boxes, then pushed on up towards the Rock Band. On the 1970 attempt the Japanese had gone to the foot of the gully on the left-hand side of the Rock Band. They failed to find a suitable camp site. Whillans therefore decided to follow a route that led across towards the right hand flank of the Rock Band, since there seemed more hope of finding a suitable camp site. They discovered one on the right-hand side of the Great Gully leading up the Rock Band at a height of approximately 26,000 feet. Above this a system of ledges and snowfields led across to the right-hand side of the Rock Band.

There was some criticism within the team and from the press that Don and Dougal were hogging the lead, refusing to let anyone else go out in front. It undoubtedly would have been better for morale if another climbing pair had been able to take a turn at making the route. Schlömmer and Axt did offer to help, but unfortunately there was an altercation between Schlömmer and Whillans after the former asked Don to send down a Sherpa to carry up his personal gear, which Don refused to do. The two Austrians claimed that Whillans and Haston refused to let them go out in front whilst the Britons put in a counter claim that they would have been only too glad to be relieved if only someone had come up from Camp 5 to do this. It is interesting that Uemura and Ito did not seem anxious to go out in front but were well content to give the two Britons their loyal support. The Sherpas, led by Pembatharke, also did a magnificent job in the final days of the expedition, working without any supervision from the climbers, most of whom had either given up or were convalescent at Base Camp. Peterson did a good job in the running of Camp 3 and John Evans, having recovered from glandular fever, returned to Camp 2 but was not able to do much to influence events.

Meanwhile Don and Dougal had succeeded in establishing Camp 6 (27,200 ft.) at the foot of a narrow gully, filled with snow, at the right-hand end of the Rock Band. Whillans went round the corner and saw that there was a comparatively easy way across to the South Ridge. They would certainly have had a much better chance of climbing this than of climbing the Rock Band itself, but they rejected the thought. After all the arguments they had had about going for the Face rather than the South Ridge route, he felt it would have left Haston and himself open to charges of hypocrisy.

The supplies coming up to them, however, had now thinned down to a trickle. They needed three bottles of oxygen a day at Camp 6, one each during the day to climb with and a bottle shared at night. They succeeded in climbing about 300 feet up the gully but then ran out of rope. It was painfully obvious that they were not going to get sufficient supplies to make a sustained effort on the Rock Band, let alone making a summit bid once that was climbed. Don had reached the high point and came sliding back down the rope to Dougal. 'I think we've had it,' he said.

And so, admitting defeat, they turned back, returning to Base Camp and all the accusation and counter-accusation that was to follow the expedition.

The arguments and the desertion of the four 'Latins' have undoubtedly clouded the real causes of failure. The decision to go for two objectives when there was barely sufficient Sherpa support for one was certainly the greatest factor. This might have defeated both attempts even if the weather had been perfect. The death of Harsh Bahuguna, linked with the ten-day storm, put the lid on it.

4

THE EUROPEAN
EVEREST
EXPEDITION

Spring 1972

One expedition had failed and the next was ready to step into the breach. Dr Karl Herrligkoffer, a Munich doctor with a long record of expedition organization behind him, had permission to attempt Everest in the spring of 1972. He contacted Don Whillans, Dougal Haston, Uemura and Ito, while they were still in Nepal, inviting them to join the team. He knew them only by reputation, and in inviting climbers whom he did not know, from another country, and who did not know the other German and Austrian members of his climbing team, he was already sowing the seeds of potential dissension which had bedevilled and, in part, damaged the chances of success of the international expedition.

Herrligkoffer, a controversial figure in the German climbing scene, first came into prominence in 1953, when he led the expedition that made the first ascent of Nanga Parbat; this was a 'German mountain' in much the same way in which Everest had become a 'British mountain', with a succession of pre-war attempts on its northern flanks. Before the Nanga Parbat expedition he was completely unknown on the German climbing scene and only had limited experience as a mountaineer. His interest in Nanga Parbat seemed to have been created by the fact that his stepbrother was Willi Merkl who led and died on the disastrous 1934 attempt when nine climbers and Sherpas were killed in a storm. Although his expedition had been successful, it was also bedevilled with arguments and controversy, particularly between the famous Austrian climber, Hermann Buhl, who reached the summit in an incredible solo bid after Herrligkoffer had called the expedition off and the climbers back down to Base Camp. The argument was so savage that it led to the law courts.

But this did not deter Herrligkoffer. He led a succession of expeditions in the next few years, six of them back to Nanga Parbat to attempt the mountain on its other faces; three of these were successful with ascents of the Diamir Face, the Rupal Ridge and finally, in 1970, the Rupal Face. Yet most of these expeditions were fraught with arguments and the Rupal Face expedition was extraordinarily similar in its pattern to that of the original ascent, with the brilliant young Austrian climber, Reinhold Messner, fulfilling the same role as had been taken by Hermann Buhl. He also made a solo dash for the summit, followed by his brother Gunter, who caught up with them near the top of the mountain. They had then found that they couldn't get back down because of the difficulty of the climbing and therefore took the desperate course of descending the Diamir Face on the opposite side. Sadly, Gunter was killed by an avalanche on the way down when nearly in sight of safety. Once again arguments flowed between summit climber and leader over a series of misunderstood signals. Once again the expedition ended in the law courts.

Part of the reason for the misunderstanding was perhaps the fact that Herrligkoffer never went far beyond Base Camp, was essentially an administrator rather than a climber and seemed to have little in common with or understanding of many of the climbers he invited on his expedition. To help finance and organize expeditions he had founded the Deutsches Institut für Anslandsforsching (German Institute for Exploration).

And so, to Everest. When Don and Dougal received this invitation, both knew about Herrligkoffer's background, but in just the same way as Buhl and Messner, they decided to join an expedition about which they were not too happy, simply because this was the only opportunity they were going to have to go to Everest in the foreseeable future.

I became involved in the expedition later on that autumn, when I received a letter from Dougal. He had just been to see Herrligkoffer in Munich, and told me that Herrligkoffer would extend an invitation to myself to join his expedition. Apparently he was having difficulty in raising funds – difficulties which were aggravated by the distrust for his expedition held by the majority of German climbers, and also a large part of the media in Germany. Dougal had mentioned that I had good contacts with the British media and could probably help him with fund-raising as well as the actual climbing. At this stage I was organizing an expedition to the Trango Tower, in which Joe Brown, Hamish MacInnes, Martin Boysen, Will Barker and Paul Nunn were to be members. The Trango Tower is a magnificent rock obelisk of 20,500 feet which would have given superb rock-climbing of a slightly larger-than-Alpine scale. The team was obviously going to be very compatible, and the expedition would have been sheer fun. However, we were having trouble in getting permission from the Pakistan Government. At this stage, I was still hopeful that we might pull it off, and therefore stalled with Herrligkoffer to give me time to see whether we were going to be able to go for the Trango Tower or not.

I actually met Herrligkoffer for the first time at the end of November, when he came over with several members of his team to take part in Don Whillans' 'This is your Life' on television. Talking with him between rehearsals, both Dougal and I were badly shaken to learn how little he appeared to know about the problems presented by Everest or, for that matter, how limited was his knowledge of Himalayan history or Himalayan mountaineering in general. I couldn't help feeling that his sole interest lay in his own expeditions and the comparatively limited fields which he had covered. It was quite obvious that money, at this stage, was very short and that preparations for the expedition had barely got off the ground. He had had an abortive expedition to attempt to climb the North Flank of Rakaposhi that summer and had presumably only just finished closing it down.

Herrligkoffer himself could speak only very limited English and the other climbers could speak none at all. They were certainly very different in appearance from the average British climber; short hair – not surprising when later we learned that most of them were in the Austrian Army – fairly 'square' clothes, and a look of earnest, clean living. Since I could not commit myself, I kept out of any of the plans or discussion. Don, on the other hand, after the programme, had a long session with the Germans and tried to get across the need for greater British participation if Herrligkoffer was to hope for more money from Britain whilst, at the same time, trying to get the planning onto a sound footing. A couple of weeks later, the fate of our Trango Tower trip was finally sealed. Due to hostilities on the India–Pakistan border, we were informed by the Pakistan Government that we did not have permission.

And so, what next? Go to Everest – even with what was obviously a thoroughly unsatisfactory expedition, which promised even more chances of failure than that of the international one? I was tired of standing down from expeditions; had even regretted, during its course, my withdrawal from the international expedition. And so I decided to go along. After all, I am a writer and a photographer. There would certainly be plenty to write about on Herrligkoffer's expedition. He needed money, which meant selling book rights, television rights, newspaper rights in this country and, possibly, the U.S. and I was probably in a position to sell these rights on the basis of my own reputation after writing up the Annapurna Expedition.

I went over to see Dr Herrligkoffer with my agent, George Greenfield. George had helped us get the money for the South Face of Annapurna and is undoubtedly the most experienced, effective expedition agent in the business. He helped Sir Vivian Fuchs with his Trans-Antarctic Expedition, Wally Herbert on his crossing of the North Pole, Sir Francis Chichester, Robin Knox-Johnston, and many others. As we flew out to meet Herrligkoffer, just before Christmas 1971, I couldn't help feeling uneasy. My motives for joining this expedition were a long way from the simple mountain challenge. This was professionalism – raising money for an expedition, writing about it and making sure that I got a fair cut of the proceeds for my writing and work for television companies.

We met Herrligkoffer at his flat in Munich. It was beautifully furnished in that slightly heavy German style, with good antiques, and its walls surrounded by statues and friezes, presumably collected on his Nanga Parbat trips. Herrligkoffer himself, with his bristling military moustache, heavily lined face and his swept-back white hair is a severe, rather cold figure. There was little feeling of shared anticipation of a great adventurer. I realized we were negotiating like a group of business men over the copyrights and how to raise money.

That afternoon we discussed and came to an agreement on the split of media rights. We left with no feeling of friendship, and I, with very little enthusiasm for the expedition. Nevertheless, in the next six weeks, George Greenfield and I set about raising the necessary support for the German–British Everest expedition. Both the B.B.C. and I.T.N. were interested, as were several publishers and newspapers. There is no doubt that we could have raised a large part of the money that Herrligkoffer needed.

Now it became increasingly difficult to deal with him and it became quite obvious that he was trying to raise funds himself which cut across the copyrights we were arranging on his behalf, in order to be independent of the British contribution. In some ways I don't blame him, but he should have told us in the first place, instead of accepting our offer of help, allowing us to raise support for him, and then revoking our verbal agreement at the last moment.

In January I went off to the Alps with Dougal Haston to make an attempt on a new route on the North Face of the Grandes Jorasses. It was a wonderful escape from the financial manoeuvring we had landed in, to the clean simplicity of a big mountain challenge with a small group of friends. Dougal and I discussed Herrligkoffer's expedition whilst tucked in a small ice-hole about a third of the way up the North Wall of the Grandes Jorasses. We both resolved to withdraw from the expedition. At this stage, Herrligkoffer still had no oxygen, nor had he ordered any Sherpas from Nepal. The expedition seemed to have no hope of success, and there seemed little point in joining a doubtful cause which was likely to give us only a series of unhappy experiences.

Don Whillans stayed on in the expedition. He, also, had many doubts about Herrligkoffer, but nevertheless had a deep and burning desire to reach the summit of Everest. Perhaps in some respects his motives were material, as mine had been. Such an achievement would undoubtedly have crowned his career as a mountaineer and established him in a very strong position. I suspect he was very aware of both this and the actual financial rewards which would have accompanied his success. But his desire to go to the top of Everest was much more deep-rooted. Throughout his climbing career, he has always favoured bold, very obvious lines; has never really bothered with a contrived route which works its way subtly up a rock face or, for that matter, up a mountain. Climbing with him over a period of time, I had found that whereas I simply enjoyed the process of climbing, and provided I was climbing, worried little about the nature of the climb, Don would only set out on a climb which he felt was worthwhile. In recent years he seemed to have lost interest in British rock-climbing, although he put up some of the best and hardest routes in Britain in the fifties. His interests had gone further afield. He had also become genuinely interested in travel for its own sake. In 1968 he had taken part in an unsuccessful attempt to climb the South Face of Huandoy. He told me subsequently that the most enjoyable part of the trip for him was the return down the River Amazon. Everest, to him, was much more than the means of making a good living or establishing himself in the climbing firmament. It represented the ultimate superlative – the ultimate strong and simple objective. To attain it he was prepared to cope with an expedition which was anything but ideal in composition.

While I was still with the expedition, we had a fourth member to choose. Don was already established as the leader of the British contingent, but we consulted with each other, in spite of an element of stress which had entered our relationship after the Annapurna South Face expedition. We had both, separately, thought of Doug Scott as the best choice for the fourth member of the team.

Doug is an extremely powerful climber with a long record of pioneering behind him. Son of a Nottingham policeman, he started to climb at the age of twelve, having borrowed his mother's clothes-line. At the age of sixteen in 1957 he had his first trip to the Alps, arriving full of ambitions to do new routes, but being avalanched off the first climb he attempted. Undeterred, he continued climbing and exploring, putting up new routes on the limestone outcrops near Derby, hitch-hiking as far afield as Morocco to look at the Atlas. In 1959 he left school to go to Loughborough to train to be a P.E. teacher, then returned to

Nottingham, getting married at the age of twenty, to teach in a local secondary school. He stayed there for the next ten years, climbing to the full, mainly with a small group of Nottingham climbers, and also taking out many of his pupils to introduce them to the hills. He remained for a time outside the main stream of climbing, partially through the fact that he tended to remain with the same group and partially through his appetite for original climbing and expeditions; he preferred to go off to the further ranges rather than hammer the trade routes in the Alps. He organized, on a shoestring budget, expeditions to Turkey, the Tibesti in the Sahara, the Hindu Kush, where he had made the first ascent of the 5,000-foot high South Face of Badaka (22,500 feet), and Baffin Island.

He also became increasingly interested in the American approach to climbing, making, in 1971, the first British ascent of Salathee Wall on Yosemite – probably one of the most beautiful rock climbs in the world. He is powerfully built, weighs thirteen stone, plays rugger regularly and keeps fit throughout the year, running and climbing. With his proven performance at altitude and expedition experience he seemed a good choice for Everest.

Once Dougal and I had withdrawn from the team, Don looked around for a replacement and chose Hamish MacInnes. Hamish was an old friend of mine. We had first met in 1953, when he took me, little more than a novice, on the first winter ascent of Raven's Gully. Since that time we had made an abortive attempt on the North Wall of the Eiger in 1957 (it would have been my first Alpine route) and both of us had met Don Whillans for the first time when we set out to attempt the South West Pillar of the Drus. Don probably saved Hamish's life when he hauled him in a semi-conscious condition up most of the climb, after Hamish had been hit on the head by a falling stone. The following year Hamish and Don made the second British ascent of the Walker Spur of the Grandes Jorasses.

Hamish has had one of the most fascinating lives of any post-war British mountaineer. He is called, by his friends, the 'Old Fox of Glencoe' and is a complete individualist who has always carved his own path, regardless of what popular opinion might be at any one time. Shortly after our ascent of Raven's Gully in

1952, Hamish took off for New Zealand with that other very hard Scottish climber, John Cunningham. They took assisted passages out to New Zealand, but only stayed there for a few weeks before working their way on a boat to India, bound for no less than Mount Everest itself. They had heard that the Swiss expedition which had made attempts on Everest in the spring and autumn of 1952 had left dumps of food and oxygen all the way up the mountain. The two Scots were hoping to use these for a super-lightweight attempt on Everest. By the time they got in position, John Hunt and his Sassenachs had already beaten them to it, so they exchanged their objective to Pumori, a very attractive, unclimbed, twenty-three-thousander, immediately opposite the Everest Ice Fall. The entire expedition had been on a shoestring. They had jumped the Nepalese frontier, had employed a Sherpa to help carry their gear for a short time, but dismissed him when he complained of carrying a load of over seventy pounds. They were already carrying ninety pounds each. They parted with the Sherpa without ill-feeling, and the latter even presented them with a fork, since they were being forced to use pitons as eating utensils.

They lived off the land, on rice and *tsampa*, until they reached the foot of the mountain, and then bought a goat to act as mountain rations. Hamish had a lightweight Boy Scouts sleeping bag and they had a threadbare tent for their high-altitude camps. Perhaps it was just as well that they were avalanched off the lower slopes of the mountain and were forced to abandon their attempt.

After a couple of years of climbing and lumberjacking, back in New Zealand, he returned to Britain. An abortive attempt on Rakaposhi with Mike Banks and some yeti-hunting in Kulu followed. He had taken photographs and was also beginning to make films. In the past few years he has established himself in his 'Fox's Lair' in Glencoe, running a climbing school in the winter, manufacturing rescue equipment, and organizing the Glencoe Mountain Rescue Team. Today he is a world authority on mountain rescue.

Hamish was an ideal choice, since he had good contacts with both the B.B.C. and various newspapers and was therefore able to raise the funds required by Herrligkoffer as entry into the expedition. The position was still as confused and as unsatisfactory as when Dougal and I had pulled out. Herrligkoffer had originally planned to travel overland, but of course as a result of the Indo–Pakistan war, the frontier was still closed. At this stage he had no other means of transport; neither did he have sufficient oxygen equipment or bottles for the expedition, even though they were now only a few weeks from departure date. Lt Col. Jimmy Roberts, who probably has some of the best high-altitude Sherpas in Nepal in his employ, was not prepared to let him use any of these; the reason for this was concern for the safety of the Sherpas. At this point, however, Herrligkoffer did have one windfall. Senator Dr Franz Burda, who runs the German publishing firm Bunte, stepped in to cover him financially. This must have relieved Herrligkoffer from many of his financial worries and, of course, enabled him to do without the British media coverage which I had organized.

Don Whillans flew out to Munich to spend a week with Herrligkoffer, hoping that he would be able to give him the benefit of his experience on the Face, and to discuss equipment for the expedition. Unfortunately this trip was to prove partially abortive. Herrligkoffer was heavily committed with his day-to-day medical practice and was also involved in a long-drawn-out lawsuit with Reinhold Messner – a by-product of the Nanga Parbat expedition. As a result Don had very little chance of advising Herrligkoffer, spending part of the time in court with him – to show Don what could happen to him if he failed to toe the line, no doubt! At all stages Herrligkoffer was extremely secretive about his plans and did not even condescend to show Don full equipment lists for climbers and Sherpas. In failing to do this, he was going to land himself in a great deal of trouble on the expedition, since as an economy measure he had not budgeted for giving the Sherpas adequate down clothing and sleeping bags. During this week's meeting, Don had emphasized how important it was to equip the Sherpas with good gear on any Everest expedition.

Somehow, the expedition got off the ground. Don had found a good contact for oxygen cylinders which, ironically, were made in Germany, flown over to Britain to have valves fitted by Sabre Safety, a small oxygen equipment firm at Aldershot, and then filled with British Oxygen. These bottles were still considerably cheaper than the French bottles available to Herrligkoffer. The British contingent also secured for the expedition a number of tents from Blacks of Greenock, and the vital Whillans Boxes from Karrimor. They had also equipped themselves extremely adequately with Don's specially designed one-piece suits, Neoprene foam overboots, and all the other equipment they were going to need on the mountain. Their gear was to prove considerably superior to that used by the Germans.

It was a question of 'on-off' right up to the last evening before departure. I have a feeling that Herrligkoffer was beginning to regret ever having invited his troublesome British members. Doug Scott had taken all the oxygen bottles and tentage to Munich in a hired Transit van. Herrligkoffer seemed to have taken an immediate dislike to Doug – perhaps because of his long hair and slightly 'hippie' appearance. He phoned Harold MacCarthy, who was his contact in Britain, to say that he wanted to drop Doug Scott from the team. Don relayed back immediately that if Doug went, Hamish and he would drop out as well. Demand and counter demand now flickered back and forth between Munich, London and Rossendale, where Don lives. Many of the quibbles were financial; the root of the problem perhaps lying in the fact that there was none of the loyalty of friendship, or even of a united cause, to join the German–Austrian contingent with that from Britain. Don had been very frank with Herrligkoffer all the way along, putting his cards on the table, that he was a professional mountaineer and therefore needed to make some money out of the expedition. His view was identical to my own when I joined and then dropped out of the expedition. Don and the other members of the British contingent wanted to cover the cost of their individual contributions, which Herrligkoffer had raised to £1,000 per head, and perhaps make some money themselves. This, of course, would involve extra work on their parts in writing, filming and sending film back. Herrligkoffer on the other hand seems to have regarded this as 'professional money-grabbing'. He did not make any profit personally out of his expeditions.

Presumably he didn't need to, since he has a good medical practice. He put all the profits from his expeditions into the Deutsches Institut für Auslandsforschung – a charitable institute, run by him from his own home address, and whose main function seems to be to finance his many expeditions. All members of his expeditions have to sign a very full contract which, in actual fact, was similar to the one used by myself for the Annapurna South Face Expedition, whose chief sponsor was the Mount Everest Foundation. In some ways you can't blame Herrligkoffer for expecting to have full copyright, plus that of all the photographs. On the other hand, he had invited climbers from a different country who had no allegiance to his institute, or to German mountaineering, and it was understandable that they would want to get hold of their own pictures and have the facility to write in their own country. This is really where the contradiction arose, in trying to form what had now become an almost bi-national expedition.

Don, Dougal and Hamish were still arguing with Herrligkoffer over the financial ins-and-outs of the expedition right up to the last evening before flying out to Kathmandu to join the expedition. Hamish was in London trying to confirm with the *Observer* and the B.B.C. the contracts that he had made with them on behalf of Herrligkoffer. Don was having a riotous farewell party in Rossendale, being dragged away every half hour or so from his cups to give his opinion on the latest gambit. It was at this stage that Don very aptly coined Herrligkoffer's nickname of 'Sterlings-coffer'. But Herrligkoffer, presumably, still needed the money that Hamish had managed to raise from the B.B.C. and the *Observer*, and therefore finally an agreement was reached between the two parties.

It was hardly the happiest atmosphere in which to start an expedition. Don and Doug still hoped that perhaps everything would turn out all right, once they reached the mountain and financial differences had been put behind them. The three British members of the team flew out, direct from London Airport, to Kathmandu on 12 March. Most of the remaining members of the team had already assembled in Kathmandu, and some of them were already at Lukla air strip ready to establish Base Camp. Herrligkoffer arrived a few days after. Don had a further shock on reaching Kathmandu when he learned that he had been demoted from the position of joint climbing leader, which he had been led to expect, leaving Felix Kuen as climbing leader of the expedition. The expedition had also acquired another name and was now known as the 'European Everest Expedition'. Presumably this was on the basis that the team comprised ten Germans, seven Austrians, three British, one Swiss, and one South Tyrol climber. The Continental element, however, were all essentially Austro–German, and the expedition split was definitely bi-national, with all the risks of 'them and us' creeping in when decisions became controversial.

By the time the three British members of the team flew into Lukla with Herrligkoffer, Base Camp was already established. The British team was amazed at the way Herrligkoffer ignored all the normal precautions one takes with acclimatization. Herrligkoffer, keen to get to Base Camp as quickly as possible, rejected suggestions that they should stop for a day or so on the way up from Lukla to Base Camp, which is about 17,500 feet. He insisted on pressing on and told the British that if they wanted to stop they would have to cater for themselves. Small things, but all abrasive to future relations. As a result of this course of action Herrligkoffer was showing some signs of altitude sickness on the way up. The Base Camp manager, Professor Huttl, had already collapsed from the altitude, perhaps partially as a result of rapid height-gain, and had to be helped back to Lukla and then returned to Germany, taking no further part in the expedition. In addition, the British members of the team had been unlucky with their health in the early stages of the expedition. Don had trouble with his old, recurring complaint of vertigo and was forced to retire to a sleeping bag on reaching Base Camp, while Doug had been knocked out with dysentery. Hamish was busy sorting out all his film equipment ready for the climb. As a result, the British members of the team were unable to take an active part either in the climbing or the load-carrying in the first few days of the expedition.

On 29 March, just three days after Herrligkoffer and the British had reached Base Camp, trouble erupted with the Sherpas. Over the years, Sherpas have come to expect a high standard of equipment. This, undoubtedly, has become one of the 'perks' to be had from an expedition. A high-altitude Sherpa who is going out on two expeditions a year – one pre-monsoon and one post-monsoon – can expect a complete set of gear each time, and of course can sell this gear at the end of the expedition. Herrligkoffer was accustomed to the Hunzas, whom he had employed on Nanga Parbat, in the Karakorum. These porters are not nearly so sophisticated as the Sherpas. On the whole, they don't give as good value for money as the Sherpas do, in the shape of determination, enthusiasm and expertise, but along with this, they do not demand quite so much. Herrligkoffer, no doubt, had planned the equipping of the Sherpas on much the same lines as had proved satisfactory with his Hunza porters. In spite of the warnings which Don Whillans had given to him, he had only sufficient down gear for the fifteen high-altitude Sherpas who would be going up on the South West Face. There were insufficient foam mattresses, and he had omitted to bring out double sleeping bags even for the high-altitude Sherpas; there was no down clothing for the Ice Fall Sherpas at all. The argument that ensued was undoubtedly motivated by the poor relationship which had already developed between the Germans and the Sherpas. The Germans tended to shout at the Sherpas and to bully them and, of course, to make matters worse there was a language barrier, since, although most of the Sherpas spoke a smattering of English, none of them could speak German and few of the Germans could speak English. The Sherpas were demanding more down clothing, refusing point blank to go any further on the mountain without it. Herrligkoffer, perhaps not unreasonably, explained that they had no more down clothing, and that therefore they could not give them any. (We were to have a very similar argument with the Sherpas during our autumn expedition.) This very nearly ended in complete deadlock and probably would have done but for Don Whillans, who got on extremely well with the Sherpas, and their excellent liaison officer, Mr Pandi, who negotiated between the two parties in the argument.

Eventually Herrligkoffer resigned himself to rushing back to Germany to collect more down equipment, and chartered a helicopter from Kathmandu to pick him up at Base Camp to speed his journey. He was very bitter when on his return from Germany with the down clothing which had been demanded, many of the Sherpas simply took the equipment and hid it away in their tents, for resale after the expedition, and continued to use the old equipment which they had said was inadequate.

No sooner had this problem been solved than another row reared its head. On the evening of 1 April, there was a meeting at which the lack of activity of the British members of the team was discussed. Don was summoned from his sleeping bag, still badly stricken with vertigo, to answer for the British. He put the case very strongly that everyone needed to acclimatize at his own rate, but the Germans remained uninterested, convinced that the British were saving themselves for later on. The real crux of the matter was the basic distrust between the two parties. Felix Kuen was a close friend of Schlömmer, who had been on the international expedition. There had been no love lost at all between Schlömmer and Don, and the former had given his version of the story to Kuen. There is no doubt that the Austro–Germans arrived on the expedition with a very strong prejudice against the members of the British team and Don in particular, being firmly convinced that their one intention was to reach the summit of Everest for their own personal satisfaction and glory.

At this stage an unofficial member of the expedition arrived – Mischa Saleki, a Persian who had originally been invited by Herrligkoffer to join the expedition, but at a later stage had been dropped from it. Mischa was extremely bitter, since he had put in a lot of work in Persia raising money for the expedition, and had also obtained a certain amount of equipment. In Doug's words:

It was hardly surprising that he was in a particularly vindictive frame of mind when he arrived, determined to avenge himself for the humiliation he felt he had received in the face of his friends in the Persian Government (which was sponsoring him in part), as a result of the leader's treatment. It was clear that if Saleki were allowed to give vent to his feelings, there would be some serious repercussions. Between us, we managed to talk him round to helping the expedition to be a success, and he became calmer when he realized that he had at least three sympathetic companions to confide in.

On 4 April, Felix Kuen, Adolf Huber, Werner Hain and Leo Breitenberger moved up to Camp 1 to make the route up to Camp 2. This foursome became known as the 'Big Four', since during the first part of the expedition they stayed in the lead, using the rest of the team as load-carriers to support them. It was a similar step to the one taken by Don Whillans, Dougal Haston and the two Japanese, Ito and Uemura, on the international expedition the previous year. There was one big difference, however, since in the case of the international expedition, it was unlikely that any other climbing pair could effectively have taken up the role of lead climbers. But on this expedition there were other candidates for the lead, though at the time the 'Big Four' moved out in front Don was still suffering with his ear trouble. He attempted to do a carry up to Camp 1 on 5 April but only made it half-way before being forced to retire. Fortunately, in the next few days he recovered fully, and the other two were also becoming increasingly well acclimatized and fit.

On 10 April, the British trio moved up to Camp 1, to be hit by a savage storm which very nearly caused several casualties on the mountain. Don had set out behind the other two and was caught in the white-out near the top of the Ice Fall. Only a freak break in the storm enabled him to see the tent at Camp 1 and reach the others; if he had not found it, he would have had an extremely unpleasant night out.

Up at Camp 2 the Austro–Germans were even more severely hit. The tents were not sufficiently strong and the plastic groundsheets quickly disintegrated as a result of the combination of wind and cold. The tents filled up with snow from underneath. The lead climbers had a desperate night and next morning retreated to Camp 1. They recovered quite quickly, however, and returned to Camp 2 once the storm was over. From Camp 1 the British trio made five carries before moving up. Doug Scott suspected that Kuen was trying to keep them one step removed from themselves out front, the whole time. On 17 April, he wrote in his diary:

Radio call from Felix taken by Peter Bednar. Felix wanted five Sherpas to come up in a few days to stay at Camp 2. Seems to be edging us out, wants us to stay here at 1 to keep Sherpas moving up loads. Suits us just now, as long as he doesn't turn round when he's in the

shit – i.e. down with altitude sickness, no supplies coming up, etc.,
and ask why we are not at the front. Seems to alternate in his thinking between us hogging the lead and not doing anything.

Perner's parting shot while I'm on the way down was to say that
Felix and Don must get together, and Felix thinks that Don is lazy !

Meanwhile, the Big Four started work on the South West Face,
running the fixed rope up to Camp 3 quite quickly and then moving up. Their progress now began to slow, and it took them six
full days to make the route up to Camp 4. Back at Camp 2, their
Austrian support group began to get impatient, demanding a turn
out in front. The British trio were quite glad to be out of the line
of fire for once and let the Austro–Germans fight it out amongst
themselves.

The lead climbers were now undoubtedly beginning to tire.
Huber developed a sore throat and had to descend to Base, while
Breitenberger, who was also on the verge of collapse, was finally
forced down. The British trio were appalled at the way the lead
climbers bullied and shouted at Breitenberger to try to keep him
going. They were more like a group of drill sergeants bullying new
recruits than climbers on the highest mountain in the world. Don
now suggested that Hamish, Doug and he should move up to
Camp 3 and establish Camp 4. Felix Kuen agreed to this in return
for a promise that the British, under no circumstances, would go
beyond Camp 4. He seemed determined to deprive them of the
glory or satisfaction of doing any lead climbing.

April was now slipping by and the team were undoubtedly
behind schedule if they were to make an effective bid for the
summit, in spite of having had one of the best seasons for years.
Part of the problem was the fact that only a limited number of
the Sherpas had been persuaded to come up into the Western
Cwm, since they still had insufficient gear and equipment. As a
result the build-up of supplies, even at Camp 2, was inadequate.
The push up the Face had also been on the slow side, especially
when one considers that the fixed ropes left by the international
expedition were still in place on the route from Camp 3 to 4, and
then up to 5; they only had to use a comparatively small amount
of their own rope to link stretches which were either covered in
snow, or where the rope had been damaged.

There was so much work to be done in building platforms at Camp 4 that the British trio, with Horst Schneider, moved up to the Camp on 30 April, and in the next two days put up two boxes and three platforms. Two of these had been brought out from Germany and were based on a design which Don had sketched for Herrligkoffer on his visit to Munich before the expedition. The other platform was already in place and was easily renovated. In view of their promise, they returned to Camp 2, having completed their task, to find that the expedition had been deprived of yet another climber. Werner Hain had been hit on the knee by a rock and had to be taken down to Camp 1. This was particularly unfortunate since Hain, as well as being a first-class climber, got on well with the British members of the team and acted as something of a mediator between them and the Huber–Kuen duo.

It was at this time that Herrligkoffer returned from Germany with the down gear demanded by the Sherpas. This precipitated another crisis. The lead climbers, who admittedly had been out in front for a lot of the time, while the British members of the team had been down at Base Camp, were now extremely tired. They felt the need for a rest, and Herrligkoffer's arrival in Base Camp seemed a good moment. Michel Anderl, the deputy leader, called the whole team back down to Base Camp to welcome Herrligkoffer, and put on 'a good show' for him. Don was appalled at this decision, since time was now running out fast; the weather was excellent, and this seemed the time for an all-out push. He favoured staying up, with as many Sherpas as possible, to keep the route going. Kuen and the German leadership rejected this suggestion and told him to come down with the others. Don, however, decided to stay on and naturally Hamish and Doug stayed with him. They were not alone, however, since Adi Weissensteiner (who had taken over the unenviable job of controlling the Sherpas), Adi Sager and five Sherpas stayed at Camp 2. Hamish, Doug and Don now resolved to move up to Camp 4, to try to establish and stock Camp 5, supported by the Sherpas. Unfortunately, however, the latter objective proved impractical since the Ice Fall Sherpas, and those working from Camp 1 to 2, had mostly gone down to see the homecoming celebrations for Dr Herrligkoffer. Doug Scott takes up the story :

The casualty list was now growing, and in theory at least, we were fortunate to have the Doctor back. Leo Breitenberger was sent back to Kathmandu in the helicopter which came to collect Hain. According to Herrligkoffer, Breitenberger had pulmonary oedema, but in fact he turned out to be suffering from pleurisy, while Hain came back to Base Camp two weeks later, having recovered from a suspected shattered knee joint ! However, the Doctor did not tend many more patients before he, too, had to be evacuated. He had flown up to 15,000 feet and had a mild heart attack from the physiological strain this entailed.

Horst Vitt, the German diplomat, had already died from pulmonary oedema, having tried to reach Base Camp too quickly to take over from the unfortunate Professor Huttl. Mischa Saleki also joined the list of evacuees, though for a different reason. Unable to stand the derision which came his way any longer, he stowed away in a helicopter, according to German press statements. Considering the machines only seated two, he must have made himself very inconspicuous, if not invisible, and presumably almost weightless ! (Incidentally, these were the highest helicopter comings and goings ever recorded as far as we know.) Finally, Hans Berger had gallstone trouble and severe pains in his bladder, but with suitable treatment he was able to come back towards the end.

On the credit side, Peter Bednar recovered from a wrongly administered cholera injection which had plagued him throughout the expedition. Luckily, a visiting band of German professors had diagnosed his problem and had treated him correctly. Peter was at last able to reach the Face after being posted for weeks at a time at the lonely Camp 1. Meanwhile, we went up to Camp 4, and in the next few days fixed 500 feet of rope up to Camp 5, using the remainder of the international expedition's rope which Dougal and Don had placed the year before. We dumped ropes, tents and oxygen at the site and chopped out a platform for two tents.

Their action in staying up at Camp 5 was severely criticized, and even described as 'sabotage' by Kuen and Herrligkoffer. Kuen states :

Finally the Englishmen left the Camp that they had already occupied for ten days. For sleeping they had used up fifteen large bottles of oxygen, in addition to a whole lot of provisions, and yet in ten days they had merely laid 40 metres of rope between Camps 4 and 5 and set up a Whillans Box and a platform. They had forcibly taken away from the Sherpas, who were on the route between Camp 3 and 4, flasks of oxygen and used them up in Camp 4. The Britons had grievously upset the provisioning plans of Camp 5 and intentionally or unintentionally had sabotaged it.

Accusation and counter-accusation. Doug Scott assures me that they only used four bottles in the entire period and that the other bottles which Kuen found when he returned to Camp 4 had been uncovered when they had dug out the platform, having been left from the international expedition. The British trio were doing their best to uphold their part of the bargain, and keep the expedition going. In the period of ten days that they were at Camp 4, they made the route up to Camp 5. Doug and Hamish went out the first day but, unfortunately, Hamish was forced to retreat with stomach trouble. Doug carried on, climbing solo, going higher than he had ever been before, using the fixed ropes of the international expedition as far as possible, joining one or two gaps with the fresh rope he was carrying. He went up to a height of almost 26,000 feet, to the head of the Great Central Couloir which is short of the point where one traverses right to reach Camp 5.

The next day Don went out with him and they made the route all the way up to Camp 5, where they started digging out a platform. Then they made one or two further carries to Camp 5. Admittedly, they did spend a long time at Camp 4 without making appreciable progress. There was, however, some bad weather during this period and they experienced a certain amount of trouble with the Sabre oxygen equipment which Don had had specially developed for the expedition.

When Kuen and Huber arrived on 10 May, there were more arguments. In Doug's words:

Huber and Kuen arrived at Camp 4, armed with a plan they had worked out at Base Camp. In effect it placed us in Camp 3, and Sherpas in Camp 4 with Peter Perner or Adi Weissensteiner if the latter's cough would allow it. Horst Schneider and Adi Sager were to go to Camp 5 and Kuen and Huber to 6. When all was ready two of us were to be allowed to join them at the front in an attack on the summit. But just how we could get enough oxygen and other equipment up there, to support four climbers, was not explained, and we grew suspicious. We had a feeling that we were being edged out again. So we worked out a compromise plan, which put us in support of the summit pair, with one other Austrian accompanying us in Camp 5. After Kuen and Huber had made their bid, we four of the support party would have a go.

After some debate, this proposal was accepted and Kuen and Huber moved up to 5. Unfortunately, Schneider and Sager were not satisfied with the new arrangements and they went to persuade Kuen to revert to his original plan. The crunch came when Schneider and Sager returned from their mission. Schneider said, 'You British are in trouble. Kuen says you must go down to Camp 3 or he will come down, call off the Sherpas and end the expedition.' Next day we went down to Camp 2 and later to Base Camp. We had come to the end, and reached the point where personality differences could no longer be ignored. Both Schneider and Sager refused to carry for Don.

It must be noted that the British trio had not insisted on having the first attempt at the summit; they had merely asked to support the summit pair from Camp 5, and that they should have the second summit attempt. The relationship between the Britons and the Austrians had become so bad, however, that the split had now spread from not only between them and the 'Big Four', but to one between them and most of the other Austrian members of the team.

On a mountain such as Everest, when one has reached the point where one pair, or group, believe that others are saving themselves solely for a summit bid, teamwork becomes impossible. It is ironic that Don, with Doug and Hamish, felt forced to take the same controversial step that Mazeaud, the Vauchers and Carlo Mauri took on the international expedition. On the other hand, on this occasion, the British trio had taken a very full and active part in the expedition, and in the later stages had done their best to make a series of compromises to keep the expedition going.

The British trio reached Camp 2 on the morning of 15 May and then that afternoon were amazed by the arrival of Felix Kuen and Huber, back at Camp 2. This was particularly ironic in the light of his threat that unless the Britons dropped back to Camp 3 he would come down and call off the expedition. One wonders whether he had lost his nerve, finding that he was out in front by himself. In an article in *Bergsteiger* he described how his sleeping bag in Camp 5 was surrounded by a crust of ice within breathing range, and stated that 'life here is unbearable'.

The three Britons had had enough, however, and went down to Base Camp the next day. Two days later, 18 May, a last attempt to reach the summit was begun. Kuen, Huber and Berger climbed straight from Camp 2 up to Camp 4, and then, on 19 May, Sager, Perner, Schneider, Huber and Kuen moved into Camp 5. They now had five Sherpas carrying loads straight through from Camp 2 to Camp 4, but supplies were undoubtedly thin on the Face and there was certainly insufficient oxygen equipment for a protracted assault. On 21 May, the five Austrians, with two Sherpas, moved up to Camp 6, once again using the ropes left by the international expedition for most of the way. Kuen, Huber, Sager and Schneider all planned to stay that night in a single two-man tent, which they had erected at Camp 6. While Schneider and Sager erected the tent in a cleft in the cliff, Kuen, together with Huber, worked his way round the corner of the rock tower to an almost horizontal stretch leading up to the snowfield. They were thus planning to by-pass the true difficulties of the Rock Band on the South West Face, to take the escape route which Don had discovered the previous year. It was now getting dark, so the pair returned to the already crowded two-man tent.

That night the weather broke and it began to hail, the temperature sinking to −40°C. The weather was still very bad the next morning and the team had insufficient reserves of either stamina or food and equipment to sit it out and wait for the bad weather to subside, so on 22 May they decided to turn back and abandon their attempt.

It is an academic point whether Kuen and Huber got higher than Don and Dougal the previous year. They had traversed round the corner whilst of course Don and Dougal had climbed straight up into the gully which seemed to penetrate the Rock Band. The two Austrians claim to have got to a point higher than that of the two Britons, but this is unlikely in the light of the route which they followed. It certainly is not worth wasting any time in conjecture on whether they did or did not.

And so another expedition to the South West Face ended in acrimony and arguments. Looking at all three expeditions dispassionately, whoever was right or wrong on the different sides of the argument, the leadership of each expedition seemed to have made several basic mistakes. The Japanese, in 1970, were undoubtedly an extremely strong and well-organized expedition, but had split their objective between the sure South East Ridge route and the South West Face. Their team, large though it was, was still not big enough to sustain two independent attempts and, as a result, had had to decide upon which one to give priority. They had decided, with some argument within the team, to give priority to the South East Ridge route, to make sure that they put a Japanese on the summit of Everest. They did, at least, have partial success by reaching the summit, and, perhaps equally important, they did return to Japan as a united party.

The following year the international expedition compounded the Japanese mistakes by taking out an expedition which was, if anything, slightly weaker than that of the Japanese, and yet at the same time tackling two objectives. One of these was the West Ridge of Everest, which was considerably harder and therefore demanded greater logistic preparations than the South Col route. Even so, the international expedition might well have succeeded had it been more fortunate with weather and had it been spared the tragic death of Harsh Bahuguna. The storm which had occurred in the middle of the expedition shattered the fragile unity of the international team, and caused the defection of Pierre Mazeaud and his friends. It is extraordinary how each expedition repeated mistakes which could perhaps have been avoided, had the expedition leaders analysed the previous expeditions.

Herrligkoffer was at least going for a single objective, but the structure of the team was probably potentially more dangerous even than that of the international expedition. In effect, there were two groups – the British trio and the Austro–Germans plus the rest of the expedition. The Austro–Germans, even though several of them were not enamoured of Herrligkoffer's leadership, remained essentially loyal to the leader's directive. The British group, coming from a different environment, without any of the automatic ties of loyalty that bound the Austro–Germans, were inevitably more critical. It seemed to me, when I was considering whether to pull out of the expedition or not, that a lack of sound preparation before the expedition, and this bi-national split during the expedition, could make failure almost inevitable. Sadly, this proved to be the case. The failure of these two international expeditions has led to an automatic condemnation of all international climbing enterprises. I suspect that in the case of Everest, this could be justifiable. So many pressures are brought to bear on the Everest climber, particularly one going for the South West Face. For a start, the expedition must inevitably be large and therefore expensive. If the money is raised from the media and commerce, naturally they want a return in publicity, and it is this very publicity that imposes the greatest pressures on the climbing members of the team. There is even a touch of the international golf tournament with individual members being given star category in the reporting and, in the event of success, the pair reaching the summit are lionized, to the inevitable exclusion of the other team members who helped them to get there. There is nothing new in this. The publicity following the pre-war Everest attempts was every bit as intense as that which follows today's epics. In 1953, it was Hillary and Tenzing who received the accolades for reaching the summit of Everest. Who, today, remembers the efforts of George Lowe, in forcing the route up to the South Col – or Evans and Bourdillon who made the first summit attempt?

Immediately the purist will say that no climber worth his salt will be concerned with such sordid matters as material rewards, fame, or a position in history. But this attitude is unrealistic; even the most modest of people like to have their efforts recognized in relation to the contribution they have made to the success of a venture.

It seems to me essential that the leader who selects a team must know the members of that team extremely well. Only then can he assess how far each member will cooperate with the others, and estimate to what degree they will be prepared to sacrifice their own ambitions for the good of the team as a whole. It is unlikely that you are going to be able to assemble a team of totally unselfish easy-going people, since the talented climber needed for forcing a route to the summit, by his very nature will have strong ambitions and is probably quite an egotist. It is essential, therefore, to get a group together who can accept each other's role within the team, and each other's ambitions, and who will also be prepared to compromise in the face of conflict. It is undoubtedly a lot easier to assemble such a group from a single country, simply because most of the climbers one knows to that degree will come from the same country as oneself.

Were these three expeditions a total waste of time? Certainly not – each expedition learned something more about the mountain. In Doug Scott's words, summing up what he learned on his first trip to Everest:

To me, the trip gave rise to few delusions of grandeur; I am simply glad to have been able to go up the Ice Fall unscathed, and to have entered the Western Cwm, that incomparable valley of snow lying between the iridescent ice of Nuptse and the hanging glaciers of the South West side of Everest. Each day I expected to succumb to the altitude; I examined myself minutely each morning for sore throat or other symptoms. Thanks to Don's guidance, all three of us acclimatized slowly, and after more than two weeks and four carries up to Camp 5, we went well to the end. One of the driving forces was a personal curiosity to find out how high one can go before the stomach starts to heave, the legs fold under, the head aches and the mind hallucinates.

Once back home the bad memories fade; one's slides and photographs bring back the haunting beauty of rock and ice swept by winds and avalanche and scorched by strong sunlight. It is an area of stark beauty where nothing grows; no trees, no flowers, no lichens even; it is a place where man's confidence is quickly shattered by a slight disturbance in the atmosphere which may transform the once-quiet Face into a whirling mass of spindrift, sending its insolent invaders scuttling to their tents, battered by the fury raging outside.

And so, climbers continued to dream of the South West Face of Everest, and in most of them, this whole mixed range of motivations encompassed a full span between idealism and materialism.

5

PREPARATIONS FOR OUR OWN EXPEDITION

Autumn 1972

The lure of Everest and the attraction of leading my own expedition had proved too much for me, even during the course of the international expedition.

I had been trying to get permission to attempt the South West Face ever since I heard of the failure of the international expedition of 1971. The problem was that a dozen other climbers, from different countries, had the same idea. The Nepalese authorities only released a list of firm bookings for Everest in the New Year of 1972. Most of these applications had been in for some years and, as a result, we weren't even on the end of the list. An Italian millionaire called Guido Monzino had Everest for both the autumn of 1972 and the spring of 1973. He was planning to make a reconnaissance in the autumn and then a full-scale attempt (apparently only on the South East Ridge, not the Face) the following spring. The Japanese Rock Climbers' Club had Everest for the autumn of 1973, the Spaniards for the spring of 1974 and the Japanese Ladies for the spring of 1975. I already knew that the British Army had put in an application for Everest, and were hoping to get permission for the spring of 1976. It seemed an awful long time to wait, though there was some possibility that some of these expeditions might fail to materialize.

My contact in Kathmandu was Mike Cheney, who was assistant to Jimmy Roberts. He is a bird-like little man, with a slightly high-pitched voice which disguises an extraordinary level of courage. Having been in the Gurkhas he had retired to take up tea-planting in India. He had then contracted cancer, and was warned that he had only a couple of months to live. A resolve to get the utmost out of life in the time left to him made him decide to go and settle in Nepal, and he drove there by Land-Rover in defiance of his doctors, who had told him he should be in bed. Like Francis Chichester, by refusing to bow down to a seemingly fatal disease, he somehow succeeded in defying death. On reaching Nepal he started working for Jimmy Roberts. Mike had access to all the latest information on expeditions' comings and goings in Kathmandu. Consequently, he was able to help me in putting in applications to the Nepalese Government, and also indicating any possibly vacant slots.

In January 1972, just after I had pulled out of Herrligkoffer's expedition, it seemed possible that Monzino might abandon his expeditions altogether. I hoped for the spring slot of 1973, since tackling Everest in the autumn presented a large number of problems. There are two periods in which you can climb in Nepal and they have very different characteristics. The pre-monsoon season is squeezed between the clearing of the winter snows, round about the beginning of March, and the arrival of the monsoon at the end of May: the post-monsoon season starts at the end of the monsoon – any time between mid-September to early-October – and then trails off into the gathering winter cold. During the pre-monsoon season the weather tends to be more unsettled than post-monsoon. However, there are two advantages in climbing in the spring. Firstly, the temperature is getting progressively warmer during the course of the expedition, so that when the team are in a position to make a summit bid, hopefully before the arrival of the monsoon, the weather is also at its warmest. In addition, the winds in the spring do not seem to be anything like as serious as they are in the autumn. In the autumn you have the converse effect; when the team starts off it is relatively warm, in the immediate lee of the monsoon, and then, as they climb higher up the mountain, it gets progressively colder. Thus, when they are ready to make a bid for the summit, the weather is considerably colder than when they started. Much more serious, however, during the autumn, are the high-altitude jet-stream winds which seem to blow continuously at an altitude starting at round about 24,500 feet. It is for this reason that the record of expeditions attempting mountains of over 26,000 feet in the post-monsoon season has been very poor. The only mountain of this category to be climbed was Cho Oyu (26,904 ft.), on 19 October 1954 by a very small, compact, Austrian expedition led by Herbert Tichy. There was, however, practically no technical climbing on this mountain – it being little more than a very high-altitude fell walk.

The story on Everest in the post-monsoon season has been depressing. In 1952, the Swiss made two attempts to make the first ascent of Everest. Their first attempt in the spring of 1952, an expedition led by Dr Edouard Wyss-Dunant, was very nearly successful when Raymond Lambert and Tenzing, who was to climb Everest in 1953, made their summit bid from Camp 7 at a height of 27,230 feet. They reached a height of 28,050 feet, roughly 1,800 feet below the summit, but were going so slowly, mainly because the oxygen system was defective, that it was obvious to them that they would not be able to reach the top and then get back before dark. They were therefore forced to retreat back to the South Col.

Having been so close to success, they resolved to return in the autumn. This expedition was led by Dr Gabriel Chevaley, and the climbing leader was now Raymond Lambert. Norman Dyhrenfurth joined the expedition as photographer and film cameraman. Base Camp was established on 2 October, but they only succeeded in repeating the route through the Ice Fall and establishing Camp 3 at the head of it (our Camp 1) on 14 October. On 20 October, their Camp 4 (our Camp 2) was established, in the middle of the Western Cwm. They were undoubtedly getting rather late in the season, and were further delayed by an unfortunate accident to one of the best Sherpas, Mingma Dorji, when a sérac on the Lhotse Face collapsed and swept him away. Several other members of the team were injured at the same time. Partly as a result of these delays they only reached the South Col on 19 November, when Lambert, Reiss and Tenzing, with seven Sherpas, did a carry up to it. On 20 November, the three climbers moved upwards, towards the South East Ridge, but were met at a height of about 26,000 feet by a hurricane of polar temperature and intensity – a barrier which it would have been near-suicidal to cross. They had no choice but to retreat. The following year, in the spring, John Hunt's expedition succeeded in climbing Everest.

Norman Dyhrenfurth returned to the Everest massif in 1955,

as leader of an international expedition which attempted a direct route up Lhotse from the Western Cwm. They, too, were defeated by savage winds in the post-monsoon season. The only hopeful factor in considering the post-monsoon season for an attempt on the South West Face was the experience of the Japanese in the autumn of 1969. They did not have any particular problems with wind at all. Whether this was a freak season, or whether they were getting some shelter from the positioning of the South West Face, it was impossible to tell, but it did give some cause for hope. The experience of the Argentinian expedition in the autumn of 1971 certainly was not encouraging, since they also were defeated by savage winds once they reached the South Col of Everest. Earlier than the Swiss had been in 1952, they established Base Camp on 15 September and found the Ice Fall with a good covering of snow which made progress easy and faster. They took a mere three days to climb the Ice Fall against the fortnight taken the previous spring by the international expedition, and by 21 September had established Camp 3 at the foot of the Lhotse Face at a height of 23,000 feet. Then, on 30 September, they had severe storms which put down very heavy snowfall – at Base Camp 50 centimetres, Camp 1 – 1·70 metres, at Camp 2 – 1·50 metres and at Camp 3 an incredible 2 metres. These heavy post-monsoon snowfalls definitely seem to be a feature of this period; most of the time the sky is clear, and even though there is high wind there is blue sky. When it does snow, it snows very heavily indeed and, as a result, the damage caused by a couple of days' snow fall lasts for several more days before an expedition can recover itself and get moving again. The Argentinians were increasingly troubled by high winds and snow as they climbed the Lhotse Face but, in spite of this, they succeeded in reaching the South Col on 28 October, and actually established Camp 5 there on the 29th. The wind was very savage however, at 160 kilometres an hour, the temperature —38° C and they could make no further progress. Their tents were being torn to bits by the winds, three Sherpas had frostbite, and so they, also, had to surrender to near-impossible weather conditions, abandoning their top camp on the South Col on 31 October. Their leader, Lt Col. Captiva Tolosa, did give us some grounds for hope, however, since he told us that the

South West Face seemed to get some shelter from these very high winds.

Another reason why I did not like the idea of trying the South West Face of Everest in the autumn of 1972 was that we would have no time at all to organize the expedition, since we could not really get under way until we had learned the fate of Dr Herrligkoffer's expedition. From initial reports in March and early April, they seemed to make good progress and there was the probability that they could well climb the mountain. I very much doubted if they would try the true South West Face, but even if they managed to get round the escape route which Don had spied in 1971 and reach the summit of Everest, we would probably have had considerable difficulties in raising funds for an attempt on the true South West Face route.

The other factor was that I felt that the quality of the Sherpa support was vital to our chances of success. The best and most reliable Sherpas available in Nepal were, without doubt, employed by Jimmy Roberts of Mountain Travel. I had already asked Jimmy, as well as Mike Cheney, whether they would be interested in being involved in the expedition. At this stage they had to warn me that the autumn was at the height of their trekking season, and that therefore neither they nor their Sherpas would be available at this period. Jimmy and Mike were hoping that Monzino might withdraw altogether, and we might be able to get the spring slot for ourselves. We were not the only climbers who were trying to jump the queue. A representative of the Spanish expedition, which already had permission for 1974, armed with a letter from Prince Carlos of Spain, was rumoured to have arrived in Kathmandu, pressing their cause for going out a year early. They, of course, were in front of us in the queue. Mike Cheney also warned me that the Canadian Alpine Club were trying for permission for Everest, though when I wrote to them their President assured me that he had never heard of any such plan. This manoeuvring for the mountain had very little to do with real climbing, and yet, strangely, it had its own special fascination, though at times it became downright frustrating. At this stage the only person involved in my plans was Dougal Haston who was always mildly amused by my obvious enjoyment of the wheeling and dealing of trying to get the mountain. Dougal was quite happy sitting back in Leysin, skiing and climbing, and waiting to see what the fates would bring.

Then in mid-April we learned that we would almost certainly be able to get the post-monsoon slot in 1972, for Monzino had definitely withdrawn. Monzino, however, still had his options open on the spring 1973 slot. Though I felt that we had to commit ourselves to this certain chance rather than hope that Monzino would withdraw in the spring also, I was still extremely worried about the prospect of trying to organize a South West Face expedition at such short notice, in such a doubtful period of the year, with the likelihood that we would not have the best Sherpas. It was obvious that a South West Face of Everest expedition would cost something in the region of £60,000 – a lot of money to collect in the course of a few weeks. But then I had another idea. Why not attempt Everest by the South Col route, with a lightweight expedition? This would mean that there would be nothing like the same financial involvement, and yet the challenge would be there, and probably with a small expedition it would be very much more fun. Immediately, I attacked the new concept with enthusiasm. Just how small can you pare down an Everest expedition? The ultimate, of course, would be one man, on his own, This had been tried back in 1934 when Maurice Wilson attempted to climb Everest from the North. No experienced Alpinist, he was a dreamer and mystic, who slipped into Tibet in native dress, with three Sherpas and a single pony carrying all his equipment. He reached Camp 3 on the North Side of Everest at a height of 21,000 feet without any difficulty, but his porters, not surprisingly, had never taken his attempt very seriously and now refused to go any further. Determined not to give in, however, he made several attempts to reach the North Col and finally died of cold and exhaustion. His body was found in 1935 quite close to Camp 3. There was another solo attempt in 1947, by a Canadian adventurer called Earl Denman. He claimed to have reached 23,000 feet – a height higher than the North Col of Everest – but there was no evidence to back up his claim. He was only away from Darjeeling for five weeks.

The scale of Everest is so vast that it is difficult to conceive of a successful solo attempt. All the expeditions to Everest have been on the heavy side, with strong back-ups of Sherpas. The only exception was another, unofficial, expedition of four climbers, three Americans and one Swiss, led by Woodrow Wilson Sayre, a grandson of the President of that name. Their declared objective was Gyachung Kang, that magnificent peak of 25,900 feet which in itself was probably beyond their capabilities. The party was comparatively inexperienced, poorly equipped and had no porters. Reaching the Gyachung Kang region, they slipped over the Tibetan frontier on to the Rongbuk Glacier, and succeeded in climbing well above the North Col of Everest to a height of 25,000 feet. This was a remarkable achievement, but the attempt was fairly heavily castigated in conventional climbing circles. Ramsay Ullman in his official book telling the story of the American Everest expedition, declares :

In retrospect, as told by Sayre, the exploit was all fun and games. It made lively reading in *Life* magazine and a good story on the lecture circuit. But it is exactly this sort of hare-brained adventuring that makes the general public think all climbers are mentally deficient. And it hasn't the remotest resemblance to what true mountaineers mean by 'mountaineering'.

But I wonder. There are quite a few mountaineers today who are beginning to feel that this type of expedition is true mountaineering, while the massive, hopefully well-organized, expeditions are getting quite a long way from it. Another challenge on Everest, of course, is to try to climb the mountain without oxygen. This is the only way that a truly lightweight expedition could succeed, since the weight of the oxygen bottles needed on the upper slopes of the mountain means that you need a fair number of load-carriers and consequently the size of the expedition must inevitably escalate. There is a certain appeal in the thought of man, unaided, reaching the summit of Everest. It would undoubtedly be a really huge challenge, since from all the evidence gained so far, particularly from the pre-war expeditions, the height of 28,000 feet seems to be a critical one without the use of oxygen. The climber who tries to reach the summit of Everest without oxygen is certainly taking huge risks, not only with his life but perhaps also with his future health – he would be making a superhuman effort on a body and brain starved of oxygen. Nobody knows just how much damage would or would not be caused by this effort.

These, then, were the lines on which I was thinking for an attempt on the South Col route of Everest. I put a great deal of thought into the matter and finally came up with what I felt was the minimum practical number for an attempt using oxygen – a climbing team of four climbers, supported by two others since you would need someone at Base Camp and at Advanced Base Camp in the Western Cwm. But this could not be a true four-man team; I intended to use oxygen and so, inevitably, the logistic load on just four men would be much too great. Therefore, one had to bring in some Sherpas as well and I planned on using six Sherpas. The team, then, would total twelve men – by no means minuscule as expeditions go, but still very much smaller than the average.

I based my planning on what I had learned on the South Face of Annapurna. One factor which made it very much easier was that the route was known. Also the length of time it would take to set up each section of the route between camps was fairly predictable. My calculations started with a hypothetical two climbers at the top camp – which would be at a height of approximately 27,600 feet – with a tent, sleeping bags, gear needed for the night and the oxygen bottles they would need for the assault the next day. You then work out how many carries it is going to take to get the pair into that position, together with the number of bottles of oxygen required by the climbers carrying the loads. You add this weight to the weight of the tentage of the penultimate camp on the South Col, the amount of spare oxygen bottles and so on that are going to be required there, and so you can work it out, all the way down the mountain.

A theory I worked out was that having established Camp 2, the Advanced Base Camp, in the Western Cwm, you can climb Everest in eight days, given perfect weather; two days to ferry requisite gear to Camp 3 on the Lhotse Face and establish four climbers and six Sherpas; two days to climb, fix ropes where necessary and ferry gear to Camp 4, half-way up the Lhotse Face. Climbers, using oxygen from the foot of the Face, would move up to Camp 4 with two Sherpas; two days for the four climbers to move up to Camp 5 on the South Col, and one day to establish two climbers in their high camp on the South Ridge. The support pair at Camp 5 would move up to Camp 6 on the day of the assault, and have a chance of either making a second attempt or a second ascent.

As far as the Ice Fall was concerned, we should, of course, need as much in the way of ladders and fixed ropes as would a mammoth expedition. The big difference, however, was that we required only a limited amount of equipment to go through the Ice Fall, since we were only maintaining approximately twelve people above the Ice Fall for a very limited period. I proposed to make the route through the Ice Fall, and then use all the climbers and the six Sherpas over a period of around four to five days to ferry all the gear required for the assault on the mountain up the Ice Fall, and then from Camp 1 up the Western Cwm. In theory, this build-up only takes about ten days.

There were many question marks, and yet many attractive features in this plan. For a start, there would not be the slightly invidious distinction between lead climbers, who have got to be saved at all costs from exhausting themselves, and support climbers and Sherpas who do all the load-carrying. Even though we would be employing Sherpas, the climbers in this situation would have to do as much carrying as the Sherpas. Because of this, I thought there would be a greater integral unity in the team with the bonus, of course, that all four climbers would have a very good chance of reaching the summit of Everest. There were also a lot of problems. A small party would be much more severely affected by some of the heavy snowfalls which could completely obliterate camps on the route. In the light of our actual experience on Everest in the autumn, it is questionable whether a small party could have maintained its drive over the period of time involved and, of course, it would have been impossible to have kept open the route behind Camp 2 while the thrust beyond it was going on. Therefore, if we had run out of supplies at Camp 2, because we were there longer than anticipated, the expedition would inevitably have failed.

Anyway, the concept of this four-man expedition was exciting. It had less the overtones of high finance and heavy publicity that a South West Face venture would inevitably entail. It was also possible to start organizing it before we knew the outcome of the Herrligkoffer expedition. We could even contemplate carrying out this expedition whether or not Herrligkoffer succeeded. And so I went ahead with my plans, formulating them towards the end of April, 1972.

Dougal was already a party to the scheme; the question was, who else to invite? Besides myself, there would be two other so-called lead climbers. I decided upon Nick Estcourt and Mick Burke. Both of them had been with me on the South Face of Annapurna and we had climbed together over a period of years.

Nick is a computer programmer aged twenty-nine, with two children. He is essentially an amateur climber, with a very traditional background – public school, Cambridge University, president of the Cambridge University Mountaineering Club, and then a job in a large organization. My invitation, however, posed him a very real problem, since he had got permission to come with me to the South Face of Annapurna in 1970 and he was naturally afraid that his employers might take exception to his going on another long trip only two years later. The lure of Everest is irresistible, however, and Nick asked for leave of absence, knowing full well that it probably wouldn't do his career any good and, at the same time, that he wouldn't get it with pay. In this respect he probably made the greatest sacrifice of any of our little group, since the others whom I was going to invite were either 'professional' mountaineers who could only benefit from the expedition, or were more independent. Nick had performed extremely well on the South Face of Annapurna – reaching a height of round about 24,000 feet. He has plenty of drive, is tremendously competitive by nature, and yet has an extremely strong conscience. I asked him to act as treasurer of the expedition, since he is always extremely methodical and has, at times, an almost pernickety sense of money values – but then, this is what you want in a treasurer.

Mick Burke had also been with me on the South Face of Annapurna, and we had climbed together on other occasions. Mick originally comes from Wigan, from an essentially working-class background, leaving school at sixteen to go into an insurance office. At the same time, he had started to climb, and quickly abandoned the security of an office for the freedom of living up in the Lake District, taking odd jobs as labourer or barman. He had never been a brilliant rock-climber, but has considerable determination over anything he really wants. As a result, he had made several outstanding routes, particularly on larger mountains. It was he who instigated the first British Cerro Torre expedition in 1967, when Dougal Haston, Peter Crewe, Martin Boysen and he, made a very strong attempt on what might well be the world's most difficult mountain. He then made his way overland up the Americas to California, and he was the first Briton to complete a climb on the famous El Capitan, Yosemite's, and for the matter, the world's, finest Rock Wall. He made the first British ascent of the Nose of El Capitan, leading all the way, and taking up as a second man Bob Wood, a talented climber who had no experience at all of Yosemite's big walls.

It was round this time that Mick got married, and started thinking of the future. Although he had practically no experience in filming, he decided to make his career in films, and managed to get a place at the London Film School. Since then he has gone steadily forward, taking an active part in making the film on the South Face of Annapurna, then going out as assistant cameraman on the ski-traverse of the Alps, led by Alan Blackshaw in the spring of 1972. There were also straight, professional jobs, working in ordinary television feature films. Mick had been with Dougal and myself on the North Face of the Grandes Jorasses, when we had tried to make a new route up the side of the Walker Spur, that same winter. He and I have always had a slightly odd relationship. He is argumentative and, perhaps having left school at sixteen and without a comfortable middle-class background behind him, is fiercely aware of what he considers are his rights and his position in the world of the climbing rat-race. Frequently we had ferocious arguments, usually over money, and yet both of us had the capacity to lose our tempers, blow up at the time and then very quickly simmer down and see the other's point of view. Our friendship has remained intact over a period of years. I had been particularly impressed by Mick on the North Face of the Grandes Jorasses; he had come with us on this primarily as climbing cameraman, and had been very happy to fill this role while Dougal and I did most of the lead climbing. We got to a point where Dougal and I were ensconced in a little two-man snow hole, a third of the way up the Face. There was no room for three and we had therefore sent Mick down to the hut, well below the bottom of the wall, with the promise that we would wait for him when the weather was sufficiently good to make a summit bid. All three of us could go to the top of the North Face together, and Mick could get the climax to the film he was making. And then the weather had improved unexpectedly and both Dougal and I felt that we could not lose a day in waiting for Mick. We set out without him, while he spent a complete day struggling and wading through thigh-deep snow to the foot of the Wall, and climbing up the fixed ropes to our high point, to receive a little note to say that we had abandoned him. In his place I think I would have been absolutely livid at this betrayal, yet Mick took it wonderfully philosophically, fully appreciating and understanding the position that we felt we had been in. This incident, plus some other very good times I had with Mick in the mountains, influenced me in inviting him to join our team. He also, of course, would be a first-class climbing cameraman, since we had no intention of taking with us a big, separate media team such as had accompanied the 1971 expedition.

In addition to my four lead climbers, I envisaged making the push above Camp 2 with our Sherpas. I needed two more climbers in a support role, who would act as long-stops and run the basic administration of the expedition while we were making our summit bid. Mike Thompson, one of my oldest friends, was an obvious choice. He had been with us on the South Face of Annapurna, in a similar support role. In his mid-thirties, an anthropologist by career, he is a reasonable, without being an outstanding, mountaineer, and is wonderfully good at getting on with other people. Mike and I had been to Sandhurst together and both of us had tired of the Army at roughly the same time. The Army released me without argument, but had felt that Mike was of greater value to them, partly because he was just completing the course at the Royal Military College of Science at Shrivenham. Mike struck on an original way of getting out of the Army by standing for Parliament. Every citizen in the British Isles (at that time anyway) had a constitutional right to stand for Parliament, yet no soldier was allowed to go in for politics, so the Army had no choice but to release him. It cost Mike about £250 by the time he had lost his deposit and paid his solicitor's fees. He even had the satisfaction of getting fifty votes in the Middlesbrough West by-election! In the spring of 1972 he was bridged between his career as an anthropologist and that of a property tycoon, just having bought a splendid derelict mansion in Bristol, which he was converting and renovating. The lure of Everest, and particularly a small lightweight expedition, was too much, however, and he agreed to come with us.

The final member of the team was our expedition doctor. I had already come to know Peter Steele, who had been the doctor on the international expedition, before I withdrew from the team. Peter, a doctor who had never been able to settle down to a steady routine of medical practice, had spent his time as an outback doctor in Labrador, then went to Nepal to work in a hospital in Kathmandu, and visited Bhutan working in that wonderful, closed land of mountains. His wife and young children accompanied him on all these adventures and he gave the impression of being a tightly integrated family man, at the same time as having an adventurous disposition. He had the double advantage of being able to speak fluent Nepali, had obviously been very good at handling the Sherpas in his experience of the international expedition, and had as wide a knowledge of high-mountain illnesses as one could possibly desire. My invitation placed him in a dilemma, since he had at last decided that it was time for him to settle down to more steady medical practice. However, for Peter, also, the lure of Everest proved too great and he agreed to come with us.

So there we were in May 1972 with permission to climb Everest reasonably assured, an exciting concept of a small expedition, and an enthusiastic team. And yet the presence of the South West Face still nagged at me. What we were trying to do was exciting and interesting and, I suspect, would have been a great deal of fun, in spite of the immense physical and mental demands which such a lightweight expedition would inevitably impose.

But the South West Face was still there! As May dragged out, it became increasingly evident that the European expedition was getting into severe difficulties, and then, at the end of May, came the news. The Britons had pulled out and, a few days later, the entire team had withdrawn from Everest. The South West Face was still unclimbed.

My mind was in a turmoil for a period of about ten days. We could be sure of raising sufficient funds for our South Col expedition – a strong body of climbing opinion in Britain strongly approved of its concept, being tired of the massive, heavily publicized expedition. It would certainly bring infinitely fewer personality problems and afford greater personal satisfaction, as I should have a very good chance of reaching the summit of Everest myself, if we were to be successful. And yet, the fact remained that we would be following the route that others had climbed before us. Admittedly, no one had climbed Everest in the autumn; admittedly, our expedition was going to be considerably smaller than any other expedition and so the odds we were piling up against ourselves would be that much greater. But these were artificial obstacles. They weren't the same as that unclimbed 2,000 feet above the high points of the two previous expeditions on the South West Face. The South West Face of Everest obviously represented a massive problem of technical climbing at high altitude, together with the logistics of getting all the gear, food and oxygen cylinders up to the foot of the Rock Band, and the problems of holding together a group of men under these circumstances. Nevertheless, the entire concept of the South West Face expedition, with all the complications, its challenges and its problems, was still extremely attractive – perhaps merely because the challenge was so very great. And so, in mid-June, I came to my decision. We changed from a relatively simple concept of a small expedition to an all-out assault on the South West Face of Everest.

From the day I made that decision, we were to have approximately eight weeks to increase the size of the team, raise all the extra money required – approximately £60,000 – and get together the mass of equipment that such a large expedition would involve. The scale of the thing we were about to undertake was tremendously exciting, even though the odds seemed to be stacked against us. The first thing was to adapt my basic planning to the larger objective. We were obviously going to have to increase the size of the team, but I was anxious to keep it as compact as possible. On the South Face of Annapurna I had had, in effect, eight lead climbers, who were capable of, and therefore expected and needed to share the lead. There were also three support climbers, two of whom were competent mountaineers yet obviously not of the same standard as the other climbers, and were therefore quite happy to adopt the role of support, without having any aspirations to go out in front. Because we had taken with us a comparatively small number of Sherpas – a mere six – the lead climbers also had to double up in a load-carrying capacity. This was primarily because the technical difficulty was so great on the South Face on Annapurna that we could not visualize being able to use the Sherpas to any great degree above 21,000 feet and this, in fact, was the case. The Sherpas never carried above Camp 4, at 21,600 feet, and by far the most arduous carry was up the Ice Ridge, in the centre of the Face, from Camp 4 to Camp 5. The climbers, therefore, had to take turns in lead climbing and load-carrying. There's no doubt about it, the lead climbers also proved to be the best load-carriers. The dual role, however, proved too much for most of the team, and by the end of the expedition there were hardly any fit members left.

The situation on Everest was very different. We knew from the experience of the previous expeditions that there was no technically difficult hard climbing, up to a height of 27,000 feet. We hoped that at least some fixed ropes were still usable, and even if they were covered in the post-monsoon snows, the very presence of these snows would make climbing on the lower part of the Face still easier. Therefore, the pressure on the lead climbers would be less. At the same time, because of the easier angle and the sheer scale of the logistic problem, it was essential that we used a good number of Sherpas for ferrying gear up the mountain. It seemed to me that we did not want to have too many lead climbers, since the real challenge of the climb was above the site of Camp 6 at the foot of the Rock Band, and it was unlikely that I was going to be able to employ more than four climbers to tackle this and then make the summit bid. The rest of the climbing below that point was comparatively routine and therefore would give the climbers who first went up and fixed ropes on this section comparatively little satisfaction. I therefore arrived at a figure of six lead climbers, of which, initially, I envisaged being one, to go out in front to take it in turns to make the route on the mountain. This would give me a reserve of two good climbers.

The next question was how many more climbers to have along as support. I decided we would need a further four. The job of the support climber is not so much that of load-carrier, but of managing the different camps on the mountain. I planned to put the burden of load-carrying on the shoulders of our Sherpas – to employ enough of them to be able to make a fast build-up of supplies to the Western Cwm and then up the Face itself. On the question of Sherpas, I arrived eventually at a figure of forty, having started with a figure considerably lower than this. My thinking about the expedition comprised a series of expansions from my original concept of a mini-expedition to climb the mountain by the South Col and I suspect this was partially because I did not want to escape too far from this concept; I preferred to keep our own South West Face venture as compact as possible, partially on an aesthetic level, and partially on one of sheer finance – the more people we had, the more it was going to cost.

And so, for my choice of a team. In the first instance, I was looking for three more hard climbers to join Dougal, Nick Estcourt and Mick Burke. This immediately raised vast problems of selection. There were so many first-class climbers in Britain and it very quickly became evident that my choice would excite much interest and a certain amount of public criticism. For the simple fact that the mountain was Everest, that we were going on the South West Face rather than the South Col route, and that I intended to select all my team members from this country, gave us the status of a national expedition, whether we liked it or not. Indeed, we needed it, since it was largely on this basis that we were able to raise the necessary funds in such a short time.

I now wanted to add four more members to the six we already had. At this stage I envisaged two of them being lead climbers so that I should have, in effect, six potential leaders and four who would adopt support roles. Although there are a huge number of very talented climbers in this country today, there are comparatively few who have real high-altitude experience. From this point of view, both Doug Scott and Hamish MacInnes were obvious choices, since they had both performed well on Everest, reaching heights of nearly 26,000 feet. There was also some hope that their acclimatization would carry through to the autumn. I therefore invited them to join me for the autumn attempt and they both accepted promptly. I had to think harder about my support climbers. They were going to prove particularly important, not only for keeping things going on the mountain, but also for helping me fling the expedition together in approximately eight weeks. Back in January, when I had been discussing the question of team selection with Dougal, he had suggested Graham Tiso as a possible person for this role. Graham was running a very successful climbing shop in Edinburgh and was also one of the main importers of specialized climbing equipment in this country. In addition to this, he was an extremely sound, steady mountaineer, with a long record of Scottish winter climbing behind him. Dougal vouched for his steadiness, and I did know him slightly – we had climbed together many years before in Glencoe, and I had met him on several occasions since. One of my biggest problems was going to be obtaining all the specialized equipment, some of which was in short supply, in time; Graham was an obvious choice and therefore I invited him. The only factor that gave me some food for thought was the worry that Graham's personality, the ebullient self-confidence of the successful businessman, might be a little too overpowering. In the event, he fulfilled an abosolutely vital role in the expedition, not only in getting the right gear together, but also on the mountain itself. We found that we worked well together, and built up a strong friendship.

My final support climber was to be Kelvin Kent. When I was organizing the Annapurna South Face expedition, I decided that I needed a person who would, in effect, be a Base Camp manager – whose role would not take him much above Base Camp, but who would take on all the day-to-day administration to leave me free to be anywhere on the mountain. The ideal person to adopt such a role seemed to be an Army Officer, one who ideally spoke fluent Nepali. Not knowing such a person, I had therefore approached Charles Wylie, who had been on the 1953 Everest expedition and was a Lieutenant Colonel in the Gurkhas, to ask his advice. He had recommended Kelvin Kent, then a Captain in the Royal Signals, stationed with the Gurkhas in Hong Kong. He was just coming to the end of a tour of duty and Charles assured me that he was both dynamic and an extremely good organizer. I took Kelvin entirely on his recommendation, and we only met personally when we arrived in Kathmandu. Kelvin fulfilled an outstanding role on the Annapurna expedition, even though he had never been on a mountain before. In the end, he reached a height of just over 21,600 feet carrying loads to support the lead team, though his chief and most important function was his handling of our Sherpas and local porters, and his general day-to-day administration of the expedition. I knew that I could rely upon him to fulfil the same function on Everest when things would be considerably more complicated and when we should have many more porters than we had on Annapurna. When I phoned him he had only recently returned from another expedition which had just completed the crossing of the Darien Gap in the Americas. He was about to take on a new job in the Army as Company Commander at Sandhurst. Characteristically, though, he responded to the challenge and accepted my invitation.

Another essential person was Jimmy Roberts. I wrote to him as soon as I decided to change my objective from the South Col route to the South West Face, to ask whether he would be prepared to change his mind and join us, in spite of the pressures of work which I knew his trekking firm would be under. Very fortunately for us, Jimmy could not resist the opportunity of going to Everest once again, and agreed to become my Deputy Leader. This meant that we would have the benefit of his vast mountaineering experience and also would be guaranteed as many of his best Sherpas as he could possibly spare. Having Jimmy with any expedition would also make any relations with the Sherpas very much easier.

This, then, was the team as I now visualized it. From the

moment I announced our intention of changing our objective to the South West Face, and the team I had selected, the phone didn't stop ringing. Everyone wanted to know why I hadn't included Don Whillans. His name had come to be associated with Everest as a result of his part in the two previous expeditions, and therefore people tended to take it for granted that any expedition to the South West Face of Everest must include him. He is undoubtedly an outstanding mountaineer but the real strength of a team is decided not by the ability of any one member, but by how well that team manages to integrate as a single unit. I did not feel that Don would have fitted into the team I had chosen, a feeling that I knew was shared by a majority of the team, particularly those who had been on the Annapurna South Face expedition.

I was now presented with a further problem. Mike Thompson phoned to tell me that he had been thinking very seriously about the expedition and his role in it. He felt that because he was trying to get established in the academic world, at the same time as developing his property in Bristol, he really could not come. The change of plan from the mini-expedition to the full-scale assault of Everest no doubt influenced his decision, since for Mike, having fulfilled a support role on the South Face of Annapurna, the same role on this expedition would merely have been a repetition of all the misery which must inevitably accompany a high-altitude siege, with none of the recompense and elation that our original small-scale adventure promised. I could fully understand Mike's feelings, and immediately started looking round for a substitute.

Our first reserve for the mini-expedition had been Martin Boysen who had also been a member of the Annapurna South Face team, and was a very close friend of mine. I therefore felt obliged to ask him whether he wanted to come on the expedition to replace Mike, even though I knew it would be very difficult for him to accept the invitation, since his wife was due to have a baby while we were away, and he had only just started teaching in a new school. For these reasons, Martin had to regretfully decline the invitation.

And so, who else to ask? There was certainly any number of

fully qualified, talented mountaineers in Britain. I did not want a brilliant lead climber for this replacement since I felt, and this proved to be the case on the mountain, that what we were really short of was good steady supporters. At the same time, I wanted someone who could take the lead if necessary. This would also have the advantage of giving us three lead pairs besides myself, yet freeing me for a support role, which is probably best for the leader of the expedition. In our discussions in January, Dougal had suggested Dave Bathgate, an Edinburgh climber aged thirty-one who had made a considerable impact on Scottish winter climbing and rock-climbing in the early and mid-sixties. He also had two expeditions behind him, both of them to Peru, one to climb Alpemayo and the other to make an attempt, with Don Whillans, Brian Robertson and Ian Macecheran, on the South Face of Huandoy. I knew Dave moderately well and had always been impressed by his quiet, unselfish manner. By profession he was a master-joiner, working in partnership with his brother, and this meant that he would probably be able to get the time off. Therefore I invited him.

A few days after this, on 17 June, we had our first Expedition Meeting in North Wales. It was to coincide with the Alpine Climbing Group Dinner at Llanberis. All the team except Kelvin Kent, who was still in Germany serving with the British Army on the Rhine, and Graham Tiso, managed to attend the meeting, which we held in the very best tradition at the Pen-y-Gwryd Hotel, the home of many of the 1953 Everest Expedition's training weekends and meetings. In spite of his decision to withdraw from the expedition, Mike Thompson had put in an immense amount of work on our behalf, planning the food, and he attended the meeting as well. We got through all the formalities, had a look at prototypes of some of the equipment including a special new box tent which Ultimate Equipment made as a rival to Don Whillans' Box (which of course had been developed in the first instance for the Annapurna South Face expedition) and everything seemed settled.

Next morning, yet another blow. Peter Steele, in his own charming, apologetic way, came to me and told me that he was desperately sorry but he, also, had had second thoughts about the expedition. The thing which really affected Peter's decision was the change from the concept of the mini-expedition to the siege of the Big Face. As far as he was concerned, it would have been just a repetition of 1971, albeit, hopefully, without any of the rows and dissension. He had been attracted by his role on the mini-expedition, where he would have been the only Nepali-speaker with responsibility, beyond that of medicine. Now I had brought in two more Nepali-speakers and administrators in the shape of Jimmy Roberts and Kelvin Kent. I could fully appreciate how he felt, especially as I knew he was also negotiating for a new job in medicine. So I accepted his resignation without any feeling of bitterness at being let down. This was made even easier for me by the fact that Peter was able to recommend someone who sounded a really excellent substitute.

Barney Rosedale was a friend of Peter's who had also worked in Nepal. Peter assured me that Barney could speak good Nepali, was dynamic and a very pleasant person. I telephoned Barney who agreed to come and see me at my home in Cheshire, and the moment I set eyes on him and had my hand gripped in one of the most powerful handshakes I have ever experienced, I took an immediate liking to him. With a shock of untidy, dark hair, intense almost haggard features which were lightened by a warm, spontaneous smile, Barney radiated both energy and sheer human kindness. He had only done a limited amount of rock-climbing and a bit of trekking in Nepal. This didn't seem to matter, since the position of the doctor on a peak like Everest is not high up on the mountain, but at Camp 2 or advanced Base Camp, ready to receive any casualties. His knowledge of Nepal, combined with the fact that he was now thirty-five and had a broad experience of medicine, most of which was spent doing interesting jobs in the outback of Africa or Nepal, made him the perfect choice. Moreover, he was used to making diagnoses on his own, without a hospital or other doctors to whom to refer for a second opinion. His enthusiasm and dedication were demonstrated by the fact that his wife was due to give birth to their first child only two or three days before the date of our projected departure, and yet he was still prepared to go with us.

And so now we had a complete team. We also had about eight

weeks to put together the entire expedition. Even more to the point, we still had nothing like the £60,000 it was going to cost, and my agent, George Greenfield, who is one of the greatest optimists I have ever met, was worried whether we should ever be able to get it. The most frightening thing was that we were going to have to commit ourselves to expenditure before we actually had the money, since we were going to have to order all our equipment and our transportation at the same time as trying to raise it. On the South Face of Annapurna I had had these financial worries taken away from me, since the Mount Everest Foundation had given us their total sponsorship. This meant that they took on any financial risk in return for taking any profits which we might make. In actual fact, Annapurna will probably have made between five and six thousand pounds by the time all the royalties of the book have come in. There didn't seem time to get this kind of support for our present expedition, however, and anyway I had received some indication that it was unlikely that the Mount Everest Foundation would want to undertake such a big risk again. The fact was we were going to have to find almost twice as much money for Everest in a very much shorter time, and also, we were going to have to take on the risk ourselves as a group of comparatively impecunious climbers. I had learned a great deal from the Annapurna South Face expedition, both on means of fund-raising and also in basic expedition organization. On Annapurna I had been a bit of a one-man band, handling the fund-raising, most of the equipment, and all the transport. Mike Thompson had taken care of the food and Don Whillans had acted as equipment designer and did a certain amount of coordination work with firms. Nevertheless, the main burden had fallen on me. This had proved too much, especially as once one gets involved in the finicky details – sizes etc. in equipment – it is very easy to lose sight of the broader picture of the expedition. Determined that this should not happen on Everest, I therefore gave Graham Tiso the onerous job of getting all our equipment together. In the early stages he was helped by Doug Scott, but then Doug, a keen climber, wanted to go off on a trip to Baffin Island and, as a result, Graham handled most of it himself, helped by Dave Bathgate in Edinburgh. Then, Mike Thompson having resigned from the expedition, Kelvin Kent took on the food organization as well as getting all our communications equipment. He attacked the task with efficiency and enthusiasm.

It would be impossible to relate the day-to-day crises which we met in organizing the expedition. Our two biggest problems, at such short notice, were getting an effective oxygen system and also getting the gear out to Nepal in time. On the oxygen front, I had decided to use the demand system developed by Dr Duane Blume for the international Everest expedition. Both Dougal and Don spoke very highly of this system, and it seemed to answer all our requirements. (The system is described in detail in Appendix D.) The firm who makes it, Robertshaw, did a special rush job for us, and succeeded in getting all the components over to Britain in early August. The question of oxygen bottles presented a greater problem. We could not possibly have afforded to use the American bottles, which were both expensive and would also have to be transported to Britain on their way out to Nepal. We therefore had to find a British firm, and were extremely lucky to come across Luxfer Limited, who offered to make the bottles for us at a very competitive price in the time available. Valves to fit the American system, however, had to be sent all the way over from the States, and this entailed a fair number of 'panic' phone calls across the Atlantic. Eventually, we got all the valves fitted and the bottles filled by British Oxygen, the day they were due to be flown out to Kathmandu! We had not had time to actually marry one of the reducer valves to a bottle, and only tried out the completed system in Kathmandu.

But by far the greatest problem was one of time. The days slipped away with terrifying speed. I wanted to get out to Nepal as quickly as possible, to be at the Everest Base Camp immediately the monsoon ended. Reading through reports of the previous expeditions during this period, it seemed possible to get excellent weather in early September, before the official end of the monsoon. The more work we could do on the Ice Fall and on the lower slopes of the mountain in the early stages, the more hope we should have of getting high on the Face before the winter cold and winds set in. The other factor was that the sooner we could get out there, the sooner the members of the team could start acclimatizing and the more leisurely could this acclimatization period be.

Normally, expeditions fly from Kathmandu to Lukla. This is both easier and also quite a bit cheaper, since air freight to Lukla costs less than employing porters to carry loads. However, since we were planning to make our approach march through the monsoon, we could not possibly guarantee getting ourselves sufficient good weather for the plane to be able to fly into Lukla. Jimmy Roberts therefore recommended that we should make the 170-mile approach march all the way from Kathmandu. This also would have the advantage that the team members could slowly get fit and acclimatized in the course of the march. I therefore planned on leaving London on 21 August. There was no question at all of sending our gear out by sea, and I had to resign myself to the expense of flying it out. In this respect, BOAC proved extremely cooperative and, without their efforts, we should never have got it into Kathmandu in time. They even flew one of their cargo planes out of schedule to Delhi to carry our oxygen, since they could not carry this on one of their scheduled passenger flights.

I had sent Kelvin Kent out to Kathmandu in advance, in order to clear all our equipment through customs – in itself a marathon task. The gear actually left Britain by cargo plane on 16 August, and by 21 August it had been flown into Kathmandu and cleared through customs – a really brilliant piece of work by Kelvin and Jimmy Roberts. We were ready to leave for Kathmandu on 22 August. I, personally, felt singularly unready for the most physically exacting climb of my career. I don't think I have ever worked so hard before in my life – not only had I been putting the expedition together, but I had also been completing – way over deadline – the second volume of my autobiography, and actually typed the last words in the hotel bedroom in London on the morning of my departure.

In those last few weeks I had worked to a routine, getting up at around 3.30 a.m., working on my book until about 11 a.m. and then transferring to the expedition, to work on that, very often until 9.30 or 10.00 at night. In the final stages I had a secretary, Betty Prentice, working full time in my office at home, to help cope with the huge volume of letters, phone calls and general administration which the expedition involved. Kelvin Kent and Graham Tiso had been under similar pressure.

I had been greatly helped in my money-raising efforts by Bob Stoodley, a friend who was chairman of a group of garages in Manchester. He wrote several thousand letters to firms up and down the country, asking for contributions and he also promoted a signed cover scheme, by which we promised to send covers back to anyone who contributed. He and his secretary Diana Lister put in an enormous amount of work on our behalf, without any thought of personal gain. Our financial backing was now beginning to look more stable. Thames/I.T.N. had taken up television rights, the *Observer* had taken up newspaper rights and we had sold the book rights both in Britain and the United States; the Mount Everest Foundation had given us an extremely generous grant and we had also received the support of the Sports Council with a grant through the British Mountaineering Council, the first time that an expedition had ever received such support. We were still about £10,000 short of my budget estimate and it was at this point that we received an unexpected windfall from Rothmans, who contributed very generously.

As I walked up the steps into the VC-10 which was going to take us to Kathmandu, I felt some of the worries that had beset me in those last hectic weeks fall from my shoulders. Despite the tight time-schedule, Graham had succeeded in ensuring that we were as well equipped as, I felt, any expedition which has left these shores. We were also fairly solvent, and the team had a feeling of excited anticipation and friendship which boded well for the future.

6

THE APPROACH
MARCH

25 August–7 September

The journey out preceding an expedition is a kind of limbo period. On my first two expeditions to the Himalayas, I had travelled out by ship – a little 10,000-ton passenger liner run by the Anchor Line, called the S.S. *Cilicia*. The charm of a boat journey, especially if one is unattached, is the way it lengthens this limbo period and all you have to worry about is eating, drinking and having the odd affair to speed the quiet passage of days and nights. The modern way, by plane, is almost too frenetic – the limbo is just a few hours in the air, before descending upon a new world, new problems and new challenges.

For us they were busy hours, for we had four thousand post-cards to sign, as part of our fund-raising campaign. We flew via Tel Aviv and Teheran, security men searching the plane and us for hidden weapons and bombs. It seemed ironic that with all the improvements in fast jet travel and cheaper fares, when opportunities for travel and adventure should be much easier, political conflicts were limiting the number of places to go and how to get there. In actual fact, the pre-war mountaineers and explorers had greater freedom. They were able to wander through the wilds of the Karakorum into Tibet and the back of China, areas which are closed to us today. We were met at Delhi by the BOAC station manager, who, just a few days before, had whisked our 16,000 pounds weight of equipment, oxygen cylinders and food through the airport and onto Nepalese cargo planes. Soon we were in the air again, this time on a Boeing 707 bound for Kathmandu.

I couldn't help feeling a little sad at the pace at which Nepal seemed to be catching up with the rest of the Western world. Twelve years before, in 1960, we had flown in from Patna, on an old Dakota, to land on a dusty air strip with a battered tin shed at one end of the field to act as air terminal. Now, the Royal Nepalese Airlines had just purchased their first jet airliner, and were in the process of lengthening their runway to take the big Boeing 707. The airfield itself was like any other modern airfield – long concrete runway, with its modern air-terminal building. And yet that day we had one of the most magnificent flights in the world, as the plane carved its way over the patchwork quilt of cloud, through which one could see the brilliant green of monsoon-fed fields, and the occasional patch of water. And then on the northern horizon – at first almost a continuation of the puff balls of white cloud – we saw the Himalayas. Dhaulagiri, a squat pyramid; the sprawl of the Annapurna range – the South Face of Annapurna itself, the mountain on which we had spent so many weeks just two years previously; Machapuchare, shapely and slender, dwarfed by the great mass of mountains behind it. Annapurna II, the mountain I had climbed in 1960, looked in some ways the finest of them all, standing in splendid isolation to the right of the Annapurna massif. I was excited, and yet my excitement was a little bit deadened, partly from a heavy mental and physical fatigue which still hung on me; partly perhaps from the fact that I had now flown this journey three times.

We landed at Kathmandu at midday; the ladder was pulled to the door of the plane and a group of the local press corps crowded around it. There was no sign, however, of Jimmy Roberts or Kelvin Kent. Everyone was very friendly and we trailed over to the passengers' entrance, the press corps clicking away with their cameras, myself tired and slightly confused, trying to gather my thoughts for the inevitable press conference. Jimmy Roberts and Kelvin arrived a few minutes later. Kelvin, characteristically, immediately took charge and shepherded us like a group of sheep into the arrival hall, where he started to chat up the customs men to get our gear through quickly and easily. At the same time, the reporters wanted their press conference there and then. What did I think our chances were; why had the international expedition failed; was there a chance for international climbing; why hadn't I taken Don Whillans, and so it went on, with me trying to field the questions tactfully and clearly, without treading on any

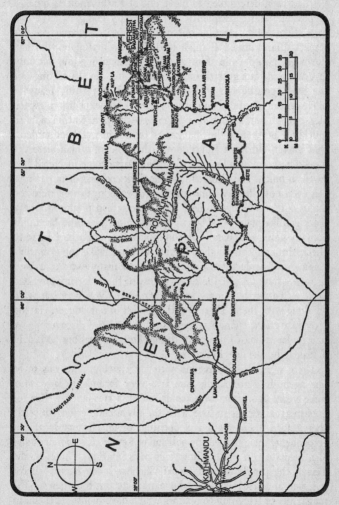

The approach march from Kathmandu to Mount Everest

toes. By the end of the conference I felt limp and yet there were still more decisions to be made.

I had been determined to move out of Kathmandu as quickly as possible, and consequently we were only going to have two days there before starting out on the approach march. In this respect, Jimmy and Kelvin, helped by Dave Bathgate who had flown out two days in front of us, had done a fine job, not only in getting all our gear through customs, but also in sorting out the loads, getting our coolies ordered, and everything ready to move on the scheduled date. I wondered if any expedition, especially one of our size, had ever moved through Kathmandu so quickly. And then to the Shankar Hotel. Set in well-kept gardens, this was an old Rana Palace, down the front of which were the mock Greek colonnades that the ruling aristocracy in Nepal had loved so much. We plunged into the dark coolness of our rooms, but even now there was no question of relaxing; there were too many different things to deal with. Jimmy had produced a very workmanlike plan, based on my own original planning brief, but actually going into details on the deployment of porters. I had to check through this so that I could at least make some sensible comments. The decisions to be made – how many extra cook-boys to take – how to split the team – most of these, fortunately, had been sorted out by Jimmy and Kelvin, and I was very happy to go along with them. There was the subject of our budget. Having only just raised enough money, already we were discovering we had under-estimated on many things. Inflation gallops as fast in Kathmandu as it does in Britain.

There were also discussions with Liz Hawley, who was to be our agent in Kathmandu. She is a very formidable lady who, some years ago, came to Kathmandu as a free-lance writer for *Look* magazine, fell in love with the place and decided to settle there, since there was a real opening for an efficient local correspondent. She obtained the position of Reuter correspondent and also helps to run the bookings side of a Safari-type hotel in the Terrai, the jungle area of Nepal. She has made herself almost indispensable to expeditions who want to get out their news to the magazines or television companies which have sponsored them. In doing this there is a split loyalty between her commitment to

Reuter, who provide her daily bread and butter, and her temporary employers for whom she acts as agent. It is, however, a loyalty which she has succeeded in bridging remarkably effectively. I still had to thrash out several intricacies involved in getting the news out as quickly as possible and, at the same time, satisfying the Nepalese authorities that they received the gist of any important news before it reached the world's papers. These were problems I could have dispensed with happily. Somehow, having left Britain, one's actual reaction was to want to drop all thoughts of day-to-day administration and the media, and get down to the comparatively simple, and much more exciting problems of climbing a mountain. If you decide to lead an expedition, however, this is one of the prices that you must inevitably pay. I also had the responsibility of writing articles for the *Observer*. The first one was due to be produced for the next Sunday, and I ended up writing it at five in the morning of the day of our departure.

At last, on 25 August, we were ready to set out on the approach march. We were to have with us, altogether, four hundred porters, recruited from villages around Kathmandu. This would have been too large a body to travel in one group, particularly at the height of the monsoon when many camp sites are waterlogged, and the porters need to find shelter in the houses of villagers. Jimmy therefore proposed splitting the party into two groups with all the climbers accompanying the first party, with two hundred porters, and then the rest following under the command of Pertemba, one of his best Sherpas. I was not too happy about this, since the loss of one vital load could influence the outcome of the expedition. In addition, there was the problem of handling money and keeping a day-to-day check on expenses. This difference of opinion brought home to me, as leader of the expedition, one potential problem in my relationship with Jimmy. He, of course, had been leader of my first Himalayan expedition, the Combined Services expedition to Annapurna II; later he had been joint leader of the international expedition. Some of our best high-altitude Sherpas were his employees, and they understandably looked to him as their boss on the expedition. This could have led to a difficult situation had Jimmy and I failed to get on together, and following those first few days when Jimmy had had to make most of the decisions in my absence, I could not help feeling a little worried that perhaps I was losing control of the situation. In fact, there was no danger of this, largely because of Jimmy's loyal friendship. We had a meeting to discuss the approach march, and since most of us were apprehensive at the prospect of half the expedition gear travelling out to Base Camp unattended, I finally allotted Barney Rosedale to stay behind. With him would be Mick Burke, who was coming out to Kathmandu a couple of days later, and Mick's wife Beth, whom I had agreed should accompany us to Base Camp.

She was coming out at her own expense at far as Kathmandu, and besides being a delightful, easy-going girl who could get on with anyone, she was also a trained nurse. This meant that she could have a very real function in the expedition, helping Barney and holding the fort at Base Camp, looking after any convalescents that Barney should send down from higher up the mountain. She had flown out with us, and would await Mick with Barney in the second party. Doug Scott, as it turned out, also went with them, having contracted a stomach upset on the morning of departure. There were, therefore, six of us in the first party: Dave Bathgate, Kelvin Kent, Hamish MacInnes, Dougal Haston, Graham Tiso and myself. Jimmy Roberts was still tied up in the trekking business, but was going to fly out to join us at the beginning of October.

The first leg of our journey was along the newly-built Chinese road, which wound its tarmac way into the valley of the Sun Kosi, and then on up towards the Tibetan frontier and, eventually, to Lhasa, the capital of Tibet. We bumped and shook in Jimmy Roberts' Land-Rover for sixty miles, to the small village of Lamosangu, where all the expedition loads had been sent out the previous day. The Sherpas had spent the night there and were in the process of sending off the porters. A little group of local reporters was grouped around the start of the footpath which was to lead over ridges, down valleys on the hundred-and-thirty-mile walk to the foot of Everest. It was a good feeling to shoulder a pack-frame and contemplate the simple day's objective of walking a few miles through the green terraced fields of Nepal to the night's camping spot. At last my own responsibilities were, for a time, almost over. Kelvin managed the day-to-day administration of the expedition with wonderful efficiency, and all I had to do, like the rest of the members of the team, was to walk through the Nepalese countryside, absorbing the host of sights, sounds and smells of this unspoilt, pollution-free land. I, for one, desperately needed the approach march, both to get physically fit, since I had had practically no exercise before the expedition, but – more important – to build up the mental stamina which I was going to require once we reached our Base Camp. Once there, I would have to make decisions constantly, and take on the full responsibility of running the expedition.

We had set out in a bright spell in the monsoon, and the sun blazed down, hot and heavy, through gaps in the piled clouds which still clung to the higher hills. Everything was green – a green much richer than anything one saw in the drier pre-monsoon season. The hillside, however steep, was carved into terraces, each one with a low mud wall imprisoning the waters of the monsoon rains. The rice shoots grew in a thick green carpet in each one of these terraced pools. There was a constant trickle of running water from the many streams coursing down the hills, and the houses clustered in little groups, brown earthen walls with a verandah across the ground floor, small wooden-slatted windows and roofs made from weathered wooden slats or thatch. Although the Everest route had now become a tourist trail, particularly in the post-monsoon period, with the constant march of trekkers, there seemed hardly any change at all from when I had walked the same path back in 1961. The Nepalese were as gentle and courteous as ever – the Nepalese girls with their golden nose studs and ear-rings had a shy and gentle beauty. The first day there was a soft, kind balm in the air after our weeks of wheeler-dealing, frantic worry and activity. We were already slipping into the easy, methodical routine of the approach march, resting beneath our umbrellas, stopping about three o'clock in the afternoon for the evening's halt.

Our first was at the side of a small lake of opaque brown waters, with a little ruined hut on a peninsula which jutted into it. The Sherpas pitched the tents, which we re-sited in the shade of a tree. Suddenly, there was a distant roll of thunder and the clouds billowed around us until the hills were engulfed, and there was just a small touch of blue immediately above us. Then that vanished as well, and the rains came down in a steady hammering torrent. Within seconds the ground was running in water. One crisis immediately presented itself. We had packed all our gear in reinforced cardboard boxes, which were especially designed for packing kippers, fish and similar products. Very quickly it became evident that they were not going to stand up to day after day of being continually soaked and then man-handled on our porters' backs; it was essential to find some way of keeping them off the wet ground, and here our aluminium ladders came in useful. We had, altogether, forty five-foot sections of ladder, and these were tied into bundles of three to make sixty-pound loads. By laying them out in a platform on the ground, we were at least able to keep all the packages clear of the water and cover them with a tarpaulin.

That first night was chaotic, yet strangely enjoyable, as we crouched under a leaking Stormhaven tent, trying to avoid the drips, waiting for a much-delayed supper to arrive. There had been a lot of talk of losing the spirit of adventure with massive expeditions to Everest – but we had very little feeling of being a large expedition. There were just seven of us crammed into the tent, and another four, two days behind. This was the sum total of the European climbers, in fact, less than we had on Annapurna, where there had been eleven climbers but also a four-man television team. On Everest we weren't bringing out any media people, but were going to do it all ourselves. This added responsibility undoubtedly increased the sense of unity felt by the entire team. It rained all night, but it was strangely reassuring to lie in one's tent and hear the monotonous, soporific drumming of rain hammering on canvas. There was something very simple, very sensual about it. I dropped off into a deep sleep, more relaxed than I had been for the past eight weeks.

We were to have, altogether, forty Sherpas on the expedition, plus several cook-boys and six mail-runners to carry film, mail and stories down to the air strip at Lukla. The Sherpas themselves were divided into two categories, that of high-altitude Sherpa, who would expect to carry loads on the South West Face itself, and Ice Fall porter, who would be responsible for carrying the gear up to Camp 2 in the Western Cwm. Of our fourteen high-altitude Sherpas, most of them were with us on the approach march. We were responsible for paying them from the day we met them in Kathmandu until the end of the expedition. They received fifteen rupees a day, plus their keep, in addition to all their equipment for the climb. The Ice Fall porters also received fifteen rupees a day and their keep, but could be equipped on a more modest scale since they would only be going as high as Camp 2 and would only be employed from the day they joined the expedition near Base Camp. I was planning to promote ten of the best Ice Fall porters to the ranks of the high-altitude Sherpas, once we saw how they performed in the Ice Fall and had brought out additional clothing and gear to make this conversion. The reason for this policy was that often some of the young Ice Fall porters are keen to get themselves established and have more drive than the older, established Sherpas; by promoting them in the field, it seemed that we should be more certain of getting the best men for the high carries.

We had two Sirdars, Pembatharke being the chief Sirdar who would primarily be in charge of directing the Sherpas on the mountain itself, while Sona Hishy, a younger man, was to be our administrative Sirdar, looking after our supplies from Base Camp, and helping to make the approach march run smoothly. This pair highlighted the changing role and development of the Sherpas. Pembatharke was very much a Sherpa of the old style. He could neither read nor write; had a rugged simplicity in his attitude to life and yet, at the same time, was highly intelligent and shrewd. He certainly had a magnificent climbing record. With the Indians on Everest in 1965, he reached the South Col on two separate occasions; as a member of a German expedition attempting to climb Annapurna I from the south, by its long, South East Ridge, he had reached their top camp, at a height of approximately 23,500 feet. Then in 1970, he had come with us on the South Face of Annapurna. For this expedition he had not been Sirdar, though he was undoubtedly the strongest personality and the strongest climber amongst the Sherpas. This had led to some tension, and towards the end of the expedition he had even become something of a trouble-maker – I suspect because he had resented his subordinate position. Even so, he had worked outstandingly well. On the international expedition he had been made Face Sirdar by Jimmy Roberts, and had been extremely successful in this role, loyal to Don and Dougal in organizing and keeping the Sherpas going on the tenuous line of communications behind them.

His opposite number and, in theory his assistant, Sona Hishy, was very different. Aged twenty-six, he had been educated at one of the Hillary schools, spoke and wrote good English, and had even visited the United States. He had done more trekking with tourists than he had climbing on expeditions. Whilst Pembatharke had a magnificent physique, and looked the very prototype of a leader of men, Sona Hishy was tall, slender built, and was a very much more complex character. He was extremely efficient, but was also to prove to be the Sherpa 'shop-steward', finding it difficult at times to reconcile his loyalty to us as – in effect – part of the management, with his loyalty to his fellow Sherpas.

Sadly, Pembatharke was the only Sherpa we had from our little Annapurna South Face team, since Jimmy was heavily committed in this autumn period to trekking, and most of the Sherpas we had had on Annapurna were also extremely good in this newer role which the Sherpas had taken. He had, however, allotted to the expedition some of his most outstanding high-altitude Sherpas, whom we were to get to know better as the expedition went on. Doug Scott had also recommended some of the better Sherpas from the spring expedition, and Jangbo was to give a particularly outstanding performance.

The routine of the approach march quickly fell into a well-defined pattern. The monsoon was certainly back with us, the rain by now having thinned out to a drizzle through the veil of mist. The porters, as they set off, looked like modern-style ghosts, each one shrouded in a plastic sheet which we had issued to keep both them, and perhaps more important, their load dry. At first there was a babel of sound and argument, particularly as the three Naiks, who were the representatives of the Himalayan Society in charge of the porters, and our own Sherpas argued ferociously about who had, and who had not, been paid. Kelvin, in the middle of the argument, bore the full brunt of this, trying to sort it out and come to some agreement with them. I was happy to stand back, take photographs and just absorb the strange beauty of the mist-enshrouded scene.

That day we had our first taste of the Nepalese leech. Dave Bathgate describes them in his diary:

Once more into the leech, dear friend

The average leech is about one inch long, has a sucker at both ends of its tubular body and travels along by somersaulting from sucker to sucker. The leech likes to sit around on dry rocks and pathways and on plants that overhang the track. Perched on one sucker, it extends itself to its full length and waves about, rather like a weed in a pool, and attempts to attach itself to a victim.

There seem to be two main types of leech common to the mountain region of Nepal, one black and the other brown, often with a yellow strip along its length. The brown one is the larger of the two, but both multiply their dimensions ten-fold once gorged. The leech can slither through the smallest of apertures. It can easily enter a boot through the lacing, and penetrate most woollen garments. Once they have latched on properly they are most difficult to detect. The larger ones can cause a prickly feeling which sometimes gives them away, but if this is not felt, they will already have used a local anaesthetic to reduce the pain while extracting the blood. If undiscovered, a leech can suck away quite happily for days, then drop off, leaving the victim bleeding freely from the wound. A leech wound should be treated just like a cut as, in damp humid climates, any kind of wound usually takes much longer to heal. If a leech is discovered just as it has attached itself to the skin, it is quite difficult to pull off, and usually it will attach itself with the free sucker to the fingers. A drop of salt on the leech will cause it to detach itself without leaving a bleeding sore. Sketofax or any other, similar, insect repellent, liberally applied, will generally deter the leech. Salt or insect repellent rubbed into the boots or on the skin is about the only safeguard, and these soon become ineffective because of walking through water or the skin sweating.

We all became thoroughly neurotic about the leeches, which in some areas seemed to cling to almost every blade of grass and would get on to the walls of the tents at night, then drop with unerring precision upon the heads of their unsuspecting victims. It took us, altogether, fourteen days to walk to Namche Bazar – a journey which is well known and well recorded. Today, hundreds of trekkers follow this trail. Making it during the monsoon gave it special character, at times an acute level of discomfort, which still managed to have a charm of its own. We never got a glimpse of the mountains throughout the approach march, and yet deprived of these further vistas one's eye was drawn to the luxuriant green of the vegetation on either side of the path, tangles of spiders' webs encrusted with jewel-like droplets of water, and the wealth of flowers which are not present at other, drier seasons.

Our route lay parallel to the spine of the Himalayas, and consequently there was a series of climbs and descents over subsidiary ridges, each undulation taking us slightly higher. A constant, imperceptible change in the style of layout of the terraced fields, the wildness of the woods and vegetation became apparent as we gained height. Our stages on the walks were all fairly short – round about ten miles a day, and some even less. This was primarily to enable the porters, who were carrying anything up to eighty-pound loads, to keep up with us. Walking in the monsoon season had many disadvantages – paths like ice rinks presented constant hazards for the bare-footed porters who were soaked to the skin for most of the time. Whereas we had our tents and sleeping bags to retire to at night, they would have to find shelter in the porches of villagers' houses, with only damp blankets to keep them warm. We were paying them the equivalent of 50p per day, but they had to find their own sustenance and accommodation at night. This does not seem much; but was quite a bit more than they would have earned had they been working for a Nepali merchant.

On 3 September – the tenth day of the approach march – we dropped down to the Dudh Kosi valley. The previous day we had crossed a pass of over 10,000 feet in the cold and drizzling rain. We now wound our way down slippery paths to the deepest bed of the valley at a height of little more than 5,000 feet above sea level – our lowest point for several days. Then, having reached the iron suspension bridge over the boiling waters of the Dudh Kosi, where the big plaque declared 'Made in Aberdeen', we knew that we were now going to gain height steadily up the valley, as we walked into the heart of Sherpa country. For the last few days there had been a transitional period, where Sherpa houses, or even Sherpa villages were jumbled with those of the Nepalis in the lower foothills. The Nepalis are essentially of Indian ethnic background, Hindu by religion, with delicately moulded features slightly reminiscent of those of the Malays or Burmese. Sherpas, on the other hand, are essentially Tibetan, having overflowed the watershed that divides Tibet from the Indian sub-continent. There are similar encroachments all the way along the Tibetan frontier with Nepal, the people having the same common Tibetan language and broad mongoloid features, yet with distinct differences in their customs and behaviour. The Sherpas form probably the largest, and certainly the best-known ethnically Tibetan community in Nepal, based on Sola Khumbu, the upper valley of the

Dudh Kosi. Before climbers started going to Everest in the 1920s, the Sherpas' economy was based on a combination of subsistence farming in the sparse, gravelly fields of the mountains, and trading between Tibet and India. They already had a substantial colony in Darjeeling at the start of the road to Everest from the Tibetan side, and it was mainly Sherpas who were employed for all mountaineering expeditions before the war – not only in the Everest region, but also across to the Karakorum. With the Communist invasion of Tibet, part of their economy was seriously disrupted. This loss in trade, however, was already being replaced by their role of high-altitude porters, as an increasing number of expeditions came to Nepal to climb in the Himalayas. Then, from the mid-sixties onwards, another development still further increased their relative wealth. Trekking became more and more popular. One of the early founders was Jimmy Roberts. In the last few years trekking has boomed, and an increasing number of Sherpas have found trekking more remunerative and less arduous than mountaineering expeditions. Nevertheless, there are still a few Sherpas, Pembatharke is undoubtedly one, Jangbo another, who prefer the rugged adventure of climbing on a Himalayan expedition, to the more sophisticated and inevitably subservient work of looking after rich American tourists on treks through Nepal. Others of our Sherpas, however, very sensibly looked upon prestigious expeditions, such as one to Everest, as useful stepping-stones in their careers as trekking Sherpas. Ang Phu, who was twenty-three and one of our most outstanding Sherpas, had been to the Hillary school, spoke fluent English and was a first-class organizer; he was determined to do as well as possible on the expedition, in order to establish his reputation and name. One could just imagine Hyram Brekenbacher from Ohio, U.S.A. basking in the reflected glory of a well-known tiger Sherpa – 'Gee, that's Ang Phu over there – he went up 27,000 feet on Everest – Yeh, he's looking after us mighty well.'

The attitude of the Sherpas to a mountaineering expedition varies from person to person, as no doubt it does amongst European climbers. The Sherpas, like most mountain people, have never been able to afford the luxury of being romantic about their mountains. Apart from anything else, having lived amongst them from time immemorial, they tend to take them for granted. The romantics are the affluent city-dwellers, be they Japanese, Indian, European or American, who come to the mountains to escape from their over-sophisticated complex lives.

Sherpas themselves are in a very similar position to that of the Swiss peasant in the 1850s, and indeed, their way of life and living standards today are probably identical. Their interest in the mountains, as with the Swiss, started only when outsiders came and offered to pay money for their help. The difference between the Sherpas and the Swiss, however, was that when the early-Victorian Alpinists started venturing into the Alps, they knew even less about the problems of mountaineering than the Swiss peasants they took with them. The Swiss peasant, therefore, initially assumed the role of guide and expert in the mountains, a role he was to keep until the end of the nineteenth century, when an increasing number of mountaineers began to feel the need for dispensing with guides and to seek out adventure for themselves. The Sherpas were employed as carriers rather than guides. The mountaineers who came to the Himalayas already had a background of climbing in the Alps or their own countries; consequently, they were the experts, and had to look after the Sherpas in the mountains, rather than vice versa. There have been, of course, some notable exceptions to this. Tenzing, who accompanied Hillary to the summit of Everest, was able to climb with the European members of the team on a level footing, especially, of course, as he had already been most of the way up Everest before the British team ever got there. With recent developments in mountaineering in the Himalayas, disparity between climbers and Sherpas has become greater. Now the mountaineers are tackling high standard technical problems at altitude, there are comparatively few, if any, Sherpas who have the technical knowledge even to think of taking part in the lead climbing and they might even have difficulty in coping with the fixed ropes on particularly steep sections. For instance, on the South Face of Annapurna, we were unable to use our Sherpas above a height of 21,600 feet since they were obviously unhappy at the prospect of tackling over-hanging Jumar pitches. It was interesting that here, it was our younger, less established Sherpas who did finally offer to try the

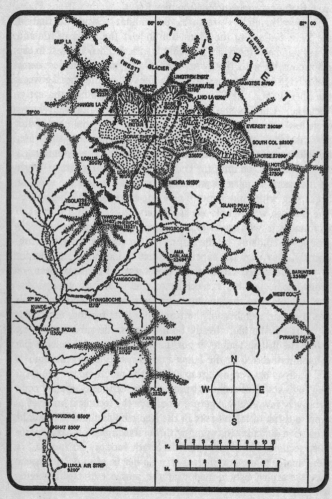

The route from Lukla air strip to Base Camp

precarious route from Camp 4 to Camp 5; in the event, we found we were unable to use their services, since they were needed lower down the mountain.

The attitude of the Sherpas to mountaineering is inevitably practical and materialistic; and it is most unlikely that a group of Sherpas would ever go off and climb a mountain on their own, for fun, as we do in Europe. They cannot afford such a luxury. With a good expedition, however, they enter into the spirit of the climbing. In my experience, the only time that Sherpas actually made an ascent for the fun of it was on our expedition to Annapurna II in 1960. We had left two of our Sherpas, Urkein and Mingma, at our penultimate camp on a shoulder of snow about a thousand feet below the peak of Annapurna IV, which we had to by-pass on our way to the summit of Annapurna II. With nothing to do for a couple of days, they decided they might just as well go and climb Annapurna IV, and went off, made their ascent and even left a bamboo wand, with a dirty handkerchief tied to it, on the summit.

On our own expedition to Everest this autumn, we had a certain amount of conflict with the Sherpas. Very often this came about through our different motives for climbing Everest, and the difficulty on both sides in understanding what the other was trying to do. For a start, the Sherpas regard every European expedition as vastly rich, since who else could possibly afford the luxury of doing anything quite as pointless as climbing a mountain. The very resources we display, the mounds of gear we bring in, the standard of life we adopt on the mountain, all contribute to this impression. The richest Sherpa, after all, is probably living at a lower standard than some of the poorest-paid workers in the countries which send out mountaineering expeditions. They come from a society where money has only very recently been used as the main means of doing business. Straight barter still forms an important part of their economy. The actual wages of the Sherpa are, in effect, in two parts – the money you pay him which, in actual fact, is not very much – 15 Rs. per day – and the equipment you give him. To us, as organizers of a mountaineering expedition, this equipment is purely functional, enabling us to climb the mountain. To the Sherpa, however, it is a lot more. It is part of his wages which he can exchange for either further goods or a straight cash transaction at the end of the expedition. Throughout Sola Khumbu, the old, traditional forms of dress are fast vanishing and the average Sherpa or Sherpani will be wearing down trousers, or a down jacket, and various other items of expedition gear. Since this equipment can only come in limited quantities with expeditions, its value has become very inflated. A down jacket, for instance, is valued at 300 Rs. or nearly three weeks' pay.

The Sherpas have become accustomed to a certain scale of issue laid down in outline in the rules of the Himalayan Society, but this has almost become a minimum issue – the Sherpas have come to expect more. Dr Herrligkoffer had had a great deal of difficulty with the Sherpas because he had not given them the gear which they were accustomed to using. The reason for the complete lack of understanding on either side was that Herrligkoffer had failed to realize the equipment he was giving the Sherpas was every bit as important as the salary he was paying them. We also had similar problems on our expedition. Team members, including myself, were very often exasperated by what often seemed to be rather petty claims by the Sherpas – whether it was for more cigarettes or for double sleeping bags, when in fact, the single good-quality sleeping bag we had given them was, in our view, perfectly adequate. It seems probable that the Sherpas took a few perks – taking perhaps a percentage of the sale of firewood or rice – or in the payment of our coolies. We often became very indignant about this, but once again, this was part of a system which they have always practised. Provided one maintained a level of control which allowed the turning of a blind eye to a certain degree, one could ultimately gain a perfectly satisfactory relationship. To me, the main factor was that whatever the Sherpas or the porters expected, they were doing a great deal for us, and the pay we were giving them was by no means exorbitant – whether it was for one of our coolies who carried an eighty-pound load, during the course of the approach march, or the Sherpa going through the dangers of the Ice Fall day after day, knowing full well that there was a good statistical chance of a fatal accident.

Sherpa society is undoubtedly becoming very much more sophisticated, with the growing invasion of visitors to Sola Khumbu. The area is becoming increasingly accessible, not just to trekkers, but to tourists, with the introduction of air strips. The air strip at Lukla has been in existence since 1967. Now they are building another air strip, just above Namche Bazar in the very heart of Sola Khumbu. The first hotel, built by a Japanese entrepreneur, is now completed and taking its first guests. No doubt there will be more in the future and Sola Khumbu will become more and more like a Swiss valley. The Sherpas themselves naturally want to share in this bonanza. They are by no means simple or primitive. They have a long history of trading behind them and have always known how to strike a good bargain, and yet at the same time they have had, and hopefully will continue to have, a rich sense of humour and a real warmth of personality. Unless the flow of tourists, trekkers and climbers into Sola Khumbu stops altogether, the people and the region must change and develop to meet this flow. Two important factors emerge, one being that the Sherpas themselves should benefit from the change, rather than a group of foreign operators or people in Kathmandu; and the other is the fervent hope that in exploiting the development of a tourist industry, they don't destroy the very landscape, way of life and architecture which attracts the tourists in the first place.

In this respect, Sir Edmund Hillary has done a vast amount to help, and has certainly put back into Khumbu a great deal of what he gained personally in reaching the summit of Everest in 1953. Over the past few years, he has set up a network of schools to give the young Sherpas a sound basis of education. He has also set up a small hospital at Kunde; has built a number of bridges, and has helped to encourage local industries. As a result of this, together with their monopoly of the job of high-altitude porter on mountaineering expeditions, and a near-monopoly in the trekking business, the Sherpas are probably one of the most prosperous groups in the whole of Nepal.

In the last days of our approach march, towards Namche Bazar, the capital of Sherpa country, we stopped for lunch and in the evenings in Sherpa houses. The basic construction of these houses had not changed very much in twelve years. There were small, but very important changes. In 1961 none of the houses had glass in their windows. Consequently, the actual window frames were very much smaller, allowing only a glimmer of light into the rooms. The crops were also limited to maize, barley and potatoes. In the autumn of 1972, however, it was very noticeable how many other vegetables had been introduced into Sola Khumbu – onions, cabbages, carrots, beans, just to quote a few. We even passed a beautifully laid-out market garden down the Dudh Kosi valley, which was being worked by a Japanese couple who had settled in Sola Khumbu, primarily with the intention of supplying fresh vegetables to the Japanese hotel above Namche Bazar. The actual structure and layout of the houses themselves, though, hadn't changed. The more prosperous ones were uniformly built on a two-storey basis; the first storey, without windows, devoted to store-rooms and byres for their cattle and sheep, and a narrow, wooden staircase in almost pitch dark, leading up to the first-floor living area. This was almost always open-plan – a big, spacious room, lit by small windows, though in the case of some of the more modern houses, the windows had been enlarged because of the inclusion of glass. At one end would be the cooking fire, on a large stone slab, without any kind of chimney stack; the smoke was allowed to find its way through the stone-tiled roof – a primitive form of space heating. The walls of the room would be lined with rough-hewn cabinets, filled with cooking pots, bowls, *chang* pots and booty from previous expeditions. At one end of the room there would be a little shrine, and the size would be a good indication of the wealth of the owner. A ceremonial prayer drum might hang from the ceiling and an array of brass cups would be lined on the front of an altar. The room itself would be full of smoke. It is not surprising that many of the Sherpas suffer from eye-complaints – and yet the houses are comparatively clean and have an atmosphere of comfort and homeliness and, what is more important, hospitality.

We reached Namche Bazar on 6 September. The village is formed in a crescent built into a wide, open bowl in the hillside. Although the administrative capital of the country, with a police station and a Nepalese administrator, it is no more than a large village. There were changes here, however, since 1961. In those days we didn't see a single European for the entire period of the expedition after leaving Kathmandu, but today, Namche Bazar has become a tourist centre, with three or four little restaurants serving omelettes, tea and *chang* at inflated prices. There are also a couple of shops selling carpets and other tourist-orientated goods. It was at Namche Bazar we paid off our four hundred porters who had been recruited from around Kathmandu, to take on local Sherpas. This, as much as anything, was a question of trade-union job delineation – once in Sherpa country you employ Sherpas. Most of our newly-employed porters were women, who carried exactly the same loads as the men. Some of them were ancient crones who looked in their sixties, and others were young girls who could have been no more than thirteen or fourteen years old. They all seemed to regard their projected journey, firstly to Thyangboche and then to Base Camp, as a glorious, well-paid holiday, a very similar attitude to that of the hop- and fruit-pickers in Kent. We also took on a certain number of yaks. These could carry a double load, 160 pounds or more, but you paid the yak owner for the number of loads carried.

I had determined to have a couple of days rest at Thyangboche, a day's march from Namche Bazar. This is the site of the main monastery in the Sola Khumbu region, and must be one of the most idyllic spots in the world. The monastery is perched on the crest of a tree-clad ridge round which swirls the Dudh Kosi river. It is surrounded by snow-clad peaks; to the north-east is Everest itself, peering over the great South Wall of Nuptse, flanked on its right by Lhotse; but at Thyangboche, even more impressive is the view of the mountains which tower immediately above it; Tamserku, a shark's fin of fluted ice, and Kantega set slightly further back, with steep, seemingly impregnable walls guarding its summit. Today, with modern transport, the European climber can be at the foot of Tamserku even faster than you could have reached the heart of the Swiss Alps a hundred years ago. In many ways this represents the most exciting climbing of the future, when small groups can go off and climb mountains like these without any of the heavyweight organization required for mountains of the size of Everest. At the moment this is impossible because the Nepalese authorities are only able to allow a limited number of peaks to be climbed. They issue a list each year of the peaks that climbers can apply for, but no doubt in future years the number of peaks which they will open up to expeditions will be increased.

We had now reached a height of 12,000 feet. I was very aware of the importance of acclimatization. In the original 1953 Everest expedition, John Hunt established an acclimatization camp at Thyangboche, where they spent a period of two weeks, exploring the glaciers in the immediate vicinity and climbing minor peaks up to a height of about 18,500 feet. This undoubtedly benefited the team later on in the expedition. This approach is strongly contrasted to Herrligkoffer's planning, the previous spring, when he flew his party into Lukla and then tried to push them as fast as possible up to Base Camp. As a result, he had acclimatization problems in the early stages of the expedition and caused a lot of unnecessary stress. We, unfortunately, were unable to take as leisurely an acclimatization period as John Hunt since we were going to have to make the maximum possible use of the comparatively warm days in the immediate post-monsoon period. However, my timing, so far, seemed to have worked out well. The monsoon, obviously, was still not over when we reached Thyangboche; the mountains were shrouded in cloud, and it was drizzling gently. I decided, therefore, to spend three days at Thyangboche, to enable our second party to catch up with us, and for everyone to dry themselves out, get their gear sorted and get used to the increased altitude.

We stayed in a small, prefabricated hut which had been left by the Indian expedition of 1965. The grass around us was lush and green from the monsoon rains, and we caught tantalizing glimpses of the mountains as the clouds rolled back and forth. Our own little group had felt a comfortable homogeneous unit on the approach march, but it was good to see Barney, Mick, Beth and Doug, on their arrival two days later.

Doug had walked all the way from Kathmandu barefoot. With his hair down to his shoulders, held back from his eyes with a head band, and a short, unkempt beard, he looked a cross between one of the early Christian martyrs and a modern-day hippie. He had a wonderfully warm and simple idealism and interest in the people around him. Inspired by the scenery about us, and the character of the Sherpas, he cooked up a scheme to organize a climbing school in Khumjung for the Sherpas to give them the necessary technical know-how to be able to work as guides in the rapidly expanding tourist industry that was developing in Sola Khumbu.

There was a further addition to the team in the form of Tony Tighe. He was a close friend of Dougal's – an Australian, who had got part-way through his studies in architecture, before feeling the wander-urge and leaving Australia to visit Europe. He had ended up at the Club Vagabond in Leysin, Dougal's base, and the temporary home of many world-travellers. Tony had settled there for a couple of years, earning enough money to live helping out in the bar and finally taking over as bar-manager. I had met him a couple of times and had spent one superb day with him, skiing down the Vallée Blanche on the Mont Blanc Massif the previous Easter to rescue some gear which we had left on the North Face of the Grandes Jorasses. He was a natural mixer, easy-going, very outward-looking and unselfish. He had written to me just before we set out on the expedition, telling me that he was planning to travel overland to India, and would be in Nepal at the same time that we would be there. He asked whether there was any chance at all of joining up with the expedition to help at Base Camp.

It is always useful having a few voluntary helpers who have joined the team on an informal basis and I had therefore accepted his offer. He was to contribute a great deal to the work of the expedition during its course.

We had nearly come to the end of our journey and the climbing was about to begin. The summit pyramid of Everest, like the keep of a medieval castle, peered tantalizingly over its curtain wall formed by the crenellated ridge of Nuptse, and the greater corner bastion of Lhotse.

Would we be able to race the winter winds and cold to its top?

7

ACCLIMATIZATION
AND PLANNING

8 September–14 September

I had not been able to relax entirely on the approach march, for I had spent much of the time, as I wandered in the rain through the Nepali countryside, thinking of how we were going to climb the South West Face and talking to the others of my plans. I had already made a draft plan; this was necessary in assessing the number of Sherpas we would require, and the amount of gear and oxygen we should obtain. I based my planning largely on the experience of Dougal on the international expedition, since Doug and Hamish, on the European expedition, had only reached the level of Camp 5. The first fundamental problem was that of how many camps we should use. Dougal recommended having a seventh camp above the Rock Band, and this seemed to make good sense, though even before leaving Britain, as I tried to make a detailed analysis of how we should establish, stock and then maintain this seventh camp, it was beginning to become obvious that with the numbers we had available – ten climbers and forty Sherpas, which might seem a small army – we should still barely have the manpower to succeed in doing this.

Oxygen was at the core of the problem. Each cylinder weighed seventeen pounds and contained just over a 1000 litres of oxygen, enough for about four hours. We planned on letting the climbers use oxygen from 23,000 feet upwards, to try to keep them going for the final summit push, while the Sherpas would start using it from Camp 5 at 26,000 feet. The problem is that once a climber or Sherpa is using oxygen, his effective payload is reduced to about fifteen pounds, since his oxygen cylinder for climbing takes up half the acceptable load of around thirty-five pounds. To achieve a fast build-up from Camp 5 upwards, one would need a large number of carriers at each camp to maintain the flow. A further complication was presented by the fact that the camp sites have a limited capacity. This was especially the case at Camp 4 (24,000 feet) which had room for only three platforms.

During the approach march, in the course of several discussions with Hamish and Dougal in particular, we decided we should have to abandon the concept of a seventh camp and plan instead on fix-roping the Rock Band from Camp 6, then making a summit bid from this lower camp.

Another fundamental decision, which to me had never seemed in doubt, was our choice of route up the Rock Band. The Japanese had headed for the left-hand side of the Rock Band, where there are two clearly defined breaks, one a ramp leading out onto the West Ridge, and the other a deep chimney-like gully cutting up through the Rock Band. Doug Scott had named it Gardyloo Gully during the European Everest expedition, and had suggested, even before we set out, that this might offer a possible line of ascent. Dougal, on the other hand, had been to the very foot of another gully which pierced the defences of the Rock Band on its right-hand side. He described this as being filled with snow and looking comparatively straightforward. It is interesting to speculate just why Whillans and Haston abandoned the Japanese line up to the left, to make their long traverse below the Rock Band over to the right. One of the key problems was that of camp sites and in the spring of 1970, the Japanese had failed to find a suitable camp site for their Camp 5 at the foot of the Rock Band. There was too little snow on the Face to cut out a platform, and they had insufficient alloy platforms to construct artificial standings for their tents. Don had detected possible sites for Camp 5 on the right-hand side of the Great Central Gully, and Camp 5 was duly established there. From their site of Camp 5, however, it would have been extremely difficult to get back across to the left-hand fork of the gully. The route to the right, across the foot of the Rock Band, however, seemed fairly straightforward, and so they had adopted this.

Since there was a line of fixed ropes, which we might well have been able to use, and since the gully through the Rock Band did not seem too difficult, there appeared to be no doubt that this was the route we should take.

The plan in principle, therefore, seemed clear-cut. My logistic calculations, made back in England before the expedition, are in Appendix B. We had even tried to work them out on a computer. A friend of mine, Ian MacNaught Davies, is managing director of Comshare, a computer company which rents out terminals to firms who can then use the central computer. He is an outstanding climber, having made the first ascent of the Mustagh Tower in 1956 with a very small and compact expedition, but more than that, he is one of the most ebullient characters on the British climbing scene. He has taken part in most of the B.B.C.'s climbing spectaculars, usually taking the part of the happy clown, a foil to Joe Brown's silent proficiency. The thought of working out our planning on his computer, like a giant war or business game, appealed to him mainly for its own interest and at the same time as a possible piece of public relations for his firm. David Walkworth, one of his best programmers, was given the task of working out a programme for climbing Mount Everest. Sadly, the pressure of work in getting the expedition together in those last few weeks was too great for us to be able to take our computer game through to its logical conclusion. I have a feeling that if we had, we should have discovered back in England that we didn't have the logistic power to establish a seventh camp.

There was nothing magic or gimmicky in using the computer. You could not work out a programme and then leave the machine to climb the mountain. We used it essentially as a very sophisticated calculating machine which could reduce the hours that I ended up spending in my tent, during the approach march, working out each step of the climb. In the event, we found that it was impractical to plan in detail too far ahead, because invariably circumstances intervened to dictate a change in plan. On the other hand, by having the outline plan based on carefully thought-out principles, and by playing through what, in effect, was a projected course for the expedition, we were in a position to alter our plans within a sound framework.

I had made my initial plans on the basis of climbers and Sherpas, without troubling about who would do what job, and how each person would fit into the role allotted to him. Now I was going to have to give people their roles on the expedition and realized all too well how critical this could be.

My team was selected on the basis that I had six lead climbers, any one of whom would be capable of reaching the summit of Everest, and who would also expect, and need, to have a share of the lead climbing if his morale and interest in the climb were going to be sustained. These were Dave Bathgate, Mick Burke, Nick Estcourt, Dougal Haston, Hamish MacInnes and Doug Scott. Then there were five of us who would have to be in support. Initially, I had given myself the role of lead climber, but then had increasingly felt that it would be better for me to stay in support, as far as possible, in the camp just below that of the lead climbers. On the South Face of Annapurna, I had found it difficult to conduct the expedition from the front, when I was forcing the route out, for then my mind was too involved in the immediate tactics of the climb, of working out the next few feet of ice or rock, rather than the operation as a whole. Back in the tent at night, the nervous exhaustion of lead climbing had been so great that it was still more difficult to pick up the strands of the entire climb. Another factor was the inevitable resentment felt by other members of the team if you spent too long out in front. Equally, though, I had found it difficult to control the expedition from Base Camp. On the South Face of Annapurna we had our greatest personal crisis towards the end of the expedition, when I had pushed Don Whillans and Dougal Haston out of turn, to the front, to make the final push. There had been a lot of hard words over the radio, and a certain degree of misunderstanding which would never have occurred had I been at the penultimate camp instead of being sick at Base Camp. And so for this climb, I resolved to stand down from the lead, but to stay as near the front as long as I could, to maintain effective control.

My other support climbers, Graham Tiso, Kelvin Kent and Barney Rosedale, were going to be extremely important, for each camp needed one European climber in residence to supervise the Sherpas, allotting loads, maintaining their morale and taking the radio calls. As it turned out, I could have used more climbers performing this role. The lead climbers were not suited by temperament to such a job, and anyway I needed to keep them as fresh as possible for the final push. My support climbers, on the other hand, could gain sufficient sense of fulfilment in feeling that what they were doing was worthwhile. In addition, they all had extra administrative responsibilities and in the case of Barney, medical ones also. On the logistic front, I merely gave Graham the list of gear I wanted at different camps and it was he who worked out the order of the loads that went up the mountain and then kept a check on their flow through the expedition. Kelvin had a constant responsibility in looking after our relations with the Sherpas and the day-to-day administration. Once Jimmy Roberts arrived at Base Camp, Kelvin was then able to move up the mountain to Camp 2, which by this time had become an advanced Base Camp, leaving Base Camp and its many problems in Jimmy's capable hands. His presence, advice and authority with the Sherpas were to be invaluable throughout the middle and later stages of the expedition.

Having settled on the lead climbers, I had to decide how best to employ them, whether to make pairings fairly permanent or completely flexible. I decided that if pairs got on well together, it was best to let them stay together. Another factor to be taken into consideration was that we had a responsibility to film for I.T.V. and Thames Television, and therefore, ideally, there should be someone interested in filming prepared to concentrate on this task in each team. Mick Burke was taking overall responsibility, but the important thing was to have a camera at the front at all times where things were likely to happen, and therefore everyone needed to be capable of having a go with it. Hamish MacInnes, also a very competent cameraman, had got some magnificent film for the B.B.C. in the spring attempt. It would therefore have been unfortunate to pair Mick and Hamish together, thus over-concentrating our filming talent. I also had to take into account how compatible each pair was going to be and how they would supplement each other's experience.

At the same time as deciding on the composition of the pairing, I had an even more basic problem to resolve. This was how far to plan ahead the sharing out of the lead climbing to ensure that team members felt, as far as possible, that they had had a fair share and consequently might end the expedition with a feeling of satisfaction. One of the factors on Everest was that we could predict movement fairly accurately from the experience of the previous expeditions. I knew that there was comparatively little technical difficulty until we reached the foot of the Rock Band. It was the Rock Band and the summit bid, which I hoped would immediately follow, that provided the real challenge of the climb – but it seemed unlikely that more than four climbers would have a chance of trying it.

I evolved a revised plan during the approach march by which we should first climb the Ice Fall with all members of the team having a turn out in front; then I intended to move Pair 1 up to Camp 1, to make the route to Camp 2 in the Western Cwm. Since this was little more than walking, I planned then to allow them to make the route on from Camp 2 to Camp 3 at a height of 23,000 feet. They would then go down for a rest and Pair 2 would move into Camp 3, erect the boxes there and make the route to Camp 4 (24,600 feet), fix the ropes and then return to Base for a rest. Pair 3 would then move up to Camp 4, dig out the platforms left by the Germans, erect their boxes and make the route up the Great Central Gully to Camp 5 (26,000 feet). I estimated that the route-making between camps would take between one and two days each, since either the fixed ropes from previous expeditions would still be in place, or if they were covered in snow, the very presence of the snow would make the climbing that much easier. The method of making the route is that the lead pair goes up and leaves a continuous line of rope all the way up the face, anchored at intervals by snow anchors, ice screws or rock pegs. Everyone subsequently climbs the fixed ropes using Jumar clamps.

Having reached Camp 5, the logical thing would be for Pair 1 to move back up, to make the route from Camp 5 to 6; Pair 2 to have the first try on the Rock Band and, if it was as straight-forward as Dougal led us to believe, I believed that, provided they felt capable, one must let them make a first attempt on the summit. This would leave Pair 3 rested and fresh to make a second ascent or attempt, depending on the success of the first attempt.

My problem was to decide upon the pairing, and then whether to just explain Phase 1, up to the establishment of Camp 5, or explain my entire plan. There were pros and cons for either course. If I merely explained Phase 1, I should have had greater flexibility in changing the plan around and adapting it to the performance of different pairs. At the same time, however, I should have created a state of greater tension in the early part of the expedition, since everyone would have been working out their position on the mountain, and their relative chances of tackling the Rock Band or making a summit bid. By explaining the full plan, I was committing myself to a definite pattern of action, but once each pair had accepted their role, I could hope that they would then work to the full within it. I decided, therefore, to follow this latter course.

I then spent many an hour considering the pairing. Dougal and Hamish, who had known each other in a casual kind of way over a good many years, had never actually climbed together. On the approach march, however, they obviously got on together, and by the time we reached Thyangboche, they also seemed particularly fit and to be acclimatizing well. I decided to pair them together. Of the remaining four, I knew that Nick Estcourt and Mick Burke did not get on particularly well; they were too different in temperament and background – Nick precise, almost niggling over small details but tremendously conscientious, Mick more slap-dash, easy-going on the surface, but very pushing underneath. Nick and Doug did not know each other overwell, and since Doug had travelled out on the second party, they did not have the opportunity to get to know each other any better during the course of the walk out. There had already been points of mutual irritation, however, with Nick's logical mind rubbing against Doug's more emotional approach to questions of basic principle. Doug and Mick, on the other hand, got on well together; they bickered constantly in an almost light-hearted, playful way; they undoubtedly made a good team.

This left Nick and Dave Bathgate, who, although they had only known each other casually before the expedition, got on very well together. Dave, like Nick, is extremely methodical and precise, with a highly developed conscience and a perfectionist attitude to any job he undertakes. And so I had three pairs who, in the course of the expedition, worked well and happily together.

The next question was more difficult – sorting out the batting order. This was not merely a question of settling on the relative strengths and abilities of each pair and arranging them accordingly, it was more a question of fitting each pair for their specific task, working out how well they were suited to it, and how easily they could accept it. Pair 1 would be having the least satisfying task, since they would merely be establishing the lower part of the Face and then making the route from Camp 5 to 6. I was hoping, however, that having made the route they would also be able to stay up, in support for the summit bid, working until they were completely finished. In a way, acceptance of this role required the greatest level of unselfishness and the highest degree of reliability, for the direct rewards were less obvious. I decided to cast Nick and Dave for this somewhat unenviable task, for I knew I could rely totally on their loyal support in what, at first glance, seemed a lesser role. In addition, Dave had less high-altitude experience than the other members of the team. There was little doubt in my mind that Dougal and Hamish were by far the most experienced pair, and Dougal particularly was recognized by the entire team as having the greatest drive on the mountain. If you like, he was acknowledged by all to be at the top of the pecking order. There was very little to choose as a pair between Doug and Mick, and Dave and Nick. Doug did have the advantage that he had been to 26,000 feet and Mick, who at the beginning of the expedition was probably the least fit, and had certainly climbed the least in the last year or so, has an amazing single-minded determination which has enabled him to screw out of the bag some very impressive performances over the years – his first British ascent of the Nose of El Capitan and, even more applicable to Everest, his achievement in leading all the way across the Rock Band on the South Face of Annapurna. Another factor which I had to take into consideration was that since Mick was chief cameraman of the expedition, I wanted to give him the maximum chance to get the best film possible, since we owed this to I.T.N. and Thames, who had sponsored us.

Bearing all these considerations in mind, I decided to designate Mick and Doug as Pair 2, with the responsibility of making the route from Camps 3 to 4 and then from 6, up the Rock Band with the first summit attempt, holding Dougal and Hamish back for the final summit attempt. This made sense and, because of the latter pair's complete self-confidence, they would be able to cope with a reserve role, knowing full well that on them would rest our main chance of reaching the summit of Everest. I had a feeling that the chances of Doug and Mick could be no more than outside, after the effort they would require to make in forcing the Rock Band.

I announced the plan once the second party had caught us up at Thyangboche. Naturally Nick and Dave were disappointed at their seemingly subordinate position in relation to the others, but it is a tribute to their loyalty to the concept of the expedition that they accepted their role without argument and fulfilled it with enthusiasm.

And so, at Thyangboche, when we were still fifteen miles from our objective, we had a plan which was to provide the basis of our efforts on Everest. The three days' rest was well spent, drying out our equipment and sorting out gear for the climb ahead. The climbers were going to use one-piece down suits, covered by a windproof outer suit. The suit had originally been designed by Don Whillans and was ingenious, having a zip round the interior of the leg so that the climber could remove or put on the suit over boots and crampons. A small slit down the back, closed by a zip, enabled him to relieve himself without taking the suit off and baring his backside to the icy blast. I had made one or two important modifications to cater for the extreme cold and wind that we were going to encounter during an autumn attempt. These included increasing the down content of the suit, having all flaps over zips padded in down and, most important, incorporating a Ventile (cotton) inner layer, underneath the outer layer of the windproof suit. This ensured that the suit was totally windproof. One thing we had failed to notice in the rush before leaving Britain, however, was that the outer suits did not have hoods. We were fortunate in having Beth Burke with us, and she hand-tailored hoods to fit all the members of the team. We had issued our Sherpas with the more conventional down jackets and trousers, with windproof outers. At the same time, Hamish was sorting out all our oxygen gear, adapting our pack-frames with a special set of straps to hold the bottles rigidly in position, and making one or two modifications on the equipment itself to strengthen what seemed some weak joints.

During our stop at Thyangboche, we visited the Chief Lama of the monastery to receive his blessing and to make a presentation of money to the monastery. I described this in my diary on 10 September:

At 11.30 a.m. we had to go up and make our official visit to the Lama at Thyangboche monastery. The official visit of the expedition is a way of giving a presentation of money to the monastery, and it is also an opportunity for the Sherpas to be blessed by the Lama. The Lama lives not in the main monastery building, but in a little side building. We went through a low door to a little yard with marigolds and flowers in window boxes around it, into the Lama's room, which was sparsely furnished with low divans round the whitewashed walls and a table in the middle. The divans were made from rough-cut wood, with Tibetan carpets on them. The Lama was sitting there, waiting to receive us, in his dark, brownish robes. He was perhaps in his mid-thirties or early forties and had a look of tranquillity about him. I was ushered in first and made my *numasti* (greeting) to him, bobbing my head; Kelvin and Hamish came in afterwards and did the same. Then all our Sherpas trooped in, in what seemed to be an order of seniority – Pembatharke first followed by Sona Hishy and then Phurkipa, the eldest of our Sherpas, and finally all the others. As all the Sherpas came in, the older ones went to him and bowed right down in front of him to have their heads touched, but the younger ones completed what was almost a yoga exercise, going right down on their hands and knees, touching the floor with their heads, and then back into the standing position – doing this three times before coming forward for the blessing. Each had with him a white ceremonial gauze scarf, in which was wrapped his offering. Between them, the fourteen had raised 280 rupees as a gift for the Thyang-boche monastery. We ourselves gave another 500 rupees for not only Thyangboche, but also the Khumbu monasteries. Having gone through this ceremonial we all sat down, and the Lama talked to us as a group. Kelvin, being able to speak Nepali, got into quite a deep discussion and the Lama was able to put across his own religious attitudes. He showed, I think, that even in these seemingly primitive surroundings, how much broader his religion is than that of many Christian priests and prelates. He said how there could be only one God, but that man had found many different ways of trying to reach him and to worship him. He then went on to talk about expeditions, saying how on the two previous expeditions, because the climbers had started arguing and quarrelling among themselves, this had led the Sherpas to become discontented, and therefore the expeditions had failed. It would be very cold for us, he said, going in the autumn, but in spite of this we should remain united.

We sat there, eating biscuits and drinking tea, for about an hour. During that time some of the tranquillity and the settled peace of the monastic's existence had rolled over us. We then visited the main *ghompa*, and were shown the inner sanctuary, a room on the first floor. It was lined with magnificent, garish mural paintings of devils, wheels of life, and other pictures associated with their mythology. Down one wall was the main altar, with three incarnations of Buddha, and glass cabinets full of idols, many of which seemed to have a strong Hindu influence in their design. On one side of the room was the monastery library, with parchment rolls tucked into little square compartments. The Sherpas, once again, went through their obeisance in front of the altar, and we admired the pictures, and made a further contribution to the upkeep of the monasteries.

We left Thyangboche on 11 September; the monsoon clouds had rolled in once again and we could see no more than the dripping trees on either side of the path, and rough stone walls disappearing into the mists. That night we stopped at Pheriche, a little collection of one-storey huts in small fields, only occupied in the summer months. The following day we walked up to Lobuje, in a rain that slowly turned to snow as dusk fell. Dave Bathgate describes the day in his diary :

There are some advantages to the depressing weather. The day started off as usual. Swirling damp mists and visibility about 100 yards, the altitude making it that wee bit colder and turning the rain to sleet as we climbed. The consolation of walking through magnificent scenery that can only be beheld in the imagination, is that one is forced to study the immediate surroundings, particularly the piece of ground in front of your nose. You walk, head down, brolly up, threading through the moraines, climbing as you peer past the boulders into the murk. Now, couldn't this just be Scotland: like some part of Sutherland to be precise, where the moraines are still not quite covered in vegetation. But stepping into a pile of yak dung you are brought back to reality. This is Nepal. This is 15,000 feet up in the mountains on the last few days of the walk into the Everest Base Camp. Yak dung is everywhere in neat piles.

Suddenly you are aware of the colours. You are walking on a carpet of yellow butterwort, little yellow stars, all interlocking, and between is green. Under a clean granite rock there are pink pom-pom flowers and one or two bright purple blooms like our bluebell. The moraine walls are covered in juniper and sheltered by the bush are edelweiss and large yellow-petalled flowers like buttercups. There are plants like fluted columns, large, leafy, green things, little clusters of red buds and many other wonders of the Alpine scene unidentifiable to the layman; a paradise for the botanist; an entomologist would have a field day. Countless millions of butterwort (an insect-devouring flower) can't be wrong. The geologist would also weigh himself down with samples of a fascinating nature; here is granite and quartz; evidence of iron and copper or schist; the stream beds are full of 'pearls' for him.

All this that has been brought to my attention would otherwise have gone unnoticed if the big hills had shown themselves.

Lobuje was no more than a couple of yak-herders' huts in a little valley at the side of a glacier. I had planned to send the porters straight through from Lobuje, by Gorak Shep, up to Base Camp with Hamish MacInnes and Dougal Haston, who seemed extremely well acclimatized and who were keen to press on and start reconnoitring the Ice Fall. On the other hand, I had wanted to give the rest of the team as much opportunity as possible to acclimatize, and therefore considered spending another two or three days at Lobuje, at a height of 16,000 feet, so that each member of the team could acclimatize at his own rate. The following morning, however, 13 September, we had no choice in the matter. It had snowed hard all night and our porters had had a rough time. With insufficient shelter in the two yak huts for all of them, we had had to make improvised shelters from piled-up loads and tarpaulins and the Sherpas and Sherpanis spent the night huddled beneath these. In spite of the cold they seemed to enjoy the experience, regarding the whole affair as a light-hearted adventure, even though most of them had little more than a blanket each in which to wrap themselves.

The next stop would have been Gorak Shep, which was not much higher than Lobuje, but in an even bleaker situation. From there to Base Camp was a three-hour walk and in the event of another bad night at Gorak Shep it would have been difficult to persuade the Sherpas to walk this distance the next day, so I decided to let them stay at Lobuje. At least it gave us a chance of issuing all their equipment to the Ice Fall Sherpas who had now joined us. Very quickly the camp took on the appearance of a bazaar, as Graham broke open the boxes and lined them up like a series of market stalls. Our temporary porters, who were going to carry the gear up to Base Camp, acted as an audience, watching the hand-out in a spirit which was both light-hearted and critical. This was the moment which had caused the crisis on the Herrligkoffer expedition, when the Sherpas had discovered that they had insufficient gear with which to climb the mountain. I was just praying that they would be happy with what we presented to them. You could tell at a glance the difference between our high-altitude porters who had been employed all the way from Kathmandu and the Ice Fall Sherpas whom we had only just hired. The latter were less well dressed, their clothes the relics of previous expeditions; very few spoke English and they looked altogether rougher and, surprisingly perhaps, older than our high-altitude porters. Jimmy Roberts' Mountain Travel Sherpas looked like mountain guides – they barely condescended to use the clothing which we had issued, preferring for the approach march gear they considered more elegant. Some of them, Pertemba particularly, reminded me of French guides, with smart peaked cap and well-cut breeches.

The proceedings started with a little ceremonial speech from myself, in which I described a bonus scheme we had worked out to give the Sherpas an incentive to carry their loads up the South West Face. I also promised magnificent *baksheesh* in the event of success. The speech was relayed in Nepali by Kelvin, through Sona Hishy, who gave it in Sherpa. The speech appeared to be well received, and then we lined up all our newly-recruited Sherpas and handed out all their equipment. That afternoon the camp resembled a factory, as Graham with one group of Sherpas assembled pack-frames; other groups fitted crampons to boots or tried on their new gear. Inevitably, the odd item disappeared, as Sherpas helped themselves, or swapped one item of gear for another. They all seemed satisfied at this stage with what they had been issued.

The following day dawned fine, and for the first time we saw the magnificent setting which surrounds Lobuje. Looking back down the valley, the twin peaks of Kantega dominated the deep-cut gorge of the Dudh Kosi. Further over to the right was Taweche, a beautiful fluted peak almost climbed by Hillary's schoolhouse expedition in 1963, and just to the right was that of Tsolatse, which was still virgin. Immediately above us were some lower, rocky peaks which would have been attainable if only we had had more time. We did, however, climb the nearest summit, which must have been at a height of about 18,000 feet. We plodded up grassy slopes which were a mosaic of Alpine flowers and mosses, and then scrambled up a rocky little ridge to the top. We had been well rewarded for our purgatorial march through the monsoons by the sheer variety and beauty of the vegetation, which would soon die in the dry, autumnal air. From the summit of our little peak we gazed across the Khumbu Glacier to the incredible turreted ridge of Nuptse which concealed Everest and the Ice Fall. Many tourists who have come only this far have made the mistake of thinking that this was Everest itself – it certainly looked sufficiently high. And then, on up the Khumbu Glacier, the 23,400-foot summit of Pumori was a shapely pyramid of snow and rock; this had been climbed by a German expedition in 1962 and was to be the target of a French expedition from Chamonix while we made our attempt on the South West Face of Everest. One couldn't help having a slight feeling of envy for them. We were under no illusions about the type of climbing we were going to have on Everest – a great deal of hard work, with comparatively little exciting climbing. On the other hand, a mountain like Pumori would obviously yield superb technical climbing, at an altitude low enough to enjoy it. Nevertheless, the scale of Everest made up for it – the problem we were tackling was so huge that this very challenge made it all worthwhile.

That day the porters and yaks moved on, up to Gorak Shep, the standard staging post on the way up to Base Camp. They were accompanied by Graham Tiso and Nick Estcourt, together with five of our high-altitude Sherpas, whilst Dougal and Hamish, with half a dozen Sherpas carrying their tentage and personal gear, moved straight up to Base Camp. And so, on 14 September, little more than three months after we had conceived our expedition, the real climbing of the mountain was about to begin.

8

THE ICE
FALL

16 September–20 September

So far luck had been with us – our timing seemed perfect; 14 September, to all intents and purposes, marked the end of the monsoon. Jimmy Roberts had seen many monsoons in Nepal and had a theory that its end was often marked by a heavy snowfall down to 14,000 feet. He appeared to be right, for the snow of the previous few days had reached all the way down to Pheriche, which is just on the 14,000-foot mark. Now the sun blazed from a cloudless blue sky and had that special, autumnal quality. In spite of the heat of the sun there was a clean-cut bite to the air, which removed all traces of haze. It was as if you were looking at the distant peaks through a magnifying glass. And it was on the 14th that Dougal and Hamish, feeling almost no effect at all from the altitude, made the long walk from Lobuje to the site of Base Camp.

Base Camp on Everest is a bleak place; it is situated on the glacier itself, amongst rocky debris carved by the glacier in the previous millennia. It resembles a vast, derelict granite quarry, whose unworked stones have been left in haphazard piles, the rocks comparatively young and unweathered, edges unrounded by erosion of wind and weather. There was rock dust everywhere, as if from a recent blasting. At close quarters it is a stark, almost ugly place contrasting with the austere beauty of the surrounding mountains; but even these mountains offer little relief, for their appeal is one of chill remoteness, a beauty unrelieved by softness. No grass in sight, none of the brilliant Alpine flowers and mosses that we had seen at Gorak Shep for the last time for some months; this was a wilderness of rock and snow and ice, whose only reminder of man was the worst possible – man's pollution of almost anything he touches. The area round Base Camp was marked by the previous expeditions to Everest. Their rubbish was everywhere – rusty tins, plastic bags, decayed packing cases.

Yet that first night the very austerity of the setting must have seemed precious to Dougal and Hamish. Both had been there before, but on the two previous occasions there had always been a mass of people around them. That afternoon, though, the Sherpas carrying the tentage and climbing gear had dumped their loads and returned to the main party camped at Gorak Shep, leaving just the two of them in a small orange tent, at the head of the Khumbu Glacier. A few days later this was to become a little village of tents, with a population of over fifty. Then, inevitably, some of the magic must be lost, for this is the problem of all large expeditions; the atmosphere of the mountains, the emotion they inspire in us, the feeling of easy friendship that you get when just a few are sharing this, are very dependent on empty solitude.

Over the way was Pumori, snow-traced buttresses stretching up towards its corniced summit. Immediately above was Khumbutse, foreshortened because of its proximity, with none of the classic proportions of Pumori; then, to its right, within easy reach of Base Camp, the pass of the Lho La, the way into Tibet and the Rongbuk Glacier. An occasional rattle, slightly muted, betrayed falling ice tumbling from its piled séracs and the western spur of Everest.

But it was the Ice Fall which commanded their attention – as indeed it does the attention of any visitor to the Everest Base Camp. The Ice Fall is a natural continuation of the Khumbu Glacier, as is the Western Cwm. It is a gigantic frozen river, the source of which is on the slopes of Everest and Lhotse. The Western Cwm must rank as the most inspiring cirque to be found in any mountain range in the world, squeezed as it is between the flanks of Everest and the incredible wall of Nuptse. The Ice Fall is the gateway to Everest, a vast frozen cataract, tumbling nearly three thousand feet between a subsidiary spur of Nuptse and one from Everest. Had it been water it would have been a gigantic waterfall, but as ice it was even more impressive. The huge but slow pressure of the glacier in the Western Cwm inexorably thrusts the ice before it, over the drop of the Ice Fall, breaking up the smooth-flowing river of ice which forms the bed of the Cwm into a convoluted chaos of ice walls, towers and pinnacles, all of which must eventually topple. Dougal and Hamish had to find a route through this maze. In addition to their knowledge of the risks and the problems, now, in the autumn, we had some grounds to hope that it would be both easier and safer than it had been in the spring. They could see that many of the crevasses which seam its surface before the monsoon had been filled in. We knew that the Argentinians, the previous autumn, had found it comparatively easy and had forced the Ice Fall in a mere three days, compared with the fortnight it had taken the international expedition and the ten days spent by the European expedition. It was easy to imagine the wonder and, at the same time, the trepidation of Eric Shipton's reconnaissance party, who first climbed it in the autumn of 1951. Entering the Ice Fall undoubtedly has an element of Russian roulette. There is no possibility of making a safe route through the Khumbu Ice Fall. All you can do is to try and pick out a route which is as safe as possible, but there will always be sections which are threatened by ice towers which, sooner or later, must collapse. You just hope that no one happens to be beneath them when the inevitable collapse occurs. If climbers and Sherpas only had to go through the danger area once during an expedition the risks would be comparatively slight – not much greater than the risks presented to any Alpinist working his way through a hanging glacier in the European Alps or any other mountain region in the world. The problem with the Everest Ice Fall is that some climbers must go through these danger areas almost every single day of the expedition. As a result, the chances of an accident occurring are increased considerably, as the death-roll on Everest has sadly proven. It is the Sherpas who are exposed to the greatest risk, particularly the Ice Fall porters whose job it is to keep Camp 2 fully stocked with food and gear throughout the expedition.

Dougal and Hamish spent a further day gazing at the Ice Fall through binoculars, resting to ensure that their acclimatization was as complete as possible. Nick Estcourt and Graham Tiso, with all our porters and some high-altitude Sherpas, walked up to Base

Camp from Gorak Shep, and that day the camp became a Base Camp indeed. The following day, the 16th, we first set foot on Everest in earnest. Dougal, Hamish and five Sherpas carrying five-foot sections of alloy ladders, rope, snow stakes and dead men (not corpses, but plates which are buried in the snow to provide a compact yet very reliable anchor), set out before dawn. There was no breath of wind, but in the dim light the temperature was in the region of −10°C; the snow was firm underfoot, points of crampons snicking into its hard surface. They had picked out a line the day before and now zig-zagged steadily up, through the gentle undulations of the approach to the Ice Fall. The harsh angularity of the ice was hidden by the covering of monsoon snows and they were able to make rapid progress, bridging the occasional open crevasse with one of their ladders. Hamish was in his element; being, perhaps, a frustrated structural engineer, he revels in making complex pulley systems, bridges and anything mechanical. By mid-day they had reached a point almost half-way up the Ice Fall, having found a route that seemed completely free from objective danger. However, the sun was now hammering down, and not only was the hard snow being softened into a thigh-deep morass, but more important, the sheer heat of the sun burning down into the giant reflector provided by the Ice Fall and the Western Cwm had an enervating effect which sapped the will and made any movement a trial. They retreated, there-fore, well content with their day's work.

That same day I walked, with Dave Bathgate, up to Base Camp from Lobuje. I was able to forget for a few happy hours my over-all responsibility for the expedition, in the excitement of walking to the foot of Everest. That evening I commented in my diary:

This morning dawned magnificently; the monsoon certainly seems to be over. Dave and I set out early, along the moraine which flanks the Khumbu Glacier, past an array of miniature Alpine flowers and plants picked out by the early-morning frost. From Gorak Shep, the route goes on to the Glacier itself, past giant white fins of ice that look like the sails of yachts. and over a sea of rubble-strewn ice. The gleaming white of the ice fins was enhanced by the drab grey of the glacier around. It is a bleak, almost lunar landscape. The Ice Fall itself is completely hidden until you are almost at the end of the

Khumbu Glacier. It turns a tight L-turn, and it is only near its end that you see it – and what a chaotic mass of ice it is. Dougal and Hamish must be somewhere amongst it. We missed the way to the camp and went much too high – very nearly reaching the foot of the Ice Fall. I was beginning to feel quite tired, and so was Dave. We were both slipping around a bit and feeling the altitude. We realized at last that the camp could not possibly be in front of us, looked back, and only after a very careful search were we able to see the camp site. It made you realize what a really huge scale this area is – there was just a collection of tiny, matchbox-like tents, lost in the barren waste of rubble on the dying glacier.

In spite of having a bad headache, Graham Tiso had been at work all day, sorting out the mass of expedition gear which was to go up the mountain. We had, altogether, five tons of gear which was destined for the Western Cwm. There were a hundred and seventy bottles of oxygen, of which I estimated we should use approximately ninety – the rest were a reserve. There was – or rather should have been – 15,000 feet of fixed rope, several hundred pitons, dead men, snow stakes, ladders and all the paraphernalia for laying siege to a big mountain. Graham had done an outstanding job in getting all the gear ready in time for the expedition, but had made one, vital mistake in failing to check the quantity of rope delivered to him against what had been ordered. Consequently, instead of 15,000 feet of fixed rope, we found ourselves with 5,000 feet – not nearly enough to climb the South West Face of Everest, and barely enough for use in the Ice Fall. The impact of this shock was softened by the discovery that Graham was, in fact, fallible! He is quite a bombastic soul, accustomed to ruling his business with a hand which is both very firm and yet, at the same time, has a touch of fun in it. Having the total self-confidence of all successful businessmen, he was happy to assure all of his infallibility. All was not lost, however, since we knew that Jimmy Roberts had about 3,000 feet of rope back in Kathmandu, and we immediately sent a message asking if we could borrow this, and for a further 6,000 feet to be air-freighted out to us from England. There were one or two other minor omissions, such as the fact that we had forgotten to supply our Sherpas with water bottles. This was easily rectified by sending down to Namche Bazar and Khumjung, and buying them from the Sherpas. There must be enough equipment stashed away in Sola Khumbu to equip almost an entire Everest expedition, though the prices tend to be inflated. We also tried to buy some rope locally, and Lindsay Strang, the New Zealand doctor who ran the Kunde hospital, succeeded in obtaining a thousand feet for us, but this was only in lengths of eighty feet or so.

On 17 September, Dougal and Hamish, with a group of Sherpas, went back into the Ice Fall, setting out even earlier than on their first visit. By dawn, as the rest of us got out of our sleeping bags, we could see them – tiny, black dots, dwarfed by the immensity of the Ice Fall. They were making good progress, having reached their high point, a good half-way up, before dawn. Once again, they moved steadily, picking their way across some avalanche debris, where they had stopped the previous day, and then climbing up a series of comparatively straightforward snow slopes, to the foot of the final steep section before the top of the Ice Fall. A sheer wall of ice barred their way. Hamish cut his way up the steep little snow gully, but by this time the heat of the sun was upon them – enervating, blazing heat, which softened the snow and exhausted the climbers. They managed to look over the top, however, and found themselves confronted by a series of moat-like crevasses. They came down that night, encouraged by their progress, but also warning us that the next section was going to be difficult.

It was now to be the turn of Dave Bathgate and myself to go into the Ice Fall to force the last section. In my diary I said:

I must say, I am a little apprehensive, in that I hope I don't make a mess of it, not having been in the Ice Fall before. Hamish and Dougal, of course, are real old hands, whilst Dave and I are novices. Still, we'll have to do our best.

There is a real feeling of friendship within the team – of people working together, and I only pray we can keep this up. It really is tremendous. Obviously, there are going to be pressures; bound to be conflicts (I have had one with Mick), and so on. But these we shy away from when we have them, realizing how bad they are, immediately suppressing them. You seem to find that when people have had a little row, they make special gestures to show this. Such as the other day, when Mick and I had a flare-up – Mick made a special point afterwards, by shoving some of the stuff I had left outside my tent in the rain, inside, to prevent it getting wet. I think it is these small things which are terribly important.

Once again, from my diary:

18 September 1972: I woke up this morning at about one o'clock, going over the various problems of the expedition. I dropped off to sleep and was woken again by a cook-boy at four o'clock with a cup of tea – certainly a civilized way to start a day's climbing, since we also have breakfast in bed. I got up at about 4.45 a.m., went over to the Sherpas and found they were all ready, and just going through their religious ceremony. In this, each one has a little thread put around his neck and an incantation is made over him with a burning ember, to protect him for the day on the mountain, and in the Ice Fall. Throughout the day, as long as the Sherpas are on the mountain, they keep small fires of smouldering herbs burning, and very often you will notice a Sherpa by one of them, muttering prayers.

Eventually we got going, just as it was getting light, at about 5.15 a.m. Seven load-carriers accompanied us, carrying ladders and other bits of climbing gear. We plodded through the dim light of the dawn – it seemed just pleasantly cool, but I suppose it was very cold, because there was no wind at all, and was absolutely clear and very dry. I felt slightly uncoordinated and still had a slight cough, with discomfort at the back of my throat. I stumbled across the broken rocks of the moraine, to the point where the Sherpas were gathered, putting on their crampons. They just leave their crampons, ropes and ice-axes out on a few rocks – which is all very fine of course, unless there is a big snowfall, when I think they would find it very difficult to locate them. It's something I am going to have to make an issue about with the Sherpas.

Being uncoordinated, I stood on my hand with my cramponed boot, cut my hand, leaving blood spewing out over everything. Having put my crampons on, I started walking and felt a lot better. I must say, I seemed to be going the fastest of all the party. Of course, you've got to remember, though, that most of the Sherpas were heavily laden, whilst we, the climbers, were not. We have noticed that as they plod up the Ice Fall they mutter their prayers. I was with Dave Bathgate; Nick Estcourt was coming up behind with Phurkipa, our 'road-mender', to improve the route.

Phurkipa was the oldest of our Sherpas. Then, fifty-five, he had been on innumerable expeditions, including the spring Everest trip with Doug. It had been Doug who had recommended him. In the spring, Phurkipa had earned the title of 'road-mender' for he had taken charge of the Ice Fall throughout the expedition, repairing and renovating the route as necessary. He was to have this function on our trip as well, and was to do an excellent job.

We wound our way up through the Ice Fall, following the trail made by Dougal and Hamish. Technically, it was fairly easy and comparatively safe, for the route was not threatened by any precarious séracs, though at one point it crossed the debris of what must have been a huge avalanche from the Walls of the Everest Spur. There was a large number of crevasses, which they had bridged, and Dougal and Hamish had done well to make such good time. The place where they had actually ended the day was below a big sérac wall. Dougal had already warned me that they had tried to go up a blind gully. We could see the tracks, but this did not seem to lead anywhere except to a huge crevasse which would require a large number of ladders to bridge. Dougal had mentioned going round to the left, up an alley-way which was below some very loose-looking séracs. It seemed a dangerous area and, as we looked, a sérac higher up collapsed – this convinced us.

Then I was tempted by the wall immediately above, which looked solid enough to use a ladder straight up it. I worked my way across, and brought Dave to me and he went to the foot of the wall itself. We started to get our ladders ready – we had five sections altogether – when one of the most impressive avalanches I have ever seen came off the very summit of Pumori. There was a great cloud of windblown, powder snow, which billowed across the glacier and seemed about to engulf Base Camp itself. But we were concentrating on the route in front, and after a struggle with our five ladders, bolted them together. This was a style of climbing I had never undertaken before. Pushing up a thirty-foot ladder from a comparatively narrow snow ledge is no joke. It was just as well we had six Sherpas with us. With all of them pushing and heaving, we finally succeeded in balancing the ladder against the wall; it reached a point about four feet below the top.

With true courtesy, partly because I wanted to get some

pictures, I gestured to Dave to have the honour of climbing the ladder first. It was a matter of balancing delicately up it – it was still very unstable. He succeeded in putting in an ice piton about two-thirds of the way up, where it come in close to the ice, fastening the ladder to it with a rope, and now that there was no risk of teetering backwards, climbed more rapidly to the top. After a bit of step-cutting, he pulled out on to the top of the sérac wall. This had taken us about three hours. I was uncomfortably aware of the speedy progress which Dougal and Hamish had made the previous day, and was worried that we were going so slowly. From the top of the sérac wall, things did not look at all hopeful. There was a wide depression, immediately in front of us, of unstable-looking snow that led to another mass of séracs; to the right, a sérac tower curled up, and there was a feeling of unpleasant insecurity wherever we looked. Finally, I picked on a line going to one side of a depression. Even on seemingly easy ground, one stepped forward very, very carefully, always uncomfortably aware that one might go rocketing down into a deep hole. Always there was the suspicion that the entire mass of ice could collapse around one, like a pack of cards.

It is strange how one's attitude to a route through a glacier or Ice Fall changes. The first time through, one's progress is slow and nerve-racking, but once the route is made, though it gets no safer, one treats the glacier in an increasingly blasé manner until finally, something happens – a sérac collapses and, perhaps, a man dies.

Another small wall barred our way. This was to be the only real climbing I was to have on the entire expedition – a mere twenty-foot, vertical ice wall. I cut a step, kicked in my crampons, forgot the altitude for just a few minutes in my concentration and apprehension as I worked my way up the sérac wall; I pulled over the side, kicking in my front points, and reached the crest. Once I had fixed the rope, Dave followed up quickly, and we looked further ahead.

The view was not encouraging. We were on a little ridge which reminded me of the crest of a breaker, frozen into immobility, brittle, fragile, about to tumble on to the lesser waves around it. To our left, this was linked with the next line of breakers by a ridge of wafery ice towers, all on the point of collapse. To the right, a trough stretched round a corner, into a broken area that was like a choppy sea. Nothing seemed stable, nothing sure. I tried the ridge to the left, but the sun was now burning down from the empty sky, sapping the will, destroying strength and energy, softening to the consistency of candy floss the snow which bound one pinnacle to another. That way seemed no good.

'Have a look at the ridge on the right,' I told Dave.

He set out, probing the snow in front of him with a long alloy pole whose function was to act as a handrail on crevasse bridges – the most effective way of feeling for hidden crevasses. I sat and stewed in the sun, trying to keep my eyes open, aware that I had been awake since three o'clock that morning. The rope trickled through my fingers. At last we came to the end of the rope, Dave secured it at his end and I clipped a Jumar clamp on to it and followed the line of his tracks, most of them deep in the heat-softened snow.

'It doesn't look too good from here,' he warned me.

It didn't; the well-defined trough had disintegrated into a chaos of holes and towers that looked ready to collapse at any instant. We returned to our starting point at the top of my twenty-foot pitch. To me, the best hope seemed straight down into the trough, to climb the other side, flanking two square-cut sérac towers which, at least, looked a good deal more solid than anything around them. A snow slope led to one side of them, but the problem here was that if one of the towers did collapse, no one below would have a chance of survival. I made a half-hearted step down into the moat which guarded them, but the snow was frighteningly soft and our own strength and determination were waning fast. We looked at each other and decided to return. I have always been intensely competitive in my climbing and could not help feeling disappointed in myself that I had not made better progress. In actual fact, during the next few days, other groups had a struggle to make much further progress in any one day. The top of the Ice Fall was to prove the crux of this part of the route.

Leaving even earlier than we had the previous day, on 19 September, after their day's rest, Dougal and Hamish once again went out in front. We were discovering that it was almost impossible to climb after midday – it was so hot. They reached my high point, and then Hamish indulged in his passion for complex engineering. He shared the same worries that I had had in the choice of a route going down into the moat and then climbing the other side. (In actual fact, this was the place where Tony Tighe was to be killed at the end of the expedition.) Hamish tried, therefore, to avoid this by making an incredible suspension bridge from several sections of aluminium ladder, across the side of the tottering sérac which I had avoided the previous day. It was a magnificent piece of engineering. Having bridged the gap they climbed a steep gully, laddered over the steep wall and got to a point where they could look across the top, over one crevasse, to what they thought would probably be the end of the Ice Fall.

That day they came down well satisfied. Up to this point, rather as on the spring expedition, Doug Scott had acclimatized slowly and, weakened by his attack of dysentery on the approach march, he had spent a couple of extra days down at Gorak Shep, to give himself a better chance of acclimatizing. However, he was now feeling better and on 20 September, with Dave Bathgate, Nick Estcourt and myself, we planned to go up and make the final push to the top of the Ice Fall.

In the early stages of the expedition almost all of us, with the exception of Hamish and Dougal, had stomach upsets, or short periods of sickness. I was struck in this manner that night, and when the time came to get out of bed I found I had lost all my strength. I spent the entire day in my sleeping bag, dosed with a variety of pills from Barney Rosedale. Meanwhile, Doug, Nick and Dave pressed on, up to the high point which Hamish and Dougal had established. Unfortunately, all the ice screws which anchored Hamish's suspension bridge had melted the previous day and so there seemed no choice but to drop the ladder across the bottom of the moat and accept the threat of the two towers above. Having done this they climbed to the top of the gully to rejoin the route made by Hamish and Dougal the previous day, and which we all hoped was to bring us to the end of the difficulties. As is so often the case, this did not prove to be so, and it was necessary to make another long traverse along an undercut ridge of ice, back towards the centre of the Ice Fall. The trio had one of their first personality differences at this point. Doug was still feeling the altitude first thing that morning, and had started out very slowly, with Nick and Dave out in front making the route. He caught up with them once they were slowed down erecting ladders. In my diary that night, after I had heard the story, I wrote the following:

Doug caught up, apparently with a new lease of life in him, pushed ahead, took one look over the top and said, 'Ah, lots of crevasses here, still, the site of Camp 1 is much further on.' Nick, however, was convinced that they were already at the site of Camp 1 – in fact they had an argument – but Doug wouldn't listen, and Nick stood down, uncertain perhaps of his own rightness, since Doug had been there before; also, Doug probably has the stronger personality. They plodded off for a mile and a quarter up the Western Cwm, about five hundred feet higher, trying to find a site.

They found another camp site which they discovered after crossing some dangerous areas, and got very close in to the side where there was the risk of avalanche, before turning back. Then, of course, they were absolutely exhausted, for it was now getting late. Meanwhile, they had another flaring argument – this time about the one-piece suits. Doug had been the original exponent of the one-piece suit, after using it on the spring attempt. Some of the team undoubtedly felt that the Erve down jackets and trousers, which we had issued to the Sherpas, were considerably superior. Anyway, Nick tried to relieve himself – the trouble is, because of the size of the slit in the back, you can't relieve yourself and have a pee at the same time, which is what you usually want to do. Nick, in a fury of rage, took his suit off, hurled it down and stamped on it, cursing it and telling Doug exactly what he thought of one-piece suits. This evening Nick admitted that the argument he had with Doug was not really about the one-piece suit at all, but was against Doug having made a false decision to push on against Nick's better judgement. Then, of course, there is a deeper connotation to all this, because I had given Dave and Nick a less attractive role than Doug and Mick, with very little chance of reaching the top.

These tensions and minor flare-ups might seem very petty when written down after the expedition – things better buried and forgotten, far from the spirit of the hills and the romance of true adventure; but if you do forget them you ignore the very reality of what an expedition is like – the tension that climbers come under, both from the point of view of personal ambition, the ways in which their differing personalities interlock, and the physical and mental stress they are under.

At first, Nick and Doug, without a doubt, got on each other's nerves, neither fully understanding or respecting the other. Nick was the more aggressive because he had been given a subordinate role in establishing Camp 6, and he felt that Doug took his, more attractive role of climbing the Rock Band too much for granted. The important thing, to my mind, was the way that in the course of the expedition, each came to respect and like the other, even though they recognized the differences in each other's personalities. An expedition is comprised of a pattern of tensions in human relationships. If these get out of hand – as they did both on the international expedition and the European expedition – the results are unhappy. If they can be contained, however, usually by the basic respect of members for each other, these little explosions during the expedition's course simply act as minor eruptions and perhaps, even, as a necessary safety-valve.

And so, on 20 September, we had actually forced the route through the Ice Fall, taking a mere five days. We now seemed well ahead of schedule. The weather was perfect, there were no signs of the post-monsoon winds, and we were all beginning to talk of reaching the summit before the end of October. The climbing now seemed very much more predictable and I could start trying to follow the logistic plan which I had originally worked out in Britain and modified during the course of the approach march.

9

TEETHING TROUBLES

21 September–29 September

We had climbed the Ice Fall, but that was barely a start. The route still had to be made safer for the porters in order to start ferrying the five tons of oxygen cylinders, climbing equipment, tentage and food through to Camp 1 and on to Camp 2, our base of operations at the foot of the Face. Although Camp 1 had yet to be established, we were still ahead of schedule, for it was now 21 September, and it was on this day that we made our first big carry, with twenty-five Sherpas, to Camp 1. At the same time, Dougal and Hamish went out in front to improve the route where possible. At this stage I was worried about Graham Tiso's acclimatization and I persuaded him to do a carry, as much as anything so that he might become accustomed to physical work at altitude. Until this point he had been working flat out, organizing all the equipment into loads to go up the mountain in the correct sequence. He explains his work and the effects of that first carry in his diary :

The effect of altitude here [Base Camp] is for the head to start thumping like fury, it wasn't too bad in the evening, though whenever I sat up the next morning, my head really started to go. However, this symptom soon went away and I felt perfectly fit. I expected that the Sherpas would want to start building their shelter and making tent platforms and other things, but fortunately they had to wait until the glacier started to thaw and loosen the boulders, so I did have the help of all of them for about three hours, and we were able to get the loads unpacked and sorted out. This was a tremendous help. They left me about midday, but that was fine. Since then, I managed to sort all the camp kits, the mugs, the stoves, the dixies and everything that is to go up to the various camps, segregated

them all, and packed them into loads. Then I had quite a lot of paper
work to do, sorting out the actual order in which everything goes
up. It's incredibly complex, this; if you take Dave, Nick and four
Sherpas, who have gone up to stay today – one can't be absolutely
certain that a Sherpa carrying a load up the Ice Fall is actually going
to make it to the camp – it is possible that he might dump his load
part-way there – so the tents they would be using had to go up the
day before. This means we've always got to work one day ahead of
ourselves, actually working this so that you don't send up a tent the
day before, that someone was sleeping in the same night. It's a nightmare, and it took me a very long time to work it all out. I think we
really should have given this some thought; this has been a bit of a
blunder, although not a serious one, in our whole planning that we
hadn't, in fact, allowed for enough tents for everyone to sleep at
Base, and at the same time to start moving tentage up the mountain.
If we hadn't had the four North Face tents and the Pete Carmen
tent extra, we would have been in the difficult position of having to
send tents up the hill the same day they were to be used that night –
hoping that they got there. Anyway, by the skin of our teeth, I
managed to work it all out so that a tent is vacated the night before
it goes up the hill. I also had to work out all the schedules; then of
course there were the changes of plan! Chris approaches very diffi-
dently and says – 'I've been thinking about this point of the plan ...'
and I have to start thinking rapidly of reasons why he can't do that,
because it would alter my plans. Then we have a little battle, and
eventually settle for a compromise. It's all been very interesting.

I've really lost track of days – it's the 22nd according to my watch
now; I just don't know how many days doing all this has taken.
Anyway, I have now got it to a pretty good state of organization. I've
managed to grab Tony as assistant, partly because I'm going up the
hill myself and I'll need somebody back here who knows something
about the equipment that's left. With his help, I got all the loads
sorted out, and him fully briefed. Then Chris was insisting I had to
go up and do some acclimatizing in the Ice Fall. That was yesterday.
I had the option of going up at 6 o'clock with the porters, 5 o'clock
with Mick and Barney – who were doing some filming – or with
Hamish and Dougal, who were just going to do some tidying up on
the route. Believe it or not, I opted for the 4 o'clock start – only
because of the heat. Breakfast was served in the tent at twenty past
three – a most incredibly heavy pancake, which sat like a great log
on the stomach; then dressed and followed Hamish and Dougal's
light up to the bottom of the Ice Fall – that's about twenty minutes'

walk through the boulder field before one actually comes on to ice – and there, had to stop and put crampons on. We found, incidentally, that the Primus Gas lanterns are absolutely fabulous for this purpose – it's just like the olden days in the Alps; a gas lantern gives far more light than a torch, and as there are no real difficulties in the lower section of the Ice Fall, it's great. You get to the start at about half past four and flog on, up the now well-beaten trail, until it gets light at about half past five.

Up until this time I was feeling quite O.K., that's an hour and a half's walk – perhaps something like a thousand feet of rise – and then I began to feel the altitude. I hadn't had any trouble at all with altitude since arriving here. Nick was flat out for one day, and other people have been pretty dodgy. You get out of breath if you start running around the boulder field, but that's to be expected – you just have to take things steady. I just kept plodding up the Ice Fall, but it really started to clobber me after this hour and a half – between half past five and six o'clock. It's a question of doing one step – then a second – then a third – and you're panting after only five minutes; I was timing myself, I could manage five minutes moving at that pace before I just had to stop, panting, to get my breath back. It was depressing because the legs weren't tired, it was the breathing which was the trouble.

Anyway, I carried on; I was just wondering how far I was going to go, was getting despondent, and then I got to the bottom of the big ladder – or Chris's Folly, as it's been called. It's the first real obstacle. Hamish and Dougal took a wrong turning and were confronted with this big crevasse – this was Chris's answer, he'd stuck up a twenty-five-foot ladder, straight up a vertical cliff. I met Hamish and Dougal at the bottom of the ladder – they'd been playing around, looking at things to see if they could make the route safer. They said it was about half an hour from this point to Camp 1 – 'One or two difficult bits in it, we don't recommend you to go.' So I thought at least I would climb the ladder and have a look and see what was over the other side. I was breathing perfectly normally, because I'd been standing at the bottom, waiting for them to come down it. And then I climbed this twenty-five-foot ladder, and just about collapsed on the face as I got to the top, puffing and panting; it was as though I'd run a mile in four minutes. Once I got to the top of the ladder, I got one or two photographs and then bombed off down – coming down is dead easy – you could almost run. I was pretty shot by this time, but as I'd come down in about an hour, this wasn't surprising.

Staggered into the mess tent, and started mooning and grumping about how hellish I felt, and they all said, 'Ah, you'll feel a hell of a lot better the next time you go up.' I don't think I'll manage to get up again. Chris has been up for the second time today and he said he felt just like I did the first time up – the second time you really begin to enjoy life. Nick said the same thing. Going up again tomorrow, I'll do a carry right through to Camp 1, then I'll move up to Camp 2 the next day, so I hope that what they say is borne out. It's funny, the body somehow seems to adapt to this lack of oxygen in the air.

It is very easy to forget the day-to-day details of an expedition and even easier to forget one's own interpretation of events as they occurred, particularly when in the decision-making position. Looking back, it is too easy to justify decisions in the light of the outcome of a certain action, forgetting the immediate pressures with which one was confronted, the change of mood from one day to another, the shifting pattern of personal relationships. All too easily this can be smoothed out into a bland, retrospective picture, and it is only by referring back to one's diary that it is possible to capture the true mood of each day of the expedition. I kept a diary, using a Sony TK 40 cassette recorder. It became my confessional – almost a psychoanalyst's couch – physically easier than writing a diary, certainly less self-conscious. In many places I have used this verbatim, to give the feeling of what it was like – not in retrospect, but actually being there, at the time. Inevitably, much of the diary is concerned with my own command problems and decisions, my opinions of other members of the team, and the role I felt they could best fulfil. This is my comment for 22 September:

Usually I get to sleep and then wake up at about midnight, or one o'clock in the morning, and start going over all the expedition problems. Certainly, yesterday was bad 'vibes' day, and there really was tension, with arguments and conflicts all through the day. Dougal and Hamish had gone off early to make the route safe. The porters had set off after them. I felt appalling, with a bad headache – perhaps through reading too much. I had taken two codeines in the early hours of the morning and another two later – probably too much, as I definitely felt muzzy first thing. Mick had sent back a mass of film and I got up at about seven-thirty and wrote a short I.T.N. report. I did a bit more work, trying to sort things out and then it was lunchtime, with row number one of the day. Mick said he wanted two porters for doing some more filming in the Ice Fall. I said we just couldn't spare two porters for this – we could spare him, but we needed the manpower. We had a tearing great row, both of us going to extremes, and at the end of it Mick's hands were trembling and he was as tensed up as I was. We then simmered down a little, finally arriving at a perfectly reasonable compromise. At this altitude, especially with the kind of work we have to do, we just can't afford this kind of throw-away of nervous tension. It's funny, Doug Scott was sitting in on the row and did his best, in his own way, to quieten it down by just asking quietly, 'Well, what do you want?' I don't think, in actual fact, that this kind of reasonable approach really works – it emerged that Mick didn't really need very much – I think Mick almost needs this slap-on confrontation.

We got through the remainder of the morning satisfactorily and I did a bit more work, but not very much. At teatime there wasn't so much a row as just tension, through a misunderstanding of different points of view. I outlined the general plan; when people were going to be moving up the mountain and then, having done this, put across the point that I would like climbers to do some carrying as well, even though they couldn't carry anything like the loads of the Sherpas. I thought it would be a good thing – it showed willing. At certain stages I think it might be absolutely essential. Immediately this opened up opposition; Dougal obviously didn't like it – neither did Hamish. They had done four days in the Ice Fall now, probably thought they deserved a rest and were bored by carrying, and they said so. I made my point, that we still needed to do a certain amount of carrying and eventually we arrived at a compromise solution, where Dougal and Hamish agreed to renovate the Ice Fall while they are down here, freeing the Sherpas for actually carrying – as good a compromise as any, probably. Anyway, we settled that one.

The weather, at this stage, had begun to look quite threatening – it had clouded over much more than it had done on previous days. A minor irritation arose when I just double-checked that the Sherpas who were destined to move up to Camp 1 knew they were going up. I had actually gone over all this with Pembatharke and Sona Hishy the day before, yet the Sherpas in question didn't know anything about it – they were just carrying ordinary loads up. This was particularly annoying, since we had actually briefed Pembatharke and Sona Hishy. Anyway, we sorted this one out – we thought.

Then Graham came to me with a problem. This was another tension thing – slightly shambolic. We had these eleven conversion kits, and had said we would like a say in the actual selection of the Sherpas to be elevated to high-altitude Sherpas. We got them lined up in a rather casual kind of way, and whether the Sirdars felt themselves affronted that we had not left it to them, I don't know. I suspect we should have just left it to Pembatharke to make the selection, to emphasize his importance. Lined up, it was difficult to remember one individual Sherpa from another, but finally we made a selection of eight men who might, or might not, be the best. The next thing was to give them their extra equipment; we'd given them lightweight padded Terylene jackets – useless, but rather attractive, and I think the Sherpas like them; we'd also given them waterproof jackets and this had obviously rankled with the original high-altitude Sherpas, since they had not had waterproof jackets on the approach march. Now Sona Hishy pointed this out to Graham Tiso. [This led to one of the most serious crises we had on the entire expedition.]

It all started so innocently. I had gone over to see Sona Hishy and Pembatharke, with Kelvin, to discuss two small, quite easy points, one, the fact that apparently Sona Hishy had complained that in up-grading ten of our Ice Fall porters into high-altitude porters and giving them additional kit, they now had two items more than the original high-altitude Sherpas, who had not beeen given the padded ski-jackets and waterproof jackets. This, of course, was completely ignoring the fact that the high-altitude Sherpas had been given Morlands Boots, Ronson lighters and wristwatches, plus one or two other extras. Anyway, we agreed that we should take the jackets back from the Ice Fall porters.

It was twilight, and we were sitting immediately outside the cook-shelter, a big, yellow tarpaulin stretched over stone walls with a long wooden pole as an eave. People were going to and fro, and then Sona Hishy, out of the blue, said 'The Sherpas going up tomorrow are not happy about only having one sleeping bag. They want two sleeping bags – they're very cold in one sleeping bag.'

I immediately replied that this had all been discussed. I told him 'We've all got the same sleeping bag – the Fairy Down sleeping bag, and the climbers are just using one sleeping bag. This is perfectly alright, and you can always get into your down suits if it's very cold.'

Sona Hishy replied, 'The Sherpas say that the down suit is outside clothing – it doesn't count. Other expeditions have given them two sleeping bags and you yourselves have two sleeping bags. We also want two.' [This is true, in so far as we had a lightweight Terylene bag which we had used on the approach march.]

'Look, Sona Hishy,' I replied, 'we explained at Katmandu.'

Sona Hishy immediately said, 'Roberts Sahib said we were going to have two sleeping bags.'

Now this is absolutely true – originally, we had planned on everyone having a lightweight sleeping bag from Blacks, for the march, but Blacks, because it was for Everest, had made the biggest flock sleeping bag that has ever been made. Fifty of these had been produced, and we had decided that they were useless – they were so bulky and heavy. We made the fatal mistake of getting lightweight flock sleeping bags just for the climbers' use on the approach march, deciding to give the heavy bags to the Ice Fall porters as their main sleeping bag. In the rush at Katmandu we had neglected to explain the change to Jimmy.

There has always been a big sleeping bag 'thing' in the Himalayas. I remember on the American Everest expedition, when the Sherpas were superbly equipped (I suspect better than ours were), there was also trouble, and they almost had a strike over this. One reason is that the sleeping bags do reach a very high market value in Sherpa country. [In the event, we were to find that you did need a double sleeping bag on the mountain.]

But the Sherpas were absolutely vehement about this – perhaps defensively aggressive – because, as the argument developed, they emphasised again and again that it wasn't the value of the extra sleeping bag they were worried about, it was the fact that they were cold at night. It's just possible that the Fairy Down bag is too large a bag, and it might well be that they are a bit cold.

Anyway we scratched and racked our brains – the argument flowing this way and that, with various suggestions being made. Then we said we could not provide extra bags immediately – we hadn't physically got them. I told Sona Hishy to call all the Sherpas and they all materialized. They'd obviously been talking about it – they looked tense, rather angry, gathering in a little group, all jabbering away in Sherpa. The trouble is, Kelvin can't understand Sherpa, only Nepali. All of them wanted another sleeping bag, and various things were suggested. I thought this was definitely a money thing and said, 'Well look, we'll fly the sleeping bags out from England – it will take about a fortnight – I'll cable straight away. The weather doesn't look as though they'll be needed on the mountain in that time,' which – hopefully – was true. But they wanted the sleeping bags immediately and were not prepared to shift until they had them.

The ringleaders were Ngati, who looks obstinate, with a squat, pushed-in type face, standing arms akimbo in his very expensive

Erve Duvet which we had given him; Pertemba, to my surprise, was also backing this up quite vehemently; Tenzing as well – and Ang Phurba, a sprucely turned out individual, wearing very smart, Austrian ski-pants, given to him by an Austrian expedition. We argued and argued and argued. At one stage I said they were asking the impossible – we did not have this gear, and if they insisted on it we'd just have to go home. But Sona Hishy had the answer to that:

'You can't afford to do that, Sahib. All it means to us is that we've lost a couple of thousand rupees if you sack us all – but for you it means many, many thousands of rupees.' [This of course was absolutely true.]

The argument got even more serious. I can't understand Nepali, but they were getting to the stage when they were being downright rude and insulting to Kelvin before I eventually thrashed out the various possibilities with them. They said they wouldn't go up the mountain the next day without an extra bag and there seemed to be only one solution. I collected ten lightweight bags from the rest of the team and said, 'Right, you can have these right now.' They had got their bags, and had on their part, won, but I went back to a very bitter, disgruntled expedition, who felt I had stood down much too easily. I don't think so – I think if I'd stood out we'd have had a situation where they just wouldn't move up the mountain. At least we've got them moving without any worry or fuss.

That night I felt exhausted from my efforts, isolated from the rest of the team who would have liked their say in the argument, without appreciating just how critical were the negotiations or how disastrous it would have been to have had a three-cornered argument. It had been bad enough arguing with the Sherpas as a group. That night, depressed, disillusioned, I spoke into my 'confessional':

Climbing Everest is a logistic problem – it's a man-management problem, a complex labour problem, and there's just a little bit of climbing in it too. If we can pull it off, we shall have climbed the mountain – it will be a challenge and I shall breathe a sigh of relief – but there's going to be little or no enjoyment in it.

And yet the mood changed from day to day, with the coming of the sun in the lee of the storm, whether it be one of words or the forces of nature. Next day, 23 September, I taped:

Kelvin came to my tent at about 6.30 – I was just having breakfast, ready for the walk up the mountain. I felt very apprehensive, because I couldn't hear any of the Sherpas and wondered whether we had another Sherpa strike! Kelvin told me that he had been up until 2 a.m. with the Sherpas in the kitchen. They had gone through everything and had got it all off their chests – I think this big row was necessary. Kelvin felt that it was, as much as anything, the fact that they are frightened of the Ice Fall. This is undoubtedly true, from the way they pray incessantly as they plod up the Ice Fall, the way they burn their incense before setting out, and hold their religious ceremonies. I think they have been building up tension about this and then, additionally, the sleeping bag thing is age-old – they've had trouble on practically every expedition about it. Anyway, the big row had come up and Kelvin had gone through it. Once again that night, the main arguers, or trouble-makers, were Sona Hishy, Tenzing – with whom he shares the same wife – and Ngati, who is related to Sona Hishy. Pembatharke, once again, was very good, shrugged and even looked fed-up when Sona Hishy got going on one of his tangents. I think Pembatharke might have been even more positive in our favour but for the fact that he has been feeling lousy for the past three or four days, with an infected leech-bite in his leg, which Barney has been treating. He hasn't been able to get out of Base Camp and doesn't like this at all. Pembatharke is a man of action and very loyal to us.

Anyway, it all seems sorted out. I set out later, plodding steadily; coughing quite a lot, but I must say I felt fairly O.K., and as I went up, felt better and better. I overtook a couple of Sherpa groups, pausing to ask the leader of one of them whether he spoke English. He did, and told me he had been on the Argentinian expedition. I asked whether the Ice Fall was better or worse now, and he said that the route we have made is superior. They seem to appreciate the fact that we've chosen a good route and a safe route for them.

Then I caught up with Kelvin – typical Kelvin – who was not only carrying a half-load similar to mine, a sixteen-pound food box, but was also carrying nine foam mats. He was going slowly and steadily and I stayed with him for a while, but when he stopped to rest I carried on up. At the top of the long ladder I waited for about twenty minutes to make sure he was alright, and then went a little beyond.

It is quite incredible, the most amazing sight anywhere in the world. There are great areas of tumbled ice – huge blocks, the size of office blocks almost, all jumbled together – great shattered areas as well, gleaming white in the snow, deep, dark, green-blue shadows – and I think we have picked the only possible route through it.

Hamish reckons, and I can see this, that we can definitely avoid one of the dangers; just short of the ladder there is a bad sérac tower that could kill someone, and we can get round it. We're going up the day after tomorrow to do this. Then the route drops into a kind of moat below another very big sérac which, if it did collapse and you were below it, you'd have had your lot; the trouble is, you're about four minutes underneath it. We're going to try to work a kind of aerial ropeway to avoid this as well. We'll see about that the day after tomorrow.

Plodded on up and was now meeting some Sherpas coming back down. Just beyond this point I'd been picking up quite a lot of gear on the way up – odd bits of rope etc., so that we have everything at the top together. Met Dave and Nick, who were coming down to meet us to collect our loads from us and carry them up the last little bit. This is the kind of friendly gesture that is tremendously warming and, I think, an important thing within an expedition. Nick and Dave are obviously very, very happy and excited to be there, at the mouth of the Western Cwm – neither of them has ever been there before – and they're going to find the route up to Camp 2. Four Sherpas are on their way to join them. We now have a great dump of gear – fifty-six loads – actually at Camp 1. It's not as many as I had hoped, but it's good, considering we're only a week out.

Doug had just set off down and I asked him to wait for me so that we could go down together. We could try to rescue some more fixed rope on the way down, and then send it up to give us enough to do the run-out to Camp 5, come what may. Even though Graham had got 10,000 feet short, it didn't seem to matter so much today. It was good going down with Doug and I must say the more I do things with Doug, the more I respect him. For instance, we'd got back to the top of the ladder and there were three long marker poles left there. He said he might as well get these back so that they can be picked up, so he collected them and went back up the hill to leave them with a bunch of marker-flags which a Sherpa would have to come down and pick up from Camp 1. We worked quietly and efficiently together, as a good team, with neither trying to dominate the other.

Everywhere, the atmosphere in the camp was good and very happy. Mick had been doing some filming with Dougal and Hamish, doing some fill-ins. Unfortunately, Tony Tighe, who is a really great chap, and has worked very, very well within the group – a strong, robust kind of character – has slipped and has torn his hand.

I saw Sona Hishy and took him aside and gave him a long, long talking to. Basically, I think he is unsure of himself – perhaps apprehensive of the climbing. He certainly wants the approbation of his fellows, and I think that although he has worked hard (there's no doubt about it – he's worked well for us), when they were all grumbling about the sleeping bags, etc., he couldn't resist the temptation of being the ringleader. I tried to get across to him – and gilded the carrot very lavishly – that this expedition was as important as the original British Everest expedition, and that he could be a Tenzing if he worked for us and with us. I gave him a lot of bull about the book – how it will be sold in every country in the world – and this, that and the other, then, looking him straight in the eye, said, 'By Christ, if there's another happening like last night, you'll regret you ever heard anything about this expedition.' Whether I got through or not, I don't know – it's always difficult to tell with the Sherpas. He is one of these semi-sophisticated Sherpas, having been in America for six months, and is particularly hard to deal with. Certainly all the other Sherpas seem happy now – mildly apologetic, almost, about last night. They've all got their sleeping bags and I think, with a bit of luck and several days' good weather, we'll be able to get the momentum going and get everything working well.

Everyone seems very relaxed and at the moment things are good – no doubt there's going to be a lot more crises – no sooner do you get one good thing going than something else happens. But today I liked walking up the hill – I felt acclimatized – it was enjoyable playing around with the ropes and it was a super, happy, carefree day.

I have described these two days in detail, not in retrospect, but as they happened. At times the pressures of holding the balance within the team between individual members and the Sherpas seemed to fill the horizon, but then, in the escape from Base Camp, just by walking through the Ice Fall to Camp 1, all the adventure and beauty of the mountain re-asserted itself. This pattern was particularly strong for myself and, perhaps, to an even greater extent, for Kelvin, who had the day-to-day contact with the Sherpas and the job of passing on my directives. I tried to keep out of this as much as possible, so that when a serious deadlock did occur I could enter into the argument as mediator, trying to find a compromise solution which would enable us to continue the climb.

Meanwhile, up at Camp 1, Nick and Dave were having their share of problems. They had moved up to the Camp with four Sherpas on 22 September, but the following day the weather began to show signs of change, with clouds swirling through the Western Cwm. Snow merged into cloud, making it almost impossible to pick out a route through the array of moat-like crevasses which stretched across the valley. They resolved to wait for the weather to clear, but next day, the 24th, there was no improvement and it had snowed during the night. Dougal and Hamish, setting out early to repair the route, discovered, about half-way up, that a big area of the Ice Fall had collapsed; ladders were twisted, ropes torn asunder – the entire area was as if an earthquake had struck it. In the driving wet snow the pair decided that it would be too dangerous to try to get any of the Sherpas across and so they turned everyone back. Our first repulse on the climb. Was this the last kick of the monsoon? Where was that perfect post-monsoon weather?

The weather continued to deteriorate, but even so, we succeeded in ferrying twenty-five loads up the Ice Fall, with Dave and a couple of Sherpas pushing down to meet the porters just short of the area of the collapse. Dougal and Hamish, assisted by Phurkipa, had made a good job of repairing the route. I, hoping to have recovered sufficiently from the cold and general malaise which had hit me, set out that morning with a half-load – a mere sixteen pounds – but I seemed to have lost all my strength. Every step was an effort; it was as if I were at 23,000 feet. I struggled up to the point where Dave had come down to meet us, and then returned to Base to collapse into my sleeping bag. Doug went on, up to Camp 1, where they had now erected one of our two magnificent Palace tents – a big frame tent one would expect to see on a Riviera beach rather than at the head of the Everest Ice Fall. With transparent plastic windows, it was about seven feet high, and had two sleeping compartments which provided a touch of luxury in these bleak surroundings. It was difficult to imagine yourself on the Riviera, however, for even this early in the season, the temperature at night dropped to −10° C. During the day, however, in the sun, the interior of the tent became oven-like, for the sun still gave plenty of heat and there was little appreciable wind. That night Dave commented in his diary:

Nothing for it but to have a swig of whisky. One bottle came up with the loads today. We were really touched when Doug Scott mentioned that this was the last bottle, but then he put his foot in it by saying that Base Camp had treated themselves to some of the goodies from the Fortnum and Mason's box. By the time Doug left our Palace, half the bottle was gone. His parting remark was 'Christ, you don't half get pissed easy at this altitude!'

Nick and Dave were left on their own in the big Palace tent, the Sherpas sleeping in the smaller Vango tents. As dusk fell it began to snow hard and they resolved to get up at intervals during the night to dig out the tent, particularly to clear the snow from the very gently eaved roof. They woke at midnight and forced themselves out into the blizzard, no pleasant task in the middle of the night. Having cleared the tent they dropped off into a deep sleep, only to be awakened again at four in the morning as the roof of the tent, forced down by the snow, touched their faces – rather like one of those nightmare stories of Edgar Allan Poe. They were lucky to get out at all, but managed to put their boots on and, crawling to the window of the tent, got out there. In the confusion Nick had forgotten his gloves and, as a result, was nipped by the frost. It was lucky it wasn't worse.

They spent the rest of the night digging out the Palace tent, which was now almost totally derelict, and then erecting a Whillans Box. By the time the 6 a.m. radio call was due they were shaken and near exhaustion – a state not improved by the fact that we, at Base Camp, failed to come on the air. We, too, had been having our crises, for several tents at Base Camp had collapsed in the night. My own role had not been particularly heroic, as I described in my diary on 26 September:

During the night it snowed steadily, and I woke up to Mick's voice saying – 'You want to watch it, the tents are all collapsing under the snow – you need to get dug out.' Then Barney got up. Barney's tent had not actually collapsed, but was very nearly buried in the snow. Mick and Beth's pole had collapsed and they had been short of breath before Mick got out. Kelvin, also, was completely trapped; he had an elaborate extension on the end of his tent – his radio house – and this had collected snow and the poles had broken. I think he was quite shaken and worried – it took him half an hour to get out, and Barney finally had to help him.

Barney turned out to be an absolute tower of strength, rounding up the Sherpas, getting shovels and trying to dig everything out. The cook-shelter had also very nearly collapsed. I wondered whether I should do the heroic thing and get out of bed – the Great Leader and all that jazz – but finally decided that it was much more important for me to get better quickly, so I snuggled down into my sleeping bag and stayed in my tent, which seemed stable. I think this happened to nearly everybody, because even Dougal said he thought of going out and helping Mick to dig himself out, but finally abandoned the idea. Anyway, Barney, a few Sherpas and Kelvin, eventually sorted everything out. Beth and Mick ended up sleeping with the Sherpas and Sherpanis, for we have staying with us ten additional porters who came up carrying loads yesterday; Beth commented on the high smell of them all.

This morning tea was delivered as usual; it's snowing hard – I reckon about three feet of snow has fallen already, and there's a lot more about. At least this bad weather spell gives me a chance to try to recover and throw off this cold and relax completely. I feel a lot better today, but think I may need two or three days more to recover completely.

Evening – 26 September 1972

In my sleeping bag – it's about 8.15 p.m., after quite a pleasant day. It stopped snowing around about mid-morning. A steady Scrabble school got going, with Dougal, Tony Tighe, Mick and Doug. I retired to my tent and started working out the best thing to do. As I thought about it, I was definitely a bit worried about Dave and Nick. There's no doubt about it, they haven't got the same breadth of experience that Hamish and Dougal have; they definitely sounded a bit worried about pushing on up the Ice Fall, or up the Western Cwm – worried about the avalanches and everything. I wanted to get Hamish up there at least. Another problem was getting the tent repaired.

So I decided to push up Hamish, Mick and Graham, to enable Graham to get the tent repaired, Hamish to act as adviser to Dave and Nick, and Mick to get some film. I called Hamish into the tent and talked this over with him, but he definitely didn't like the idea of going with anyone but Dougal. He and Dougal have formed a superb pairing, in the same kind of way, almost, that Don and Dougal clung together on Annapurna. But this, I think, is a much better, more well-ordered and equal pairing, with each respecting the other. I agreed that Hamish and Dougal should go up together to support Nick and Dave. Although worried about Mick's reaction to this, whether he would start getting all aggressive, wanting to be out there filming, I finally decided that we would keep him back – I don't want more people than absolutely necessary out there in front.

Then we started working out ways of repairing the tent at Camp 1. Someone – I think it was Graham – suggested that they send the broken frame back down here and meanwhile, another frame is taken up to replace it. We could then repair the frame down here, and use it as a permanent Base tent. This had the advantage that we did not have to send Graham up.

I sat down and worked out the basic movements this afternoon. With a bit of luck, everyone will be moving up in two days' time and I sincerely hope I shall be fit and well enough to keep going for the rest of the expedition. I announced my plan just before supper, and Doug, very characteristically and very nicely, said, 'Well, can't Dave and Nick make it to Camp 2 by themselves?' I know he was thinking of their disappointment if they were to feel themselves outclassed the moment Dougal and Hamish got there. Nevertheless, I think we've got to make sure of getting the right site for Camp 2, and of getting there as quickly as possible. Anyway, they have got one day to do it – maybe this will act as a spur to them – they might just do it tomorrow, before Dougal and Hamish arrive, in which case it will all be finished. Then, of course, they will be going on by themselves to establish Camp 3.

27 September 1972

Yesterday evening there was a good forecast – the weather cleared with the evening, and it was a brilliantly clear, very cold night. We were called slightly late this morning, about 5.30 a.m., and Mick, Doug and two Sherpas set off. Mick got about a hundred yards away from the camp and said, 'Appalling this, we'll never get up.' I then sent two Sherpas to increase their party to six, and they kept going.

Nick came on the radio at 6 a.m., sounding very abrupt – I think he was probably in a bad temper, feeling rather self-righteous about how hard they were having it, how easy we were having it, and how much we were expecting from them. Anyway, they said that they were going to send three of them forward and two down to break trail. There was no sign of the trail-breakers until about 9.15 a.m., when they appeared at the top of the ladder.

This evening, at the five o'clock call, Nick said they had got about two-thirds of the way up the Western Cwm, in very bad conditions – very deep snow, very heavy going. When I said I was sending Hamish and Dougal up to give them a hand he said 'Oh,' obviously resenting the inference. I'm not sure how I could have put it better, or more kindly – I just said 'to give you a hand, perhaps – you've already had two days at it'. Anyway, tonight both Mick and Doug talked about this. Mick is obviously very worried, and I think this must have got into Nick's mind, as well, that Hamish and Dougal will be pushed in front whenever others are a bit slow or, perhaps, if the issue seems to be in doubt. Perhaps I didn't get across well enough the fact that at this stage of the game it's just a matter of pushing the route out, and when you have the manpower to do so, it's ridiculous to leave a large party just sitting doing nothing at Base Camp. If the front pair are delayed, it's much better to use the climbers to help with the climbing when they're not carrying loads.

The night of 28/29 September

In my conversation with Doug and Mick yesterday we arrived at a plan, in principle, and this is one of the issues which could cause argument. As Doug and Mick, very sensibly, pointed out, if they spend two days on the Rock Band and then find it's going to take longer, what do we do? Do I pull them back? If I try to pull them back at this stage, there will inevitably be an argument, with Hamish and Dougal impatient to get up there in front to force the route. I think, therefore, providing our communications system is working effectively, and providing Doug and Mick are making some kind of progress, somehow I am going to have to keep them going on the Rock Band – even if it takes four or five days – pumping up more oxygen so that they can do it. What we want, in a way, is to put our 'B' team out in front first, giving them the first chance of getting to the top of Everest, though the odds would be very much against them because, of course, they will have exhausted themselves on the Rock Band. They've got this huge carrot of making the first British ascent of Everest, but on the other hand, Hamish and Dougal will be in position for the final push when, and if, they are exhausted. This could create great pressures, because Hamish and Dougal, champing at the bit to get out in front, will also be critical of the progress being made by Doug and Mick, perhaps fearful of losing the ultimate accolade of making the first ascent. It's going to take a lot of controlling of these two pairs, but I think this could give the ingredients for the greatest success.

29 September 1972

After a really good, deep sleep, I was woken up at 6 a.m. The massive doses of Vitamin C seem to be succeeding in getting rid of my cold, though I am coughing quite a bit even now. By this time Dougal and Hamish had already set out; I went to the kitchen and, after a Sherpa breakfast, waited about for a while, planning to go up with the Sherpas. They showed no signs of getting ready fast enough, so I finally set off by myself. It was still very cold – there are extraordinary temperature contrasts here at Base Camp, ranging from about −11°C first thing in the morning, to the seventies once the sun hits us.

I plodded up – certainly going infinitely better than the previous occasion, when I had stalled and staggered back down. Kept going, slowly and steadily. I had only a light load, just a cine-camera belonging to Hamish and a few bits of film, but I passed some bamboos which had been left on the side, so decided to take them up too – a really awkward load because they stuck straight up above my head, and every time I got on a steep bit they stuck into the snow.

I caught Graham up about three-quarters of the way up. He'd set out about an hour and a half earlier, and was going very, very slowly. He really is finding load-carrying a very hard, purging experience. He was muttering to himself, swearing that this was the last time he would ever carry up. I gave slightly too tart a reply, saying, 'Well, if you're not going to carry, then you're really not much use to anyone.' Immediately I realized how wrong this was, because in fact Graham is extremely useful and important, just in getting all the gear organized.

Having plodded behind him for a bit, I passed him, then passed the Sherpas and kept going to the top. I found it hard work because of the heavy snowfall – even though the trail had been broken yesterday, Dougal had had to break it again afresh – which just shows how strong and fit he is. I was very tired by the time I reached Camp 1.

Camp 1 is a fantastic situation. It's on a huge block between great crevasses – completely safe though, because it's right in the centre of the Glacier, well away from the big avalanches which could come down either from the Nuptse or Everest Faces. Dougal and Hamish were already there. Hamish had felt very rough on the way up, caused, he thought, by his breakfast, and so Nick and Dave had been left to make the route by themselves. They had set out earlier, with their four Sherpas, and with a bit of luck will have made the route to Camp 2 and sited the Camp. I waited up there. There's a very impressive load now – already eighty-five loads, and another thirty-five coming up today, making it a hundred-and-twenty.

Graham staggered up and said he really could not face doing this again, so he's staying up here tonight, and I hope, tomorrow, will get all the loads organized. At the moment they're in a great big heap, an absolute shambles. I waited for the porters to arrive, all thirty-five of them; this is one of the biggest carries, I should say, ever to have been made through the Everest Ice Fall.

A week had gone by since we had first reached the top of the Ice Fall, and although still only two-thirds of the way up the Western Cwm, we were all optimistic. Surely that snowfall must be the last heavy snow of the season! We now looked forward to weeks of uninterrupted sunshine – hoped that we should be able to get into position to make our summit bid before the winter cold winds became too intense. The next day I was planning to move up to Camp 1 with a strong force of Sherpas and the rest of the lead climbers. We were on the move once again.

10

UP
TO CAMP 3

30 September–8 October

'I know it's inevitable, but I can't help resenting the arrival of the big team,' said Nick. 'When there's just two of you and a few Sherpas, you live a hell of a sight better, and you get on together so much better – especially with the Sherpas. I feel we've really established some kind of rapport with them, especially Jangbo and Pertemba.'

I could sympathize with Nick's feelings. We were standing just above Camp 1, which now resembled a small village, with the big Palace tent dominating the cluster of two-man tents standing around it. It had been re-erected that day, on the undamaged frame brought up from Base Camp; a Stormhaven tent had also been erected, and a babble of voices intruded on the peace of the late afternoon. The surrounding scenery was the same as it had been for the last three days or, for that matter, from time immemorial, but the mere presence of the tents and the sound of twenty-five people somehow diminished the sensuous quality of mystery which is such an important part of the beauty of mountains. As always on any big expedition, the satisfaction of isolation can only come in small doses, though during the course of the expedition, as camps are established, the lines of communication become more extended and the numbers are stretched up the length and height of the mountain, the feeling of solitude returns. Certainly, we were not a big expedition by Everest standards, but in those early days, when the entire manpower of the expedition was first compressed into Base Camp and then spread between Base and Camp 1, we still felt we were on an overcrowded planet. But Nick and Dave could look forward to escaping from the 'crowds' – if only for a short time. It was 30

September and on the following day they were going to move up the Western Cwm to establish Camp 2.

A week had gone by since we had succeeded in climbing the Ice Fall, but a single day's heavy snowfall, combined with a few more days of bad visibility, had set us back about four days – days which did not seem to matter too much at the start of the expedition, but which were to prove all-important later on. The previous day Dave and Nick, helped by Hamish and Dougal, had marked out a route through the maze of crevasses which guard the lower part of the Western Cwm, and now we were ready both to push them up to Camp 2, so that they could start work on the Face itself, and to start ferrying loads up the Western Cwm to Camp 2. I had moved up to Camp 1 that afternoon, with Doug Scott and fifteen Sherpas, to join the five climbers and four Sherpas already in possession.

Next morning, 1 October, the entire party set out for Camp 2 with Nick and Dave, the two Sherpas, Jangbo and Pertemba, carrying their personal gear so that they could spend the night there. Most of the Sherpas were using snow-shoes for the first time. Three days had elapsed since the last snowfall and in that time the surface had already formed a slight crust which would have broken under the pressure of a boot, but with snow-shoes it remained firm. Nick Estcourt and Dave Bathgate led the way, with the seventeen Sherpas who accompanied them trailing behind, roped together in groups of three. I also went up, with Hamish and Dougal, to help repair the route and get photographs of the Western Cwm. It was a wondrous sight – the tiny figures of the climbers giving a scale and perspective to the gigantic size of the Cwm. They formed ever-changing patterns as they zig-zagged through the crevasses which stretched across the deep-cut valley like so many moats in some kind of natural fortification. A powder-snow avalanche started as a little puff, high on the steep walls of Nuptse, and then billowed out into a great cloud as it swept down over a couloir and spread across the floor of the Cwm. The cloud of snow particles hovered over the Cwm for a few minutes and then seemed to dissipate in the air, leaving no trace. The avalanche might never have occurred – but of course it had, and we had seen that it went across the line of our proposed route, which was squeezed in towards the right-hand side of the Cwm.

It was only when you started walking that you began to gain a true idea of the gigantic scale of the Western Cwm. At first, the South West Face was hidden coyly behind a subsidiary spur from the West Ridge of Everest, then, as you worked your way up and across to the left-hand side of the Cwm, it came slowly into full sight, foreshortened, massive, the Great Central Gully leading upwards like an arrow, into the guts of the South West Face – the Rock Band which stretches across the wall. The Rock Band looked deceptively short and even more deceptively close to the summit. For Nick and Dave the excitement at the prospect of being the first of the party to set foot on the Face was tempered by fatigue, as they forced the route towards what was to be the site of Camp 2. They reached the end of the main crevasse area around midday and, looking up the Cwm, the Face seemed comparatively close; then, as they started plodding up the long, easy slope that led to the centre of the Cwm, they began to realize the vast scale of the place. After an hour's walk they didn't seem to be much closer.

Doug Scott had accompanied them, and he and Nick pushed on towards what had been the site of the German camp that spring. Reaching it at about three o'clock that afternoon, they glanced back and saw that their Sherpas had already made up their minds for them; Pembatharke had stopped in a slight depression about two hundred yards short of their high point, in an area which had been Camp 2 for the international expedition. This was to be the site of Camp 2.

The Sherpas quickly dumped their loads and headed back down the Cwm. They had had a long, hard day. Nick and Dave were left with Pertemba and Jangbo. It must have been a precious moment as they sorted out their gear for the night, and erected two box tents. Once again, they were out in front, just four people dwarfed by the immensity of the Western Cwm.

I had planned on their taking just one day to run the rope out to Camp 3 but, after our experience of the last few days, hardly expected them to make such fast progress. It was a delightful surprise, therefore, the following evening to learn that they had succeeded in reaching their objective. The site of Camp 2 was about half a mile from the foot of the South West Face. Having used snow-shoes to reach the Camp, they discovered that once on the Face itself, the snow became firm and solid, perfect for crampons. They worked their way across it to the Bergschrund which marks the foot of the Face proper, and were able to climb it easily, since it was filled with snow. From there, a straightforward snow slope swept up towards the little rock buttress that guarded the site of Camp 3. There was no technical difficulty, it was just a question of front pointing on the hard snow, at an angle equivalent to that of a steep hillside in Britain. Dave and Nick made a beautiful, text-book job of the fixed roping, leaving dead men snow anchors at distances of about a hundred and fifty feet up the slope all the way to the Rock Buttress, which they reached at 3 p.m. It was here that they found the first signs of previous visitors, in the shape of a few lengths of partially-covered rope, and some pitons hammered into cracks. After hammering in their own ceremonial peg, they slid back down their ropes and returned to Camp 2 just in time for the evening radio call at 5 p.m. At last our onslaught seemed to be rolling out according to plan.

The following day, Doug Scott and Mick Burke moved up to Camp 2, accompanied by five Sherpas and myself, while Nick and Dave dropped back to Base Camp for a well-earned rest. It was to be the job of Doug and Mick to establish Camp 3, and then make the route up to the site of Camp 4. I wanted to be at Camp 2, which was already the focal point of the expedition. Here I could keep an eye on the arrival of the flow of supplies up from Camp 1, and at the same time be in touch with Doug and Mick on the Face.

For me, that day was one of the most satisfying of the expedition up to that point of time. I left Camp 1 late, having been delayed by the necessity to write a report for the *Observer* and wanting to wait for the arrival of mail from Base Camp. As a result I completed the walk from Camp 1 to 2 on my own, and in this solitude could enjoy the euphoria of being in the Western Cwm, surrounded by some of the most magnificent mountain scenery I had ever seen. Behind me, framed by the flanks of Nuptse and the West Ridge of Everest, was Pumori, its summit appearing ever-ready to topple down on to the Khumjung Glacier.

On either side were the steep retaining walls of the Cwm, grey-brown granite, fluted ice slopes, crested by top-heavy cornices, and in front was the duo of Everest and Lhotse, seeming easy angled in comparison with the sheer sides of the ravine leading into the upper part of the Western Cwm.

The only signs of man were the tracks in the snow and the bamboo marker wands placed every hundred yards or so. Camp 2 itself was tucked discreetly in a slight depression, invisible until only a hundred yards from it. It was already growing, with four tents and boxes pitched to absorb the fresh arrivals. The following day we all made a carry up to Camp 3 to dig out tent platforms and prepare the camp for Doug and Mick to move into the following day. For me it was to be one of the most testing days of the expedition. Doug and Mick, both fairly lightly loaded, set out first; I followed about half an hour behind them, having made the mistake of trying to carry too much, about thirty pounds. I have always found the height of 22,000 feet to be critical for me – a height barrier which has to be broken through painfully. The approach to the foot of the Face was easy-angled, little more than a walk along a well-defined track, but almost immediately I felt the effects of the altitude. It was not so much a feeling of lack of breath, as a lassitude that stole over my limbs, making each step a separate effort of will. The party behind were rapidly gaining on me and then, even more depressing, some Sherpas who had left half an hour after me stormed past, hardly seeming to notice the altitude. Although still only half-way to the Bergschrund, I was reduced to trying to force myself to take just twenty-five paces without a rest; all too often I failed to make even this limited norm, and would collapse over my ice-axe, resting for two or three times as long as it had taken to make the previous twenty-five paces, before struggling on again. I had been going quite well the previous day and had hoped that I had, at last, broken through the acclimatization and fitness barrier. But now I seemed to have slipped right back again. At the Bergschrund, and the foot of the fixed ropes, I clipped on with one Jumar, and started plodding up the slope. By now the others were nearly half-way up – about four hundred feet above me – no distance at all at sea level, but here, at 22,500 feet, they seemed forever unattainable. My progress had been reduced now to ten paces at a time without a rest, and I was finding it difficult to reach even this target, often making only six or seven steps before sinking on to the snow. It is difficult to imagine just how punishing this experience of altitude can be. Each step needs a separate effort of will, and progress is so slow as to be almost imperceptible. The target, in this case the rock buttress guarding Camp 3, never seemed to get any closer; the gap between myself and the others out in front, however, became wider, and before I was a third of the way up, they were already below the buttress, digging out a platform. My own discomfort was now compounded by a constant bombardment of snow blocks which they dislodged in digging out the camp site. I shouted out for them to stop digging until I got out of the danger zone, and slowly plodded on upwards; but it was obvious that I was going to be in the line of fire for at least another hour at my present rate of progress. Mick Burke at last put me out of my misery, shouting down to suggest that I dumped my load and got back down, out of the line of fire. In suggesting this he offered me a let-out that I had thought of adopting, but was loath to do so on the grounds of pride and, perhaps more important, the feeling that as leader of the expedition I could not afford to give in. I tried to keep going, but finally collapsed on the snow in a paroxysm of coughing. Able to go no further, I just dumped the load about two hundred feet below the site of the camp and then staggered down the fixed ropes. Even going downhill, I had to stop and rest every hundred feet or so, and it was all I could do to walk those last few hundred yards over fairly level glacier to the site of Camp 2. I crawled into my tent and dropped into a doze, only waking on the return of the others. They had had a hard day, digging out the platform for Camp 3, and yet they were all in good spirits, and it was strange, that night, in spite of my failure to reach the Camp, even I felt relaxed and satisfied. I wrote in my diary:

Physical effort is, oddly enough, a great palliative to worry and the nerves. On the surface, for instance, today has been a very unsatisfactory day, and the fact that I failed to reach my objective – I didn't get to Camp 3, and had to come back – doesn't stop me feeling tremendously more relaxed than I did yesterday. All the worries about day-to-day administration seemed expurgated. I suppose the problems are still there, but they don't seem to matter so much and I am concentrating on putting my plan on the mountain into practice.

I think I am certainly in the right place, up here at Camp 2. Even if I'm not going brilliantly well, it doesn't really matter because my job is to direct. This is the real focus of activity. Further back, one would not have this feeling for what is really the 'being' of the expedition – the people who are pushing out in front – in this case, Mick and Doug, who are going out tomorrow. I am simply going to try to keep simmering on, keeping just behind the front pairs, being very careful not to exhaust myself, and even though I know that this height, between 22,000 and 23,000 feet, is a bad height for me (I'm not a brilliant high-altitude goer, there's no doubt about that), I do know that once I get on to oxygen, from Camp 3 onwards, I should be all right. I go very well on oxygen, and I'll be able to move up to Camp 4 to supervise the vital traffic of supplies from Camp 4 to Camp 5.

You've certainly got to be very careful when in this kind of supervising/directing role, that you don't tire yourself too much. For instance, for the four o'clock radio call, I was definitely not totally compos mentis, unable to take in everything as fast as I should because I was so tired. This is something one is going to have to watch more, as one gets higher up the mountain, looking after oneself well so that one can take intelligent decisions.

That same day, nineteen Sherpas carried loads from Camp 1 to Camp 2 while, back at Base Camp, Jimmy Roberts had now arrived and had freed Kelvin to move up to Camp 1. Another arrival at Base Camp was Ken Wilson, editor of *Mountain Magazine*. He was a close friend of several members of the team and, in a light-hearted moment during the preparations for the expedition, I had told Ken that if he managed to reach Base Camp at his own expense we would make him welcome. A keen rock-climber, he had done a certain amount of climbing in the Alps, but had no direct experience of expeditioning or high-standard Alpinism. He is extremely outspoken, forceful in his views, and of course, through the pages of *Mountain* has considerable influence in the climbing world. I felt, therefore, that it would be good, both for him and for mountaineering in general, if he were able to come out and see how an expedition like ours performs in practice. At the same time, I must confess to having had some doubts, since Ken is splendidly argumentative, and I could not help worrying that he might upset the fine balance of personal relations on which an expedition depends. In the event he was to prove a positive asset. Anyway, he had just arrived at Base Camp and, at this stage, was in no fit state to vent his opinions on anyone, so severely was he affected by the altitude.

On the following day, 5 October, Mick and Doug moved up to Camp 3 to make the route up to Camp 4. This time I succeeded in plodding up to the Camp, travelling with a very light load as far as the point where I had dumped my load the previous day. Two Sherpas, Tenzing and Ang Dawa, were going to stay up at Camp 3, whilst the other three, Anu, Ang Phu and Ngati, carried loads and returned to Camp 2. It was on this day that Ang Phu really began to show his determination to do well on the expedition. Not only was he one of the youngest of our high-altitude Sherpas, in some ways he was the least experienced. He had been on the international expedition but had only carried loads as high as Camp 3. He spoke very good English and had been a teacher at one of Ed Hillary's schools before deciding that there was more money to be made as a trekking Sherpa. While working for Jimmy Roberts he had, for a time, acted as Jimmy's personal servant. We found him to be extremely helpful, going out of his way to look after any of the climbers on the expedition, helping them with their rucksacks, bringing them a welcome cup of tea, and similar small services, and yet there was nothing obsequious about his approach – one had the feeling that it was from sheer good nature.

I had, however, wondered just how tough he was going to be on the mountain. In the previous few days he had been complaining of severe headaches, and he certainly looked desperately ill. He refused to give in, however. That morning I tried to persuade him to take a day's rest, but he wouldn't hear of it. Then I suggested that at least he took a light load, but no, he was determined to carry as much as anyone else. Once we started, he was obviously walking with difficulty – as tired as I had been the previous day – but he kept plodding on doggedly, until he reached the long slope below the Bergschrund leading to the fixed ropes. This was not steep, but the snow was hard, requiring precise use of crampons. Half-way across the slope, the unfortunate Ang Phu tripped and slipped, sliding about two hundred feet back down into the Western Cwm. There was no risk, but it must have been a frightening, humiliating and depressing experience, especially losing all that painfully gained altitude. Many of our Sherpas, and even the climbers, would probably have called it a day, and returned to Camp. But not Ang Phu – he slogged, painfully, back up to the track and continued slowly up the line of fixed rope.

That afternoon, as we enlarged the platform for the boxes, wispy clouds chased across the sky, a sign perhaps of yet another change in the weather. Nevertheless, there was a feeling of immense satisfaction as we gazed over the slowly expanding view. From Camp 3 we were tightly blinkered by the great retaining walls of the Western Cwm. At 3, the view to the South was still barred by the great wall of Nuptse, but to the West we could gaze down the great sweep of the Western Cwm, gaining some idea of its scale from the tiny cluster of dots which represented the tents of Camp 2, and the even smaller specks that were our porters carrying loads up from Camp 1. The crevasses, part-covered, looked little more than ripples on the surface of a slow-flowing river, and the sweep of the Cwm led the eye across the hidden void of the Khumjung Glacier to Pumori, whose summit was now very nearly level with us, the great hog's back of Cho Oyu, and the serried ranks of lesser peaks, many of them still unclimbed.

We returned to Camp 2, well content, leaving Doug and Mick ensconced at the high point of the climb so far; but we were to be delayed once again, by a change in the weather. Next morning I woke to find the skin of my little two-man tent forced down towards my face. It had been snowing all night and our camp was nearly engulfed. The South West Face could not be seen, nor, for that matter, could any other mountain. A hundred yards above us a cluster of séracs loomed occasionally out of the gusting snow, but we could have been almost anywhere in the world. There was no question of movement that day – we could only sit out the storm, hopeful that it would not delay us too badly. At least it gave time for reflection, reading and letter-writing – the eternal pursuit of all Himalayan climbers. Up at Camp 3, Doug wrote to his wife, Jan. It is a letter which perhaps reveals more of the climber's thought-processes, and how he reacts to an expedition, than even a diary, and I have therefore included it with very few cuts :

6 October, 9.45 a.m.

Hello darling,

Here I am, back at Camp 3, overlooking the Western Cwm and Pumori. The wind is howling outside, and spindrift is pelting the sides of the box more or less continuously – just as it did in that Tunnel tent on Baffin Island with Denis. The box is khaki-coloured and the roof is sagging in with the weight of the snow. I'm here with Mick. He's had a bad night – we most certainly have come up to sleep at 23,000 feet too fast, only two weeks since arriving at Base Camp. I'm O.K., but Mick's drugged up to his eyeballs on headache and pain-killers and sleeping tablets, so he's not much company to-day. Think I'll go out and rouse the two Sherpas who are in the second box we put up yesterday. It took us five hours to cut into the snow and ice under this bulge of rock. It was like an archaeological dig, bringing up old tents, axes, cylinders, etc., from the German, international and Jap. expeditions. We have two more boxes to put up and also to make the route to 4, but this weather is really going to knock us back, and is what could finish us – the whole Face is a mass of spindrift, coming down to here, but then spinning round this little rock-step so that to open the box zip means we get covered inside.

Feel guilty lying here, so think I'll go out and put up some more Whillans Boxes. Follow that by dinner of chicken-breast, peas and powder potato and Oxo. Might be able to cheer up Mick, whose headache isn't going away yet; he may have to go down. Still no mail from you in two weeks – pissed off, especially as I'm lying here with nothing else to do but worry about you both. [Jan and his nine-year-old son, Michael.] Look, about me working after Christmas. One or two things you should think about. Most of the expedition lectures will be over by the end of January. I could do my book by half-term, though Easter is more practical. Would it be best for us all if I got a job at half-term (Feb), or after Easter, at a Primary School – yours ! ! ! – or one nearer home? I even feel like getting my hair cut and getting stuck into teaching as a career. I think I'd make a good headmaster ! I don't want to come here again – on this Face. Tozal Del Malo [a mountain Doug climbed in the Hindu Kush] was far more enjoyable and satisfying at the time. Here I am again a prisoner of my own ambition, very much so, as it's impossible just now to stand up properly outside this tent. We all want to get up and off – Hamish, Dougal, Mick and me, all prepared to rush it out of the way.

Same day, 4 p.m.

Well, I plucked up courage to go outside; the two Sherpas looked really bad, Tenzing and Ang Dawa. So as to enjoy my food and sleep unaided by pills, I got stuck in and dug out another platform, and put up another box with the thing blowing all over the place, with only me to hold it. Anyway, that's one more job done to get me nearer home. The spindrift beyond these canvas walls is terrible, I have to take my glasses off as they steam up. Gave the Sherpas their ration packs, with instructions to make potatoes, etc. Got Mick his oxygen bottle, so that he can take some now, as apart from going down, it's the only way he's going to make it tomorrow up to 4. He's gone off to sleep again, looking like a first-world-war pilot. He's got the *Lord of the Rings* open on his chest; I don't want to read it until I get home to Mike. Apart from wanting to finish the job off, reading it to Mike, it makes me very homesick to even see it.

Seeing as there are no books for me to lose myself in, I'll tell you both about the Sherpas. They are generally a good lot, and any tricks they get up to – well, so would I, if I saw a crowd of Europeans come into their valley, obviously so much richer. So they did go on strike for an extra sleeping bag. But that was sorted out. They are working harder than in the spring, when they had one day on, one day off, for 50p per day, regardless. Now they are working three days and one off. One or two high-altitude Sherpas didn't turn up, so we promoted a cook-boy, Dorjee, who looks about fourteen years old, but is, in fact, eighteen. He looked so proud when he was handed his high-mountain clothes, and even prouder when he came down through the Ice Fall, having carried a very heavy load of 45 lbs. The other Sherpas made sure he got the heaviest load! They don't put up with any softies!

It's getting quite dark in this olive-green hell, as the snow is piling up all round. I'll get dinner ready over a primus gas stove – much better than the Bluet Gaz, especially the double burner that we have down at Base Camp. I'd love to be sat down in our kitchen right now, and have you put some cauliflower-cheese or corn-beef hash, or stew and dumplings, or fresh herrings in front of me. Still, I expect that you're glad for the rest from that. Michael's probably rushing out on a bread butty, to be up on the field. I expect Goose Fair, and then

Bonfire Night are all in your minds; if all went well, I could just about make 5 November, but of course there will be weather problems, so it's unfair to make you think of such an early date. I'll get on with the dinner. I love you, love you both.

7 October, 9.00 a.m.

Well loves, I started getting the dinner ready and Mick said he couldn't eat any, then I heard these horrible groans from next door, and all the time the drifting snowstorm piled up outside the tents. Then I heard the zip frantically open and honk! Both the Sherpas were sick! What a team at the front! Well, I had my Surprise peas, surprisingly soft and sickly sweet chicken-breast, Oxo and Smash. It took me two hours in the confined space of these boxes. Then I dug out a tin of Nestlé's cream and had that with sugar. Too lazy to do apple flakes. Mick had a bad night, and this morning he was coughing blood up from the inside sores in his mouth. He kept taking oxygen, but it didn't help much. He still has a headache. Still no-one answering the radio, so I think I'd better get everyone down to Camp 2 – at least they can recover down there, provided we can get through the storm lashing around. I don't like it here! Now the roof is dripping from cooking a brew – all over. My bag is quite wet from the condensation as is Mick's, but he couldn't care less any more – trying to wring some comfort out of an oxygen bottle. Trouble is, Camp 2 won't be much better, we'll have to put tents up in the storm and then I'll have to come back here to do the route to 4 with someone. Main thing is there may be a letter from you, and I can post this and find myself some good books. No other way out but to grin and bear it. Well, hold on, it's 2.00 p.m.

The Sherpas weren't happy. I looked in their box and there was Ang Dawa. Well, there was a balaclava, covered in spindrift, right by the door and in the darkest far corner there was Tenzing, holding his head. 'Go down, lads,' I said. 'Sahibs go down, O.K. all go down.' It took three hours to get them ready. Then to take off, down the fixed ropes in white-out conditions. Unable to see out of my steamed-up goggles, so took them off! Like Blind Man's Buff! Snow and air and moving air surfaces were all one, but we got to the bottom of the Face with nothing worse than burnt hands from sliding down the rope. Then we had to rope up as one of the Sherpas had fallen off the lower slope and gone a quarter of a mile out of his way! He wasn't hurt, but it shook us all up, and no-one wants to walk through up to a quarter of a mile of soft snow. Then we got into the bottom of the Western Cwm, and the snow came up to our waists, wading along very much out of puff, with unseen avalanches pouring over Nuptse, which we felt the wind of. Luckily, we found the marker flags and eventually stumbled into the embryo Advance Base Camp, half covered in snow.

Chris was there; he had been on his own for three nights, with four Sherpas, and was glad to see us. He gave me your letter and Michael's. Glad you love me – never thought you didn't, really. Anyway, the saga goes on, now in better spirits, as the Sherpas cook us powdered spuds, ham and beans, and eating sweets robbed from ration packs. The snow continues to fall, and there will be no more travel up the Ice Fall, nor up the Cwm, for a few days. So I can get down to some serious reading and good thoughts about you and Michael. Christ, it's cold here just now, water bottles frozen, and so is this rotten ball-point pen, and now they've sent the dinner in back to front, having cooked the ham in potato powder, not in the ready-made Smash. So I'll make do with Kit-Kat and ship's biscuits.

The in-word here, among the Sherpas, is 'Why not indeed', as Mick hands round fags and they offer each other food and what-not. The 'Goon Show' is on the tape, and Neddy Seagoon is off to find the yeti on the Yorkshire moors! We're sitting in our box, Mick and Chris and me, with a cooking canopy over the front, and all the Sherpas cooking and eating *dahl*, rice and yak meat. They are chattering together, with the Sirdar, Pembatharke, getting all the laughs and others bursting out slapping him on the back and thighs. Strange to see them touch each other the way they do – something we seem to be ashamed of. They certainly don't look effeminate – far from it – tough guys of the mountains with the snow licking round their backs in the candle-light.

8 October, 7.30 a.m.

Morning. The storm seems to have blown itself out, although there are high clouds at 30,000 – an uncontrollable whirlpool of misplaced gases. There's a big breaking of the trail today, some up, some down from 1, 2 and also up to 3. Mick's throat is still bad, and he is now on some strong pills to put him out of his misery. We'll go up to 3 tomorrow, to do the route to 4. Our two Sherpas are still not very happy.

Why on earth do we do it? Doug's feelings would be mirrored by almost every single member of the expedition; the homesickness, worries about letters from our wives, promises that we'll never land ourselves in a similar situation again, and then, a few days after getting back home, most of us are planning the next time. Part of the reason is the shortness of human memory for things unpleasant, part the speed of a change of mood in self or surroundings; the elation of the good days' climbing, when the route is forced out another thousand feet or so; the impact of a golden sunset; the reward of the ever-expanding scene as we gain height; the satisfaction of facing up to adversity and overcoming it – all are there.

11

THE RUN
OUT TO
CAMP 5

9 October–14 October

The second storm; only two days of snow, but it set us back four days in our race against the winter winds. It was 9 October before Doug and Mick were able to move back up to Camp 3. The site of the camp was a shambles, with all the loads buried and the boxes sticking out of the snow like three sinking ships, their frames warped and broken, the fabric torn. It was an unpleasant shock, for we had hoped that the Whillans Box would stand up to almost any weight of snow. This had been the case on the South Face of Annapurna, but unfortunately, in an effort to reduce the weight of the box, the manufacturer had reduced the gauge of the aluminium tubing of the frame. In addition, we had specified a ventile wall material, which was not quite as strong as the canvas used on the boxes for Annapurna. On further inspection of the boxes at Camp 3, it was discovered that two of them were repairable, but one was a total write-off.

While the two Sherpas dug out the platform and patched up the boxes, Doug and Mick set out to start their route up to Camp 4. The way ran out to the left, beneath the rock buttress, across fairly easy angled snow slopes and over a couple of small rock steps, towards a snow field leading up into the great couloir that swept down from the centre of the Face. It was a fine effort on the part of both of them, but particularly on that of Mick; he had found the trip up to Camp 3 exhausting, making slow, laborious progress. They worked into the dusk, seen from Camp 2 – now in the chill grip of the shadow of Nuptse – two tiny dots against the sunlit snows of the Face. The shadows were like the rising tide, for as the sun dropped behind the wall of Nuptse, the shadow crept inexorably up the Face and the snows changed from dazzling white, through a rich yellow, to a dusky pink that faded imperceptibly into grey as the sun dropped below the far horizon. The difference between sun and shade was cataclysmic. There was still some warmth in the sun, and if there was no wind you could lounge around without wind-proofs or down gear, but the moment the sun dropped behind Nuptse the temperature took a nose-dive, down to −10°C., and during the night it was already beginning to drop to −20°.

That evening, Mick and Doug worked until dusk before returning to their Whillans Box, repaired by the Sherpas. Above Camp 2 we always cooked for ourselves, and the food was arranged in two-man day packs; while at Camp 2 and below, we had our Sherpa cooks and the cooking was carried out centrally. It was dark before they had finished melting snow for brews and cooking their supper; the next morning they were out of the boxes before the sun struck the Face, determined to reach Camp 4 that day. In an effort to avoid the possibility of anyone dropping out from exhaustion before the final push, I had decided that the climbers should use oxygen from Camp 3 onwards. Once you get badly run-down at altitude, there is very little opportunity for recovery, since even Base Camp, at 17,800 feet, is situated at too high an altitude for real rest and recuperation. During the spring expedition Doug had not found it necessary to use oxygen until above Camp 4, and even from there up to Camp 5 the benefit he gained from the set was dubious, since it was faulty for most of the time. He was sceptical on this occasion as to how much good it would do, taking into consideration the weight of the cylinders against the benefit gained from the use of the oxygen, but nonetheless decided to give it a try.

They pulled across the fixed ropes left the previous night, to their high point, and then started to climb the long snow slope that led into the centre of the Face. Their two Sherpas, Anu and Ang Phurba, followed, carrying spare reels of rope. Each reel was three hundred feet long, and Mick and Doug took turns to run out the full reel in a single pitch at a time, kicking slowly, laboriously, up the hard snow slope. It was typical of Mick that, after nearly being forced back down to Base Camp by a combination of appalling mouth sores and altitude sickness, he rallied in the face of the challenge, not only of forcing the route out but also of trying to get it on film. Both he and Doug worked through a long, trying day. The sun was blazing down out of a brilliant-blue sky, but any feeling of warmth was illusory, for a high wind was playing over the upper slopes of the mountain, dislodging the freshly-fallen snow and sending it down the central couloir in a continuous cascade of fine spindrift which penetrated every chink in their clothing. It got behind goggles, into their mitts and, perhaps most serious of all, filled the sacks on their pack-frames carrying the oxygen bottles, thus near doubling their loads. Doug finally abandoned his oxygen set, preferring to climb without its benefit and thus reducing the weight he had to carry by over twenty pounds.

As they gained height, gusts of wind reached down, tearing at their clothing, driving the ice particles, which were as sharp and painful as a thousand minute needles, into their faces. The climbing now became more awkward, over a series of ice rock steps. There was insufficient snow to use the dead-man anchors, and even ice pitons were difficult to place. They were on the front points of their crampons, the wind tearing at their clothing, trying to push them back down the slope. Looking down, the Western Cwm was now in deep shadow and its lapping tide was creeping up the slopes of the South West Face. The two Sherpas were on their way back to the camp, but Mick and Doug kept going into the dusk. Now on their last three-hundred-foot rope, it came to an end still seventy feet below the site of the camp. They could see the gleaming corner of one of the platforms sticking tantalizingly out of the snow just above them.

The slope was littered with the flotsam of previous expeditions, tattered fabric, warped alloy poles from the tents and boxes sticking out of the ice – black and yellow from the Japanese attempt, red from the international expedition, and blue from that of the spring. For the first time they caught sight of the white hawserlay nylon rope from the spring attempt, wherever there was a rock stop protruding from the snow. Dropping down, they managed to pull some rope, left from the spring attempt, out of the snow, and then, by ripping it through the crust of snow, were able to use it for those last seventy feet to the site of Camp 4. They found the camp devastated by rockfall since Doug had last been there just five months before; the Japanese platforms, rather like bedsteads dumped on a scrap-heap, were hanging from their anchor points at an angle. The German platforms, however, looked as if they would be usable once they had been dug out, and the mutilated box tents, now little more than distorted skeletons, had been hacked out of the ice and cast down the slope. Given another few months, Everest would have erased this insolent, man-made rubbish from her profile. Mick, tired and cold, turned to race back down the fixed rope to start a brew at Camp 3, but Doug, more reflective, sat amongst the ruins to watch the setting sun :

A moment to myself, for the first time in two months. A place, high in the Himalayas, to watch the quiet evening turn into night – doubly moving after a hard day's climbing. The wind had stopped and the mountains around me were at peace. The sharp line of shadow and sunlight crept up towards me from far below, and then, with a flourish of white, bright light, the sun dropped out of sight behind Nuptse. The cold struck into me almost immediately and forced me to scuttle down the fixed ropes, into the steamy warmth of our tent.

In just one and a half day's hard work, Doug and Mick had forced the route to an altitude of 24,600 feet. And things had also been happening down below, for although the making of the route is the most obvious sign of progress, and certainly gives the most dramatic part of the story, it is just one small segment of an expedition. The flow of supplies behind the lead climbers is every bit as important, and can present as much risk and perhaps an even greater physical and mental challenge.

By now, Camp 2 was beginning to resemble an Advanced Base Camp. Dougal and Hamish were ready to move up behind Mick and Doug to push the route on, up to Camp 5, near the foot of the Rock Band. Kelvin, Barney, Graham and Nick, with a further fifteen Sherpas, had also come up with the big Palace tent and the green cook tent. The dump of supplies was impressive and we were now ready to start ferrying them up the South West Face. But we were also faced with some problems. The Ice Fall was not nearly as static as we had hoped it would be, in the post-monsoon period. Crevasses were opening constantly, and then re-opening, séracs tottering. Dave and Nick had tried to improve the route on their way back up the mountain on 10 October, after their rest at Base Camp, with unfortunate consequences to Dave. He described it in his diary:

Just about sun-up, I enter a very broken section. The first few ladders are O.K., but then signs of activity. A crevasse has opened. The two ladder section spanning it has parted – it was not bolted together. A section hangs either side, connected by a piece of cord. The handrail rope is wire-tight. I wait for Phurkipa and his pals.

'Not possible,' he says. 'Ladders too small; we have no rope.' But there is some rope dangling down on the other side of the crevasse.

'I go, Phurkipa, O.K. You hold rope.'

Swing down on the ladder, grab for the other one swinging in space, and pull up, breathless – high trapeze act at 20,000 feet. The rest is easy. With the extra rope we make a swing ladder bridge.

The next long bridge requires adjusting, and a few cracks dodging. Then I'm back to breaking trail through the spindrift, ice-axe probing for the invisible hard stuff below the fluff. Every time I sink up to my crutch, having missed the covered path, I have a fit of coughing, and every time I cough I feel as if I've broken a rib.

The last obstacle beyond the big ladder, the violin bridge, lives up to its name – evidence of movement here, and on the rise to Camp 1. Five and a half hours from Base, breaking trail all the way, but it's nice to see Graham again.

11 October 1972

Very cold night, very little sleep. Still got catarrh and my back is a gonner. I was really pleased with myself for all the work I did in the Ice Fall yesterday, and what do I get for it? – the way I feel, a severely strained back, lower spine. The rope I salvaged from the snow slope was attached to a wooden stake. I tried to pull it out, used all my strength, but obviously the wrong way. Couldn't budge it, so started to dig. The stake was five feet long. Didn't feel any pain at the time, but later sitting in Graham's tent, cooking the evening meal, I started to ache.

Today has been murder. If I cough I can't straighten; if I lie flat it takes ages to bend again. Meanwhile, I'm missing all the fun up the hill. Today the weather was perfect. Graham did my job, taking the mail up to Camp 2, while I lay in the tent, slowly drying up in the heat; it's a major effort to transfer into Graham's tent to make a brew.

12 *October* 1972
From the door of my tent I can see it's a beautiful day, so why me?
Why do I have to be the one immobilized? I complain too much.
Just have to make the most of it when I can move again.

The agonized cry, which any of us in a similar state would have
made; but then, the selfless admonishment, so characteristic of
Dave. When Graham brought news of Dave's back injury, Barney
was desperately worried that he might have slipped a disc, and on
13 October dropped back down to Camp 1, to see how badly injured he was. Barney himself was in a bad way, having cracked a
rib from the violence of his bouts of coughing. He was hoping to
spend a few days at Camp 1, taking advantage of its slightly
lower altitude to recover. Fortunately, he found that Dave had
only strained a muscle, and would probably be fit in a few days'
time, and commented wryly:
'You're a fitter man than I.'
But he was not to be allowed his rest. On 12 October, Dougal
and Hamish, with the Sherpas Pembatharke and Pertemba, had
moved up to Camp 4, to build the camp site and start forcing
the route up to Camp 5. The following day, four of our Sherpas,
staying at Camp 3, carried loads up to Camp 4, and on the way
down one of them, Ang Dawa, was hit on the mouth by a gas
cylinder which must have been dislodged by one of the party at
Camp 4. When he got back down to Camp 2 his face was a terrifying sight, covered in blood. I mopped it up gingerly, to find that
his upper lip had been split in two by the flange of the falling gas
cylinder. It was as if he had been given a hare lip. I cleaned it up
as best I could, and tried to put a dressing on it – no easy task on
the face. There was nothing more I could do until Barney got back
and so I put him to bed with a good dose of painkillers and
sleeping tablets. That night, on the evening radio call, I told
Barney of the bad news, and even though he was in desperate
need of rest he agreed to return the next morning to patch up
Ang Dawa. He must have set out early, for he reached Camp 2
at ten in the morning, his face haggard with pain and fatigue. At
every coughing spasm, and they were frequent, he hugged his
chest and winced with pain from the cracked rib.

But he wasted no time and turned the untidy Palace tent into a surgery, sterilized his gear and gave Ang Dawa a local anaesthetic. Soon he was stitching away on Ang Dawa's lip, while Ang Dawa, wonderfully stoic, sat motionless, mouth wide open, accepting Barney's ministrations. Once the operation was completed I asked Barney:

'When can we send Ang Dawa back down to Base for convalescence?'

'Convalescence?' said Barney. 'He'll be right as rain in a couple of days. You can keep him up here, and he'll be carrying as if nothing had ever happened to him.'

And Barney was right. Within a week, Ang Dawa's wound had healed completely, there wasn't even a sign of a scar – a tribute to Barney's sewing, and the remarkable healing powers of the Sherpas. This was especially remarkable at that altitude, for any wound takes a long time to heal, and often becomes septic.

This accident emphasized the risks involved on the South West Face. Anyone climbing up to Camp 4 spent some hours in direct line of the camp site and gully above, so that anything dislodged from the camp could easily hit them. At Camp 4, there were no level spaces, and even the ledges cut in the shallow covering of snow quickly filled in with spindrift which became instantly iron hard. You had to use constant vigilance, both to avoid slipping yourself, or dropping anything. Had it been an oxygen cylinder, rather than an empty gas can that had been dropped, Ang Dawa would undoubtedly have been killed.

Up at Camp 4, Dougal and Hamish dug out the platforms left by the German expedition, and erected two of our Ultimate Boxes. These were on a slightly different design from the Whillans Box, were more compact and lighter but, unfortunately, they had one major fault in the design of the corner joints. A hardened steel screw held together the three alloy pins which socketed into the poles of the frame, and this became more brittle in extreme cold. Several broke during the expedition, causing us considerable worry.

At this stage, however, the weather was still clement; hardly a breath of wind brushed the upper part of the Face, and on 13 and 14 October, Hamish and Dougal pushed up the great snow couloir leading up towards the Rock Band. On their second day they ran out of oxygen about half-way up, having started out with cylinders only half-full. They hung the empty cylinders on the fixed rope, to ensure they could not go tobogganing down the slope on to the camp and the climbers below, and continued without oxygen.

'We were almost glad, afterwards, that we had run out,' commented Dougal. 'It showed us that we, also, could climb without oxygen, like the Sherpas who were carrying our ropes.' Of course, Pembatharke and Pertemba were still going without oxygen.

Two days work and they had run out the rope to a point just short of the site of Camp 5. Although both were climbing very strongly, they had used up all their stock of fixed rope, and so turned back. It was still only half-way through October, and yet we had now reached a height of approximately 26,000 feet. On the surface we were in a very strong position. The morale of the Sherpas was excellent. In my original planning I had allowed for the Sherpas to do just two carries from Camp 3 to 4, before they returned to Camp 2 for a rest. This was the most they had ever done successfully on either of the two previous expeditions; but Pembatharke, on his way back down to Camp 2, after helping Hamish and Dougal make the route up the couloir, volunteered, out of the blue, that the Sherpas would be prepared to make three carries in succession without going back down for a rest. This made a considerable difference to my own logistic planning, for though we had a total of forty Sherpas, there had already been several inroads into our numbers. I had had to keep Sona Hishy back at Base Camp, to supervise all our local purchases; Phurkipa had to stay in the Ice Fall to supervise and repair the route. There were always a few who were sick or recovering from illness and, as a result, we never had more than twenty Sherpas at Camp 2 and above. Carrying all the oxygen, food and rope we were going to need was undoubtedly going to cause us some severe problems later on in the expedition.

At this stage we only had twelve thirty-five-pound loads at Camp 4, of the seventy I had calculated we should need. Camp 5 was not even established, and I had calculated that we should need forty-three thirty-pound loads there. It was no use, therefore, trying to push the route out any further before we had at least built up the stockpile of gear, at both Camp 4 and Camp 5. With this in mind, I had planned to move up to Camp 4 myself, with four Sherpas, and spend four days carrying loads up to Camp 5, before Nick and Dave (provided his back recovered in time), moved back up the mountain to occupy Camp 5 to make the route to Camp 6.

In spite of the two spells of bad weather, we still seemed to be comfortably ahead of schedule, with a good chance of making a summit assault before the start of November. On 14 October, I was ready to move up to Camp 3 on my way to 4. I decided to wait until the load-carriers from Camp 2 arrived, for they were bringing up the mail, and so lazed through the day in the sun, watching through the binoculars as the tiny, ant-like figures of Dougal and Hamish pushed the route up towards Camp 5. It was difficult to imagine that the weather would ever change. There was not a breath of wind in the Western Cwm, not a single plume of spindrift blowing down from the ramparts of Nuptse. The interior of the tents was uncomfortably hot, and outside you only needed a light sweater.

The mail arrived, and with it were some cuttings from the short reports I had written for the *Observer*, and an article by Chris Brasher from the Colour Supplement, summing up what we were trying to achieve. He ended the article with an extract from Norman Dyhrenfurth's description of his attempt on Lhotse in the autumn of 1956:

The following days were terrible. During the night of 16 October, the storm rose to new heights. It was a miracle that the tents were still standing ... what had happened to the weeks of good weather that usually follow the monsoon? One stormy night followed another, the days were no better ... another day passed, and another night straight out of Dante's *Inferno*. In the early morning hours I made up my mind to go down to Camp 2 before losing my sanity in this constant rattling of the tent and the wild howling of the storm ... We had reached the limits of human endurance.

Reading this, in the afternoon sun, it sounded a different mountain from ours, and yet, just two days later, on 16 October 1972, we also were to have our first taste of the post-monsoon Everest winds.

12

OUR
WORST ENEMY,
THE WIND

15 October–26 October

The wind, like a raging torrent, cascaded down the great central couloir, lapping round the box in which I was lying at Camp 4; it was a river of racing spindrift with lumps of ice and rocks, which had filled the gap between the wall of the box and the snow slope behind, bounding and hammering over the flat roof. Had I been sharing the box with anyone, we would hardly have been able to hear each other speak. There was no question of calling down to the four Sherpas who were in the two boxes just below. Words would have been plucked away in the wind. The only possible means of communication was to get out of the box and visit them personally, a minor expedition in itself, with the wind so savage and the situation of Camp 4 so precarious.

The boxes of the Sherpas were perched on an alloy platform left by the Germans. We had also dug out a system of ledges and platforms, but all these were now covered in spindrift, which immediately hardened to the consistency of concrete. It was like living on the pitched roof of a skyscraper. A slip would have been fatal and it was necessary to clip into a network of safety ropes whenever you ventured outside the box.

And yet, the previous night, it had been possible to relax, once we had dug out a platform and erected my own box tent. There had been no breath of wind, though a bank of high grey cloud did augur a change in the weather. Although desperately tired, at the same time I had been strangely elated to be on my own with four Sherpas, at the highest camp on the climb so far; probably the highest man on earth, for my box was just above that of the Sherpas. That night I had been too tired even to cook and had been touched when there was a call from outside and Ang Phu arrived with a plateful of stew and a mug of tea. I snuggled down into my sleeping bag, still wearing my down suit and all my clothes, ate the meal and then started fiddling with the oxygen equipment. During the day I had used oxygen to reach Camp 4. Though it undoubtedly improved my performance, it had not helped me as much as I had hoped. Part of the reason, perhaps, was that my personal gear weighed in the region of thirty pounds before I added the seventeen pound oxygen bottle. The benefit gained from the oxygen, therefore, was in part cancelled out by the extra weight I had to carry. The flow of oxygen had, however, removed that feeling of total lassitude I had experienced on some of my carries up to Camp 3. I had climbed very slowly up to Camp 4, much slower than the Sherpas who had not had the benefit of oxygen, but I had, at least, felt in control of my body, had been able to cut down the number of rests, just plodding slowly, one foot in front of the other.

Using oxygen to sleep on at Camp 4 was a questionable subject since we wanted to conserve our supplies on the mountain, but planning to stay there for some days, I decided at least to give it a try. I had brought in a half-empty cylinder for this purpose, attached my reducer valve to it, and then plugged in the little sleeping tube, which bypassed the demand valve and gave a fixed flow of about one litre of oxygen per minute into a light plastic mask. The continuous hiss of oxygen was strangely reassuring, as I cocooned myself in my sleeping bag. Full of food, I felt comfortably warm and sleepy and quickly dropped off into a deep sleep.

At about midnight I awoke to the deafening rattling roar of the wind and spindrift avalanches – the noise was so great I couldn't tell whether the oxygen was flowing or not, fumbled for my torch in the dark, found it, then lay back panting, willing myself to sit up and check the pressure of the oxygen cylinder. At altitude, each separate action takes three times as long as it would lower down, and you tend to think about the simplest task for a long time before actually carrying it out. The cylinder was empty. I didn't want to use another, and anyway there was no question of getting out of the tent in the middle of the night to get one. And so I just lay back in the box and listened to the ice blocks pound down over the roof. It was a frightening experience.

We had brought up a length of chicken wire to Camp 4, on Hamish's advice, to erect an avalanche fence to guard the camp. It had been the task of Dougal and Hamish to erect this before coming back down to Camp 2 for a rest, but somehow they had not got round to it. The weather had been so perfect when they had been up there that probably it had not seemed as necessary as it had been on the spring expedition, when there had been a lot of stonefall; then again, at 24,000 feet everything is such an effort that one inevitably tends to take the easiest way out, and postpone work if possible.

That night, it had been all the Sherpas and I could do to erect the third box, and in the subsequent days that I was at Camp 4, the wind was either too wild for us to even contemplate going out to try to make a fence, or if the weather was good we were fully occupied, digging out the camp or actually making a carry to Camp 5. That night I just lay and listened to the wind hammering the box, praying that nothing big would hit it.

In the morning the wind didn't let up. Just opening the sleeve entrance of the box to dig some snow to melt for a brew was an agonizing experience. The spindrift drove into my face like a thousand tiny daggers, and welled into the entrance of the tent, penetrating clothing. I filled a plastic bag with snow, all of which had to be chipped away with an ice-axe, for the spindrift formed into a concrete-like mass wherever it settled. Find the lighter, light the primus, and then just lie back exhausted, the mind a near-blank. It took an hour to melt a panful of water for the first brew of the day. I nibbled some nuts, couldn't be bothered to cook, and listened to the wind; imagined what it would be like struggling against the torrent up towards Camp 5. And the route wasn't even made all the way. Dougal had warned me to be careful of the last length of rope. It was anchored to a very poor rock peg. What would it be like in this wind forcing the route, playing around with risky fixed ropes? Time for another brew; I postponed the decision. And then came the desire to relieve myself – the most dreaded moment of the day. I opened the sleeve entrance a chink, and a gust of spindrift blasted in. The thought of baring my backside to the wind and cold was too much. There is some recompense in having a tent to yourself. I found a plastic bag, and held it carefully. Peeing was a lot easier, we each had a pee bottle and it was just a matter of emptying it afterwards outside the tent, but you had to be careful you didn't let it freeze solid! The temperature inside the box, even with the gas stove going full blast, was only −10° C, and once frozen it would have been difficult to thaw it out.

I glanced at my watch – 10.30 a.m. – half the morning gone already and I hadn't even dressed. There was a shout from outside. Gingerly I poked my head out of the sleeve entrance. Ang Phu and Ang Phurba were fully dressed – 'Ready to go, Sahib?' Ang Phu asked.

Feeling a rush of shame that I was not, I thought of the top of the fixed ropes anchored to that uncertain peg, and temporized. 'We wait for an hour, see if it gets better.' They shrugged, impassive, and crawled back into their box. I got out *The Lord of the Rings* and slipped away into Tolkien fantasy, the world of Tree Ents, and Isengard, and the terror of the Nazguls, which was nothing to the real, tearing terror of the wind and snow and rocks outside.

An hour went by, but the thunderous torrent of ice and spindrift didn't let up. I didn't even bother to shout out to the Sherpas, but just curled up in my cocoon, put on another brew and started another chapter. And then came a shout from below. A Sherpa had arrived from Camp 3; a sneaking twinge of guilt – if they had fought their way up here, couldn't we have gone to Camp 5? I poked my head out of the box and shouted to him, through the wind, where to put his load of two oxygen bottles. He yelled something about Sahib coming. That made me feel even more guilty, for Kelvin, ever determined, ever willing, was at Camp 3, supervising the build up of equipment. I had been a little worried about his enthusiasm. He had, of course, less experience of the mountain than any of the others, never having been climbing before the Annapurna South Face expedition. I knew how determined he was, how much he wanted to reach Camp 4 with a load – in a way this was his 'Everest'. And yet at the same time, knowing that he had extended himself to the limit, just to get as high as Camp 3, I was afraid that in trying to reach Camp 4, he could take himself well beyond his limits.

But there was nothing I could do about it. I returned to Tolkien. Then, at about midday, there was a shout from below; I poked my head out once again, and there was Kelvin, trying to pull up over the lip of the platform. He looked all in, fumbling helplessly with the fixed rope. I knew that if he tried to unclip his Jumar he would, perhaps, slip and fall unprotected.

'Hold it there, Kelvin!' I shouted, and started the cumbersome process of forcing on frozen boots and slipping on my windproof over-suit, before crawling out of the box and swinging down the rope to him.

He was not wearing the hood of his down suit, his head was merely protected by his now iced-up balaclava. Icicles clung to his nose and beard, but the most worrying factor was that he was obviously having difficulty in using his hands. Pulling him up onto the small ledge outside the lower box I said, 'Let's have a look at your hands.' Kelvin pulled off his Dachstein mitts, and as I had feared, his fingers were white right the way down the palm of his hand. He had quite severe frostbite. I'm afraid I laid into him verbally, from a whole mixture of motives, some of which arose from my own sense of guilt, however irrational, that I had not fought my way up to Camp 5; also I had let Kelvin hold the fort at Camp 3, in a position where he could put himself at risk as a result of his lack of experience. It is unlikely that any of the other, more experienced members of the team would have got frostbite in similar circumstances. For a start, Kelvin had made the mistake of only using woollen mitts, when he would have been better off with the windproof polar mitts. Even then, he would probably have avoided frostbite if he had noticed his fingers becoming numb, and had stopped to warm them by putting his hand inside his down suit, or just by rubbing them. But he had been fixated by the need to fight his way through to Camp 4, had pushed himself to the limit to get there, not just for his personal satisfaction but primarily to get vital supplies to us. He felt that only by his own personal example could he possibly persuade the Sherpas to make the carry, and this was undoubtedly true.

1 Too much rain, too many leeches; the team pensive

2 Lunch break on the approach march. MacInnes playing
chess

3 Most of the streams were in spate

4 Nepalese hill-woman

5   Tamserku, 21,730 ft

6   Barney Rosedale climbing in the Ice Fall ▶

7 Sherpas at work in the Ice Fall

8 Nick Estcourt climbs up fixed rope using Jumars above Camp 5

9 Camp 4 with boxes partially collapsed after the big storm. Cho Oyu in the background

10 Making the route through the upper part of the Ice Fall

11 Haston inspects the South West Face

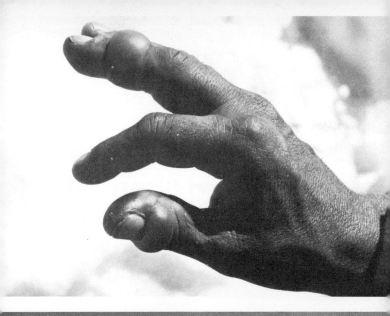

12 Kent's hand immediately after getting frostbite

13 Taweche and Tsolatse, 21,130 ft, from Base Camp

14 Camp 2 after the storm – and yet morale remains high

15 The effects of the post-monsoon winds – Everest Ice Fall ▶

━━━ Route taken up South West Face by '72 Expedition	••━••━ West Ridge Route climbed by American Everest Expedition '63
━ ━ ━ Possible routes on South West Face through Rock Band to Summit	
	A Line attempted by Japanese
━•━•━ South Col Route first climbed by British Everest Expedition '53	**B** Chimney attempted by Whillans and Haston
••••• Out of sight round corner	**C** Escape route towards S.E. ridge

He was bitterly hurt by my verbal attack, and in retrospect, I regret it, but at the time I, also, was under stress. Feeling I could not let Kelvin go back down on his own, I wanted to send someone whom I could trust to look after him, and therefore sent him down with Ang Phu, by far the most humane and reliable of our Sherpas. In doing this, I lost another reliable man at Camp 4.

Because we were running short of true high-altitude Sherpas, I had brought up the best of our converted Ice Fall porters, a broad stocky individual who always had such a wide grin we had nicknamed him Nippon Wide. But he had a grin no longer. Having been affected very badly by the altitude, he was now lying groaning in his sleeping bag. I tried to persuade him to go down with Kelvin, but he muttered that he was too ill to move. And so Kelvin went down with Ang Phu, and reached Camp 2 in the late afternoon, to be treated immediately by Barney.

After being put in a warm sleeping bag with a hot water bottle, he was given a steam inhaler to breathe in hot steam, in order to increase his body temperature as quickly as possible. He was then put on oxygen, a bowl of water was warmed to a temperature of $43°$ C so that he could immerse his frostbitten fingers and bring back the circulation as quickly as possible. This proved an extremely painful process and that night he slept little because of the pain.

The following extract from Kelvin's diary and letters home written three days later on 19 October from Camp 2 show how he felt:

... So much has happened. Thank God I can still write, even with Barney's Dachstein mitts on.

We're still hemmed in here by a storm which buffets everything. The fact that this Safari-type tent and some of the others are still standing is a miracle. Outside the full fury of an Arctic gale carries on unceasingly. Awe-inspiring perhaps, but you'd have to be a madman to appreciate it.

I've written to Chris up at 4 to try and explain or justify my carry-up there on the 16th. He was pretty annoyed at the time and let fly freely. I wanted to retaliate but didn't have the bloody strength. Anyway it took my mind off the immediate problem. I think frostbite in any circumstances tends to numb the brain as well as the limbs concerned. Physical exhaustion outweighs any thought of potential damage and in any case just standing out on the tiny platform at 4 nearly 25,000 feet up in the face of a howling sub-zero blizzard is madness. The whole thing I suppose is madness! Perhaps you've got to put on the right expression of bliss and joy. Some people do, but for me it's like some gigantic minor key composition by Shostakovitch where you seem to be falling deeper and deeper into a bottomless pit of despair and suffering. The only difference is that with music it's all in the mind, but here it's a reality – a grim reminder of man's capability to go just so far and yet know that when he ventures past his own defined limit something will happen.

Chris is still up at 4. I don't hold much against him for his out-burst. In fact, any leader would have gone to town on me, especially after two days by himself above Camp 3 in appalling conditions. Just to exist there in this storm must be an exercise in survival. It doesn't appear to achieve anything if they can't move forward, but we all know that if he abandons the camp it will be torn to shreds.

I suppose I'll look back on that trip to 4 as the climax of my non-mountaineering career. It was a funny set of circumstances which pressed me to go (in addition to my own personal ego!). That morning (16th) Chris did not come on the radio set. This was unlike him even though he may have been sleeping. I was especially worried because Camp 4 was crucial to the expedition's Comms and in any case Chris – as leader – couldn't do much without being able to keep in touch with other camps. I was fairly certain that his walky-talky had broken or that he'd failed to get a good battery connection. In any case I wanted to take up a spare set. Also, we had quite a stockpile of stores at 3 and certain things were running short further up. The Sherpas had specifically requested sugar and the inevitable equal priorities of food packs, oxygen, rope and ironmongery had to be shifted sooner or later – preferably sooner.

I felt O.K. when we left although the weather was not good. All four Sherpas at Camp 3 with me reluctantly decided to go up as well. I know they would not have left had I stayed in the tent. As it was I set out by myself a little ahead of them once I was pretty certain that they would follow. The wind was really howling and unlike the day before there was no sun at all. Even with my windproof suit on I was cold but thought that I would warm up a bit later. It must have been nearly −30°C. I remember that we couldn't cut the corned beef with a knife and we had a breakfast of muesli and coffee. To move out required a lot of will power.

Coming round the corner from the shelter of the rock overhang

I had my first real taste of Everest wind. The spindrift was being hurled into my face like someone throwing ice-cold sand. The little traverse into the open had been hard enough for me and being alone I felt extremely insecure. Round the corner it was worse. I couldn't hear a thing and kept on questioning my ability to go on. The trouble was that any forward progress was so slow that even being well wrapped up it was unbelievably cold and unfriendly. No warmth from the sun and visibility so poor that I couldn't see my objective which was some 1500 metres straight up the Face. Even the fixed ropes were steeper than I'd ever been on before. The whole effect was worse than the 3–4 ASFE and this was much higher. Funny, it never occurred to me to set out using oxygen. I wasn't in that class anyway. Perhaps it would have made all the difference.

Anyway, after about two and a half hours my hands and feet started to go numb. Visibility was now only a few yards and even less when the great rollers of spindrift came rumbling down the face like a surfer's wave. It was impossible to look upwards into the driving wind. But occasionally I could just see over to the shoulder of the West Ridge which the American teams traversed in '63. We were actually on a sort of vast elongated snow slope about 200 metres wide with exposed rock on either side. Sometimes small icy outcrops would jut out in the middle of this slope which had been blown hard and jagged like. But there were still patches of deep driven snow and loose blocks of ice.

Below me I could see the four blurred shapes of the Sherpas catching up fast. It was impossible to look right down to the top of the Cwm where the tents of Camp 2 might just have been visible had the weather cleared. I wanted to keep ahead but my body refused to take me forward. Sometimes for five minutes at a time I'd just stand there accepting nature's blows without wanting to fight back. When the rollers came it was like being in the middle of an asteroid belt being bombarded with stone and pieces of ice – some as big as golf balls coming straight at me at eighty m.p.h.

After another half hour of grind up this never ending steep slope I looked down and saw that there were only two Sherpas on the rope – now about fifty metres below. I couldn't understand this for a while but later realized that the other two had turned back. Heaven knows I wanted to do the same but now the first two Sherpas were right behind me goading me on. They were grumbling and eventually I had to stand aside and let them pass. By this time my right hand was hurting from pain and my bloody camera annoyed me intensely as it swung from side to side dangling from my neck. I wanted to throw it away but equally wanted to try and record on film these incredible conditions which I didn't think anyone else would believe.

You know, I kept thinking that I must be weaker than the others. Doug and Mick as well as Chris plus some of the Sherpas had all got up to 4 earlier and had made no great song and dance about it. They must have some guts and far more physical and mental determination than I. I really admire them.

Eventually I struggled up to the site of 4. It had taken me nearly five hours. The whole place looked really windswept and deserted like a scene I remember from the film *Scott of the Antarctic*. Everything not actually buried or anchored to the ground was flying horizontally in the wind. The two Sherpas had already dumped their loads and had passed me on their way back down. No word was uttered. Even they looked shattered. But for me, the last two or three lengths of fixed rope was the hardest thing I've ever undertaken. I frankly didn't think I'd make it and especially on the sections where the wind had blown all the snow away from the rock, I doubted my ability to heave up to a firm foothold again or remain in balance as I attempted with more and more difficulty to transfer the karabina and Jumar from one rope to the other. The trouble was that the thumb, index finger and middle finger of the right hand were virtually useless and even the fingers of the left hand, which I used to help keep open the ratchet, were all freezing up. The more pressure I used the more useless they became. My feet too were numb and hurting. Also my inexperience in using crampons on the rock sections didn't exactly help! It was all pretty pathetic.

I hadn't ever shouted for help before in my life but this time I was beyond being a hero. Just below the bottom tent I blurted out a plea for assistance and just collapsed in a heap waiting for something to happen. The wind was really ferocious and I could hardly speak. Hertzog's words about man not belonging here in his Annapurna book went through my mind vividly. Ang Phu came out of the bottom tent and immediately started to help. He called up to the top tent and I heard him telling other Sherpas to get a brew on. I was hauled up to the top platform and Chris came out. His immediate reaction was hardly cordial. I think he shouted 'You bloody fool – you've gone and got yourself frostbite haven't you?' He seemed more annoyed that I'd let the expedition down by writing myself out of the H.A. action than anything else. This meant of course that he had to give up a Sherpa (Ang Phu) to escort me down. In short I had succeeded in messing up the middle camp's manning plans. He wasn't in the slightest bit interested in my load of sugar, spare radio and

Coolite chemical light tubes – which incidentally are proving very good indeed. To Chris I was just an inexperienced fool trying to prove something to myself to the detriment of the expedition as a whole. He almost made me feel that this was in fact the case, but ironically, had his radio worked he evidently was going to say that conditions were so wild at Camp 4 that any carry-up from there was out. Equally to carry to 4 was not on! Hardly surprising really when I think of it now. I truly reckon the wind up there was as fierce as the two typhoons I have experienced in Hong Kong. And yet it was rewarding – I knew that.

Getting down to 3 and then on to 2 was not exactly easy as you can imagine. Without Ang Phu I don't think I could have done it. He was so good and I owe him a lot.

About half past four I staggered in to Advance Base and was greeted by Barney who immediately went into action. Dougal and Hamish are here as well and have been a great help. Barney is absolutely wonderful. He's had me on oxygen, penicillin, pain-killers and hot water treatment, and I know that no one could do more. He is always cheerful, sympathetic and understanding. In many respects I think he's the strongest member of this team.

Next day I looked at Chris's radio. All that was wrong was that the circular dial which you pull out to adjust frequencies had not been pushed back in properly – a five-second job!

... Still the wind rages. It will be this that stops us. Not the mountain or the kit or the climbers. Perhaps if it eases I can go down to Base tomorrow although trying to get through the Ice Fall with both hands out of action and no feeling in my feet will be interesting. I think Dougal and Hamish will probably escort/winch me down. I could hardly be in better hands! It's hard to say what the outcome will be. My feet will be O.K. and the left hand looks only superficial. There's nasty blistering and discolouring but with luck I shouldn't lose too much. At any rate I'm not depressed. I think that at any level the warm feeling of achievement, of getting a load to its destination surpasses the temporary feeling of cold and fatigue. You can feel good even if it hurts ...

Back at Camp 4, I was already feeling remorse for having been so unsympathetic and wrote Kelvin a letter apologizing for biting his head off. At the same time though, I was worried about losing him from the expedition. Ironically, I could afford to lose my support climbers less than the leaders, the immediate problem being that there were no climbers at Camp 3, which needed constant supervision, just to keep the boxes from being engulfed in the snow. The Sherpas, left by themselves, tended to huddle inside their boxes until they collapsed on top of them.

In addition, Nippon Wide seemed to have taken a turn for the worse and was lying in the Ultimate Box in a state of semicoma. I put him on oxygen and at the evening call asked Barney's advice. He recommended a number of drugs, and I persuaded Nippon to take them. He was in such a poor state that he was unable even to eat or drink. It was very noticeable that once the Sherpas did go down with sickness, or became frightened, they had very much less power of resistance or recovery than the European climbers.

The following day it was blowing as hard as ever. There was no question of going up to Camp 5, and it was now becoming increasingly important to get Nippon Wide back down the mountain. At midday I succeeded in getting him dressed and sent him down with Anu, just leaving Ang Phurba and myself up at Camp 4. On the way down, Anu abandoned Nippon Wide and made tracks for Camp 2, as fast as he could get down. The unfortunate Nippon Wide barely managed to get down to Camp 3, taking a bad fall on the way and as a result got frostbitten hands. He could every easily have died from exposure.

This failure to look after each other was a feature I had noticed before among some Sherpas. It was perhaps a symptom seemingly endemic in the East, of the lack of care for an individual's life created in part, no doubt, by the sheer harshness of day-to-day living. In this particular case, the other Sherpas were as angry as we were at Anu's callousness.

Back at Camp 2, they had tried to force the route up to 3, and I had hoped that Graham would be able to get there to spend the night. The Sherpas, however, had turned back. The conditions in the bottom of the Cwm were nearly as bad as they were on the Face, with fresh deep snow covering the track, and spindrift gusting across the foot of the Face. That evening one of the five Sherpas staying at Camp 3 dropped back to the lower camp, reporting that one of the three boxes had collapsed under the weight of snow. Four Sherpas were still there, but it seemed unlikely that they would keep the boxes clear of snow without one of the climbers there to help them. That night therefore, the party at Camp 2 resolved that Nick and Graham would reach Camp 3 at all costs the next day. Nick described their arrival at Camp 3 in his diary:

It looked as though a bomb had hit it. No sign of gear pile or the two tents at the right-hand end of the ledge. We started digging and dug from 1.30 to 4.30, but the spindrift had set solid and we only succeeded in extracting one Whillans Box.

19/10/72. Wild night – either Graham or I were up every forty-five minutes to clear snow off roof – only spindrift but the amount incredible. Also told Sherpas to do same thing. However, I was very angry when I got up this morning and found that they had not bothered, and that one of the boxes was now even more badly damaged.

Various problems – one working stove between six of us – a lot of snow in our box.

The stove we were using had a damaged burner that was obviously giving off carbon monoxide, but Graham persisted in using it and I nearly passed out. Just after two sips of coffee I puked – unfortunately into the billy which held the rest of the hot water. At least this convinced Graham that I wasn't malingering and I was allowed to have the stove off and the ventilator open.

Various radio calls occupied the morning and at 11.00 we agreed with Chris that two of our Sherpas would carry half-way up, to be met by his four, who would take their loads and the ones abandoned on the 16th, when Kelvin had got frostbite. The other two, Graham and I, would dig out the camp site.

Our Sherpas must be the laziest, thickest four on the entire trip. When the time came, the two that were meant to do the carry disappeared into their tents without saying a word. The others did no digging. The Sherpas in the other Whillans Box attempted to repair it by putting a pole into a small rip in the side. Naturally after three minutes the rip was three feet long.

I am deeply depressed about prospects – it seems this expedition is going the same way of all Autumn expeditions – things looked so good, as recently as the fifteenth.

Later we decided to abandon the other box and sent two Sherpas down with it, with two Sherpas from Camp 4, who also had to go down because their tents had collapsed – things look even worse.

Things also looked bad at Camp 4. One of the Ultimate Boxes

had collapsed completely, failing at the corner joints which had already proved to be a weak spot in the design. I had had no choice but to allow Ang Phu and Anu to return to Camp 2, leaving Ang Phurba, Jangbo and myself at Camp 4, to try to sit it out till the weather improved sufficiently for us to establish Camp 5 and make a carry. In my diary I commented:

It's an absolutely perfect, azure blue sky with a blazing sun. In theory it should give perfect conditions. Looking out over the mountains, mile upon mile of peaks, absolutely clear; very very beautiful, very peaceful, and yet this fiendish wind makes it as harsh a mountain situation as I think I've ever been in.

It wasn't a continuous wind, but came in gusts. Every now and then there would be a lull, complete silence. You'd think, 'the wind's finished – it's going to be a perfect day' – but then there would come a reverberating roar as the next gust hurtled down the slope and engulfed the box.

It was difficult to maintain an overall picture of the expedition from my solitary eyrie at Camp 4. I should probably have been better off with a companion, so that at least I had someone with whom to discuss plans, rather than being dependent exclusively on the radio calls for each step of my planning. As the days went by, my nerves were becoming more and more taut. Merely dealing with the hour-to-hour crises of survival in the camp were enough to stretch me to the limit. And yet I felt I was in the right place, for this was the crucial point for the expedition at that moment: whatever crises developed down below could be solved by the people involved, without affecting the crisis point which the expedition faced forcing supplies up to Camp 5.

That night [19th] Hamish, back in Camp 2, had suggested that we should abandon the Face until the weather improved, taking the boxes down and storing them under the platforms to prevent further damage. The tent situation was getting critical with nearly fifty per cent of our tentage written off either by wind or weight of snow. I was loath to agree to this, however, since once we abandoned Camp 4, we could then waste two good days in getting back up, and if we were only to get the odd good day, it seemed essential we should stick it out at the top camp, taking maximum advantage of any break in the weather when, and if, it arrived.

That night I temporized and said:

'Well, let's think about it, and discuss it again tomorrow, there's absolutely nothing we can do about it tonight.'

That night I commented in my diary:

I have a feeling that once we abandon this camp, we've lost the battle. It all depends on whether this is the average wind direction. If it is, I think we've had it, because we now seem to be in the period of the high Autumnal winds and you certainly can't climb the mountain in these conditions.

With this depressing prediction, I tucked down into my sleeping bag and began to massage my toes to try to get some kind of life back into them. Just going out of the box a few times during the day was enough to freeze toes to such a degree that they never really came back to life, even after a night in the sleeping bag. Although using oxygen helped in this respect, I used as little as possible, and during the six nights I spent at Camp 4 during this stint, only used it twice.

That night was the worst of the lot. The wind built up into a crescendo of violence. I took two sleeping tablets but they had no effect. I just lay, tucked into the inside wall of the box, listening to the thunder of ice blocks rattling across the top of the tent. Nerves stretched to the limit, I was on the point of screaming into the noise-filled opaque void.

By morning I had had enough. At the morning radio call, I agreed with Hamish that it would be best to evacuate the Face. Hamish and Dougal were going to return to Base that day, and Mick and Doug would probably do so as well.

Then suddenly I noticed that everything had become silent; there was no wind. I poked my head out of the entrance of the box. It was a brilliant, clear day, just as it had been for the last three, but the important factor now was that there was no wind. The sun even seemed to have a little heat in it. Everything was different from what it had seemed early that morning; the nightmarish night was forgotten. This was a day to go up, not down: and so I called out to the Sherpas.

'It's a good day, Ang Phurba. We go up.'

They accepted my decision without expression, and by ten o'clock we were ready to make the first carry up to Camp 5. I had decided to go up using oxygen, taking a very light load, so that I could fix the final stage of the route to the site of the camp, while I gave Ang Phurba and Jangbo loads of rope, and oxygen cylinders weighing about thirty-five pounds each.

I set out in front with the two of them close on my heels. In theory, the oxygen set should have reduced the altitude to the equivalent of 17,000 feet, but it certainly didn't seem to be doing this. I was taking a couple of pants for each step and, after a dozen, wanted to take a rest. Perhaps the cold had affected the function of the demand valve. At my first rest, the two Sherpas steadily gained ground on me and stormed past, Ang Phurba making particularly good progress. I shouted out for him to wait at the top of the fixed rope, and warned him that the top peg might be badly placed. He showed no sign of having heard me, but just kept plodding on up the slope, and I had little enough breath to spare to shout after him. That night in my diary I commented.

You just plod on up this endless, great wide snow gully. Part of you is wondering why the hell you're doing it – it's absolute misery, one step, then another and then another – the slow monotony of it; yet when you do rest and look round, the view is fantastic. You look down, into the Western Cwm, sweeping down again to this ever widening vista of mountains – Cho Oyu quite close now, only a bit higher than ourselves. Swinging across to the west, Menlungtse, a perfect pyramid; Gauri Shankar, round humped, with sheer-seeming walls on every side – these two peaks still unclimbed – and then mile upon mile of other mountains, a lot of them in Tibet. Gosainthan, I think, in the distance, the last 8,000-metre peak to be climbed. This ever-expanding view makes up for all the misery and effort.

You plod on, see the Sherpas getting farther and farther ahead. By the time I reached Dougal's high point, Ang Phurba had already got out one of the reels of rope he was carrying, and had run it out across to a shoulder on the right, behind which Camp 5 was hidden. By the time I had followed it to the camp, the two Sherpas were already hard at work digging out the camp. An overhanging rock wall gave excellent shelter from any rocks or spindrift from above. A dozen oxygen bottles from the International expedition were left over on one side of the ledge. The Sherpas had already tunnelled down to a part-wrecked tent left by the Germans the previous spring. They offered me some sweets that had been lying there for the last six months; they could have lain there for a further year or years and would still have been edible.

All the effort and struggle to reach that point was made infinitely worthwhile by the incredible view. We were now level with the summit of Nuptse, on the other side of the Western Cwm, could even glimpse snow peaks on the other side of the long crenellated ridge. It was strange to think that I had stood over there, just eleven years before. At that time I could not have foretold that I should ever be at 26,000 feet on Everest or, for that matter, the course of my life which had led me to this point.

I was content. We had carried two loads up to Camp 5, and that single day of fine weather brought all my optimism back to life. Perhaps we had a chance of reaching the summit after all – just a few more days like this and we could get Camp 5 stocked, and the route run out to the foot of the Rock Band. I set out behind the Sherpas to return to Camp 4, sliding down the fixed ropes, sitting down every hundred feet or so, both to rest and to watch the sun drop down towards the western horizon, bathing the mountains in a rich, yellow glow which slowly turned to orange. The following day the wind was back, but that single day of activity had given us new strength. I was now determined to maintain our toe-hold on the Face.

At this stage I still hoped that I should be able to continue to sit it out at Camp 4, pushing Nick and Dave through to Camp 5 as soon as I had managed to do another carry with the Sherpas. But two days went by and we were unable to make any further progress. Ang Phurba had had enough and wanted to go back down, and so I sent him down, replacing him with four fresh Sherpas, Pembatharke, Pertemba, Ang Nima and Ang Phu. Unfortunately, however, Pembatharke was feeling the altitude and Ang Nima complained of headaches. I, too, was reaching the end of my tether – the isolation and the continuous shriek of the wind were beginning to have an effect and I longed to escape, if only for a few days. So I decided that we should have to abandon all hope of getting Camp 5 stocked before Dave and Nick moved up to make the next push forward, and bring them up to Camp 4 to take over from me.

Meanwhile, down below there was no shortage of incident. Dave had made a miraculous recovery from his back injury and had moved up to Camp 3 to join Graham and Nick. Barney, ever faithful, was holding the fort at Camp 2, while Mick and Doug had retreated to Base Camp. There seemed little point in using them to carry loads up to Camp 3, which was well stocked anyway. At Camp 1, Ken Wilson was in charge. It was an important but incredibly dreary role, for Camp 1, though a vital link in our communications, was a depressing place in which to spend any length of time, as uncomfortable as any camp on the mountain yet with none of the excitement associated with the camps of the Face. In addition, the Ice Fall porters who were looking after Camp 1 spoke practically no English. Ken is a very gregarious person who thrives on argument and discussion, and to put him, in effect, on his own was a refined form of torture. There was a plaintive note in his voice on the radio, when he asked when he was going to be allowed to move up to Camp 2. Nevertheless he did a magnificent job at Camp 1, organizing the flow of loads up the mountain and looking after the needs of the Sherpas. There was no doubt that we needed a Camp 1 manager, but I had no-one with whom I could replace Ken, and yet it was obviously unfair to keep him there for his stay with the expedition, especially as he had come out to Everest at his own expense to see as much as possible of what we were doing.

I decided, therefore, to risk leaving the camp unsupervised, on the supposition that the Sherpas based there had the comparatively simple task of ferrying everything they received straight through to Camp 2, and allowed Ken to move up to 2, to keep Barney company.

Having made my decision to move back down for a rest, I longed for Dave and Nick's arrival, but this was to be delayed for yet another day. On 22 October, the wind blasted across the face with hardly a break. I could have got down myself, but dared not leave the Sherpas on their own, since almost inevitably, and quite rightly, they would have wanted to go down as well. And so I just sat it out. I commented in my diary:

The wind is the appalling enemy, it is mind-destroying, physically destroying, soul-destroying, and even existing in the tents, which I think are now pretty weathertight, is still very, very hard. This will certainly be the most exacting test I have ever had to face, and I only hope it is one that the others will be able to face.

One worry here is that having pushed Nick and Dave up to Camp 5, I shall have to push Graham up to here. One problem is his relationship with the Sherpas. He can be very outspoken and could rub them up the wrong way. At the moment it is vital that we keep the Sherpas happy and bend over backwards, just to keep them up here, carrying. Also, how long will he be able to take this kind of wind battering? He might be able to take it better than I – he has less administrative problems, and, I think, is a more phlegmatic kind of person.

Oh, the absolute lethargy of 24,600 feet. You want to pee and you lie there for a quarter of an hour making up your mind to look for your pee bottle. I've no appetite at all and it's an effort to cook anything for yourself. I suspect it is high time I did go down for a short rest – I think if you try to stay up high the whole time, to conduct operations, you end up being ineffective in that you are just getting weaker and weaker, more and more lethargic. Part of me wants to stay up here, because this is the focus of events, but I think I really should go down.

And so I waited, longing for a temporary release from Camp 4 and, perhaps equally important, the company of my fellow climbers.

Nick and Dave came up to relieve me on 23 October, yet another brilliant clear day, with the wind tearing out of the empty sky. They came up without using oxygen, engulfed in clouds of spindrift. Nick first, with Dave dragging a little behind him. Nick commented in his diary:

Main worry was my toes, which were numb all the way up to 4. I would stop every thirty steps to wiggle them but it didn't seem to help. Got up in three hours, Dave in about three and a half. Chris seemed pleased to see us. I suspect more because he could now go down, than because of our company. He said he had been furiously spring-cleaning the inside of the box, but it still looked pretty grim to me. Afternoon spent sorting out box. However, it will always be cramped as the upper wall bulges with snow and the lower one over-hangs space and you don't like getting too near it.

It had been cramped for one, was even worse for two. During the night, condensation formed an icy armour on the ceiling of the box, above the frost liner; then, during the day, with the stove going full blast, it would start to melt, dripping onto the frost liner which provided a supplementary ceiling. Fortunately this was semi-impermeable and would therefore collect little lakes which could be channelled off to the sides. The main problem was storing all one's gear, radio, first-aid kit, spare clothes, cine and still cameras, which had to be hung from the frame of the tent or wedged round the sides. And then there was the food, stove and pans, which took up one corner; it was all too easy to knock over a full pan of soup. You needed relentless self-discipline to keep the box in any kind of order.

I plunged down the fixed ropes in a mere hour and a half, all the way back down to Camp 2, partly in my anxiety to reach semi-civilization and partly to get the film I had taken, of Nick and Dave arriving at Camp 4, back down to Base Camp that same day. Camp 2 was a different world. Our Sherpa cook thrust a big mug of tea in my hand. You could sit outside; didn't have to watch where you put hands and feet – but most important of all there were people to talk to – Ken had now joined Barney at Camp 2 – Ken full of impressions of Everest, full of enthusiasm; Barney, forever cheerful and helpful, even though he was still having trouble with his chest, and in a way, had the most ment-ally exacting and yet least rewarding job on the entire expedi-tion. Holding the fort at Camp 2 entailed directing our Sherpa force in their efforts to supply Camp 4, arguing with them about rest days, keeping records of our bonus schemes, and supervising the camp.

That night, Ken cooked a magnificent three-course dinner over the gas stove and then we lay in our sleeping bags in the com-fortable sleeping compartment of the big Palace tent, talking of subjects connected and unconnected with the expedition. Ken is obsessed with climbing, not just from the actual physical process, but the ethics and politics. It was refreshing having a ferocious argument on the use of artificial aids on British rock, in the wild confines of the Western Cwm.

Up at Camp 4, Nick and Dave were not so comfortable. Nick wrote:

I had a lousy night's sleep – not more than one hour altogether – cold toes, desperately cramped (the floor was shaped for one person, not two) and the continuous howling wind. (At the moment I am reading *Wuthering Heights* – appropriate !)

The following morning was fine with very little wind. Nick in his diary continued:

It seemed a warm and pleasant morning though the thermometer outside the tent read −17°C which just shows how we are getting acclimatized to the cold. Just before leaving, a large chunk of ice hit the box and bent part of the frame.

They were obviously going to be able to make a carry up to Camp 5, but unfortunately they were only to have two Sherpas available to go up. Pembatharke had been steadily deteriorating for the last three days, ever since reaching Camp 4, and it was obvious that he was going to have to return. Ang Nima had also been complaining of headaches, and although he seemed to be fit and strong, insisted on going back down. Maintaining our numbers at Camp 4 had become a real problem and I had no-one down at Camp 2 with whom to replace them immediately. We had made another change in tactics, since the Sherpas preferred to live at Camp 2, making their carries straight through to 4. They travelled lightly-laden up to Camp 3, where Graham was still ensconced, then picked up a load there and pushed on to 4. It made a gruelling day, but they were prepared to do this every other day, and, of course, were very much more comfortable down at Camp 2.

That day, Dave Bathgate decided to stay behind at Camp 4 to receive the Sherpas carrying up from Camp 2 and to sort the camp out while Nick went with the Sherpas up to Camp 5. Nick described the day in his diary:

Pertemba set up a fast pace and the three of us kept close together taking four hours for the trip. I didn't use oxygen but only took one coil of rope. The weather was magnificent – no wind, hardly a cloud in the sky and the view was unbelievable. The greatest moment of all was when I could first look over the Lhotse-Nuptse ridge and see range upon range of peaks stretching on the other side. I am pretty sure I recognized Annapurna away in the distance. It was one of those days when I felt really strong, and thought for a change that we might get up this bloody mountain.

But next day the weather had reverted to normal; the wind was hammering the tent, and, more ominous, a scum of high grey cloud covered the sky. They would have liked to have taken a rest day, but the two Sherpas said that under no circumstances were they prepared to spend another night at Camp 4. They were prepared, however, to make just one more carry up to Camp 5, before going down. And so Dave agreed to go up with them, while Nick rested and did some work on the camp site. Dave also went up without using oxygen, a sterling effort; but conditions were less pleasant than the previous day and by the time he returned to the box his feet were numb with cold. Nick warmed them by putting them in his crutch, using body heat in an effort to get back the circulation, but they remained numb, none the less.

Everyone on the mountain felt encouraged by their effort. We now had enough gear at Camp 5 for Nick and Dave to take up residence. I was planning to send up a further four Sherpas the next day to help them move up. But as so often happened on this expedition, just as the tide seemed to be turning in our favour, the weather took a hand once again. By dusk, the camp was engulfed in cloud, with the wind tearing at the box. They took Mogadons to try to deaden their senses into sleep in the face of the constant roar of the wind. Dave Bathgate described what happened that night in his diary:

An almighty crash: immediate wakening – everything covered in snow; the bottom end of the Whillans Box torn, the framework broken and sheared through; it must have been a good-sized rock that had hit us. This was taken in, in seconds. I remember Nick saying, 'Well, there she goes.' Both of us trying feverishly to think of what to do, though still half drugged with Mogadon and, anyway, at an altitude of 24,600 feet, constructive thought is difficult.

Eventually Nick sat at the broken end of the box, holding it up with his head. I put boots on over duvet socks and crawled out to inspect the other boxes for possible habitation. It was pitch dark outside, and the beam of my torch hardly cut through the rushing particles of snow. Both boxes had rips or broken zips and were rapidly filling with snow. The temperature was −25°C, and God knows what the strength of the wind was. The only thing I could grab to help with repairs was a shovel, and spare piece of framework. The shovel helped to prop up the damaged corner. Everything was in chaos, but we managed to find some matches, a stove and brew materials – and then, ironically there was a shortage of snow to melt in the cooking pot.

We brewed for two and a half hours, and this raised the temperature in the box to an almost bearable level. Outside the wind was still whistling past, bringing with it a torrent of spindrift and rocks. At 8 a.m. we made radio contact with Camp 2, and Chris agreed that we should abandon Camp 4. He asked whether we could transfer to one of the other boxes, but we told him that they also were damaged and were now part filled with snow. In addition, all our gear was covered in spindrift and we could never have got it effectively dried out.

By 11 a.m. we were ready to go. Down the ropes with numb hands and feet, a river of snow rushing past, ankle deep. During the big gusts it was total white-out conditions, and if you could manage to open your eyes, you could see black objects rush past. At one point Nick tried to warn me of stone fall. Dozens of rocks, anything from the size of golf balls to that of footballs, whizzed past our ears. We were very lucky not to be hit.

Eventually we got round the rock buttress, to the relative safety of Camp 3, and Graham was waiting for us with gallons of hot drinks. He seemed quite happy at 3 where it was sheltered from the full force of the storm. We left him and clipped on the fixed ropes once again; visibility averaging fifty feet, arrived down at the Bergschrund safely, and traversed the slope before walking blind for a while. Began to wonder about our chances of finding Camp 2, and chances of survival if we didn't. Then suddenly, during a clear spell, we saw people coming towards us, Barney, Chris and two Sherpas. Our gratitude was indescribable. The Sherpas took over our bags. Everything was laid on at Camp 2.

We were almost as relieved to see them as they were to see us. Even down in the Western Cwm the weather was frighteningly savage. Had they missed Camp 2, they would have had little chance of surviving a night out. Camp 2 was relatively luxurious compared to 4, but it was hardly a holiday camp. The tents were being threatened with destruction from the sheer weight of snow building up around them, and at night one wondered just how long our Palace tent could stand up to the battering of the wind.

Things looked black. We had been forced to abandon Camp 4, and had to face the prospect that all three boxes would probably be destroyed in the storm. Graham was sitting it out on his own at Camp 3, hoping to preserve the box he was living in, at least, and the rest of us were at Camp 2. Communications with Base Camp were broken, both on the Ice Fall, and the routes between Camps 1 and 2.

I could not help wondering whether we had reached the end of our resources, but then put the thought behind me. None of us was prepared to admit defeat.

13

THE STORM

27 October–30 October

'Check mate' – another game over, our fifth that day. Barney and I were lying in our sleeping bags in the sleeping compartment of the big Palace tent, which rocked and shook in the wind. The little cassette recorder, kept inside the sleeping bag to warm the batteries, was playing Bach's Orchestral Suite – the music both of us found to be the ideal palliative to taut nerves. We were both relatively warm and comfortable, just as long as the tent stood up. Nick and Dave were in the sleeping compartment beside us, but the living area which filled the rest of the tent was anything but luxurious; spindrift found its way through every single chink, covered the food, piled rucksacks, cooking pots and stoves in its powdery film.

Our cook, Pasang, was crouched over a primus stove, trying to persuade it to work. Muttering imprecations in Nepali, he was pumping furiously, tried to light a match, but the head broke off; he grabbed another and the same happened. By this time the primus had cooled off and the jet of vapour had turned to liquid paraffin – a match smouldered into flame and suddenly the whole tent seemed full of yellow flames. Pasang continued to pump. 'For Christ's sake turn down the pressure,' we shouted. 'You'll burn the tent down if you're not careful.'

Reluctantly, Pasang turned down the pressure and the flames vanished, to be replaced by the pervasive fumes of hot paraffin. The cook's tent had finally been engulfed in the snows that morning and he had been forced to move the communal kitchen, with all its accompanying fumes and mess, into the 'Palace'. This tent had therefore become the communal home for all twenty

Sherpas and the four climbers at Camp 2. At night everyone packed into it to eat the evening meal, listen to the radio and talk. With twenty Sherpas and four climbers crammed into the tent, there was hardly room for everyone to sit down but the warmth of close-packed bodies, and the heat from the primus stoves which were burning without a pause throughout the day, raised the temperature to a warm -5° C! We played chess, read and talked. I had left *The Lord of the Rings* up at Camp 4 – it had been too heavy to contemplate carrying it down and then all the way back up again. I'd moved on to *Cider With Rosie* by Laurie Lee – another escapist and rather improbable book for the Western Cwm of Everest. On Nupste, back in 1961, my main reading had been Apsley Cherry Garrard's *Worst Journey in the World* which told the story of his experiences on Scott's last expedition to Antarctica. Whenever I had thought that life on the mountain was unbearably tough, I just had to read another chapter to realize how much harder it had been for those Antarctic pioneers. On Everest the conditions and stress from cold and wind were probably every bit as bad as those experienced by Cherry Garrard, though of course we did have better equipment and food, and the experience was not so long drawn out. We were all looking forward to the end of our ordeal and yet, at the same time, there was real enjoyment in each other's company, in the moments of intense exhilaration caused by the stupendous beauty of the mountains around us, of having made a good carry or, perhaps greatest of all, the thrill of pushing out a few hundred feet of the route. It was in this respect that Barney possibly had the most exacting job of all. He had very little of this type of stimulus, since he was landed at Camp 2 with the nerve-racking job of controlling the Sherpas, keeping a check on the build-up of supplies and administration, all on top of his duties as doctor. He was sparely built before the expedition, but now his face was carved into hollows by the stress of living at over 21,000 feet for a fortnight; he was still coughing, and every single cough caused a stab of pain from his damaged rib. With none of the spur of possibly making a vital section of the route, or the final summit bid, he just had to keep going with only the occasional trip up to Camp 3 to change his horizon. Nevertheless, throughout, he remained wonderfully cheerful and kind – a good and very soothing companion.

We started another game of chess, changed the cassette to some Mozart, and tried to ignore the wind outside. There was no movement anywhere on the mountain. Graham, in solitary state, was up at Camp 3, sounding remarkably balanced and content with his lot when contacted on the radio. Barney, Nick, Dave and myself were at Camp 2. Ken Wilson, having made a single trip up to Camp 3, had returned to Base with the comment, 'You're mad – you're all mad. I'm not involved in this expedition, and I'm going to get out of it as fast as I can!' And yet there was no doubt that he had gained a tremendous amount from the experience and had, of course, fulfilled an invaluable role during the lonely week he had held the fort at Camp 1. A gregarious rock-climber, Ken has never had aspirations to being a big expedition man. He was due to leave for home anyway, and did so inspired, and certainly enlightened by his experience, but without regret.

Mick Burke and Doug Scott were at Camp 1, on their way back up the mountain, and the rest of the team was down at Base Camp, which was now being ably run by Jimmy Roberts, assisted by Kelvin Kent and Tony Tighe. Bob Stoodley had also just arrived there. We had paid for his trip out to see us as a recompense for his efforts in raising money in Britain. Having contracted a stomach upset on arrival at Lukla, he never recovered from it, being unable to hold anything down for the entire week he stayed at Base Camp. Consequently, he spent much of the time in his sleeping bag, felt desperately ill throughout, and yet still ranked it as one of the greatest experiences of his life! Beth cared for him, together with all the other convalescents and invalids down at Base, referring the symptoms of each patient to Barney, at Camp 2, for his radio-diagnosis and prescription. Barney finally recommended Bob to start back for civilization, since he was just wasting away at Base – by the time he got back to England he had lost twenty-one pounds.

Base Camp was certainly a busy place at this stage. Chris Brasher had arrived – he was going to take over my role as expedition writer, sending reports back to the *Observer*. By now the expedition seemed to have turned into a monster with a minute head, in the shape of Graham at Camp 3, a puny body, our team of four climbers and twenty-one Sherpas at Camp 2, and a massive tail sitting at Base Camp. There were several disturbing factors, the most serious being our shortage of tentage. It seemed probable that all the boxes at Camp 4 would be written off, leaving us with hardly any spares. Hamish was designing a special, reinforced box, which he hoped to prefabricate at Base Camp before it was dismantled and carried up to Camp 4. He had already ordered suitable timber in Namche Bazar. Meanwhile, Dougal and Tony Tighe were on their way to the Base Camp of the French Pumori expedition, to see if they had any spare tentage which we could borrow, or buy.

Up at Camp 2, I tried to work out our most effective moves once the storm blew itself out. We were now losing tents even at Camp 2 – the kitchen tent, of course, had already foundered, the fly-sheets of the Vango four-man tents were being ripped to bits in the wind and these, also, were fast vanishing under the snows, in spite of our efforts to keep them dug out. The Palace, miraculously, stood up to the hammering, though at night we were all careful to have our rucksacks packed, ready for a hasty retreat in the event of it blowing away. The constant flapping of the canvas, the all-pervasive spindrift, and the savage wind and snow when you ventured outside to dig out the tent or relieve yourself, were all beginning to drive us to a nervous edge.

And then, on the morning of 28 October, there was an improvement. You could see the top of the Rock Band through swirls of cloud and spindrift. The wind in the bottom of the Western Cwm had dropped, and it looked as if we might be able to re-establish the route between Camps 1 and 2. This had become critical, for we were now low on some foodstocks, particularly *tsampa* and sugar but, more serious still, we had only two gallons of paraffin. To melt all the snow necessary for brews and food for twenty-four people, Pasang had to keep the stoves burning twelve hours a day, using a battery of three primus stoves to melt a single big pot of melt water. At this rate we had barely twenty-four hours' fuel left. Barney had been worried about fuel stocks for some time, but there was a fuel shortage all the way back to Namche Bazar, and a fresh consignment had only just reached Base Camp. At Camp 1 they could only spare two gallons, but this would keep us going for a few days until supplies from Base reached us. Consequently, I resolved to organize a carry from Camp 1 to 2, and hoped that there would be a carry that same day from Base. I sent Dave Bathgate down towards Camp 1 to meet the Sherpas coming up, wading through the thigh-deep snow. At the same time, I told Doug and Mick, who of course were at Camp 1, that they could come up to Camp 2. In retrospect this was a mistake, since though the weather showed signs of improvement, it certainly was not settled, and allowing them to come up to join us meant that Camp 1 was, once again, without a European in charge and, even more important, take the radio calls. We could possibly have taught Ang Dawa, the Sherpa in charge of the seven porters at Camp 1, to use the radio, but somehow had never thought of it, though later on we were to do just that.

The weather had closed down before Doug and Mick reached us at Camp 2. Once again, it was near white-out conditions, and as dusk fell, the wind built up to a new fury. The Palace tent shook and bent under the force of the wind, and all of us took the precaution, once again, of packing rucksacks preparing for a quick retreat – though where we could have retreated to, I am not at all sure! Nick and Dave, in an effort to build up their stamina, slept on oxygen and as a result slept through the storm.

Next morning, it was still gusty but the clouds had at last cleared and the sun was blazing down from a deep blue sky – but any feeling of warmth was illusory. Outside, it was −10°C and even with the stoves going at full, fumy blast, the temperature inside the tent never attained freezing point. But the sun was welcome as we crawled out of the tents, shook ourselves and assessed the damage. The camp was almost entirely buried, with the ends of the tents sticking out of the snow like the prows of sinking ships after a U-boat attack on a World War II convoy. We took stock. Banners of spindrift were blowing from the ramparts of Nuptse, forming huge, inverted whirlpools over the Western Cwm. It seemed unlikely that the boxes at Camp 4 could have survived their ordeal. I examined the camp through binoculars; it looked as if they were still standing, but it was difficult to assess just how damaged the tents were. Dropping down to Camp

3, I saw no sign of Graham's box – it seemed completely buried by the avalanches of snow which must have poured down the Face during the night. What was more worrying, he did not come up on the eight o'clock radio call. This did not mean too much, however, since Graham often overslept the first call of the day. Even so, I was worried, and opening up an hour later was very relieved to hear Graham's voice, still full of sleep, slightly belligerent, very matter-of-fact.

'What's all the fuss about? Slept like a log up here. The box could take any amount of snow and I'd be fine if I didn't have to worry about you buggers down there !'

'Sounds good, Graham. Do you need anything?' I asked. 'We'll try to get up to you today.'

'I'm running a bit low on coffee and biscuits – and could do with a gas lamp – but there's plenty of food up here.'

'We'll try to get them up to you. You've done a great job sitting it out.'

'It's given me plenty of time to think. I've come up with one or two ideas that we can discuss when I get back down.'

'Do you want to come down for a rest?'

'I could do with one. You get a bit tired of a six-foot long box after a time, but I'll be fine until you manage to send someone else up to take over.'

One problem solved, I then got on to Base Camp. As always, Tony Tighe answered the radio. He took all the calls at morning and dusk throughout the expedition, was always calm and cheerful, and very often did an excellent diplomatic job, softening demands for more supplies which came from the mountain to Jimmy, or complaints at a failure to send something up from Base Camp. They, also, had had a rough night at Base Camp, with tents collapsing under the snow. What was more serious, they were low on food supplies, expecting the latest consignment to arrive that day, but with the snowfall the route was blocked all the way back to Lobuje, and it looked as if it would take some days to force a new trail out, diverting manpower from the equally crucial job of re-establishing the route back up the Ice Fall.

I wanted to get into communication with Camp 1, to ensure that the Sherpas there had survived the night. From previous experience, we knew that the winds and snow-drifts at this lower camp could be even worse than in the Western Cwm itself.

'Tony, could you tell Hamish and Dougal that I'd like them to force the route up to Camp 1 today. Apart from anything else, we must get some more paraffin up as soon as possible,' I said.

'Could you wait a minute, I'll see what they think.'

A few minutes later – 'Hello, Chris, are you still on the air, over.'

'Yes, over.'

'I'm afraid they don't think there's much chance of getting up today. The snow's very deep and apparently the Ice Fall has shifted quite a bit near the top. They reckon it'll take a couple of days to clear the route. They say why not send someone down from your camp?'

'O.K. fair enough, I'll do that.'

I had no choice but to agree – it had taken two days, earlier on in the expedition, to clear the Ice Fall after a storm that had been considerably less serious than the most recent one. The question was who to send back. Whoever went down would almost certainly have to stay the night, perhaps longer. It would have been easier had I kept Doug and Mick back at Camp 1, but since I had let them come up the previous day, making the trail afresh practically all the way, it seemed a bit much to send them all the way back again. Nick and Dave, on the other hand, might even benefit from a trip to a slightly lower altitude, especially if these high winds were to persist for several days, holding us down in the Cwm. And so I decided to send them back to Camp 1, knowing full well that they would not be too keen to go.

They agreed without argument, however, and got ready that morning for what was obviously going to be an epic descent. Dave Bathgate described their experience in his diary, immediately after reaching Camp 1.

Only the top third of the green Stormhaven kitchen-tent at Camp 1 protruded from the white expanse of new spindrift. The canvas was taut, and where it disappeared under the snow, a thick layer of ice had formed. The ridge pole, although strengthened by odd sections of metal, sagged alarmingly. All the sleeping tents were buried under ten feet of snow, likewise the expedition gear and food supplies.

Nick and I arrived at this scene of devastation after a four-hour trip down the Cwm from Camp 2. Normally, the journey from 2 to 1 takes an hour, but ploughing through the deep powder, after a four-day Himalayan holocaust, was strenuous work, even with the aid of snow-shoes. Most of the way, only the top few inches of our six-foot marker flags were showing, and there was a half-mile section where they had disappeared altogether. This we put down to a huge, powder-snow avalanche from the Nuptse Ridge. The wind often whipped the spindrift into an opaque cloud which blinded us completely, penetrating clothing, stinging our faces, so that we just had to stop in our tracks until it cleared. Our breath froze to our beards and our beards froze to our clothing. It was bitterly cold.

From their past performance, we knew that the Camp 1 Sherpas were a competent bunch, but even so, we could not be certain that they had survived the last storm. The surface area around Camp 1 was flat, and so the snow had drifted evenly to a depth of about ten feet. Nick and I stood on the wind crust and peered down at a Sherpa who was digging out the remains of a Tunnel tent. The orange roof was just visible and the hole was already four feet deep. Strangely enough, the tent seemed to have retained its shape – a tribute to the robust Tunnel design.

Great clods of hard-packed snow were being tossed by invisible men from several other holes nearby – it was just like an archaeological dig. The Vango tents, which are the conventional triangular shape, were in a much more pitiful condition than the Tunnel tent. They had collapsed, foundered under the pressure of tons of compact snow. Surely, if anyone had been in those tents they would have suffocated. One of the diggers lifted his goggles onto his forehead, and smiled up at us.

'Hallo, Sahib, you want tea?'

It was Ang Dawa, the Sirdar of the Camp 1 Sherpas. Our first concern was to ascertain that there had been no casualties and Ang Dawa assured us that his team were all well and in good spirits, but there was much hard digging to be done. It was a terrific boost to our morale to see how well they had coped with the situation and we congratulated them on their survival.

We descended a snow staircase and entered the narrow entrance of the Stormhaven kitchen-tent. At the far end an enormous dixie of water was bubbling on the top of two roaring primus stoves. It was warm in the tent and a pleasant relief to be sheltered from the buffeting of the wind and spindrift, which was still swirling outside. With the rise in temperature, the ice which was caked on our beards and woollen hats melted, and dribbled down our fronts. The steaming mugs of tea warmed our insides, and our hands clasped round the hot cups began to thaw out. We sat on some gear salvaged from the abandoned tents, which was arranged along the sides of the tent, with the Sherpas' personal kit. Ang Dawa told us how, during the worst night of the storm, they all had had to evacuate their tents in favour of the kitchen-tent and how, to save this last refuge from destruction, they had taken turns throughout the night, working in pairs, to keep it clear of snow.

We could imagine how miserable this experience must have been. The spindrift penetrates every nook and cranny of clothing, freezing whilst you are exposed to the cold and the wind, and then melting and soaking everything once you return to the warmth of the tent.

Fortified by the strong tea, we spent the rest of the day uncovering as much equipment as possible and then retired once more to the kitchen-tent, where the Camp 1 cook had been preparing a meal. He served up a special corned beef hash for Nick and myself, which we washed down with scalding, sweet tea. There were ten of us, all sitting shoulder to shoulder, knees up to our chins, because all available floor space was taken up with steaming dixies, pans of rice and plates of *sempi* – the porridge-like dish of *tsampa* that the Sherpas live on.

At about 8.30 p.m., after everyone had eaten and drunk their fill, Ang Dawa said, 'You sleep here, Sahib.' I had expected to spend the night crouched in my present position. How on earth could we all stretch out in this confined space?

'We do whatever Sherpas do,' I said.

At a word from Ang Dawa, the entire tent erupted into activity. Kitchen and eating gear was polished clean, large kettles and dixies were stacked inside one another and placed neatly aside, rucksacks were retrieved from behind food packs, and soon plastic-covered foam mattresses were spread out on the icy floor. Next, sleeping bags and all sorts of down equipment began to fill the area, and the floor level seemed to be raised a couple of feet. We joined in all this, and soon ten bodies were securely, warmly covered in down, lying head to toe, side by side, one on top of the other.

Sherpa heads popped up in the most unlikely places, between piles of down. Ang Dawa took the responsible position beside the tent entrance. We all chatted and smoked for about half an hour after we had settled in, as the light from a single kerosene candle flickered across the frost-encrusted canvas roof. Everything was organized. There was nothing to do but to get some sleep.

Back at Camp 2, although our situation was not nearly as uncomfortable as that at Camp 1, we had a much more tense day. It had started that morning, before Nick and Dave set out for Camp 1. A number of Sherpas had been sitting around in the Palace tent and Nick was trying to pack his rucksack, searching for gear in the chaos of kitchen equipment, other people's gear and the general clutter of a camp. Suddenly, he had erupted into a fury that was nearly hysterical.

'Come on, get the hell out of here, all of you – straight away !' he shouted at the Sherpas.

'Nick, for God's sake, calm down,' I said. 'We can't afford to put their backs up. They're only sheltering from the wind. They haven't got a communal tent.'

'Well, how the hell do you expect me to get all my stuff sorted out to go down to Camp 1?' he muttered. But his outburst had subsided. It had had very little to do with the presence of the Sherpas in the tent; it was the suppressed nervous tension of four days' hammering by the wind that had burst out, and it was to occur again before the day was out.

Just after Nick and Dave had left, Pasang was struggling with his recalcitrant stoves and allowed one of them to gush flames up to the roof, and throughout the kitchen compartment. This time it was Barney who blew up. He had become increasingly irritated by Pasang's low morale, and the trouble he had been having in keeping the kitchen going during the storm.

'Switch off the kerosene, before you burn the tent down,' we all shouted. Pasang did so but then, in a fury of rage, kicked the fuming stove across the tent smashing it beyond repair in the process. Barney's self-control broke down, and he told Pasang in fluent, and very violent Nepali, exactly what he thought of him. We could not understand it, but the meaning was all too clear !

Half an hour later, I was outside the tent, helping to dig out another buried tent, when I heard a babble of voices build into a crescendo of anger. Normally, I tried to keep out of day-to-day disputes, leaving them to Barney, who could speak the language and was handling all daily administration, but this was obviously something serious. I hurried over to find Barney surrounded by a group of shouting, near-hysterical Sherpas. It looked as if it could easily turn to violence.

'What's happened?' I asked.

'They say I hit Pertemba,' Barney said, looking drawn, near the point of breakdown.

'Did you?'

'Yes, but not on purpose. Pertemba had taken the tarpaulin covering the dump of gear, to mend his tent. I was trying to persuade him that we needed it for the gear – if we have another snowfall we could lose a lot of stuff, if it's not covered up. I was explaining this to him, and in gesturing with this bit of tent pole, accidentally hit him on the hand. I dropped the pole immediately, and apologized, but you'd think I'd stabbed him for all the fuss he made.'

'He did it on purpose,' Pertemba broke in furiously. 'Doctor Sahib hit me!'

'I saw it – it was on purpose,' shouted Anu. 'Doctor Sahib does not like Sherpas; he shouts at us and is rude to us. He doesn't treat us when we are sick.'

'Look, calm down, all of you,' I shouted over the din. 'Pertemba, Doctor Sahib is the good friend of the Sherpas. He would never hit you, it was a mistake.'

'It wasn't; he did it on purpose,' said Pertemba. His hands were trembling and I could see he was on the point of tears. There was no sense at all in any of the Sherpas. They were in a state of hysteria, created by the hammering we had received in the last four days. All I could do was to try and soothe them and Barney down. I talked for half an hour, trying to bring home to them the wonderful, selfless work Barney had done on their behalf in looking after them when they had been sick or injured, and in running Camp 2 generally. Eventually, they all calmed down, and Pertemba even shook hands with Barney. I felt completely drained by the experience, and was trembling myself when I got back into the big Palace tent.

I suspect we needed that outburst, for that night, when all the Sherpas piled into the Palace tent for the evening meal and chat, there was a feeling of renewed optimism and real friendship. Everyone went out of their way to be pleasant to each other, as if to make up for the fury of the morning. The wind had dropped, and there was hardly a puff of spindrift blown from the summit walls of Nuptse and Lhotse. There was not a cloud in the sky, and as the line of sunlight crept up the South West Face of Everest and the great hanging glacier of Lhotse it turned from a rich yellow to a mellow rose. The sky darkened into the deepest purple and a sickle moon hung poised over the South Col. It was difficult to believe there had ever been a storm and wind, and savage argument in the still, silent dusk. That night Pasang excelled himself in his cooking and we excelled ourselves in the expression of our appreciation. The unity of the group, so fragile under stress, was restored.

But I could not relax completely. I had to plan our next moves, was beginning to wonder already if I had been over-pessimistic about the progress we could make in the lee of the storm. That night, on the radio, we agreed that Dave and Nick would go down to meet the Sherpas and Dougal, who would try to re-open the route up the Ice Fall. That day they had only got half-way up, to find that another sérac collapse was endangering the route. Meanwhile, Mick and Doug were going to move up to Camp 3 on their way up to Camp 4, and Graham, who had now been alone for a week, was to return to Camp 2 for a rest.

We all slept well that night, the first quiet night for a fortnight. The next day, Jimmy Roberts reported that the French were making their summit bid on Pumori. We could see them through the binoculars, tiny little black dots moving slowly but surely up the summit snow cone of the mountain, which was only a little higher than our Camp 3. They had completed their objective; we had barely started. This did mean, however, that we should be able to borrow some of the box tents they had with them. Talking it over with Hamish on the midday radio call, we agreed that since we could buy at least three box tents from the French now that they had succeeded and would need them no longer, we could abandon our plans for using his own reinforced, home-made box, and concentrate on making progress as fast as possible up the mountain.

It is amazing how quickly pessimism can turn into optimism with a change in the weather. At the height of the storm, although

I don't think any of us contemplated giving up our attempt, everything had seemed as black as possible. Camp 4 would be a total write-off, it was going to take several days to resume communications through the Ice Fall, and at least a week to deploy; and yet, once the storm ended and the sun blazed down once more into the Western Cwm, it all seemed so different. We were full of hope once more. Perhaps the boxes at Camp 4 could be salvaged; perhaps we could start pushing the route out in the next day or so.

Next day, Doug and Mick were due to go up to Camp 3 on their way back up the mountain, while I was going down towards Camp 1 with four of our Sherpas, to meet those sent up by Dave and Nick. In turn they were going to drop down towards Base, to meet the Sherpas coming up. In carrying out this seemingly innocuous task, I had my own narrowest escape on the mountain. The Sherpas were all roped together but, in common with all the climbers, I had not bothered and was stepping off the beaten track from time to time to take pictures of the Sherpas plodding through the snows, silhouetted against the sun which was hanging over the parapets of Nuptse. We were about halfway down the Western Cwm when I stepped off the track once again and suddenly found myself with my head just below the surface of the snow. It happened too suddenly for me to be frightened, but I realized that I did not dare move or struggle, for fear of disturbing the surrounding snow which held me in place over the hidden crevasse.

'Give me a pull,' I shouted, and the Sherpas edged towards the hole I had made, tossed me a loop of rope and pulled me out. I was landed, like a panting codfish, shaking slightly from the shock of my near-escape. I was even more shaken when I looked into the abyss I had uncovered. The crevasse, dark and bell-like, stretched out into black shadows from the tiny hole I had made in its roof. Had the snow not held me, I could have fallen a hundred feet or so. I took a photograph of the hole and we trooped on down the Western Cwm, careful to stay on the track. That moment of inattention, caused by concentrating on photography rather than the route, had very nearly cost me my life. Down we went, to the porters who had come up from Camp 1, full of grins, laden with much-needed food and, even more important, the mail. I shoved the latter in my pack-frame so that I could let Doug and Mick have their letters before they set off for Camp 3.

About half-way back I began to feel the need for a rest. Pausing, I sat on the pack-frame and then, like a small boy looking for Christmas presents, went through the mail to see if I had a letter from my wife, Wendy. There were two; I opened them with frozen fingers, clumsy with cold and excitement, fumbled with the envelope, dropped it and saw it blow away, across trackless snow. With no thought for hidden crevasses, I just dived after the letter, spreadeagled in the snow as I grabbed at it, reached it and then lay there as I read, tearful in my emotion at hearing from home.

Once at Camp 2, there were decisions to make. On the way down and back, I had spent much of the time deciding how I could speed up the run out towards Camp 5 and yet, at the same time, readjust the pairing so that each pair would be getting the objective which they had come to accept as their own. I described my predicament in my diary that night:

1 November 1972 – Wednesday.

A right bloody mess I've made – a real cock-up. The problem is, I've sent Nick and Dave, slightly against their wills – or rather, very much against their wills – down to Camp 1 when, in actual fact, it would probably have been wiser to have sent Doug and Mick straight back down even though they had just come up the previous day. The trouble is, by sending Nick and Dave back down, now that the weather's really good, I've got two carefully balanced teams out of sequence. Now that we've got some movement going, the obvious thing is for Mick and Doug to be pushed up to get Camp 4 started. Originally, we agreed that they should do this, and spend two or three days sorting out Camp 4, so that Nick and Dave could move through. But there shouldn't be three or four days' work – we really need to be pushing out as fast as we possibly can, taking advantage of what good weather we have in the few remaining days before it gets desperately cold.

Doug and Mick went up yesterday with the agreement that they should just spend two or three days, and then come back. But then, last night, Graham came down from Camp 3 bubbling over, obviously having done a lot of thinking, and he put across the very strong point of view that we should be pushing out fast. I had already been thinking of sending up two Sherpas today from Camp 2, straight up to 4, so that Doug and Mick would have their help to speed things up. Graham made me think that we really should send four Sherpas and get the whole camp sorted out so that, ideally, they could make a carry to Camp 5 tomorrow and thus hurry the move up to Camp 5. But, of course, this immediately brings up the problem of Nick and Dave. One way, of course, would be for Doug and Mick to do the route from Camps 5 to 6 and for Nick and Dave to do the Rock Band – they are undoubtedly quite as capable as Doug and Mick – but, and this is a very big 'but' – Doug and Mick have always been promised the Rock Band, and have come to accept it. In addition, although I don't think Doug and Mick are any better mountaineers than Dave and Nick, they might be just that bit more determined – I don't know.

Anyway, it has caused an unholy row, and the most obvious thing now seems to be to get the thing back to its original pattern – to give Dave and Nick the route to Camp 6, and Doug and Mick the actual Rock Band. I pushed around various ways of doing this last night, slightly defensive against Graham urging me to change my plan but, at the same time, feeling that it was necessary and saying so at the seven o'clock call last night.

The problem I was trying to solve was how to get Nick and Dave back into the front, without holding up our advance. It was 1 November, the day that Mick and Doug were to move back up to Camp 4. Having sent four Sherpas up to Camp 4 that same day, I was hoping that on the following day they would be able to make the carry to Camp 5 and the day after that, actually move in. Nick and Dave, however, were only due to reach Camp 2 that day (1 November), having the previous day fulfilled an important task in going down to meet Dougal and Hamish and then transporting the loads by means of an aerial rope-way across the big crevasse immediately below Camp 1. This crevasse had opened up, from being about three feet wide, to fifty feet, in a matter of weeks. Getting back to Camp 2 on 1 November meant that the soonest they could possibly reach Camp 5 would be 4 November, the day after Mick and Doug had reached it. This seemed a sound compromise, for it seemed unlikely that Doug and Mick would be able to run the full route out to Camp 6 in the day they were there by themselves, and this would give Dave and Nick the satisfaction of completing that route as originally planned.

I explained all this on the radio call of the morning of 1 November. Unfortunately, Doug infuriated Nick by making the claim that, 'We do want the Rock Band because we've been planning on it, and Mick wants to film it,' a sentiment which was perfectly fair. (In fact, I also wanted Mick to film it.) This, however, made Nick see red; he wrote in his diary:

This remark made me fume with rage. I switched off the radio in a huff. Fumed all the way up the Cwm and, as a result, did the walk in three and a half hours, in spite of drifting and a not very good path.

I knew all too well that I was going to have an angry Nick on my hands when he arrived at Camp 2, even though I had tried to restore the original plan. My fears were amply justified. I had taken the precaution of keeping an eye out for him and went down to meet him, getting in the first broadside by apologizing for having had to send him down to Camp 1. Nick was literally trembling with rage, feeling that he had been supplanted by Doug and Mick. The root of Nick's indignation was the fact that I had given Doug and Mick the key role in the first place and was now maintaining it, when Nick had every right to feel that he deserved such a role every bit as much. He also pointed out that he had probably made the greatest sacrifice to come on the expedition, having come without pay. In actual fact, this put him in the same position as the rest of us, with the exception of Kelvin. On the other hand, all of us who earned a living partly around climbing would benefit very directly from the expedition.

In the mess tent I was backed up by Barney and Graham, as we cooled Nick down and tried to show him that in reality the original plan had hardly been changed. Even so, I could fully sympathize with his anger, and suspect that I would have felt much the same had I been in his shoes. Dave Bathgate, who arrived at Camp 2 about half an hour after Nick, was much more resigned than his partner, murmuring: 'Well, someone had to go down there – I suppose it might just as well have been us.'

The argument had cleared the air and, anyway, the objective combined with our residual friendship was too strong to disrupt our effort. That night we settled down to our evening meal with a feeling of restored harmony. The weather was perfect; Graham in a single day at Camp 2 had reorganized the camp, sorting out all the loads, putting up a special store tent and creating his own logistic empire. Success, once again, seemed within our grasp.

14

RETURN TO
THE FACE

31 October–7 November

Across the face, the wind gusted at over sixty miles per hour, blowing up clouds of spindrift, blinding the climbers and making any form of work on the wrecked camp site impossible. Mick and Doug had taken four hours to plod up the line of fixed ropes to Camp 4 – ropes which had to be cleared of snow every foot of the way; Jumars were perpetually iced up, so that they slipped ineffectively on the ropes. Behind the climbers were fifteen Sherpas, all of whom had come up from Camp 2, to pick up loads stockpiled at 3, to carry them on up to Camp 4. This meant that they climbed 3,600 feet in the day, a truly magnificent effort on their part, and one which they were to repeat on alternate days for the next ten days.

The tension and arguments born from our five storm-bound days were forgotten; we were looking forward once more, full of optimism in spite of the cold and wind, and the lateness of the season.

It was five o'clock in the afternoon before Doug and Mick reached Camp 4. Down in the Western Cwm, Camp 2 had been plunged into shadow for some hours, and the shadow line was already lapping up the Face. The Sherpas who had carried loads up to the camp dumped them wherever they could, tying them to the frames of the platforms, digging out little ledges in the hard snow, and then went whooping down the fixed ropes towards the relative comfort of Camp 2. But Doug and Mick with the two Sherpas Ang Phurba and Anu, who were staying up with them, had a long task in front of them before they could creep into the shelter of the boxes.

From below, the boxes had looked in reasonable shape, slightly misshapen, but still erect, brightly coloured huts clinging to the slope. On reaching them, however, Mick and Doug discovered that the boxes were filled with spindrift, like snow cubes parcelled in canvas. The frames of two of them had collapsed, and the snow inside had set as hard as concrete, hiding all the stoves and cooking pans left behind when the camp had been abandoned. There was no sign of any of the stores which had been carried up to Camp 4 before the storm; these, also, were concealed under the compacted spindrift. In some ways it was worse than establishing a camp from scratch; poles were bent, sockets jammed with ice, vital pieces missing – and the line of shadow creeping up the Face was a tide of darkness that would bring an instant drop in temperature. Fingers and toes were already nipped, but you couldn't hurry; everything had to be systematic; anything dropped was lost for ever. If you slipped, having forgotten to clip onto one of the safety ropes, you'd go all the way down to the bottom of the Cwm, smashed and dragged to bits over broken rocks protruding from the slope.

They dug out the tents, hacking away with the picks of their axes, then clearing the rubble with gloved hands, sifting it for parts of cooking stoves, movie cameras, pots, and items of personal equipment. Then they had to re-erect the boxes, manipulating frames to make the canvas fit over them. Six o'clock; time for the radio call. Doug opened up.

'Hello 2, this is 4. Can you hear me? Over.'

'Yes, you're loud and clear, how's it going?'

'Bloody desperate. We still haven't got anywhere to sleep tonight. Must close now; we'll open up in a couple of hours.'

And they went back to digging in the mellow evening sunlight, which gave only the illusion of warmth.

It was dark before they had patched up two boxes for the night – they still had to sort out stoves and cooking pots, collect snow for the evening brew and lie and wait for it to melt. It was ten o'clock at night before they had completed their meal and could curl up in their sleeping bags for a well-earned sleep. Not surprising that they missed the eight o'clock call next morning.

Even though tired from the effort of the previous day, Doug, with two Sherpas, made a carry up to Camp 5, while Mick, with the other two, did his best to dig out all the gear left at Camp 4 before the storm. I was particularly anxious to learn exactly what we had at Camp 4, for my own planning of the build-up to Camp 5. With Doug's carry, we had just enough gear at 5 for him to move up with Mick on the following day, and this is what they did.

And so they had another camp established, this time from scratch. A platform had to be dug, tents erected, all in the chilling cold. But at least Camp 5 was a more relaxing place than 4; it was situated in the shelter of an overhanging rock wall, on what must have been a broad rock ledge, covered in snow. While Mick dug out a platform, Doug ranged around taking photographs.

Attempting to get more in the frame of the camera, he stepped back, but still not getting quite enough, stepped back again, over the edge! Unroped, without his axe, it was fortunate that he had removed his gloves to take the pictures. He shot down the fifty-degree slope of hard snow, towards a vertical drop of about two thousand feet leading to the slopes below, a fall which he could never have survived.

With bare hands clawing at the snow, he kicked in with his cramponed boots and somehow, on the very brink of the drop, brought himself to a stop. He was still sufficiently cool to take a unique photograph looking straight down at Camp 4, fifteen hundred feet below, before kicking back up to the ledge!

Mick, digging away at the snow, had been blissfully unaware of this near-fatal accident. That night, they were both badly shaken by the experience, exhausted by the effort of making the camp, and chilled by the bitter cold of Camp 5. Up to this point Doug had fought shy of sleeping tablets, never trusting them, but now, perhaps in a state of shock and because of the savage cold, even inside the tent, he took three, which knocked him out for the night.

Next morning, 5 November, dawned fine, without a breath of wind on the mountain. My build-up seemed to be working out. Nick and Dave had spent the night at Camp 4 and were moving up to 5 to join Mick and Doug; Graham Tiso was moving up to Camp 4 to look after the camp and supervise the Sherpas. I was still at Camp 2, anxious to supervise the build-up from the orchestra stalls, though I was planning to move up to Camp 5 when the route had been established to 6. Things never go completely according to plan, however. I spent most of the morning examining the upper part of the Face through binoculars, anxious to see Mick and Doug start out on making the route back across the great snow gully towards Camp 6. It was easy to be impatient in the hot sun at Camp 2. It was very different up at Camp 5.

Because of the overhang guarding the camp, the sun did not reach it until two o'clock in the afternoon. Before that time, the camp was held in a vice of cool shadows which made movement outside the tents a refined form of torture; hands inside gloves, feet inside boots and overboots froze in a matter of seconds, once outside the shelter of the tent. That morning Doug, having missed the eight o'clock call, finally came up at nine o'clock, sounding punch-drunk with cold and altitude; the sleeping pills, also, must have had an effect.

He reported that they had managed to pitch a tent but had got mild frostbite in the process.

'You don't get the sun up here till after two. It's bloody cold at the moment. Your hands and feet freeze even if you go out of the tent for a couple of minutes.'

'Will you get out today?'

'We'll try, but you've no idea how cold it is.'

That had to satisfy me. It seemed a perfect day, not a breath of wind, not a sign of spindrift from the peaks around us. I spent most of the day gazing up at the great gully leading up to the Rock Band above Camp 5. To reach the snow rake that led across the base of the Rock Band, they would have to traverse back to the left over the top of the gully, to get beneath a subsidiary rock wall, before traversing back again over the camp and on towards the site of Camp 6. I could see the slow-moving figures of Nick, Dave and two Sherpas, the latter doing a carry to Camp 5, the former moving up to join Doug and Mick – but there was no sign of movement from Camp 5. As the day wore on, it became increasingly obvious that they were not going to leave camp. I felt all the frustration of the Commander sitting in the lush comfort of his headquarters, watching and wanting to drive on the troops in the frontline. Not being there myself, I was unable to implement my plans, not being fully aware of just how savage were the conditions there. In the last day or so, we were becoming aware that we barely had the carrying capacity and drive to make more than one serious attempt at cracking the Rock Band and then making a summit bid.

So far, in keeping with my basic plan I had held Hamish and Dougal back, but could I afford to hold them back as reserve any longer? I felt that I could not – they were fit, the most experienced pair I had, and raring to go. Whichever pair moved up to Camp 6, they were going to have to move quickly and decisively on the Rock Band, if they were to make a summit assault. A delay at this stage meant that our chances of making such an assault must inevitably recede, for we simply did not have the capability of sustaining the supply of oxygen bottles from Camp 4 to 5, and then to 6. The trouble was that even climbers resting at Camp 5 used up oxygen, for it was essential to sleep on oxygen, not just for sleep itself, but also to retain warmth. The human body without extra oxygen is unable to sustain its warmth at that altitude, no matter how much down gear covers it.

And so I knew that I should have to adapt my plans; use Mick, Doug, Nick and Dave to establish the route to Camp 6, and then supersede Mick and Doug by bringing Hamish and Dougal straight through for the push on the Rock Band. I was under no illusion about the problems that this change in the plan would cause, for I knew that Mick and Doug had set their hearts on having first go at the Rock Band.

That evening at the five o'clock call Doug told me on the radio, 'I'm sorry we didn't get out today. Mick has got bad piles. We're buggered; we're going to have to come down for a rest.'

'Can't you stay up for just a few more days – just to support Nick and Dave in making the route up to Camp 6.'

'It's no good, we're in a really bad way. Both of us have mild frostbite. It's been a hell of a job just getting the camps up. We've had to work into the night. You've no idea how bloody awful conditions are up here. We must have a rest before tackling the Rock Band.'

Then I made a tactical mistake.

'Look Doug, I'm going to have to push Dougal and Hamish up

to try the Rock Band; we just can't afford to keep them in reserve any longer. Can't you keep going for just a few more days to make the route up to 6 and then keep them supported?'

There was a silence for a couple of minutes – Doug was obviously talking it over with Mick, and then Mick's voice came over the radio:

'Up to your old tricks is it, Chris?' he said.

This was a reference to my decision on the Annapurna South Face expedition to push Don Whillans and Dougal Haston through to the front, when the rest of the team seemed to be tiring.

'It's not a question of that,' I said. 'It's simply that you and Doug are obviously tired and that we can't afford to hang around. Dougal and Hamish are the best-rested pair and it's time they had a go out in front.'

'But they're not acclimatized,' said Mick. 'If they come straight up here from Camp 1, they're going to have trouble and will probably go no better than us.'

'I'm sorry, Mick. I disagree. They've been once to Camp 5 without trouble and I think they'll do it again. We can carry this argument on when you get back down.'

And so it ended. I didn't relish Doug's and Mick's return when, no doubt, they would present me with the full broadsides of their arguments. That night Nick, who had reached Camp 5 in the late afternoon with Dave, commented in his diary:

Mick and Doug both invalids; I suspect a bit psyched out by cold and altitude. Doug had a headache and Mick, piles. Also their stove kaput. They want to go down tomorrow.

It was a long evening as we had to cook for them as well – very cold (suspect less than −30°) and there aren't enough foam mats. More to say, but have cold hands.

Next morning Nick was so impressed by the cold that he broke into the eight o'clock call while I was talking to Graham at Camp 4.

'This is Nick at 5, this is Nick at 5. I must come in please, I must come in.'

'O.K. Nick, what's the trouble? Over.'

'It's quite incredibly cold up here. You can have no idea how cold it is,' he said. 'We must have more sleeping bags and foams. You need two sleeping bags each and a double thickness of foams. One of the stoves has broken down as well. We must have two stoves to each tent.'

'O.K. Nick, we'll get these up to you as soon as possible. Can you get out today?'

'Doug and I are going to run the rope out towards the Rock Band, while Mick films us, and Dave sorts out the camp site. We've only got two oxygen sets working at the moment. Doug's has packed up, and one of those we brought up from Camp 4 isn't working properly. Doug and Mick want to come down today after doing their bit of work.'

'O.K. Pertemba and Jangbo will join you today. They've got Graham's and my oxygen sets.'

Doug had felt a lot better that morning and was keen to contribute to the day's climbing before coming back down for a rest. Dougal and Hamish, also, had been influenced by the previous evening's radio call. They had heard Mick's comment about their lack of acclimatization, and, perhaps partly to prove him wrong, had come storming up to Camp 2 in a mere hour and a half from Camp 1. The previous day they had spent trying to safeguard the route from the Ice Fall.

There was no wind, but a light veil of cloud hid the top of Everest as we all prepared to sit it out, gazing up, impotent to influence events, at the climbers working from Camp 5.

Nick described the day in his diary.

Woke 5 a.m. when the oxygen ran out, shivered for one and a half hours, and then got up to make a brew; view at sunrise, mind-blowing. Eventually, set off with Doug to make the route. It was very cold for the sun was hidden by cloud clinging to the top of Everest.

We ran out about six hundred feet of rope diagonally, back left across to the end of the little Rock Band, at the start of the long rake going back below the Rock Band. Here there were a few old ropes draped across the bare rocks left by the previous expedition. My turn to lead. I climbed the rocks, partly pulling on the ropes, until a few feet up. I must have pulled too hard; a peg came out and I teetered backwards, almost off balance, but somehow managed to lunge into the rock. After that I stopped using the rope and climbed the pitch more or less properly. It was quite hard and the first really technical climbing I had done since the Ice Fall. It wasn't made any easier by the oxygen kit upsetting my balance and the mask and goggles constantly frosting up. Right at the top the rock became crumbly and I had to make a very precarious mantelshelf on to a ledge covered with ice.

Doug then came up and ran out the next reel of rope all the way to the foot of the Rock Band. I followed but my oxygen gave out when I still had a hundred feet to go (I had started out on a three-quarters-full tank). I suppose there wasn't really much point in my struggling up to Doug's high point, but somehow it seemed such a tangible end to the day, to be there at the foot of the Rock Band. There was, too, the thought, always in the back of my mind, that perhaps I would never ever get any higher. Moreover, having a few pegs with me it seemed logical to leave them at the high point, though that was a justification more than anything else. I just wanted to get there and touch the Rock Band. Without oxygen, every step was an effort – only a hundred feet, yet it never seemed to get any closer; I was shattered when I reached it. That day we had run about 1200 feet and reached around 26,700 feet. Also I had come up from 1900 feet in only five days.

I was very tired by the time I got back to Camp 5. Doug had already pushed on down for Camp 2. Graham Tiso was there and said that the temperature that morning at Camp 4 had been −38°C. That means that our temperature must have been around −45°C.

Graham had new crampon straps for me and I put them on then and there, while the camp was still in the sun, scared of how cold it would be in the morning. Even so, I nearly got frostbitten fingers in the process, and my fingers were tender all next day.

At about 8 p.m. the Sherpas who have replaced Doug and Mick, called me out, asking about how their sleeping oxygen gear worked. I gave them half-an-hour's pep talk and blundered around in the dark looking for the oxygen kit.

It was a very tiring day.

Meanwhile back at Camp 2, Doug and Mick had arrived. That night they accepted my change in plan without comment, though Doug asked several searching questions about my plans for the next few days. Next morning, however, he came into the sleeping compartment I was sharing with Barney.

'Can I talk about our role on the mountain?' he said.

'Yes.'

'Look, I've been looking forward to doing the Rock Band for two and a half months now, and had got it firmly fixed in my mind that I was going to do it. I don't see really why we shouldn't – I don't see that anything's changed. We could go straight up tomorrow.'

'But Doug, if you needed a rest so badly, how can you possibly have had one if you stay down here only a day? It just doesn't make sense.'

'But you've been planning this all along; it's as Mick said, you're up to your old tricks again. In some ways you're no better than Herrligkoffer in the way you're manipulating people.'

And so it went on. Eventually I saw red and suggested that if that was how he felt he should start heading for Kathmandu. Barney just sat there quietly, sympathetic and friendly, the mere presence of him providing a calming influence.

As Doug and I reached a climax to our argument, we temporized, each of us realizing that we could not afford to break up the expedition, but more, I think, we both valued the relationship and friendship we had built up over the previous weeks and realized the danger of destroying this. I tried to explain to him how badly we were up against it, and how this now seemed the only course open.

Eventually Doug said, 'Well it'll take a day or so to get used to the idea,' and we left it at that. I felt grateful to him for his acceptance of something about which he obviously still disagreed. Later on that day Mick looked in.

'I disagree with what you've done, but I've had enough of arguments.'

'Thanks Mick,' I said, 'I appreciate how you feel.'

This had been a real test for the expedition. Whether I had been right or wrong in my decision is immaterial. The important factor was that Doug and Mick, though believing me to be wrong, were able not only to accept my decision but to then give Hamish and Dougal their loyal support. Perhaps most important of all, we remained friends, after having had what could easily have been a bitter row.

Meanwhile, back on the Face it was as cold as ever. Graham at

Camp 4 was matter-of-fact and cheerful, having made a carry to Camp 5 without using oxygen, admittedly with a nominal load. His main function was just to sit it out at the camp, supervising the Sherpas. Up to this point the Sherpas had two successive carries before returning to Camp 2 for a well-earned rest. We were trying to persuade them to make three. We were getting magnificent help from the Sherpas at this stage of the expedition, both on the 2 to 4 run and the one from Camp 4 to 5.

Up at Camp 5, Dave Bathgate was going to try to force the route out towards Camp 6. That night he wrote in his diary.

Up as early as possible, then start to kit out the Sherpas (Pertemba and Jangbo) with oxygen. They have not used it before; what a place to learn! We wasted almost two hours in the freezing cold, fitting them up before we set out, just after one thirty in the afternoon. My oxygen set started to pack in (iced up); I managed to fix it so that day I did get a proper flow. At Nick's high point, I decided to run out the old nylon (I think German) rope. It was iced up and tangled but if I hadn't done it others might be reluctant to use it under these conditions. Just as the sun dropped below Nuptse I had run out the nylon and started on the big white reel. It's a clean run on snow all the way up to Camp 6, but it was also very nearly dark. We got back to 5 before total darkness, very cold and tired but Nick had the brew on.

They were cold and tired but they knew the kind of contentment you always gained when out in front. The struggle was simple, rewarding and very positive.

Back at Camp 2, I was grappling with the problems of our supply line. Chris Brasher had arrived the previous day, after a night at Camp 1, bustling with energy.

'It strikes me you've got very little time to make your summit bid. Shouldn't you get Hamish and Dougal up there fast?' he suggested.

'It's not quite as simple as that, Chris,' I replied. 'It's no good having them up at Camp 6 unles they have the wherewithal to actually make some progress with enough oxygen, fixed rope and food to keep them going. At the moment we still haven't even got the route run out.'

The problem was that we could only just sustain four Sherpas at Camp 4 with Graham; in turn, these could barely keep up with the needs of four climbers actually in residence at Camp 5, let alone build up the stockpile of oxygen and fixed rope needed at Camp 6. There seemed only one solution, to build up Camp 5 before sending Hamish and Dougal up, supported by Doug and Mick. And then I thought of a way of speeding up the process at least a little. The Sherpas at Camp 4 should be able to support two climbers at 5, and at the same time, build up enough gear for the two at 5 to start ferrying loads up to Camp 6. And so I made my plan. I hoped that Nick and Dave would complete the route to Camp 6 that day, and I, with the Sherpa Ang Phurba, was going to set out on the journey up the Face, to occupy Camp 5 and, hopefully, make the three carries that I calculated would be needed to stock 6, ready for Dougal and Hamish to move in. It would take me three days to reach Camp 5, but in that time the Sherpas at Camp 4 would have further time to stock the Camp. What a web of logistics – and yet these have their own fascination. The problem was to implement these plans, forcing one's resolve against the harsh wind, the effects of altitude, and the growing fatigue caused by the two months' struggle.

Back at Camp 5, it was to be Nick's and Dave's big day; for them, in all probability, the end of the expedition. Their goal was not the summit of Everest – just the site of Camp 6. That night, Dave headed his entry in his diary – 'Tuesday, 7 November. This is the day of triumph and disaster.'

On this, their third day at Camp 5, they knew their strength and determination were being steadily drained by the bitter cold. Nick wrote in his diary – 'This was to be our big day. All four of us were to make a shit or bust attempt for 6 using the French oxygen. We were set up, and ready to leave at 10 a.m.! Quite an achievement.'

But as so often happens at altitude, there were endless delays. They were planning to use the French oxygen bottles we had brought with us for the final stages on the mountain. We had two types, a hundred and seventy bottles made by the British firm Luxfer; each weighed seventeen pounds and had a capacity of around 1200 litres. The French bottles, left over from my Anna-purna South Face expedition, weighed only twelve pounds, yet carried nearly a thousand litres. Since they had a definite capacity–weight ratio advantage, we were hoping to use the latter high on the mountain, where the weight on your back becomes critical. We had a specially designed thread converter, which enabled us to use the French bottles with our American oxygen units. Hamish had tried these out at Base Camp, where they had worked satisfactorily but now, at altitude, perhaps because of the extreme cold, it was impossible to screw the adaptors tight enough either to the French bottles or to the American reducer valves. There was no choice, therefore, but to use what British bottles there were. Unfortunately, there were only three, one of which had a pressure of only 200 p.s.i., when maximum capacity was 3,000; another had a pressure of 1800, and the third was full.

By this time, Nick and Dave were both cursing but there was nothing they could do about it except make do with the bottles, for they were still determined to make the push for Camp 6. They explained the problem to the Sherpas who agreed to take one hundred-metre rope each (weighing about fifteen pounds a time) without using oxygen, a truly magnificent and very loyal gesture. Dave took the full bottle and Nick took the half-full one, but just as they were ready to set out, Dave began having trouble with his demand valve – it was not functioning properly. They had already lost half the morning; and so Nick set out with Pertemba and Jangbo, leaving Dave to catch up. But Dave's misfortune was not finished. Fingers and mind numbed with cold, he fumbled with his pack-frame, trying to pack it, then dropped it, and watched it toboggan down the slope, out of sight. But he didn't give up – there's a dogged quality in Dave. He improvised a harness for the oxygen bottle and set out after the others. He never caught up with them, however, and continued to experience trouble with the set until it finally packed up altogether. By that time, he was so far behind that he could fulfil no useful function on the climb and therefore decided to return. On the way back he improved the fixed rope, safeguarding some of the long traverses by placing intermediate anchor points, one of them his own axe. As it turned out, it was providential that he did turn back.

Meanwhile, out in front, Nick was making good progress, reaching Dave's high point at about 1 p.m. The view was incredible, for he could now look over the wall of Nuptse at the serried peaks beyond, Ama Dablan, slender and delicate, Kangtega more massive and a hundred other mountains he couldn't identify. In the far distance, to the south, mountains merged into the haze of the Indian plains. There was no wind and the sun even seemed to have a touch of warmth in its empty glare.

Uncoiling one of the hundred-metre ropes, he set off round the corner, Pertemba paying it out as he climbed, scrambling over a series of small rocky outcrops that protruded from the snows just below the base of the Rock Band. The Rock Band itself towered above, grey black slatey rock, steep, seemingly unclimbable at that altitude – it was hard enough crossing comparatively easy snow slopes. Having run out a hundred metres, the rope tugged taut and Nick looked around for somewhere to anchor it. The snow was shallow, a crusty shell over the slate-like rock. He found a rocky encrustration, managed to hammer a rock peg into a crack and tied the end to it.

Whilst the two Sherpas climbed to join him, using the rope as a handrail, he could regain his breath, watch Dave, now far behind, still plodding very, very slowly up towards them; then he looked across the snow slope stretching beneath the Rock Band, towards a rocky spur that thrust down from the barrier which barred our way to the summit. That marked the site of Camp 6. Somewhere up there, folded in the angle of the wall, must be the gully which Dougal had assured us led through the Rock Band, a snow paved gateway through Everest's most formidable obstacle. Nick looked across, but his curiosity was dulled by the sheer fatigue of altitude. His target was Camp 6.

The Sherpas arrived, going strong in spite of the fact that they were without oxygen. Nick set out once again, trailing the second hundred-metre rope behind him. The going was now quite straightforward, across a slope of crisp snow, little more than forty degrees in angle. His cramponed boots bit reassuringly into the snow and it was just a question of plodding slowly, one foot in front of the other. But after only fifty paces, his oxygen ran out, leaving fifteen pounds of useless metal on his back. Taking off his pack-frame, he disconnected the cylinder and hurled it down the slope; because of the long traverse, there was no risk of hitting anyone lower down on the mountain. He carried on, immediately feeling much colder because of the lack of oxygen, but at least the pack was lighter.

He climbed a further hundred metres and was now about halfway across that final slope. He anchored the rope to a snow stake and the two Sherpas followed up. There were now only two ropes left – no point in both of the Sherpas staying, so Nick sent Jangbo back, to start making a brew for Pertemba on his return. Nick tied together the two ropes, one length of a hundred metres and the other forty, and set off once again.

He wrote in his diary:

I was obsessed with the need to reach Camp 6, and didn't notice the time. Eventually, forty feet short of 6, the rope went tight, so assuming I had run out all 470 feet, stopped to put in a dead man. I took my rucksack off, to take out the dozen pegs that were in it to leave at the high point. I fumbled and dropped the rucksack, which held my oxygen unit and spare gear, and watched it cartwheeling down the slope out of sight. I very nearly cried, I was so disgusted with my mistake; I'd never dropped anything like that before in all the time I'd been climbing. Then I pulled in the rope so that I could tie it as tautly as possible to the dead man, and fully forty feet came in – it must have been sticking somewhere when I had pulled it before and I could have got all the way to Camp 6 after all. In retrospect, though, it's just as well I didn't, since that last forty feet could easily have taken half an hour, and later on that length of time could have made all the difference between being dead and staying alive.

It was only then that I realized how late it was getting. The sun was dropping below the mountains on the far horizon. I actually said to myself, 'That is an absolutely fantastic view – but you shouldn't be seeing it – not from here anyway.' It's incredible how much colder it gets the moment the sun goes down. And it chose that very moment to start blowing. At first it wasn't too bad, but by the time I had got back to Pertemba, the wind was unbearable. We were having to go back straight into it, and it wasn't in gusts; it was a continuous blast of spindrift; you couldn't open your eyes, couldn't face into it.

Pertemba seemed in a befuddled state from the long wait, and the lack of oxygen. I said, 'We'll get down fast now Pertemba', and led the way down. The descent was a nightmare; it was pitch dark and you were handling the karabiners with totally numb hands. It wouldn't have been so bad if we'd been going straight down, but most of the way back entailed traversing with long gaps between the anchors. If we'd slipped, we'd have fallen quite a distance before the rope went tight. You couldn't wait for the gusts to die out, for the wind was now continuous; you just rushed on down, completely blind, into the wind. It was a matter of each man for himself; there was nothing we could do for each other. We were both very tired and I must admit I just charged off and left Pertemba behind. I feel a bit guilty now, but at the time if anything had gone wrong I don't think I could have done anything about it anyway; he just came about ten minutes behind. It was fantastically cold, pitch dark, with that howling wind and driving spindrift. God, I was relieved to see the tent, and hear Dave and Jangbo shout 'Hello, hello.' The zip door opened and there was this black hole, through which I just threw myself, crampons and all, and lay down in the dark. I cried in my relief at getting back.

Dave was very relieved to see me. He had spent the last hour holding the box up. A whipcrack of wind had lifted up the floor of the box with him lying on it, and had smashed the frame. After this he had had to hold it up braced across the box. Even so, he had a brew ready for me. We sat there, holding the sides of the tent up; I had a lovely hot drink clutched in my hands, but my hands, not just my fingers, were numb, likewise my feet from my ankles downwards: I was very worried about them. I thawed my hands out, gradually over the course of the evening; I was too cowardly to do it quickly; it's too painful that way.

And then Pertemba got back; that was a relief; I should never have forgiven myself if anything had happened to him. I crawled into the Sherpa tent next door, which was as warm as toast, being a double-skinned Tunnel tent, not a box like ours. We then had our evening pill ceremony; this was a regular feature, in which we gave them sleeping tablet, vitamin tablet, iron tablet, salt tablet, and a headache pill if they needed one. It showed that we were concerned about them, and helped to build up a real friendship. We got very close to those two Sherpas in those few days on the expedition. I felt we had built up a real friendship.

I had a long chat with Pertemba. He made a very relevant remark when he said: 'We nearly died.'

And we bloody well did. If I had been able to pull that extra forty feet of rope through first time off and had actually reached the site of Camp 6 – and I should have done, I was in that kind of mood –

we should probably have started down two hours later, and I think under those circumstances we should have been lucky to survive.

But at last they did have some luck. After they had sat up for a couple of hours, holding their box up against the gusting wind, it dropped, then vanished. Using the remainder of Dave's oxygen bottle, they were able to drop off to sleep till next morning.

There was no question of their staying up at Camp 5 to help build up supplies. Next morning Nick's hand and feet were still numb and white. He undoubtedly had frostbite; it was just a question of how bad it was. Dave's feet also were numb. As far as they were concerned the expedition was over, for it was unlikely that either would recover in time to be able to return to the Face before its outcome was decided one way or the other.

There is a wind chill scale which gives the effective temperature caused by wind, combined with cold. That previous night the temperature had probably been around about $-40°C$ and the wind had been gusting at anything up to a hundred miles per hour – the special Indian weather forecast had given winds of 220 kilometres per hour over the summit of Everest that night. These conditions are described as 'unbearable' on the wind chill scale.

Nick and Dave had certainly taken themselves beyond normal limits, in an effort to make the summit, not for themselves, but to make it possible for two others to move up to Camp 6, for that summit bid. That day had been the equivalent of their own summit push – a very unselfish one, for there was no chance of personal glory or that special satisfaction of standing on the highest point of the mountain. We all owed them our gratitude, and they had earned that personal fulfilment at having completed a task as well as anyone could possibly have done.

15

BUILDING UP
CAMP 6

8 November–13 November

It was a long road back to Camp 5. I had set out in the early evening from Camp 2 on my way up to Camp 3, the first staging post. We had spent most of the day watching the progress of Nick and the two Sherpas through the binoculars. Down in the comparative luxury of Camp 5, it was difficult to conceive just what it was like up there. The bottom snow slope of the Face was now engulfed in grey shadows, with the rocks of the Rock Band and the snows above dyed a rich yellow which faded into pink as dusk fell. That night, as I plodded up the fixed rope, there was no hint of the gale tearing across the slopes above. Here, I was protected by the great walls of Nuptse, was still below the cruel winds of the jet-stream which laps round the summit of Everest. The night was needle-cold, but at this altitude there was no wind. At the very time that Nick and Pertemba were fighting for their lives, I was able to sit on the snows, just four thousand feet below them, enjoying the utter peace of solitude after the previous crowded days. Action is so much easier than direction.

Camp 3 was unoccupied. I was to have the solitary remaining box to myself. Ang Phurba, who was going to join me at Camp 5, was to set out next morning from Camp 2, to make the journey to 4 in a single push. The solitude of that night was a peaceful balm; at Camp 2 there had never been any privacy, with the continuous chatter, and the complicated decisions affecting the course of the expedition which had to be made. Now, for a few hours, I was in a vacuum, out of contact with people. It was pitch-dark when I reached the box; I tumbled in with a sense of luxurious satisfaction, fumbled in the dark for a box of matches and eventually found one. Graham, the last tenant, had left everything in immaculate order. I found a candle, struck half a dozen matches before I finally coaxed one into life and lit it. The gentle glow filled the box. The stove alight, I shoved a panful of snow on it and got my sleeping bag out of the pack-frame. Soon I was ensconced, drowsy, listening to the purr of the stove. For me life was good, while three thousand feet above, Nick and Dave were sitting crouched in their box, trying to hold it together against the fury of the wind. Such are the contrasts of Everest!

I met them the next day as I pulled up the fixed ropes on my way to Camp 4. First were Pertemba and Jangbo, moving quite quickly and precisely, then going much slower, sitting down for rests every few yards. Nick and Dave, their faces worn with fatigue, ice clinging to their beards. It was good seeing them. Nick warned me of the conditions I should have to face at Camp 5, but somehow, I didn't really take it in; you couldn't until you had experienced it for yourself.

And then on up to Camp 4 – push the Jumar forward on the rope, pant into the oxygen mask, take a step forward, step up – slow but rhythmic – blank off the mind, think of anything but Everest. Although very slow, I got there in the end, to see the boxes of Camp 4, brightly coloured in the afternoon sun, clinging to the rocky slope. After passing the debris of the camp, empty tins, tattered pieces of tent, poles sticking out of the ice, I reached camp itself, pulling over the lip of the plaftorm to a mocking laugh from Graham.

'You took your time,' he said.

But he also had a mug of tea ready. I had become accustomed to Graham's hectoring manner by this time, had come to know and like the warmth under his bombastic exterior. Under his command, Camp 4 was beautifully organized. He knew the whereabouts of every single item of kit, had made the box tent as comfortable as possible, with a piece of pole in its middle pushing up the roof, to prevent it sagging. I crawled into the box with him, to be fed with mugs of tea and a magnificent three-course meal of soup, a hooch of fried steak-and-kidney pudding with mashed potato powder, followed by apple flake washed down with coffee cognac.

Next morning was a brilliant windless day. Graham and I

played with the little synch-sound super 8 mm. cine camera, trying to make a documentary of what life was like at Camp 4. It was one o'clock in the afternoon before I was ready to set out for Camp 5. This time I threaded my demand valve down inside my one-piece suit, the inlet from the tank coming into the suit through the side pocket slit, and then reaching the mask up the front, on the inside of the down suit. I hoped that by keeping the valve warm I should get better performance from the set. This was to prove the case. For the first time at altitude on the mountain, I seemed to be going strongly, didn't feel the need for rest, just put one foot in front of the other, and plodded remorselessly up the great gully. I seemed to have passed each landmark almost before I expected to see them, reached the top in just over the hour. As I came to the little red Tunnel tent, Ang Phurba, who had set out earlier, poked his head out, gave me a smile and then thrust out a big mug of tea. It was almost warm in the late afternoon sun and I felt enough spare energy to potter around the camp site, checking oxygen bottles for their pressures, stacking our meagre pile of supplies on the rocky shelf at the back of the ledge holding the Tunnel tent and the ruined box.

That night a deep sense of contentment swept over me as I snuggled into my sleeping bag and listened to the purr of the two gas stoves. Ang Phurba cooked the supper and then I fixed him up with his sleeping oxygen. To sleep on, we had a half tank, which I had used to reach Camp 5, with another half-tank to change onto when we ran out half-way through the night. Plastic masks cupped over our faces, the gentle hiss of oxygen was hypnotic, gently lulling us to sleep. We had double sleeping bags at Camp 5, a special Mountain Equipment sleeping bag inside the Fairy Down bag, each one of them normally amply warm enough for any conditions.

I woke up at 3 a.m. to a numbing cold that didn't so much come from the outside as from right inside of me and which then seeped slowly outwards, through my limbs. The hiss of oxygen was gone; I lay back for several minutes just summoning up the determination to change cylinders and at last took the plunge, opened the sleeping bag, feeling the cold air rush in – it was probably −40°C outside. After fumbling for the torch, I grabbed the fresh cylinder, fiddled with the valve of the dead bottle with fast numbing fingers and after a struggle changed them over. Reassured by the steady hiss I dropped back into sleep, feeling the life-giving warmth of the oxygen flow through my body.

At about six o'clock, the oxygen ran out once more, and I woke up again, lay cold, vacant-minded for a couple of hours. The roof of the tent and the upper parts of our sleeping bags were rimmed with hoar frost, which would melt once we lit the stove. Ang Phurba moved, grunted, then rolled over and lit one of the gas stoves; the frozen cylinder gave off little more than a glimmer. He heated the other stove over it, thawing out the gas until it started burning with a stronger flame, then reversed the process till both stoves were burning strongly. He had filled a pan with snow the previous night, and now we both lay back, dry-mouthed, waiting for the snow to melt, then boil, for the first brew of the day.

At least there was no wind, but even so it was bitterly cold. Nearly eight o'clock, time for the morning radio call – unless you warmed the batteries of the walky-talky, the radio wouldn't function at all. I emptied the little pen-light batteries into a frying pan over the stove and heated them up till they were warm to touch, slotted them back into the radio, which I had kept inside my sleeping bag, with my cameras and inner boots all night, and shoved the radio back inside my down suit until the time of the radio call. Only with these precautions could we be sure of getting communication with the camps lower down on the mountain. Tony Tighe's voice came through first, very clear and close, though he was eight thousand feet below and about six miles away at Base Camp.

'Hello Chris, you sound loud and clear, how are you this morning?'

'We're fine today Tony, there's hardly any wind up here, though it's bloody cold. How're Nick and Dave?'

'They got down last night. Beth's been giving them the full treatment, soaking their feet in hot water, the lot. Dave is O.K. but Nick has frostbite in two toes. Pertemba and Jangbo are fine.'

'Do you think there's any chance of getting Pertemba and Jangbo back up the hill?'

'I'll ask Jimmy. Pembatharke is a lot better now and is going to go up to Camp 2. He'll be able to keep things going.'

'That sounds great Tony, well done. Hello Camp 2 are you on the air, over?'

'Hello Chris, this is Barney, how are things up there?'

'Great, but bloody cold, are you all right at 2?'

'Everyone well, and Sherpa morale good. We're having a big carry to 4 today.'

'Sounds great, Barney; hello 4, are you on the air yet, over?'

Graham's voice, always grumpy in the early morning, came on:

'What are you so bloody cheerful about? It's not civilized this early!'

'Are you making a carry today, Graham?'

'Yes, we'll be able to get four Sherpas up today.'

'That's good, well done!'

At last things seemed to be slotting into place. After the radio call, Ang Phurba and I had another brew in order to postpone the grim moment of crawling out of warm sleeping bags, and start the slow process of dressing. You didn't need to put on any clothes, you had them all on already. It was the footwear that took time. My inner boots, having spent the night at the bottom of my sleeping bag were already warm, I slipped these on while still in my sleeping bag and then started to thaw out the outer leather boots; they were frozen, rigid as steel, icy to the touch. I held them over the gas stove letting the heat go up into the boot. After five minutes they had softened but were still cold to the touch. I forced them onto my feet, tucked the sleeping bag round them in an effort to retain the warmth and started warming up the foam over-boots, shoved these on over the boots, then the nylon outer boots. Including my socks, this totalled five layers. Knowing I could delay no longer, I pulled on my windproof outer suit and overmitts and crawled out of the tent. It was now eleven o'clock in the morning. The sun was glaring down, but we were hidden from it, barred from what little heat it gave out by the overhanging rock wall. Within a minute of getting out of the tent, in spite of all precautions, my feet began to feel the cold, and within five minutes were numb, to remain so for the rest of the day. I had to sort the oxygen bottles and the loads we were going to take up to Camp 6 that day, and then crampons, fiddling with the straps with fast-freezing fingers. It was so cold that bare skin stuck to the metal – you had to try to put them on without taking off your windproof mitts.

It was midday before Ang Phurba and I were ready to set out. A few days before, safely back at Camp 2, I had been impatient at the slowness of Nick and Dave in setting out from Camp 5; now I knew the reason why. Everything took three times as long as it would have done lower down on the mountain.

We set out across the fixed ropes. We were carrying similar loads of around thirty-five pounds each. The trouble was, of course, that half that load was the oxygen bottle which, by the time we reached Camp 6, would be empty, fifteen pounds of useless scrap alloy. My oxygen set seemed to be working well. I could feel the breath of oxygen mixed in air each time I breathed through the mask. Determined to stay out in front this time, I set Ang Phurba firmly behind me. He was always there, close on my heels, a reminder that he was probably fitter than I.

And on we plodded, up to the rock step: tiptoed carefully across the sloping, slabby ledges, leaning out on the rope that led across and away from us, then straight up towards the foot of the Rock Band. Although going slowly, I felt in control of myself, it was just a question of putting one foot in front of the other, ignoring the slowness with which one reached each landmark on the route, ever aware of the incredible, expanding vista of mountains stretching ahead. As we crawled above the barrier wall of Nuptse, we could look across to the mountains south of us, as well as the more familiar sight of the peaks in the far, far distance to the west.

We had now reached the final section of the route. Nick, single-minded and determined to finish the route in the day, had not had time to make intermediate anchor points. The rope stretched out in single leaps of three hundred feet, stretching across the snowfield below the Rock Band. I had brought up several snow stakes, and now my interest was held by the job of safeguarding the route by placing anchors. In fact my progress was probably slower, but time passed much more easily in my concentration on the simple task I had to complete. Almost without noticing it, I reached Nick's high point, just fifty feet or so from the rocky spur which dropped down from the foot of the Rock Band. There were a number of ledges set into it, on one of which I should have to find a camp site. At this point I was able to look straight up into the gully which Dougal had described as the way through the Rock Band. He had said that in 1971 it was a straightforward snow gully, but now, looking up, I could see very little snow. Indeed, it barely seemed a gully at all, was more a fissure in the rock wall, narrow, steep, in places overhanging. It looked hard; but then I shut the problem from my mind. I had programmed myself to establish Camp 6, and just completing this simple task was taking all my own resources. The gully was Dougal's problem. It was there, and however difficult, there was nothing I could do about it. Should it prove too difficult in the circumstances, he could always try to find a route round the corner, bypassing the Rock Band.

And so I gave my attention to the more immediate problems of finding a suitable camp site. It all looked very exposed to the wind. Down the side of the spur, underneath each little overhang I could see how the wind had sculpted out hollows from the snow. Eventually I decided that it was unlikely that anywhere at the end of the icefield would be truly protected from the wind; better to choose a site where at least there was plenty of sun to help setting out in the morning.

At last I was going to get a little lead climbing, as I tied onto the end of the rope left dangling by Nick, and started to pick my way across towards the rocky spur, kicked steps up a steep little snow slope and then pulled over a rock step. A length of rope, left from the spring expedition, protruded from the snows and was attached to a big boulder on a ledge reaching out to the crest of the spur. It was undoubtedly exposed to the wind, but got plenty of sun and what a situation! Just round the corner we could gaze down on the South Col, over a thousand feet below; immediately across from us was the great mass of Lhotse, its summit only a little higher than the site of Camp 6, and around us was the endless vista of mountains.

I took off my pack and found that I had run out of oxygen – I didn't know for how long. On the other hand, when Ang Phurba arrived he still had three-quarters of a tank left. His set could not have been functioning correctly and yet, in spite of this, he had followed close behind me all the way up. In a way it was a plus, for it meant we had some extra oxygen here at Camp 6.

But time was slipping by; it was now three o'clock in the afternoon and we wanted to get back to Camp 5 well before dusk. We turned round unburdened, and set off down the ropes. I stopped every few hundred feet, partly to rest, but also to gaze once more over the vista of mountains. Their beauty alone was enough to make up for all the effort and discomfort of the past few weeks.

And so, back to Camp 5. Ang Phurba had already got down and, as I arrived, thrust a steaming mug of lemon tea into my hand. I felt a wave of gratitude for his thoughtfulness. When we had first met Ang Phurba we had no idea of how outstanding a performance he was to produce on the mountain. Slightly built, a bit of a dandy, always elegantly dressed in gear issued by other expeditions, he was a far cry from the simple peasant; it had been difficult to imagine him having the endurance to keep going at altitude and yet he was proving to be one of our most outstanding Sherpas.

That afternoon I felt well content with our performance. There had been hardly a breath of wind all day, and now, bathed by the late sun Camp 5 was a pleasantly relaxed place to be in. I was anxious to organize our loads for the morning, and was testing the pressures of the oxygen bottles that littered one end of the ledge. I described what happened that night in my diary:

Then I went over to find some full oxygen bottles. All the bottles have been left in an absolute bloody shambles – empties mixed up with full ones. I was testing one of them, to find out whether it was full or empty – enough to go up the next day. It was tied onto a rope, reasonably full, certainly O.K. for sleeping, and so I tried to get it untied. There was a big pile of other oxygen bottles lying alongside it – not very safe, not very well jammed, and I swung this one up and hit three of them. They cannoned down the slope and there was a tremendous crash as one of them exploded. Camp 5 is almost directly over Camp 4, and I had this horrible vision – Christ, they could have wiped out Camp 4 – I could have killed someone! It was the most agonizing thought and Ang Phurba, who had just come out of the tent, shook his head and said, 'Very dangerous, sahib – very, very dangerous.' He told me that one bottle dropped from Camp 5 on the international expedition had gone straight through one of the tents. I went through absolute agony for about an hour and a half, was unable to raise Camp 4, but Camp 3, occupied by Dougal and Hamish came over the air. It was the five o'clock call. We heard that Graham had had to go down – hit by a stone; it could not have been our oxygen bottles, thank God, because it had happened at about 3.40. Quite honestly though, I think it could well have been a stone that either I or Aug Phurba dislodged on our return from Camp 6, because it was impossible to avoid knocking them down occasionally – they are embedded in the snow. Fortunately, Graham wasn't badly injured, but we didn't yet know whether Camp 4 had been hit. Hamish, who was at Camp 3, said he didn't think it possibly could have been.

Graham had had a narrow escape. The stone had come crashing through the wall of the box, hitting him on his forehead. He was knocked unconscious and does not know for how long he was out. Coming to, he found himself covered in blood, lying inside the box. He called out to the Sherpas, and one of them helped him back down to Camp 2, where Barney was able to stitch his wound. Had the stone hit him on the side of the head, where the skull is very much thinner, he might well have had a fracture.

It could have been a lot worse, but this meant that I had lost yet another climber from the Face. That left Dougal and Hamish on their way back up to Camp 5, Mick and Doug still down at Camp 2, and myself. Hamish and Dougal were due to move up to Camp 4 the next day; I should then learn whether Camp 4 had been hit, since, having lost their camp manager, the Sherpas were unlikely to come onto the radio on the morning call.

The wind built up once again, rattling and hammering the tent throughout the night. Next morning Ang Phurba and I began to get ready for another carry. We were both weary from the previous day, but nevertheless determined to make another trip to Camp 6. Already worried about the Sherpa replacement situation, I was going to have to find replacements for Ang Phurba at Camp 5, as well as for the Sherpas at Camp 4 who would be making their second carry that day and, in all probability, would want to go back down. Then there was the problem of the oxygen cylinders, accentuated by the failure of the adaptors for the seventeen French bottles which were sitting at Camp 4 and, of course, on which I had been relying.

That morning, at the nine o'clock call, Mick Burke came up with:

'Look Chris, I'm going to be pessimistic here, to offset your optimism – I just don't think we've got enough oxygen cylinders on the mountain to last beyond the 14th November.' We tried to work it out over the radio, but it is not easy to do mental arithmetic at 26,000 feet, one's mind being a little addled by altitude.

Finally, I said:

'Look Mick, I'll sit down and work things out again and we'll open up in an hour's time.'

I sat down in my sleeping bag, with Ang Phurba watching me impassively, trying to calculate our oxygen consumption. I knew we had one and three quarter bottles up at the top camp, four cylinders at Camp 5, five were being carried up from Camp 4 that day, four at Camp 4 and so on down the mountain. But when I started trying to work out the rate of consumption at each level of the mountain, a calculation easy enough at sea level, however hard I tried I simply couldn't work it out – the mind was too slow.

Ten o'clock came, and I opened up on the radio.

'Have you worked anything out?' asked Mick.

'Look I'm still working on it,' I replied. 'We'd better open up again at midday.'

I decided to send Ang Phurba on up to Camp 6 by himself, while I tried to work out our logistics. I should have to make my carry to Camp 6 the following day. Ang Phurba, ever loyal, set out without protest and I went back to my figures. Twelve o'clock came, and we talked it over once again on the radio.

Barney suggested that we should try to sleep without using oxygen. Mick agreed that this would be possible. In the meantime we ordered another twenty bottles to be carried up from Base Camp to 1, first thing the next morning, holding back the Sherpas at Camp 1, so that we could push them straight through to Camp 2 on the same day. Mick ended up saying:

'Look, we realize that there isn't a hope in hell's chance of Doug and I having a second attempt on the summit, but even so, we'll do our best to keep going and help Dougal and Hamish.'

That afternoon, as I continued to try to calculate our logistic position, I knew we were up against it and commented in my diary:

'You know, we might pull it off, but by God, if we do, we'll have done it against absolutely every kind of odds that you could possibly imagine.'

Just after one o'clock three Sherpas arrived with loads from Camp 4. This was their second carry to Camp 5, and they said they wanted to go back down for a rest. I used all the inspiration I had in me to persuade them to make just one more carry before going down. They listened impassively and said they'd see how they felt next morning. I felt drained from the emotional effort I had put into trying to inspire them. It was now one-thirty and the sun still had not struck the tent. I had come out without putting on overboots and, as a result, my feet were numb with cold. Back in the tent I lay cold and exhausted until at last the sun lit the nylon fabric and some warmth began to filter into the tent.

A few minutes later Ang Phurba arrived back; he had been very fast, taking under three hours for the round trip, but he looked very tired and told me that the wind had been bad on the upper part of the carry. He had shown considerable courage in going up on his own, for the Sherpas prefer company when they're climbing. I prepared a brew for him and he crawled into his sleeping bag.

In spite of the logistic crisis that morning, everything seemed hopeful; it was a beautiful evening, with that rich, rather yellow, mellow glow as the sun went down. I decided to do some filming and got out the little auto-load camera, filming Ang Phurba heating the wireless batteries and preparing a brew. I crawled outside to sort out the loads which had arrived that afternoon, and do some more filming.

And then I needed to relieve myself – and this was my embarrassing, very humiliating downfall. I described it in detail in my diary and I include it here, for I hope it brings home some of the grim, perhaps sordid, and yet in a weird kind of way, the funny experiences that are all part of a Himalayan expedition. It is comparatively easy to cope with the dramatic crises, the savage storms, the sheer ice pitch at 24,000 feet, but less easy to cope, day after day, with the basic problems of living at 26,000 feet in sub-zero temperatures.

Now we've got these one-piece down suits; it's not too bad, in fact it's comparatively easy to relieve oneself when wearing the down suit by itself. If, however, you are wearing the down suit *and* the outer suit, it is absolutely desperate, trying to get the two slits in both suits lined up. Deciding to make it easy for myself, I peeled off the top windproof suit, leaving only the down suit to worry about. Afterwards, without thinking, without looking back, I stood up and shoved my windproof suit back on. Pushing my left hand, which was gloved, through the sleeve, I did not realize anything was wrong – until I poked my hand through the cuff!

I tried to scrape it off – rub it off – but by this time the sun had gone, it was bitterly cold and it had frozen to the consistency of concrete. Poor old Ang Phurba – he's feeling a bit rough anyway, and I said 'I'm sorry, Ang Phurba – I've made a mistake!' He just buried himself in his sleeping bag and then there was a horrible gasp as he dived for the entrance. And so I took off my down suit as well as the outer suit, and after an attempt to clean them up, shoved them into the collapsed tent next door! I got into my sleeping bag and eventually we dropped off to sleep, though Ang Phurba insisted on having the door open, and it was bloody freezing!

Next morning Ang Phurba woke up and felt ill. I was meant to be doing a carry, while Ang Phurba had said he was going down anyway, and this clinched the deal! It was all I could do – at least he made the breakfast and the morning tea which, I must say, was a nice luxury, while I lay back.

By about 10.30 a.m., Ang Phurba was ready, and he went down. I should have gone up, but Ang Phurba shook his head – he told me that yesterday had been very, very cold and conditions very bad. Today seemed much worse – windy all day, but by this time it was 12.15, getting late for a push all the way up to Camp 6 and back, especially thinking about Nick Estcourt's frostbite, and I'm afraid my willpower died. I did not think I could do more than two carries anyway, so decided 'Well, let's get the camp sorted out, help Hamish and Dougal, and then I can go up with them tomorrow.'

I only hope that when, and if, Hamish and Dougal turn up, they don't wrinkle up their noses, put me in quarantine and refuse to come anywhere close to me.

Here is your dynamic Leader of the British Everest Expedition, sitting at 26,000 feet feeling rather like a social pariah. I wouldn't say I'm feeling sorry for myself, but I don't know – I'm not so much muddled-thinking – my mind in some ways feels quite sharp. I think it's more that you're slow in thinking – very, very forgetful; I find it very difficult to master the logistics of our problem. And now I'm just mastering the very simple problem that Ang Phurba has also left all the flipping dirty plates and pans and I'm having a session cleaning these.

The sun's just hit the tent. Life's a lot more bearable now, and when I've done this washing-up, I'm going to get out of the tent and start sorting things out.

And these were my feelings at Camp 5, as I recorded them over a period of twenty-four hours, into the cassette recorder. It's very easy to forget just how you felt, from hour to hour, once you get back to civilization. One's thought processes are undoubtedly muddled and slow at this altitude – just how slow is only evident when you read back the transcript of recordings made at the time. Hamish and Dougal arrived that evening; it was wonderful seeing them again, having their companionship. Dougal was the first to arrive and I crawled out of the tent to greet him and then started helping him to pitch a new Tunnel tent to replace the box which had collapsed around Nick and Dave. The wind was now scudding round the corner and although the Tunnel tents, which had been designed by Doug Scott, were magnificent once erected, you needed a B.Sc. in engineering to work out how to put them up. Dougal and I did our best though both of us being far from mechanical by nature, our attempt was a little pathetic. Finally, fingers frozen, we retired to my tent to await Hamish, the expedition engineer. He came up about an hour behind Dougal, having had trouble with his oxygen set, and having been hit on the leg by a stone. He put the finishing touches to their Tunnel tent and then we all gathered in my tent for a communally cooked meal of corned beef hash washed down with coffee cognac. In spite of the cold and wind we were all full of confidence and I felt warmed and cheered by their presence.

We decided that we should set out next morning, Dougal and Hamish to move into Camp 6, myself to carry a load for them. That night, though, the wind blew fiercely. My own tent was pitched securely and was partly protected by that of Hamish and Dougal. Theirs, however, was not nearly as well pitched, and during the night was flapping around to such a degree that most of the time the walls were resting against their faces as if it had been an ordinary bivouac sack. As a result they got practically no sleep. There were other problems as well, as I commented in my diary.

The idea at this stage was to get Dougal and Hamish up to the site of Camp 6. The only problem here was that it became increasingly obvious that we barely had the manpower to do it – we'd only, after all, got three loads up – two loads that Ang Phurba and I had carried, then Ang Phurba's load. Dougal came up with a suggestion that Hamish and he should consolidate today, that Mick and Doug should come up, and then that the five of us should go up to 6 next day, with Dougal and Hamish staying there. This would mean bringing another tent up, however, and I didn't like the idea of this, feeling the fewer people we have up there, the fewer people we have to feed and give oxygen. Therefore I came up with the idea that I should do the carry by myself on the 13th, while Mick and Doug move up to here, and then the next day Mick and Doug should carry Dougal and Hamish into Camp 6. I must say, I'd quite like to have done this myself, but you can't have everything, and this does seem a sensible way of doing it.

And so, I prepared for my own final fling on the mountain, going through the slow, painful process of getting dressed, sorting out my oxygen kit. Unfortunately, the set I had used on my trip with Ang Phurba had belonged to Mick Burke and I had sent it back down the mountain for him to use for his return to Camp 5. This meant I had to use the set which Ang Phurba had been using, one that was suspect anyway. In addition, the mask did not fit sufficiently closely for enough suction to shift the valve, when breathing in. Consequently, a certain amount of precious oxygen was lost round the sides of the mask.

Before I had walked a dozen paces, it was obvious that the mask was only working for part of the time, and I was having to breathe very hard to get any oxygen at all. You could tell when it was working by the sound of the valve opening and closing.

I made my lonely way up the fixed ropes; there was a feeling of exultation in the very lonely emptiness of the world around me – a rope that stretched for ever in front, mountains stretching for an ever-increasing, expansive distance as I slowly gained height. The wind hammered and buffeted at my back, as I slowly plodded towards my goal. There was room for fear in the very loneliness of my position, in the demoniac force of the wind that was so much stronger than I; time was slipping by; it was three fifteen and I was still a long way from the rock spur at the end of the Ice Field; could I get there and all the way back to Camp 6, in time? The oxygen set seemed to have packed in completely but I still had some strength in reserve. I was very, very slow, one foot in front of the other, and yet I could keep going without taking rests, felt better than I had done earlier on in the expedition, on my way up to Camp 3.

The sun, low on the horizon, had that warm yellow light that was so meaningless in the constant blast of icy wind. I pulled up over the step, teetered across the narrow rock ledge leading to the little platform I had chosen for Camp 6, and crouched down beneath the slight drift of snow to remove my pack. I had carried up two French oxygen cylinders and a rope, about forty pounds in weight, too much for that altitude. My pressure-gauge still read 800 p.s.i.; it had only been 2,400 when I had started, only three-quarters full – so I had used barely half a tank to reach the high point! For well over half the time the set must have been malfunctioning. I felt a faint glow of satisfaction at having forced myself on, but the satisfaction was quickly replaced by doubts about my prospects of getting back down. Could I face into the savage wind, had I sufficient strength for those long traverses?

I started down, blown off track as I stumbled over the long traverse. Pushing myself as hard as I could to reach Camp 5, I could not imagine myself getting all the way down to Camp 4 that night. I was so tired that I cried with exhaustion as I pushed my weary body the last few feet into the camp. Mick and Doug had arrived and had found a snow hole just above the camp. As I came in, Mick poked his head out of a hole in the snow. Doug, matter of fact, commented :

'You'd better get a move on if you want to get down to Camp 4.'

Quite obviously, there wasn't any room at Camp 5. Hamish thrust a mug full of soup from out of the tent. I gulped it down, and quickly packed my rucksack with a few belongings; I didn't even need a sleeping bag for these were back at Camp 4.

Fortified by the mug of soup I set off down the great central gully to Camp 4. I was so tired that even going downhill I had to sit down and rest every few feet. And yet, tired as I was, I felt enthralled by the view. The light was beginning to fade from the rocks around me, and the distant peaks were silhouetted against a sky that was gold on the far horizon, merging into a deep red and then an opaque blue-black. For me, whatever the outcome of the expedition, this day had been the climax. The experience, my own peace of mind, having taken myself to the limit and beyond, made everything, all the worries of leadership, stress and discomfort, completely worthwhile.

It was pitch-dark by the time I reached Camp 4. I let out a shout, and a cry came back.

'In here, Sahib.' It was Ang Phu. He had cleared the box in readiness for me, had a panful of water heating on the stove and a sleeping bag lying out ready. His thoughtfulness was truly wonderful, bathed me with a warm glow, as I crept into the box, lit a candle and made some lemon drink. I was so tired that I couldn't face cooking or even eating anything. I just curled up in the sleeping bag, wondered if there was a second one anywhere, but had neither strength to search, nor even the energy to find my sleeping tablets. Blowing out the candle, I lay back, feeling icy fingers of cold creeping round my legs, crawling over my body. Even though I had arrived back warm, even slightly sweaty from my exertions, now the cold penetrated everything. I could not take any oxygen and longed for another sleeping bag. Too tired, too cold to sleep, I just lay shivering in the dark – so cold that I shouted out into black space 'I'm cold' but it didn't help. I had not had enough to eat that day, and unless one has taken in enough fuel, especially at that altitude, there is not enough residual warmth in one's body to stay warm, however many layers of down one is covered by. I just lay there waiting for the morning. Commented in my diary next day:

I was very depressed this morning, the 14th, when I felt I had lost control of the expedition. In a way I felt I had lost control of myself, just wanted to be at home, in my own big double bed with my love, under a nice big warm quilt.

There's a hole in this box that I am in at the moment, made by a stone – I think it was the stone that forced Graham to go back down. Spindrift was pouring through it all night and in the morning everything was just covered in spindrift. I was bitterly cold and it was hours before the sun came on to the tent. Life couldn't have been more miserable.

Now though, having been up at nine – then the ten o'clock call – I can look at things more rationally – there's no doubt about it, we've only got about four or five days. We're not in a position to supply our front climbers. We've really pushed Dougal and Hamish out in front a bit too soon, for we can barely keep them supplied – I think everyone is in a mood of, 'Let's have done with it.'

The weather forecast, last night, at 9 kilometres, which is just over the top of Everest, was 'winds of 200 kilometres per hour', and certainly the winds were something like that yesterday. I think the chimney through the Rock Band is very sheltered, but if it is technically difficult it's so bitterly cold that I don't think they're going to be able to really contend with it. But at least we'll be able to get above the high point of the international expedition, I think, and it's just possible we'll be able to climb the Rock Band. I suppose miracles do happen – the miracle could occur, where we could reach the top of Everest. The big problem is supplying this pyramid of oxygen which the lead climbers require to keep going.

Anyway, Dougal and Hamish are getting a French box which is, by far, the best piece of tentage we've got on this expedition, up today, and let's just pray they can have a really good night and tomorrow make some good progress. It will be very, very exciting to hear how they've got on tomorrow.

In the meantime things are very, very thin here. I've got Jangbo and Pertemba coming up today to Camp 4. Ang Phu is going up to Camp 5. It's going to be very critical, just how tired Mick and Doug are, and whether they can do a carry, because it does need a two-man carry each day, to keep the people out in front supplied. I think we're on a last ditch, forlorn hope at the moment. I'm going to hold out here, at 4. At least today, I think, I've managed to make my standard of life a little pleasanter than last night and this morning. I also intend to feed myself up, and I think a rest will make all the difference, But it really takes an effort of will to get out of the box and into the cold. It also takes about two hours to get your feet warmed up once again, after you've done it. Your feet get much colder hanging around the camp than they do in a single kind of push or carry.

Anyway, four to five days of this and, success or fail – we can't do any more. Quite honestly, I just want to get home. I think the effort's been worth it – we've had a really fine, great effort, and I think everyone has done their very best and will have taken themselves to their limits, and slightly beyond. But I think the thing we want to do most of all now, all of us, is just get home.

I recorded these comments early in the morning of 14 November, while up at Camp 5. Fifteen hundred feet above me, Dougal and Hamish were preparing to move up to Camp 6, supported by Mick and Doug. We had been struggling for too long, our resources were too thin, and yet still in the bottom of our hearts we had some hope left.

16

DEFEAT

14 November–16 November

14 *November*. Jimmy Roberts was sitting near the summit of Kalipatar, a small peak which commands a magnificent view of the upper reaches of the South of Everest, above Gorak Shep. He had gone there a few days previously to watch the final stages of the expedition; Kelvin Kent, Nick Estcourt, Dave Bathgate and Graham Tiso, all more or less injured, certainly out of the expedition from a climbing point of view, were convalescing at Base Camp. Tony Tighe and Beth Burke were also there, managing administration. Barney was at Camp 2 and I was sitting it out at Camp 4. Both of us had now been above Base Camp for six weeks, and were desperately tired. Hamish, Dougal, Doug and Mick were at Camp 5. They realized that chances were thin and yet, when I had left them the previous night, morale had been high and we all had felt that long as the odds were, we still had a chance.

Dougal Haston wrote a description of his experiences in those last two or three days of the expedition, and of that final push towards Camp 6:

Rocked gently by the wind, Hamish and I moved up the familiar highway with its overnight stops at 3 and 4, towards the decision-making at 5. The altitude scarcely seemed to matter. I barely remember the journey as my mind was too full with the problems of the Rock Band and above. Logistics were stretched. Tucked away in my rucksack was a tent sac. I didn't show it to many people and it wasn't in case we got lost between 2 and 5. Slowly, as a positive plan began to appear through the maze of possibilities, a bivouac above the Rock Band became a distinct possibility in any scheme with a chance of success. This wasn't a crazy decision caused by oxygen starvation. We'd talked away many nights at Base Camp on the subject. It's just that a bivouac at 28,000 feet or above is something you don't consider lightly, or make the decision to attempt easily. You're pushing calculatedly close to the overbalance of the survival seesaw. I'd thrown it out, casually and jokingly, to Doug and Mick and seen their faces assume that funny, vague look that you sometimes see when friends think you've temporarily flipped.

With such thoughts whirling, I moved in an easy, occupied manner into Camp 5, to find Bonington in an occupational sleeping bag. Crawling into the tent, I got the good news that there was a lot of material at the site of Camp 6, then the not-so-good – that we still had to pitch a roof next door for Hamish and I to sleep in. Meanwhile Hamish arrived, muttering about a troublesome oxygen set. It seemed a long and different time since I'd spent so many days there with Whillans in 1971. There was no sitting, watching the evening sun, only a constant roaring, cracking wind projecting spindrift in great clouds throughout the camp. We were still erecting the tent as darkness was falling; fumbling frozen-fingeredly with a good, but intricate design system. It was still badly pitched as the final appearance of darkness forced us into Chris's tent for some thaw-out drinks. Hamish and I did pass the night in the new tent – or maybe it passed the night on us. It's all pretty vague. Anyhow, it almost qualified as a bivouac, since the framework collapsed in the night and the windcracking roof spent the rest of the time keeping us awake and beating on our heads. No sleep, and a long excavation emergence in the morning put us in no shape to journey towards Camp 6 that day. Chris did a lone carry. Doug and Mick arrived. An incoherently irate Doug fixed his own special brand of tent, with his own special system which was unfortunately only in his head and not in the instruction manual we carried in ours. Mick and I played at snowholing. Hamish fiddled with oxygen. Chris came back and disappeared towards 4, down pointing for ever. Slowly, a plan and order came through and we were all asleep and organized for the move up on the next day – Hamish and I to occupy 6, Doug and Mick to carry in support.

It was a strange new day as I moved onto the fixed ropes. Sun, yes, but not in the camp, with only the warmth of a gas burner in a banquet hall when eventually reached. I was alone and a good way up the ropes before seeing the others emerge and prepare to follow. On this part there was no explanation for me, only memories of previous struggling, and an awareness of being in much better physical shape than before. Three weeks above 24,000 feet might be a record for high-altitude holiday camping, but it doesn't do wonders for you physically. Flashes of emaciated effort came back as I moved easily on, upwards. But with all the sense of physical well-being, there were many other not-so-good factors to counteract a light-hearted journey up towards Camp 6.

The wind – always the wind, was viciously asserting its authority. This was no silent journey up a crisp snowfield in the pure high air. I had visions of storms on old trans-Atlantic cutters. The constant banging in your ears would suddenly be intensified with a huge crack, as an extra gust smashed over the West Ridge and pulled at the figures on the ropes. This cracking was at least a warning. The axe was banged in and you crouched and held on. Once I was toppling on a long, loose section of fixed rope and went twanging down onto my Jumars. Doug told me later that at one point he was caught unprepared, picked up and thrown for a few feet, before clattering onto the ever elastic fixed ropes. I continued quickly, with a mind going almost as quickly as the wind. I had experienced many bad storms, many high winds, but this was a new dimension of wind speed, and it was basically fine weather ! The sky, when you could see it through the spindrift, was blue. A storm thought was quickly eliminated from mind.

I reached the position where the equipment was dumped and at just above that point the wind stopped gusting and moved into continuous movement. Thinking was difficult. I had to turn away and crouch. Two things were blatantly self-evident. There was no way we could attempt to climb on the Rock Band and no way a tent could be pitched. I looked up at the couloir that we had followed before. Another disillusioning surprise. Whillans and I had climbed a hundred metres of it, mainly on snow and easy rock, with the potential continuation also on snow. Now it was bare rock. To my confused head this seemed a total contradiction. The rest of the Face had much more snow on it than it had had last spring, but now this part which should have been filled with snow, had none. Even given the possibility of continuing, which now seemed zero to me, the Band was obviously going to take much more time than even the slowest of our plans had allowed.

Grappling with this thought, I remembered the possibilities of escape onto the relatively easy ground of the South East Ridge. A quick move – out of the Face, and round the corner. It was no survival scene. The wind seemed to screw round and blast me on the face. I backed quickly round the corner and the prevailing blast hit me again. A sudden bad thought: I knew that without an oxygen mask I wouldn't have been able to breathe on that particular corner, and just hoped that the cylinder didn't run out at that particular moment. Another thing seemed reasonably certain, the so-called escape route was an escape only into something worse. On the flattish slabby ground, it would have been suicidal to attempt to move. Any gust would have blown one off immediately. Turning back to try to find some kind of shelter, I saw Doug at the top of the ropes. We just muttered a few obvious things. He took some pictures. Hands were turning white, even with double gloves. There was nothing to do but turn around. I jerked my head downwards. He nodded. Setting off down I met Mick. He knew what was happening – there was no real need to say anything. Moving past, I left him with the extremely difficult task of trying to record the scene on film.

Back at Camp 5 I found Hamish, who had turned back because of a faulty oxygen set, and as everyone crowded in to drink tea we started to talk about the decision made. It was obviously final. Even if the wind had stopped miraculously, we did not have the back-up for another push. And one wind-free day was not enough. That night I put our decision to Chris on the radio.

I knew that something was wrong, for I was in direct radio contact with Jimmy Roberts, six miles away, and six and a half thousand feet below me at Kalipatar. Through his powerful binoculars he had been able to watch the drama taking place on the long traverse across to the site of Camp 6. It had been like watching a movie with no sound, and just as confusing; although able to pick out the arms and legs of the climbers, it was not possible to identify them. You could barely do this from three-foot range, so well-disguised were they by shapeless suits and oxygen masks.

Jimmy had seen and reported the retreat of one figure fairly early in the day, and had then given the fatal news – that the remaining three had also turned back. The weather had now been fine for over a week and, as a result, all the loose spindrift had been blown from the Face; yet there were no tell-tale clouds of snow to betray the savage winds. Down at Kalipatar the winter sun blazed hot from a cloudless sky; there was no wind at that level. Up at 4, however, I did at least have some hint of the winds that were being experienced above Camp 5; it was a bitterly cold, blustery day, but I still had some shelter from the great wall of Nuptse. Anyway, it is the top two thousand feet of Everest that juts into the jet-stream blasting with an ever-increasing force through the high airs of the earth.

I knew they were coming back down, that they had not occupied Camp 6 – but why? I surmised that afternoon in my taped diary:

I'm lying here in the gathering gloom (it's about half past five), just waiting for the seven o'clock call, to find out why they didn't establish Camp 6. Can't help being worried that I could have made a mistake. For instance, I know I didn't actually tie down the two parts of the French boxes. Certainly they were there yesterday, but could they have blown away – could I have done something wrong which could have prejudiced the expedition? Logically, I don't think so. I think it's more likely that it's just too cold and windy; perhaps they're having trouble with their oxygen sets. But until you know, you can't help being a bit worried.

I think really, this – the whole thing – has become a real battle of attrition and we've all been here too long. We're tired, we're fed up with it, and I think we're all just looking forward to a decision – one way or another. I don't think we've got a chance of getting to the top of Everest – conditions are just too inhuman up there – the human frame cannot cope with hundred-mile-an-hour winds, and a temperature of about −30°C. When I went up there yesterday afternoon, I don't think I could have erected a tent; I think this might well have been the trouble that Hamish and Dougal got.

And so, Dougal's news on that seven o'clock call wasn't really a surprise. I just accepted their decision straight away, and said, 'Yes, O.K., we go down.' I had experienced the wind the previous day, had learned for myself how insufferable it had been. Lower down the mountain they found the decision more difficult to accept. It's strange how quickly the human memory forgets just how savage an experience can be. That night, Nick wrote in his diary:

'My own feeling – emotional I know – is to wish that they had at least spent a night at Camp 6, and tried – somehow. I feel cheated and let down. I know this is stupid; it's partly Base Camp frustration. In some ways it's better, in some ways worse, for the front four. I feel sorry for Chris.'

Jimmy, also, was disappointed. From Kalipatar the climbers

looked more like puppets than humans. It was so difficult to appreciate the effect of the wind and cold on the human body and mind. That night I had a feeling of complete peace of mind. We had done our best, had taken ourselves to the limit, and now that it was all over I just longed to clear the mountain safely, and get the hell out of it, back to home.

The front four came back down to Camp 4 that morning, carrying mammoth loads. At the same time, a big party of Sherpas came up from Camp 2 to clear the camp. By evening we were all back down at Camp 2. There was no sense of depression, no regrets – there was almost a feeling of elation, everyone confident that it had been the wind and cold which had beaten us – a wind and cold that I am positive no human being could have struggled against. We were like a pack of school-boys at boarding school, about to go on holiday after a particularly long and arduous term. The experience had brought us closer together, rather than weakening our bonds of friendship. We had experienced some friction during the course of the expedition; we had had conflicts, but knew these to be inevitable – perhaps essential as a safety-valve to the stresses of such a venture. Every single person on that expedition, Sherpas and climbers alike, had done more than could possibly have been expected of them in the normal course of events. Of the Sherpas, the performance of Ang Phurba, Pertemba, Jangbo and Ang Phu had been exceptional. There was a wonderful feeling of unity, not only between the climbers but also between climbers and Sherpas, and through the throes of the expedition we had emerged as a single, close-knit group.

I wanted to clear the mountain as quickly as possible. On 16 November, Dougal, Hamish, Doug and I were setting off from Camp 2 to return to Base. Mick had gone down the previous evening to send film which he had taken at the site of Camp 6 back to Britain, and to prepare our reception from a filming point of view. Chris Brasher had abandoned Camp 2 in the Western Cwm after a couple of days, to go to Kunde to complete an interview with Sir Edmund Hillary, but had come rushing back to Base Camp to get the story of our retreat. This was to leave Barney with the unenviable job of holding the fort to the last. He was to have one more night at Camp 2 while the Sherpas stripped it, and was then to drop back down to Camp 1 and then to Base Camp.

We set off at dawn, when the Western Cwm was still in deep shadow, held in the grip of the winter cold. A flurry of vapour was blowing off the summit of Lhotse, sure sign of the ever-present wind. But down in the Cwm, the air was still. I walked down, without regret, very tired yet still marvelling at the incredible architecture of the Western Cwm. The sun, creeping behind the great mass of Everest, lit the upper ramparts of Nuptse then crept above the South Ridge of Everest to throw long shadows down the Cwm itself, emphasizing the dark void of crevasses, picking out pinnacles and airy ridges of ice through and over which our route lay.

Camp 1 was rather sad, stripped of all its tents – just the scattered debris of an expedition. Hamish and Dougal were in front. I went down the Ice Fall with Doug Scott, finding the upper part changed from when I had last seen it six weeks before. Crevasses had opened out, séracs had fallen and the route wound its way through the debris. Strangely, we had little sense of danger, perhaps becoming immune to the feeling after our weeks on the mountain. I spent an hour photographing a particularly spectacular section of the Ice Fall which, only two hours later, was to collapse – with disastrous results.

We were over half-way down when we met Tony Tighe on his way up the Ice Fall to meet us. He was tremendously excited at the prospect of getting a glimpse into the Western Cwm. He had spent the last eight weeks at Base Camp fulfilling unexciting but invaluable duties, taking all the radio calls, helping Jimmy Roberts with general administration and the assembly of loads for the mountain. At times he had even taken on the role of diplomat. It is all too easy while on the mountain to resent people having the easy living at Base Camp, to wonder why supplies were not coming up to the front line more quickly; grumbles were passed back to Base Camp all too often over the radio. Tony would soften them down and, in passing them on to Jimmy, would take the sting out of them. In every way he had fulfilled an important role on the expedition through his mature good sense, his kindness and his efficiency. The last day I felt I had to give him some kind of reward for everything he had done for us, knew how much he longed to see into the Western Cwm, to get an inkling of the excitement and struggle we had known and enjoyed all these days. And so I had invited him to come up and meet us.

He was brimming over with happiness when we met him. He had come up with twenty Sherpas who were going to Camp 1 to meet those bringing loads down from Camp 2. Having dropped behind them, being less fit than they, he was now on his own – nothing unusual since the track through the Ice Fall was clearly marked, and all the crevasses bridged, all difficult sections fixed roped.

We passed him, got back down to Base Camp, to the first wash in six weeks, to mugfuls of tea, to Brasher's debriefing. There was a feeling of the start of the holidays, talk of the meals we were going to have in Kathmandu, dreams of getting home. The afternoon wore on, light-hearted as ever and then suddenly there was a rising babble of voices amongst the Sherpas. They were obviously worried – they seem to have an almost extra-sensory perception of trouble. Kelvin called me over.

'There's some kind of trouble in the Ice Fall,' he said.

'What is it?' I asked.

'I'm not sure. They're not at all certain, but seem to think there's been a big collapse.'

Some of the Sherpas were already on their way down, having picked up their loads at Camp 1. A few minutes later Phurkipa arrived and told Kelvin there had been a big collapse in the Ice Fall just above him. At this stage we could not tell if anyone had been involved – we could see another group on their way down, however. From their position we estimated that they must have been above, or somewhere in the area of the collapse when it occurred. We were all worried about Tony. Phurkipa and he had passed each other, going in their opposite directions just short of the area of collapse and Tony could have had time to get into the danger area. But there was nothing we could do but sit it out and wait.

The large party came in sight; one of them was seen to be wearing a one-piece suit. There was a shout from Mick Burke:

'It's O.K. – it's Tony!' I felt a wave of relief come over me, unable to stop the tears; Dougal, normally so unemotional, gripped my shoulder and said,

'I couldn't have taken another Annapurna!' (An allusion to Ian Clough's tragic death in the Ice Fall at the end of the Annapurna South Face expedition.) But this is exactly what we were going to have to do. Almost at the moment Mick had called out, someone else shouted, 'It's not Tony – it's Barney – Tony isn't with them!'

We hurried forward to where Barney was coming into the camp with a dozen Sherpas.

'Have you seen any sign of Tony?'

'No.'

'Yet you've come all the way down from Camp 1?'

'Yes, but there's been a hell of a collapse in the Ice Fall; we had to make a bit of a diversion to get round the debris. I don't think we could have missed him. Was he on his way up?'

'Yes, he was last seen just short of the collapse.'

And so it went on. We were all badly shocked but slowly we pieced together what must have happened. Tony had last been seen by Phurkipa at about midday, on his way up what we knew as the 'Ice Pitch ladder'. Phurkipa had probably been through the Ice Fall that year more times than any one else on the expedition, for he had been in charge of the Ice Fall Sherpas in the spring, also. He was the last person to see Tony alive.

Meanwhile, another group of six Sherpas had just reached Camp 1, where Barney was supervising the distribution of loads to be carried back down to Base Camp. The Sherpas set off down the top of the Ice Fall for Base. Barney was still packing loads for the retreat when, just after midday, he heard a dull crump from the Ice Fall. This was followed by a huge cloud of ice particles which boiled up like some gigantic explosion, then hung in the still air for a few minutes before dissipating to leave the Ice Fall basking, once more, under the cloudless sky. A few minutes later the Sherpas came rushing back. They were hysterical in their panic, but Barney gathered that they had nearly been killed when the ice ridge they had just started to cross had collapsed beneath their feet. More serious, they had left one of their number suspended in mid-air on the fixed rope! Barney reacted immediately, taking with him Pertemba and Jangbo, who had come down from Camp 2 with him. On reaching the area they found that a complete ice ridge, which our route had followed, had collapsed. Fortunately we had always realized that this section was dangerous, being badly undercut beneath, and had therefore put a fixed rope along its length. There was a notice at one end urging everyone to clip on to the rope with their safety sling and fortunately the front Sherpa, Ang Tande, had done so. As he had started out across the ridge it had collapsed beneath his feet, leaving him hanging in mid-air about seventy feet above the debris. Had the rope pulled its anchor, or had he failed to clip in, there is little doubt that he would have been severely injured, perhaps killed. Even more fortunate was the fact that had the Sherpas been two minutes earlier, or the collapse two minutes later, all of them could have been on the ice ridge and the rope would almost certainly have been pulled from its anchor under their weight.

They had had a miraculous escape, but as we talked to Barney and the Sherpas there was a terrible, growing certainty that Tony had been engulfed in the collapse. The front Sherpa, Ang Tande, had seen no sign of him which meant that Tony must have been in the Trough, just below the ridge.

Barney, having assembled all the Sherpas at Camp 1, had then led them back down to Base, finding a safe way round the disaster area. None of them, of course, had any idea that Tony – or anyone else – had been below them at the time of the sérac fall.

Although there seemed to be little hope, while the faintest vestige remained we could not give up entirely. That afternoon, even though it was getting late, Mick Burke and Dave Bathgate, with four Sherpas, went up the Ice Fall to investigate the scene of the collapse, reaching the area at about eight o'clock that night. Eerily lit by moonlight, they could see the Trough filled with huge blocks of ice, the remains of another sérac tower hanging crazily over the scene of disaster, threatening the searchers. They looked and listened, praying that Tony might just have been trapped by one of these huge ice blocks, some of which were as big as houses, and yet somehow miraculously protected. But there was no sound except the occasional creak of the glacier as séracs shifted and ice

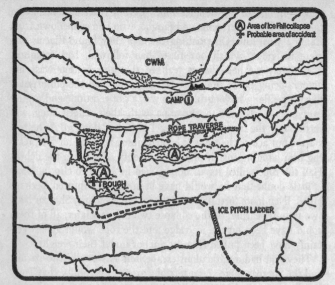

Diagram drawn by Dave Bathgate on the night of the accident
to illustrate what happened for our official report

blocks moved. Mick said afterwards that it was one of the most
frightening experiences of his life, for the whole area was obviously ready for a further collapse.

First thing next morning we sent another search party up –
Hamish, Doug Scott and a further group of Sherpas. But in the
light of the dawn there was no sign of Tony; he had vanished
completely under the tons of ice.

And so, we had to face the cruel loss of a very good friend, in
the very last hours of an expedition which, although unsuccessful
in its direct objective had proved to be a profoundly worthwhile
and happy experience. Originally, Dougal had know Tony well,
Mick and I had known him only casually, from times spent in
Leysin, the rest had come to know him during the course of the
expedition; but you get to know a man, come to depend upon
him in such circumstances to a degree which would be impossible
back in civilization. We had all come to respect Tony and had

built up a series of strong friendships which went a lot deeper than mere acquaintanceship.

As we walked from the Everest Base Camp we fell prey to a whole mixture of emotions; sadness at the loss of a close and respected friend, elation from our experience on the mountain but most of all, unity in the face of the adversity we had endured.

17

CONCLUSIONS

We had tried and failed. We knew when we snatched that vacancy in the queue for Everest that we would be fighting against long odds, that chances were thin, but then surely this is part of the challenge of climbing, attempting the seemingly impossible and proving it wrong. There had been some grounds for optimism, the hope that there would be shelter on the Face itself, the fact that the Japanese reconnaissance in the autumn of 1969 had made fast, easy progress to the foot of the Rock Band and had found it much easier than they did the following spring.

But for us the Face had proved impossible. We had been beaten by a combination of high winds and extreme cold. I am confident that no other party could have done much better that autumn, but even this does not mean that the Face is impossible in the autumn. Given the right trick of circumstances, a few days of freakish, windless weather at the right time, a party could climb the South West Face of Everest at this time of year.

The vicissitudes of the four expeditions which tried and failed on the South West Face could well have masked the greatest problem of all, however, since no expedition – for one reason or another – has reached the foot of the Rock Band in a condition to make a serious attempt to overcome its defences.

In the spring of 1970, the Japanese attempt was undoubtedly half-hearted, with the main effort of the expedition being put into the near-certain success of the South Col route. The attempt was finally called off on the grounds of stonefall, though I suspect this to have been no more serious than that experienced by the European expedition of spring 1972, or even our own expedition. Once again, in the case of the international expedition, the tragedy of Harsh Bahuguna's death, the appalling weather, a high rate of sickness, and friction within the team all contributed to delaying both the initial ascent and build-up on the Face, so that finally Whillans and Haston were forced to retreat without really having made any impression on the Rock Band. In the case of the European expedition they did not attempt the Rock Band, but tried to by-pass it, traversing round to the right to escape on to the South East Ridge. This offers a comparatively easy way out and it is arguable that Kuen and his team, with a little more determination and in spite of the British contingent's defection, could still have succeeded in reaching the summit by this route. In doing so, however, they would have avoided the challenge presented by the South West Face for up to the foot of the Rock Band the climbing cannot be considered difficult and the escape route, though probably no push-over, could still be climbed quite quickly.

We, also, were in no fit state to make a sustained attempt on the Rock Band when the time came, having taken too heavy a hammering from the combination of wind and cold. Dougal Haston had described how, on the spring attempt of 1971, they had been able to sit comfortably in the sun, even at Camp 6; there was no question of that in the autumn of 1972. I had never before experienced such a combination of savage wind and intense cold over a sustained period. There was certainly no question of being able to undertake high-standard rock-climbing nor could we have supported a lead pair at Camp 6 in a siege which might have lasted several days in those weather conditions.

Can the South West Face be climbed? I am confident that in the pre-monsoon season it can; the escape route round the side would give an almost certain way to success but in taking this, the real challenge of the South West Face would be evaded. Tackling the South West Face will require a combination of high-standard technical climbing at an altitude higher than almost any other mountain in the world, together with the logistic build-up necessary to support at least two climbers – and ideally, four – at Camp 6, with oxygen, food and equipment.

It is interesting to note that the pattern of failure is very similar to that experienced by pre-war expeditions attempting the first ascent of Everest. Nearly all of these reached a height of around

27,000 feet to be defeated by the technical difficulties of the Yellow Band and the altitude. Today we can cope with a very much higher standard of difficulty at altitude, thanks to improvements in equipment, but I cannot help wondering whether these improvements are yet sufficient to enable climbers to tackle what, in effect, is a high-standard Alpine problem at an altitude of over 27,000 feet. The critical factor is oxygen, both the reliability of the supply and, even more important, the weight of the cylinder. If this weight could be reduced by half, the logistic problem also would be reduced by very nearly the same proportion, making it that much easier to sustain climbers in a siege at altitude. Developments are being made in this direction, particularly with the introduction of a chemical stick oxygen which avoids the need for carrying a heavy cylinder. This type of oxygen works on the principle of igniting a chemical substance which gives off oxygen in its combustion. Unfortunately, however, it also gives off other, noxious gases, as we discovered in the summer of 1972 when investigating the possibility of using it; the system would require a heavy filtration plant to isolate the oxygen. An improvement and reduction in weight of the oxygen system would enable an expedition to reduce the number of Sherpas required to make and maintain the build-up on the Face itself, thus easing the problems of the climbers out in front.

Another important factor is the choice of the route itself. Whillans and Haston had adopted the right-hand route up the Rock Band primarily because they had found a convenient site for Camp 5 on the right-hand side of the great central gully. From here it would have been difficult to get back across to the break on the left-hand side of the Rock Band, the line that the Japanese had favoured in 1969 and 1970. This latter line seems to have some distinct advantages. Throughout its length it appears to be a snow and ice gully in photographs taken over a period of years. The gully on the right, on the other hand, seems less reliable. The left-hand gully also has the advantages that it is shorter, being approximately five hundred feet in length, while the right-hand one is probably about eight hundred feet. Camp 5 could be situated near the foot of the Rock Band where there seems to be a snow-covered ledge on a small promontory, though even if this were to prove unusable, platforms such as those at Camp 4 could always be constructed. The great advantage of this step would be that Camp 6 would then be above the Rock Band, somewhere on the broad snow field that stretches back to the right-hand side of the upper part of the Face, where an easy-angled snow gully leads to the Col between the South summit and the main summit. The route would be more pleasing aesthetically, for there is not the easy option of an obvious escape off the Face and, at the same time, it might prove more practicable.

And so the siege goes on. Is it worth it – worth the expense – worth organizing large expeditions (for you would never climb it with a small one) – the discomfort – the possible loss of life – and all the ballyhoo which must inevitably accompany an Everest expedition? I think it is. The South West Face is a major mountaineering challenge which must continue to nag mountaineers until it has been solved, in just the same way that the Walker Spur of the Grandes Jorasses, the North Wall of the Eiger and the North Face of the Matterhorn did mountaineers in Europe before the Second World War. It is all part of the evolution of mountaineering. Today there is a strong trend in favour of lightweight expeditions, one which all the members of our own team would most certainly support, for there is, without doubt, a greater feeling of adventure and a closer empathy with the mountains when there are only a few other people around. But the only way to climb the South West Face of Everest is with a big expedition – in fact, during the later stages of our expedition we felt anything but over-crowded – each camp being manned by the minimum number of people.

On the question of cost, in my opinion it is impossible to estimate financial worth on any one adventure of man, whether it be reaching the moon, sailing round the world single-handed or climbing the South West Face of Everest. Our expedition cost in the region of £60,000, a sum considerably lower than that spent by many other Everest expeditions. The money was raised from a number of sources – from the media, Rothmans, the general public, the Government in the shape of the Sports Council and the Mount Everest Foundation. I believe our sponsors are satisfied that their money was well spent.

Then there is the publicity always surrounding any Everest expedition. This is necessary on two counts, firstly because this is the return our sponsors get for their support and secondly because both the general public and our fellow climbers are interested in what has happened. There is nothing new in this. Pre-war expeditions to Everest were extensively covered by newspapers, carried out lecture tours and excited interest similar to that of today.

Is it worth the risk of life? One could well ask whether any form of climbing is worth such a risk, and in so doing would challenge the very basis of the sport, for an integral part of the game – indeed one of its attractions – is the element of danger, and that very element must on occasions cause loss of life. Himalayan climbing has a greater level of risk than climbing on lower mountains; the climbers take themselves to greater physical limits and the scale of objective danger from weather and avalanche is that much greater, particularly on Everest where, in what must be the most dangerous Ice Fall in the world, climbers must expose themselves to risk of avalanche over a long period of time. Anyone who climbs on Everest must accept this fact. You reduce the risk factor as far as possible, but you can never eliminate it completely.

And so the challenge of Everest remains, not just that of making a first ascent of the South West Face, but even repeating the well-trodden route to its summit by the South Col. The Italians, with a mammoth-sized expedition, which has also established the controversial precedent of using helicopters to carry some supplies up into the Western Cwm, concentrated their gigantic effort on climbing Everest by the South Col route, placing eight climbers on the summit, just one less than the Indians in 1965. In the autumn of 1973 a strong Japanese expedition made another attempt on the South West Face. They started much earlier than us, reaching Base Camp in mid-August, and they also had a considerably larger team. They succeeded in making the route through the Ice Fall and establishing their Advance Base at the foot of the South West Face during the monsoon but were then delayed by heavy late monsoon snowfall. Tragically they had an accident when Jangbo was killed in an avalanche just below

Camp 3. He had been one of our most outstanding Sherpas in the autumn of 1972.

The Japanese went for the right-hand route through the Rock Band, which the three previous expeditions had followed, rather than choosing the left-hand route selected in 1969–70. In spite of their earlier start they established Camp 5 only a short time before we had established Camp 5 in the Autumn of 1972. Then, discouraged perhaps by the accident and the bad weather, they decided to put in a parallel attempt on the South Col route. This was a spectacular and very impressive success with two members of the team reaching the summit of Everest in a single push from the South Col, the first time the mountain had ever been climbed in the autumn and also the first time the ascent had been made from as low as the South Col. They paid for their achievement however, with severe frostbite. This does at least show that Everest can be climbed in the autumn.

The following spring of 1974 a Spanish expedition sponsored by a commercial firm called Tsimist also attempted the South Col route but were defeated by bad weather conditions – an indication that the South Col route cannot yet be dismissed as an easy day for the Ladies. In the autumn of 1974 an expedition of Chamonix Guides is attempting the West Ridge of Everest and in the spring of 1975 the Japanese Ladies will attempt the South Col.

Our own turn comes once again in the autumn of 1975. The Canadian Alpine Club had this slot but cancelled it in the winter of 1973. After a lot of thought and discussion with Doug Scott and Dougal Haston, I decided that it was worth having yet another attempt on the South West Face of Everest. It would mean returning in conditions that had driven us to reluctant submission in the autumn of 1972, but we had learnt a great deal from that experience and by setting out earlier, improving our equipment, particularly the tentage, on the Face itself, and with some of that luck which is so necessary on the South West Face, we felt it was worth yet another try.

We have already made one effort, contributing something to the knowledge of the Face, in exactly the same way in which three previous expeditions have done – in the way that subsequent expeditions will do, until one expedition, hopefully our own in 1975, will come up with the right cocktail of planning, timing, determination and dash of luck. Ask any member of our team or ask any mountaineer, whether he would like to go to Everest. The answer would almost certainly be 'yes', for a whole gamut of reasons: to finish off a job well started; to work out the complex formula required for success on this immense problem of logistics combined with high-standard technical climbing; to stretch body and will-power to the limit; to capture the approbation of his fellow men – a vanity to which almost all of us are a prey to some extent. But perhaps the reason, above all, is to gaze at that vista of peaks after laboriously crawling, higher and higher, up Everest's South West Face and then, if lucky, to reach the summit, to enjoy that climactic moment when the mountain drops away on every side and you are standing on the highest point on earth.

APPENDIX A

I The Team

CHRIS BONINGTON, *Leader* Age at time of expedition, 38, a photojournalist living near Manchester. Married with two children. Reached Camp 6, 27,300 feet.

JAMES ROBERTS, MVO, MBE, MC, *Deputy leader* Age 55, Director of Mountain Travel, Kathmandu : Base Camp 17,800 feet.

MICK BURKE Age 32, film cameraman living in London. Married with one child. Reached Camp 6, 27,300 feet.

NICK ESTCOURT Age 31, Systems Analyst from Manchester. Married with three children. Reached Camp 6, 27,300 feet.

DOUGAL HASTON Age 33, Director of International School of Mountaineering in Leysin. Married. Reached Camp 6, 27,300 feet.

KELVIN KENT Age 32, Major in the Royal Signals, has served with the Gurkhas and speaks fluent Nepali. Married with one child. Reached Camp 4, 24,600 feet.

HAMISH MACINNES Age 43, writer, photographer and equipment designer living in Glencoe. Reached 26,500 feet.

DOUG SCOTT Age 32, school-teacher from Nottingham. Married with two children. Reached Camp 6, 27,300 feet.

GRAHAM TISO Age 38, retailer and designer of mountaineering equipment living in Edinburgh. Married with three children. Reached Camp 5, 26,000 feet.

DAVE BATHGATE Age 32, master-joiner, married, living in Edinburgh. Reached 26,700 feet.

DR BARNEY ROSEDALE Age 37, married with one child. Reached Camp 3, 23,000 feet.

DR R. B. SUBBA Liaison officer.
BETH BURKE Base Camp.
TONY TIGHE Base Camp.
BOB STOODLEY Chairman of a group of garages in Manchester
– Fund Organizer.
BETTY PRENTICE Expedition Secretary.
DIANA LISTER Fund Secretary.

II British Everest High-Altitude Sherpas, 1972:

Jimmy Roberts

	Name	Age	Village	Times to Camp 5 and performance
1.	Pembatharke	34	Phorche	Sirdar – once to Camp 5
2.	Sona Hishy	32	Namche	Asst. Sirdar (little H.A. experience) Camp 2
3.	Pasang Namgial	33	Namche	Cook, Camp 2
4.	Phurkipa	45	Namche	Ice Fall duties
5.	Ang Phurba	27	Khumjung	Five times and Camp 6 twice
6.	Ang Nima	25	Phorche	Three times
7.	Anu	24	Khumjung	Four times
8.	Pertemba	25	Khumjung	Five times and Camp 6 twice
9.	Ang Phu	24	Khumjung	Eight times (!)
10.	Ang Dawa	33	Phorche	Twice
11.	Jangbo	29	Namche	Four times and Camp 6 twice
12.	Tenzing	37	Namche	Three times
13.	Ngati	30	Takto	Camp 4, fairly experienced
14.	Chongrinzing	24	Namche	Camp 4
15.	Pasang Tenzing	39	Khunde	Three times, experienced older man
16.	Tenzing	23	Namche	Five times. New, son of Phurkipa

17.	Mingma Rita	28	Phorche	Three times. Newish
18.	Nima Sange	36	Phorche	Three times. Newish
19.	Nima Rita	33	Phorche	Twice. Newish
20.	Nima Kanchha	24	Jharak	Twice. Newish
21.	Lhakpa Gyalu	22	Phorche	Camp 4. Very young
22.	Mingma	30	Pangboche	Camp 4
23.	Karsang Tile	42	Namche	Camp 4
24.	Nima Tenzing	42	Pangboche	Camp 4

1. Of the fourteen first selected, nine carried to Camp 5. Neither the Asst. Sirdar nor Cook went above Camp 2, and Phurkipa was confined to important duties in the Ice Fall.
2. System of selection: Jangbo and Tenzing (12) recommended by 1972 expedition, and also Phurkipa. Remaining seven men were Mountain Travel Sherpas, ex international expedition 1971, six having then carried to Camp 5 more than twice and Pertemba also to Camp 6 once. (1) was on Annapurna South Face, 1970 (5) (6) (7) on Manaslu with Messner in spring 1972. Pertemba reached top camp Annapurna 1, north side, 1970. Ang Phu was new, considered too young to go above Camp 2 on international expedition.
3. Ten men added at Base to make twenty-four (nos (15) to (24) on list). Judging from the villages the Sirdars selected people they knew, only one or two men not being from either Phorche or Namche. However, they did well, all going to Camp 4 and six to Camp 5.
4. In all, out of twenty-four men, fifteen reached Camp 5 and twenty-one reached Camp 4. Of the men who reached Camp 5, three went to Camp 6 as well.
5. About fifty-three Sherpa loads seem to have reached Camp 5, plus those carried by members. On international expedition the total was fifty-five – 1972 figure not known, but I don't think more than four or five Sherpas carried to Camp 5 that season.

Some Notes on Sherpa Performances
on Everest from 1924 to 1972:
Jimmy Roberts

The time is the morning of 3 June 1924, the scene, Camp 5 at
25,000 feet on the North Side of Mount Everest. It is a crucial
morning for the 1924 expedition. Two days before a summit
attempt by Mallory and Geoffrey Bruce had petered out when the
porters had refused to carry loads beyond Camp 5. Now, Norton
and Somervell have, in their turn, reached 5 with four porters
and after a bad night the porters are sick and dispirited and un-
willing to continue.

In *The Epic of Mount Everest* Sir Francis Younghusband tells
the story.

All having fed, Norton addressed himself to the task. The struggle
which now ensued between him and the four porters was essentially
a struggle of spirit ... Norton ... appealed to the imagination ...
There was no holding a pistol to their heads; no physical force; no
threats; nor even bribing by money. He simply painted for the
porters a picture of themselves covered with honour and glory and
receiving praises from everyone: and he told them how their names
would be inscribed in letters of gold in the book which would be
written to describe their achievement if only they would carry loads
to 27,000 feet.

Three men responded, the fourth was too ill, and Camp 6 was
established that day at a record 26,800 feet. However, afterwards,
the Mount Everest Committee seems to have run out of funds for
buying the necessary gold leaf, as we are asked to turn the black
printed names into gold as we read them: Napboo Yishay,
Lhakpa Chedi, and Semchumbi.

As a postscript to this story, after the 1953 ascent of the mountain the Himalayan Club instituted a search for Lhakpa Chedi,
who was believed to be still alive. He was discovered in Calcutta,
working as a poor watchman in some obscure factory or store-
house. Small wonder that the modern Sherpa, sometimes described
as being 'mercenary', prefers cash to fame, and does not, as some
people would like to imagine, risk his life for the fun of the game

or out of automatic and unreasoning devotion to his 'Sahibs'.

It is easy enough to write somewhat cynically now, of what one great man wrote of another great man and mountaineer fifty years ago. What is certain is that the transport of three loads to 26,800 feet that day of 3 June 1924 did mark a major breakthrough in Himalayan Mountaineering. But I guess it was respect for Norton and Somervell, rather than the promise of fame, which drove the Sherpas upwards and not down, and Younghusband, while emphasizing the honour and glory line, does hint at this in a passage I have not quoted. That 'nor even bribing by money' bit reads now like a nasty crack at modern methods, but the modern Sherpa will still respond to a personal appeal from someone he respects and who seems to be doing his best – not necessarily a lead climber, whom he may shrewdly suspect of using his services for selfish ends.

Of course during the fifty years since the 1924 expedition the standard of Sherpa performances on Everest has gone up and up and I have collected together here a few facts and figures and comparisons spaced through the years.

By the end of May 1973 eight Sherpas (some as expedition members but all former porters) had reached the summit of Mount Everest, and one of them, Nawang Gombu, reached it twice. Real fame (and some affluence), the fame and glory said to have been promised on that morning of 3 June twenty years earlier, has come to only one Sherpa, Tenzing. First is first, and one may murmur legitimately enough about luck, and being in the right place at the right time. However, in 1953, in the case of Tenzing, there is no doubt that the finger of fate also pointed at the right and most deserving man.

The comparison in progress between the 1924 and the 1953 expeditions is not very typical, as in 1953 only three Sherpas (including Tenzing) climbed higher than 26,000 feet, whereas in 1924 seven reached Camp 6 at 26,800 (another four having gone up with Mallory and Irvine on 7 June). However, in 1953 the top camp was higher and the climbing more difficult: also a much greater number of men reached 26,000 feet (the South Col) than on any pre-war expedition. Ten years later, during the 1963 American expedition, we find sixteen Sherpas reaching camps on two separate routes above 27,000 feet, including one man to the summit. A total of twenty-three men reached the South Col at 26,000 feet, but four of these men did the carry three times and eleven men twice, so in all forty-two loads of about forty pounds reached the Col. Again in 1965, with the Indians, the number reaching the top camp has increased to twenty and there are more men carrying to the South Col, one man making the trip no less than five times.

Turning to the South West Face we have more precise records of the 1971 (international) and 1972 (British) expeditions. Both expeditions had about the same number – forty – of Sherpas working above Base Camp, of which about twenty to thirty were stationed at or above Camp 2 for work on the face. In general the calibre of the men was better in 1971 than in 1972, although in 1972 the Sherpas had far better cooperation and help from the European members than in 1971. Both expeditions experienced spells of worse than normal weather conditions.

Confining statistics to Camp 5 (at 26,000 feet, the equivalent of the South Col) and above:

In 1971 seventeen men reached Camp 5 or higher, and between them they delivered a total of fifty-five loads to that camp, the best performances being by seven men who carried between camps 4 and 5 four times each. Two men reached Camp 6 at 27,000, without oxygen.

In 1972 fifteen men reached Camp 5, the total Sherpa loads reaching that camp being fifty-three – much the same figure as in 1971. The best performances were put up by one man who did eight carries, and three who did five each. One man went to Camp 6 twice, and two men helped to make the route to Camp 6.

Comparing the 1963 (American) with the 1971 expedition, both of which I had personal experience of and both of which employed about the same number of Sherpas, it is interesting to note that more loads reached 26,000 feet in 1971 than in 1963 although the route was technically more difficult and the weather was far worse in 1971. The conclusion is that once the Face route is made and roped (and of course this proviso is important) it is less demanding to carry a load from Camp 2 to 5 on the South West Face than it is to 5 on the South Col. Despite this the Sherpa record on the often criticized 1971 expedition was really very good. Whereas seventeen Sherpas reached Camp 5, only four expedition members made it to that point.

Turning to the matter of 'bribing by money', the principle was built into the strategy of the 1972 expedition, with handsome rewards for reaching the higher camps publicized from the outset. In 1963 and again in 1971 rewards were only introduced towards the end, to maintain the momentum of the carries, and were at best pretty tight-fisted. In 1938 I can remember paying off the Sherpas after a ten-week expedition to Masherbrum in the Karakorams and they received about £10 each. Of course money went further in those days, and also the men had received a small advance of pay before the expedition. But the pay was very little, about ten new pence per day, and all clothing and equipment was taken off the men. Today a high-altitude porter would earn about £50 in pay for a similar expedition, plus possibly £30 or more in rewards, plus about £120 worth of equipment – say £200 in all. Provided he can cash in on the equipment, that is good pay in Nepal, although not high by western standards, nor expensive for the services rendered by the better men. And of course the second-rate man will receive less in rewards. An increase in rates of pay in the near future is not unlikely. Unfortunately, rich expeditions tend to pile on the 'baksheesh' and incentive money, and thus make things difficult for poorer people who follow them.

The matter of the clothing and equipment has been a bone of contention between expeditions and Sherpas in the past. I have no idea of the policy followed by the pre-war Everest expeditions, but certainly up to about 1948 the men did not expect to keep their clothing and equipment at the end of an expedition. The gifting of equipment, first started by an affluent Swiss expedition coming to India after the war (it was easier to give away the stuff than to take it back to Switzerland), soon caught on, and now there is no surer way of creating poor relations with expedition Sherpas than by short-dealing them (as they think) with inadequate clothing and equipment. In 1963, on the very generously equipped American expedition, sleeping bags were the trouble: in 1971 my expensive advice was followed, and all was well: in 1972 we were in trouble again and although the complaints were soon rectified the need should not have arisen. The irritating aspect of this business, especially to a newcomer to Nepal, is that the complaints may begin before the men have themselves done a stroke of work, and those that start the trouble often turn out to be those who least deserve good equipment.

The porter long ago disappeared from the Alpine scene and these days guideless climbers far outnumber those employing guides in Europe and America. However, the conduct of Himalayan expeditions has changed very little in the last fifty years, the routes being climbed or attempted are more difficult but the general strategy employed is the same. Instead of the small compact party doing most of its own carrying, which many of us hoped to see once the giants had been climbed, expeditions have grown bigger and bigger, employing armies of men. For the Sherpas, this is all to the good, and should he tire of expedition life, there is more regular and only slightly less lucrative employment available to him in the trekking and tourist business.

I seem to have strayed from my subject of Sherpa performances on Everest, but I wonder if we have not already seen the most interesting years. No doubt the loads will continue to pile up on the South Col. Climbed fairly and correctly by any route Mount Everest continues to maintain its value, but how long the public will continue to stomach large and costly 'assaults' on the easiest way to the summit, on the lines of the 1973 Italian expedition, remains to be seen.

The South Col route would become exciting once again if the Nepalese authorities could be induced to place a limit on numbers going beyond Base Camp. Fifteen would not be too few – high mountains have been climbed by less – and within this limit it is amusing to work out the optimum composition of the party.

If I suggested one plus fourteen Sherpas I might be accused of being facetious, however five plus ten Sherpas would make a very strong team, and no topping up of numbers with additional 'Ice Fall Sherpas', and the use of helicopters or light aircraft for dropping supplies would be strictly forbidden. From these rules I must however exclude the 1975 Japanese Ladies expedition, that year let sheer manpower have its final fling – there will be more than mere loads to shift up the mountain.

APPENDIX B
Planning Instruction
(Prepared July 1972)

1. The team and responsibilities.

Bonington	Leader and co-ordination in this country.
Roberts	Deputy Leader, organization in Nepal.
Bathgate	Assistant, Equipment.
Burke	Cine and photographic.
Estcourt	Treasurer, insurance details, visas.
Haston	Any work needed on Continent.
Kent	Food and communications – Base Camp Manager.
MacInnes	Oxygen and technical design.
Scott	Equipment.
Tiso	Equipment.
Rosedale	Doctor.

  1 Liaison Officer.
  2 Sirdars.
  7 High-altitude Sherpas.
 30 Ice Fall Sherpas – with 14 high-altitude conversion kits to make the best 14 Ice Fall porters into high-altitude Sherpas.
  1 Cook (high-altitude).
  2 Cook-boys.
  4 Mail-runners.

2. Factors affecting choice of timing.

(a) *Weather*. The monsoon bad weather can end at any time from the start of September into early October. There is no regular pattern from year to year but September is often a fine month. In 1971 the weather was good in September, and the Argentinian expedition, which reached Base Camp at the start of September, made rapid progress through the Ice Fall, but were then hit by bad weather in October. By the time the weather settled in November, they had used up most of their supplies and had lost the ability to keep going. November usually seems to be a fine month, but of course it is getting progressively colder, with shorter days. There is usually a high wind coming from the North East. We should get some protection from this on the Face, but could be troubled by spindrift.

The Swiss, in 1952, abandoned their attempt on the summit from the South Col on 26 November, at a height of 26,600 feet, where they were beaten back by an icy blast of wind.

Mike Ward reports that a temperature of −40°C. has been recorded on the South Col at midday in early November, with a wind speed of 30 m.p.h. – this would give a very high wind chill factor.

It is obvious that the earlier in the season we can get into position to make a summit assault, the better chance we have of success.

(b) The scale of the logistic problem on the South West Face dictates a relatively slow build-up. To make an effective assault from Camp 6, seventy thirty-pound loads must go up to Camp 5 – See Note A. Based on these calculations, given perfect weather, it will take approximately twenty-four days to fully stock Camp 5 for the final summit assault.

(c) *Acclimatization*. It is essential that the team has time to acclimatize at a height of around 12,000 feet, working up to 18,000 before moving up to Base Camp.

(d) *Preparation time*. It is essential that the expedition leaves Britain with the best possible equipment and food correctly and logically packed. The time we have to prepare the expedition is very short, and this must affect the timing of our departure from Britain.

(e) *Transportation problems*. We shall be flying the gear out on a Space Available basis, with BOAC. This means we must let them have the expedition baggage over a space of ten days well before our own departure date.

3. Timings Chosen.

Bearing the above factors in mind, we shall try to reach Lobuje, the best place for acclimatization, as early as possible in September, so that we can either have a long period in which to acclimatize if the monsoon is late in breaking up or, in the event of fine weather, make an earlier start on the South West Face, to give us maximum chance of getting high while the weather remains fine.

We shall, therefore, aim to set out on the approach march on 25 August.

4. Approach March. 25 August to 9 September.

The party will consist of the ten climbers. Beth Burke and whatever Sherpa contingent Jimmy has organized to accompany us from Kathmandu. *Jimmy – could you please advise on this?* I estimate we shall need a total of 400 porters. Mike Cheney suggested that it might be a good idea to split the porter force, so that we have a front party with the bulk of the climbers and comparatively few porters, and then a second party, with most of the porters and perhaps two of the climbers – Kelvin plus one other? This could have the advantage that the lighter party could travel quicker, and therefore have longer to acclimatize, and make it easier over all, for finding camp sites. *I leave this entirely to Jimmy.* We could hold back the food needed for Base Camp and Advance Base, from early October onwards, and have this flown in with Jimmy when he comes out to join us. *Jimmy – your opinion on this? ? ?*

5. Acclimatization Period.

We shall march straight through to Lobuje and set up acclimatization camp there. It is impossible to predict how long this period will be, since this will depend on the monsoon. If the weather is settled, an advance party will move up to the site of Base Camp as soon as possible, commensurate with being reasonably acclimatized, to start work on the Ice Fall – on the other hand, if the monsoon seems to be lingering and the weather is bad, the entire party will remain based on Lobuje, getting what acclimatization training is possible.

At the same time, the Ice Fall Sherpas will be sorted out, equipped and given any basic training that seems necessary.

6. *The Assault.*

Phase 1: Making route through Ice Fall – four to ten days.

Four climbers and four Sherpas and eight Ice Fall porters with local porters will move up to the site of Base Camp as soon as the weather seems to be settling, to start work on the Ice Fall. They will make the route fit for porters and warn the main party to set out for Base Camp in time for them to be ready to start ferrying through the Ice Fall as soon as the route is completed.

Phase 2: Establishing advanced base – eight to ten days. (Manpower available – 49).

(a) A small advanced party of two climbers and two Sherpas will move up to the site of Camp 2, and then make the route to 3; the two climbers will move up to Camp 3, and make the route to 4.

(b) The Ice Fall route making party will rest as necessary, and then join the ferrying parties to Camp 2.

(c) The entire party, less the advanced party will be split between Base Camp and Camp 1, to ferry all the food and gear required on the Face, to Camp 2.

Phase 3: Establishing and stocking up to Camp 5. Approximately fifteen days.

(a) The best fourteen Ice Fall Sherpas will be selected and equipped as H.A. Sherpas towards the end of Phase 1.

(b) Towards the end of Phase 1, the numbers at Camp 2 will be increased, and as all the gear needed on the Face, and at Camp 2, arrives, the carrying force will be deployed as quickly as possible between Camps 2, 3 and 4. We should have thirty men available at Camp 2 and above – eight climbers, eight H.A. Sherpas and fourteen newly promoted Sherpas. They will be distributed between the three camps, with eight at Camp 4, ten at Camp 3, twelve at Camp 2. This gives a reserve in the lower camps to replace anyone who falls out in a higher camp, but we want to avoid more movement between camps than is strictly necessary.

(c) This leaves two climbers, one H.A. Sherpa and sixteen Ice Fall

Sherpas who can be used to maintain the day-to-day flow of supplies to Camp 2, and work around Base Camp. At least one of the two climbers represents one that has gone sick. We need one fit and responsible support climber at Camp 1, to keep an eye on the Ice Fall and flow of supplies. Beth can run Base Camp once Jimmy moves up to Camp 2. If the sickness rate is higher than we predict, the build-up will take longer, but the principle remains the same.

(d) In this Phase, Camp 2 becomes an Advanced Base, is made as comfortable as possible with centralized cooking organized by our H.A. cook, and as much good, fresh food as possible.

Phase 4: Climbing the Rock Band – Approximately six days.

(a) Towards the end of Phase 3, a lead pair is filtered up to Camp 5 to make the route to Camp 6. A pair will then move up to Camp 6 and try to force the line through the Rock Band. I shall allow four days for this effort. If they are unable to make any progress on the Rock Band, they will then work round the side and fix rope diagonally up towards the South Ridge.

(b) At the same time, the numbers in Camp 5 will be increased to six. These will ferry up all the food and gear required for the final assault.

(c) Once the lead pair at 6 have completed the route up to Camp 7, ideally in the snow bay at the top of the Rock Band, but should this prove impossible near the crest of the South Ridge, a pair will move up to 6, and from this four, one pair will be selected to move up to 7, supported by the other pair, to make the summit assault.

Phase 5: First Assault.

(a) The summit assault should be made from the top of the Rock Band. The first assault pair will take enough rope – 600 ft. – to fix awkward sections. This is essential for their retreat and in the event of having to put in a second assault. It is possible that the first assault pair could be so badly delayed by a difficult section that they do not have time to reach the summit in the day. They will have to watch their oxygen very carefully.

(b) At the same time that the assault goes in, it is essential that the pair at Camp 6 do another carry, taking up a further 4 bottles of oxygen, which the assault pair can use on their return to Camp 7, 2 bottles for the night and 2 bottles to get back down the next day. They should use this oxygen as little as possible, since this would be invaluable for a second assault.

Phase 6: Second Assault.

It is important that we have the ability to make a second assault, ideally, with a fairly rested pair. This will be mounted as soon as possible after the first assault.

Bad Weather: In the event of bad weather, particularly when the team is deployed up to Camps 5 and 6, I shall have the difficult decision of deciding whether to sit it out, using up oxygen, or putting everyone back to Camp 2. In principle, if it means only a short spell of bad weather, it is best to sit it out, using the minimum of oxygen.

Rests: We shall try to avoid people coming back down to rest more than is absolutely essential. It is best for team members to take regular rest days at the camp they happen to be in. I have calculated on an average of 1 in 5 days resting. We must try to keep up the momentum of the deployment on the mountain.

7. *Oxygen.*

(a) 3 to 4. Climbers to use it for climbing and carrying, if they feel they want it.

(b) 4 to 5. Climbers use it for carrying and climbing, and occasionally at night if they really feel the need for it. Sherpas carry without it, but can use some at night if necessary.

(c) 5 to 6. Climbers and Sherpas (if we use them that high) carry and climb with it, and sleep using one bottle between two.

(d) 6 to 7. Climbers use one bottle a day for climbing or carrying, one bottle each at night.

(e) 7 to top. The summit pair will spend one night at Camp 7 with a bottle each for sleeping. They will take two bottles each on the summit push. It is vital that the support pair at 6 get a further four bottles up to 7 on the day of the summit push, to be used by the summit pair, if needed, on their way back down. We shall use the French bottles for the summit push, since they have 1000 litres of oxygen in them and therefore have a better capacity–weight ratio than the Luxfer bottles.

8. *Food.*
See Note B for detailed food planning.

9. *Wireless.*
As described in my newsletter 2.

10. *Tentage.*
As described in newsletter 2.

Note A – Weight Statistics

Summit Push

Oxygen	4 bottles – French	48	
Regulators	2	2	
Pack-frames	2	4	
Cine gear	1	4	
Rope and iron	500 ft	18	
		76	2 × 38 lb. loads

To Camp 7

Oxygen – Sleeping	2 bottles – French	24	
Tent	1	6	
Foams	2	2	
Cooker+Pan+1 Gas	1	4	
Food	2 man-days	4	
Personal gear	2	16	
Radio	1	2	
Oxygen carrying	4 bottles – French	48	
		106	
		76	
		182	4 × 45.5 lb. loads

Oxygen for return or second ascent	4 bottles – French	48	
Oxygen carrying	2 bottles	24	
		72	
		182	
Oxygen bottles – running total=16		254	

To Camp 6

Oxygen – climbing	8 bottles – British	120	
– sleeping	14 bottles	210	
– spare	4 bottles	60	
Boxes	2×12 lb.	24	
Foams	2	2	
Cooking kit	1	2	
Gas Cartridges	10×1½ lb.	15	
Food	16 man-days	40	
Rope	2,000 ft	40	
Ironmongery		8	
Radio	1	2	
Personal gear	2 man	20	
Film		8	
First Aid Kit	1	1	
		552	
		254	
Oxygen bottles – running total=42		806	33×25 lb. loads

To Camp 5

Oxygen – carrying to 6	33 bottles	495	
– sleeping	23 bottles	345	
– making route	4 bottles	60	
– spare	4 bottles	60	
Boxes/tunnel tents	3	48	
Cooking kits	3	6	
Food	40 man-days	100	
Radio	1	2	
Gas cartridges	20×1½ lb.	30	
Rope	3,000 ft	60	
Iron		15	
Personal gear	4 men	60	
Film-cassettes etc.		20	
First Aid Kit	1	1	
		1302	
		806	
Oxygen – running total=106		2108	70×30 lb. loads

To Camp 4

Oxygen – carrying	20 bottles	300	
– sleeping	20 bottles	300	
Rope	2,000 ft	40	
Iron		15	
Boxes	4	64	
Cooking kits	3	9	
Gas cartridges	26	39	
Food	50 man-days	125	
Personal gear	6 men	60	
Radio	1	2	
Cine gear		20	
Extras		60	
First Aid Kit	1	1	
		1035	
		2108	
Oxygen – running total=146		3143	105×30 lb. loads

To Camp 3

Oxygen	20 bottles	300	
Rope	2,500 ft	50	
Iron		15	
Boxes	4	64	
Cooking kits	3	9	
Gas cartridges	40	60	
Food	90 man-days	225	
Radio	1	2	
Personal gear	6	60	
Cine gear		20	
Extras	1	60	
First Aid Kit	1	1	
		866	
		3143	
Oxygen – running total=166		4009	115×35 lb. loads

To 2 – Initial Stock

4 Man tents	4	80
Personal gear	8 men	80
Gas Cartridges	30	45
Rope	1,200 ft	22
Ironmongery		30
Food – Mountain	40 man-days	100
Spare oxygen	20	300
Extras		600
Big tents	2	160
Cooking kits	1	60
(including 2 space heaters)		1477
		4009
		5486

140 × 40 lb. loads + 180 man-days of food/gas/paraffin allowance to get above to Camp 2 at 5 lb. man-day 23 loads.

2–4 man tents + cooking kit left at 1 = 2 loads.

Grand Total: 165 loads to 2.

This represents the quantity of food to go to above Camp 2 and all gear to 2 and above.

186 bottles oxygen.

At Base Camp 11 bottles.

Note: Once Camp 2 has been initially established at the end of Phase 2 the 16 Ice Fall porters, left to service Camp 2, will be sufficient to keep it stocked on a day-to-day basis, with fresh food, etc., and at the same time bring up extra cine equipment, personal gear and other items, to convert Camp 2 into an effective Base Camp.

Note B – Food

1. *Quantities.*

See following breakdown.

2. *Approach and Base Camp ration.*

(a) Allow 1 lb. per man-day from England but the effective European ration could be higher than this, since the Sherpas would not want the breakfast foods and some of the other purely European foods.

(b) Put ration from England in twelve man-day boxes so that we can open a fresh one each day.

(c) This can be supplemented by reserve boxes containing such things as dehydrated meats, egg, vegetables, potato (lots of this) for when we cannot purchase fresh food for one reason or another.

(d) Plan each day's menu to combine the items brought from England – which should be unobtainable in Kathmandu – items bought in Kathmandu, and items that can be purchased on the march, so that each day's menu is varied and interesting.

(e) IT IS VITAL THAT WE EAT WELL ON THE APPROACH MARCH AND AT BASE CAMP.

3. *Advanced Base ration.*

(a) Allow 2 lb. per man-day from England.

(b) Think on lines of eight man-day ration boxes.

(c) The increase in weight from England should be made up with dehydrated meats and some tinned meats, good breakfast foods, and dried vegetables, plenty of mashed potato powder.

(d) Good bulk fillers are important for both Base Camp and Advanced Base. We should be able to get plenty of potatoes in Khumjung, but remember that these will freeze solid on way up to Advanced Base. We might be able to get over this by pre-cooking.

(e) Plan on fresh foods being sent out from Kathmandu – cheeses, salami, good vegetables – once Lukla is open. Liaise with Cheney on this.

(f) Another excellent staple is noodles and all types of pasta – I believe these are obtainable in Kathmandu.

4. *Mountain ration.*

(a) 2½ lb. per man-day – GROSS – packed in two man-day packs from England.

(b) Mike's first proposals on right lines, but replace tinned products by dehydrated foods, if possible.

(c) Include effervescent multi-vitamin tablets in each pack. They make a pleasant drink. Talk this over with Barney.

(d) A high-quality box of matches in each pack – remember our troubles on Annapurna?

(e) A slow-burning candle – Price's patent candles – address from Tiso – in every other pack.

(f) Some tissue paper in each pack.

(g) Good cough sweets in each pack – talk to Barney.

5. *Packaging.*

Packaging wants to be light as possible, but must be strong. Make all food loads into 70 lb. units, with an outer covering that is *robust, completely waterproof yet as light as possible.*

Approach and Base Camp rations. Make up containers of five 12 man-day packs.

Advance Base ration. Band together two separate containers each containing 2 eight man-day packs. 1 eight man-day pack should weigh 16 lb., the twin packs with packaging will weigh say 34 lbs. (right for carrying through Ice Fall). The complete load will weigh 69 lb.

Mountain ration. Band together two separate containers, each containing 6 two man-day packs – 1 two man-day pack weighs 5 lb., the 6 two man-day package will weigh say 32 lb., the total porter load will weigh 64 lb.

Individual packing of items. Investigate vac packing, sachets and plastic. We want stuff to be compact as well as light.

6. *Research.*

We haven't much time but check with Services research departments, and contact all the major food firms that make any kind of dehydrated foods. Check with Mike Cheney on foods obtainable in Kathmandu.

7. *Marking.*
Mark all packages and containers clearly.

8. *Supplier of Food.*
I have got one more possible line of getting a single big food complex to take over supply and packing of food. I shall give them till 30 June to make up their minds, then we must go to Andrew Lusk, pay them to do the entire job of getting food together and packing it. Kelvin, you might have to order highly specialized foods – Kendal Mint Cake, some dehydrated food – you could start work on that immediately.

9. *Deadline.*
I want all food packed and ready by the 1st August.

Everest South West Face – 1972

Food Calculations – allowing for 15-day approach march and 70 days at Base Camp and above.

Approach	12 Europeans	(10 climbers plus Beth + 1 extra)	
March	12 Nepalis	(9 Sherpas, LO, 2 cook-boys)	
	24 For 15 days at	1 lb. from England	360 lb.
		3 lb. from Kathmandu	1080 lb.
	360 man-days		
Base	12 Europeans	(10 climbers plus Beth, Extra)	
Camp	45 Nepalis	(9 Sherpas, 30 IF Sherpas, LO, 3 kitchen, 2 mail-runners)	
	57 For 30 days at	1 lb. from England	1710 lb.
		3 lb. from Kathmandu	5130 lb.
	5 Europeans	(Beth, I & II supervisors, 3 sick or visiting)	
	17 Nepalis	(10 Sherpas I & II, 2 sick, 2 kitchen, LO, 2 mail)	
	22 For 50 days at	1 lb. from England	1100 lb.
		1 lb. from Kathmandu	1100 lb.
		2 lb. local	2200 lb.
	2810 man-days		

Advanced   8 climbers, 21 Sherpas for 20 days
Base   29 at 2 lb. from England   1160 lb.
                              1 lb. from Kathmandu   580 lb.
                              1 lb. local   580 lb.
           4 climbers, 10 Sherpas for 40 days
                        14 at 2 lb. from England   1120 lb.
                              1 lb. from Kathmandu   560 lb.
                              1 lb. local   560 lb.
           1140 *man-days*

Assault   8 climbers, 14 Sherpas for 40 days
Ration   22 at 2½ lb. from England   2200 lb.
           880 *man-days*

           Totals   From England   7560 lb.*
                                 From Kathmandu   8450 lb.
                                 Local   3340 lb.
           Porter loads from Kathmandu (first 45 days)   212 loads

Total man-days on Expedition:

           Approach   15 × 24 man-days = 360
           Mountain   70 × 56 man-days = 4265 man-days
           Food allowed for expedition   = 5175 man-days

* Make up to 8000 lb. with Luxury boxes+dried meat to
supplement Base Camp ration.

APPENDIX C

Equipment:
Graham Tiso

The manufacturers and suppliers of the equipment we required responded magnificently to our call not only for price concessions but principally for delivery on time. Ordinarily normal delivery times are so extended it would have been impossible to get together such a vast quantity of specialized equipment in eight months let alone eight weeks. The equipment left Britain on time with not one single item missing, proof that in times of crisis people respond. The expedition acknowledges an enormous debt of gratitude to all these people to whom the word 'impossible' did not exist. It may be invidious to single out some for special mention but their response was so outstanding, the risk is worth taking.

Frank Brownlie and Cyril Workman and their assistants at BOAC Cargo Centre, Heathrow, who treated our stores as though they were the most valuable, most fragile, most important goods ever to pass through their hands. No V.I.P. ever had treatment like our stores!

Dave Crooks and Charlie Boyle of L.E.P. Transport Edinburgh who responded to every demand made on them even though on occasions it was only remotely connected with transport and customs clearance.

Mike Devereux of Ashton Containers who designed and produced special waterproof cardboard boxes out of an already overfull pre-holiday production commitment in an incredible seven days.

Alastair Veitch of the Alna Press whose personal attention to our printing and stationery requirements saved Chris Bonington and myself so many valuable hours.

Squadron Leader Simon Baker of R.A.F. Carlisle who refused to be beaten by the problems of packing down suits and foam mats in a vacuum packing machine designed to pack shirts, vests and handkerchiefs.

Black and Edgington Ltd who made specially, at the height of their season, some of the most important of our camping requirements including the tentage which was to perform so well on the mountain.

And lastly, my wife and children who, knowing I was to be away for three months, never complained though I was only to be seen on my way to and from bed for the preceding two months.

We knew that we would have enough problems to cope with even if we had no equipment failure at all. Proven equipment was essential; Everest is not the place to prove new ideas. Doug Scott's recent experience and Bonington's Annapurna knowledge were married to my knowledge of what it was possible to obtain in the short time available and the equipment requirement was drawn up.

The scale of issue of equipment to climbers, high-altitude Sherpas, Ice Fall Sherpas, cook boys, mail-runners, the liaison officer and the conversion kit to equip selected Ice Fall Sherpas to high-altitude standards was drawn up. It was then tossed back and forth between Chris Bonington, Jimmy Roberts and myself until we all agreed. The result is reproduced below. The kit for climbers, high-altitude Sherpas and the liaison officer was packed in personal boxes for issue at Kathmandu, the remainder packed with general equipment for issue on the approach march.

All the equipment was supplied through my own retail organization and goods for which we had to pay were sold to the expedition at net cost price. All equipment was assembled and packed in my warehouse in Edinburgh and all my staff worked exceptionally hard, often in their own time, to ensure that the gigantic task of assembling and packing about 10,000 lb. of equipment in eight short weeks was completed on time. Without their help Dave Bathgate and I could never have coped. The expedition in this, as in many other cases, is extremely grateful for the assistance of faceless, nameless helpers.

Personal Equipment – Scale of Issue

		Climbers	H.A.S.	I.F.S.	C.K.	L.O.	CB/MR.
Windproof suit	Mountain Equipment	1	–	–	–	–	–
Down suit	Mountain Equipment	1	–	–	–	–	–
Ventile anorak	R. L. Harrison & Co. Ltd	–	1	1	1	–	1
Ventile trousers	R. L. Harrison & Co. Ltd	–	1	1	1	1	1
Egger Expedition duvet jackets	ETS Roger Egger	1	1	1	1	1	1
Egger duvet trousers	ETS Roger Egger	–	1	1	1	1	1
Tiklas padded ski jacket	Pindisports Ltd	–	1	1	1	–	–
G.T. zip cagoule	Graham Tiso	1	1	–	–	–	1
Foam-back cagoule	Ultimate Equipment Ltd	–	1	1	1	1	1
Nylon overtrousers	Ultimate Equipment Ltd	–	1	1	1	–	1
Damart suits	Damart Thermawear (Bradford) Ltd	2	2	1	1	2	1
Helly Hansen Polar jackets	Helly Hansen (U.K.) Ltd	1	1	1	1	1	1
Helly Hansen Polar trousers	Helly Hansen (U.K.) Ltd	1	1	1	1	1	1
Bukta track suits	Edward R. Buck & Sons Ltd	–	1	1	1	1	1
Clarks Craghopper trousers	H. Pickles & Sons Ltd	–	–	–	–	–	–
Levi jeans	Levi Strauss (U.K.) Ltd	1	1	1	1	1	1
St Michael sweaters	Marks & Spencers Ltd	2	1	1	1	2	1
Pringle Houston Merino sweaters	Pringle of Scotland	2	–	–	–	1	–
Everest Shetland sweaters	W. Bill Ltd	1	–	–	–	–	–

Personal Equipment – Scale of Issue – *(continued)*

		Climbers	H.A.S.	I.F.S.	C.K.	L.O.	CB/MR.
Summerland sweaters	Jersey Knitwear Co.	1	–	–	–	–	–
Joe Brown shirts	Joe Brown	–	1	–	–	1	–
Viyella shirts	William Hollins & Co. Ltd	2	–	–	–	–	–
Balaclava helmets	Robert Sim of Stewarton	1	1	1	1	1	1
Helly Hansen Polar mitts	Helly Hansen (U.K.) Ltd	2	2	1	1	1	–
Dachstein mitts	Viktor Derkogner	2	2	–	1	1	–
Miloré silk gloves	Miloré Ltd	2	–	–	–	–	–
Janus mittens	C. & L. Towers	–	–	1	1	1	1
Star North Wall stockings	Star Sportswear Ltd	3	3	1	3	3	1
Helly Hansen polar socks	Helly Hansen (U.K.) Ltd	1	1	1	1	1	–
Down socks	Mountain Equipment	1	1	1	1	–	–
Galibier Makalu boots	Richard Pontvert	1	1	1	1	1	–
Kastinger Nordwand boots	Vango (Scotland) Ltd	–	–	–	–	–	–
Niagara walking boots	A. L. White & Co. Ltd	1	1	–	1	–	–
Morlands sheepskin boots	Morlands of Glastonbury	1	1	1	–	1	–
Millet gaiters	Sacs Millet	1	1	–	–	–	–
Millet overboots	Sacs Millet	1	1	–	–	–	–
Foam overboots	Karrimor Weathertite Products Ltd	1	1	1	1	1	–
Karrimor nylon overboots	Karrimor Weathertite Products Ltd	1	1	–	–	–	–

Product	Manufacturer					
Stop Tous	J. E. Barlow & Co. Ltd	–	1	–	1	1
Aries insoles	E. A. Chamberlain Ltd	2	2	1	1	1
Downhill goggles	I. & M. Steiner (1950) Ltd	1	1	1	1	–
Folding goggles	I. & M. Steiner (1950) Ltd	2	1	–	1	1
Champion goggles	I. & M. Steiner (1950) Ltd	–	1	1	1	1
B.A.O. sunglasses	British American Optical Co. Ltd	2	1	1	1	–
Fairy Down Polar sleeping bags	Arthur Ellis & Co. Ltd	1	1	1	1	1
Dacron Fibrefill sleeping bags	Black & Edgington Ltd/Du Pont (U.K.) Ltd	1	–	1	1	1
Stuff bags	Tulloch Mountaincraft	3	3	–	2	3
Camp Trails Astral packframe and bag	Camp Trails	1	–	1	–	–
Karrimor Eurotrekker pack-frame and bag	Karrimor Weathertite Products Ltd	–	1	1	1	–
Inter-Alp Chouinard Frost ice-axes	Codega Nicola & Figli snc.	1	1	1	–	–
Inter-Alp Cerro Torre ice-axes	Codega Nicola & Figli snc.	–	1	1	–	–
Chouinard crampons	Salewa	1	1	1	–	–
Salewa crampons	Salewa	–	1	–	–	–
Whillans harness	Troll Products	1	1	1	1	–
Jumars	Robert Lawrie Ltd	2	1	1	1	–
Wire brushes for Jumars	Myles Brothers	1	1	1	1	–
Pile Wonder head torches	Pindisports Ltd	1	1	–	–	1

Personal Equipment – Scale of Issue – (continued)

		Climbers	H.A.S.	I.F.S.	C.K.	L.O.	CB/MR.
Aluminium water bottles	Marsteller & Killman	1	–	–	–	–	–
Seiko wrist watches	Seiko Time (U.K.) Ltd	1	–	–	–	–	–
Fero wrist watches	S. B. Schlesinger & Co. Ltd	–	1	1	–	–	–
Ronson Windmaster lighters	Ronson Products Ltd	–	1	1	1	–	–
Feudor stick lighters	R. Barling & Sons Ltd	3	1	1	1	–	–
Swiss Army knife	Swiss Cutlery (London) Ltd	1	1	1	1	–	–
Housewives	Scottish Infantry Depot	1	1	1	1	–	–
Umbrellas	Kathmandu Bazaar	1	1	1	–	–	–
Aiguille extendable sacs	Karrimor Weathertite Products Ltd	–	–	–	–	–	1
Pee bottles	Black & Edgington Ltd	1	–	–	–	–	–

H.A.S.=High Altitude Sherpas
I.F.S.=Ice Fall Sherpas
C.K.=Conversion Kit
L.O.=Liaison Officer
CB/MR.=Cook-Boys and Mail-Runners

N.B. Spares are required to cover losses and extra mitts, socks, and goggles should be taken plus a few extras of some other items to cover changes in plan or requirements. For instance, we planned to give the mail-runners the Aiguille Extendable Sacs but found they required bigger ones – we had extra pack-frames and bags and were able to issue these.

Notes on personal equipment

Outer clothing must be windproof but must not be so water repellent that condensation occurs on the inside. For climbers a one-piece suit with outer of breathing nylon and lined with Ventile was chosen. Basically the idea worked well but the outer nylon wore badly and a superior quality would have been better. Closer attention to detail points of design and cut would also have been desirable. The pockets were not big enough, were not capable of being fastened securely and the opening of the lower ones was covered by our harnesses. The long front zip should have been capable of opening from the bottom to form a fly. The zip sliders should have had bigger pullers to allow them to be gripped with a gloved hand but a more serious fault was the omission of a hood. The suits were very baggy in the nether regions though our harnesses acted like a corset and held the spare material in place.

For the Sherpas we chose conventional double-texture Ventile anoraks and trousers as they would be of more use to them after the expedition than a one-piece suit. They were totally satisfactory.

Down suits of similar design to the windproof suits were used by climbers. They were very good and had hoods though again detail design could have been better. The nylon was not completely downproof and this caused thin spots and speckled under layers. Egger (Erve) expedition duvet jackets and trousers were given to Sherpas and were much appreciated. A padded ski-jacket was given to Ice Fall Sherpas, which with the foam-backed cagoule to keep the wind out, heavy serge trousers and nylon overtrousers, provided adequate insulation.

Damart vests and longjohns were worn by everyone for just about all of the time although it is perhaps significant that the two most experienced cold-weather climbers, Bonington and Haston, changed to woollen underwear when it got really cold.

Everyone wore their *polar suits* almost all of the time, and found them excellent. It was felt, however, that they should have had pockets; indeed some members added them themselves.

Although *Dachstein mittens* had previously been thought the best, almost unanimously, *Polar mittens* with nylon outers were found to be superior for swarming up fixed ropes and working around camps. *Miloré silk gloves* are knitted from silk rather than made from a woven fabric and everyone sang their praises.

Down socks are used principally as bed socks but it was felt that the plastic sole transmitted cold and should be replaced with a good insulating material.

Galibier Makalu boots (previously Hivernale) are considered to be the best available. The team felt that one or two detail design changes could be made which would significantly improve the insulating properties of these boots and the factory have responded by making prototypes incorporating changes suggested by us. Although one member enthused about *Millet overboots*, no one else wore them as they have to be permanently fixed to the outer boot and thus preclude the use of the foam overboots. Probably we would have been better to take Chouinard 'Supergators' as they are not a permanent fixture. These would give additional insulation above the sole of the boot and with a nylon overboot with an insulated sole would probably give the best protection against cold for high-altitude climbing.

Nylon overboots are invaluable from Base Camp up, not only for wearing when climbing as an additional insulating and protective layer but also around camp for slipping on over whatever footwear one is wearing in a tent to go outside for a short spell.

Kastinger single boots used by the Ice Fall Sherpas were supplied big enough to take two or three pairs of socks and proved perfectly adequate up to Advance Base Camp at 21,800 feet. *Morlands* sheepskin boots are welcomed by aching feet after a hot day's walk or a day in the Ice Fall. They would have been most useful at Camp 2 and we envied the Sherpas who had the foresight to take them this high.

The expensive *'Downhill'* goggles used by the climbers were found to give insufficient protection on their own and an additional spare lens from the *'Champion'* goggles had to be added to cut down glare to an acceptable level. The cheap *folding goggles* however were much appreciated by everyone as disposable adequate protection. It was also found necessary to double up on the lenses in the 'Champion' goggles and undoubtedly the best protection is given by the virtually unbreakable B.A.O. *sunglasses*.

Sleeping bags caused us some concern. We considered that high-quality single bags in conjunction with our down suits would be adequate but the high-altitude Sherpas demanded an inner bag and, as we found when it got colder, they were justified in doing so. Fortunately some members had taken their own personal bags with them and we were able to rush out from Britain some special *Mountain Equipment* bags to supplement our stores. The *Fairy Down* polar bags were too bulky and too heavy, but this was because we had given insufficient thought to their size; they were too big. Had they been the correct dimensions they would have been very good indeed. Probably a good combination would be a very high-quality lightweight, low-bulk down bag supplemented by a light synthetic filled bag which could double as a bag for warmer temperatures such as those encountered on the walk-in.

Although the experimental *Dacron Fibrefill II sleeping bags* seemed to satisfy the Ice Fall Sherpas, when the climbers used them doubled up at Base Camp they found them inadequate. Fibrefill II is an experimental sleeping bag filling which theoretically should be much better than any other synthetic filling. It did not perform as well as expected and on return to the U.K., investigations showed that the bags were not constructed in such a way as to allow this filling to give optimum insulation.

We chose the *Camp Trails 'Astral' pack-frame* as the 'V' strengthening at the top as opposed to a bar joining the two uprights right at the very top allows the wearer to look up more easily. These frames and bags were completely trouble-free as were the *Karrimor Eurotrekker frames* which carried an astronomical load up the mountain.

We chose the *Chouinard/Frost Bamboo shafted axe* for the high-altitude Sherpas and ourselves as being the best available. As the Ice Fall Sherpas were likely to do anything with their axes except cut steps we chose *Cerro Torre axes* with high-strength metal shafts. No breakage was incurred in either model in spite of considerable abuse.

The only problem with the new *Chouinard crampons* made by Salewa was with the bar which holds the centre posts; breakages were not uncommon. The fault which caused this has now been rectified at the factory. *The Salewa crampons* basically stood up very well though a vast stock of the serrated bars which joined the front and heel parts was needed as there were two or three breakages a day in the latter part of the expedition. This is possibly due to the crampons being used constantly on ladders and bridges in the Ice Fall putting an unnatural strain on this part.

The *Whillans harness* was considered indispensable and the only criticism made was that the crutch strap which is now made from 1½" web was more comfortable when it was 1". We understand that there are manufacturing problems in using the 1" web. The *Jumars* worked perfectly; no trouble was encountered in slipping on iced ropes. It was found that a single Jumar attached with a short length of webbing to the Whillans harness was the easiest way of ascending fixed ropes.

The *Pile Wonder headtorches* were only used on the walk-in and around Base Camp. Most of them fell to pieces and were considered to be inadequate for the job.

The *wrist watches* kept excellent time in spite of severe weather conditions. This is important when radio schedules have to be kept.

Lighters are an essential not a luxury. Matches fail to function in the rarified atmosphere of the higher camps and the little 'Stick' lighters are ideal. Provided that they are kept in a warm pocket or warmed for a moment in the hand they work first time even in the coldest conditions.

An *umbrella* serves to keep off the rain on the walk-in and the sun once one gets on to the mountain. Definitely another indispensable piece of equipment on a trip such as this.

The *Karrimor Aiguille extendable sacs* were used as day sacs in the Ice Fall and were satisfactory except that it was found that the harness was set too wide at the top. The factory are taking steps to rectify this failing.

The *pee bottle* was perhaps the most used piece of personal kit. A wide necked polythene bottle of thirty-five fluid ounces capacity was found adequate for all but the most prolonged stays in one's sleeping bag. It is essential to empty them whilst they are still liquid; a frozen pee bottle was an almost insuperable problem.

Climbing Gear

5,000 M	Edelweiss 8 mm. tensile rope	M. Teufelberger
150 M	Edelweiss 6mm. tensile rope	M. Teufelberger
300 M	Edelweiss 5mm. tensile rope	M. Teufelberger
100 M	Edelweiss 4mm. tensile rope	M. Teufelberger
12×150'	Viking 9mm. climbing rope	British Ropes
1,000'	Tigers Web R2X 1" Soft	Black & Edgington Ltd
1,000'	Tigers Web R2X ½" Soft	Black & Edgington Ltd
300	Bonaiti 12mm. alloy karabiners	Guiseppe & F. lli Bonaiti
100	Tubular aluminium snow stakes	Aalco (Glasgow) Ltd
25	Deadmen	Clogwyn Climbing Gear
45	Salewa drive-in ice pitons	Salewa
90	Salewa tubular ice screws	Salewa
30	Stubai ice screws	Stubai
40	Stubai ice pitons	Stubai
100	Chouinard rock pitons	Chouinard
16	Hiebler Prussickers	Salewa
1	Parba bolt kit	Troll Products
24	Troll Etrier steps	Troll Products
1	Avalanche probe	Salewa
20 prs.	Snowtread snow-shoes	Sportsman Products Inc.
39	Sectional aluminium ladders	Lyte Industries Ltd
100	Marker flags	Ultimate Equipment Ltd
300	Marker canes	Kathmandu Bazaar

Notes on climbing gear

High tensile strength auxiliary climbing rope is less elastic than a normal climbing rope and was found ideal for fixed ropes. 8mm. diameter rope was used up to Camp 6 and from there it was intended to use the 6mm. to save weight. The 8mm. rope was also cut into sixty-foot lengths as the Sherpas insist on tying themselves together in ropes of three for going up the Ice Fall and along the Western Cwm. Although it was intended that climbers leading should use 9mm. climbing rope single, in practice, they invariably led out on the 8mm. rope.

Webbing is used for a wide variety of purposes as are the smaller sizes of rope. Tigers Web was found to be satisfactory provided that the ends were taped after the knot had been tied otherwise it was found that the knot worked loose.

After a typing error, which resulted in our taking five thousand feet of rope instead of five thousand metres, had been rectified we found that our supplies of rope and webbing were just adequate. All the rope intended for use as fixed rope was taken on 100-metre drums which eased running out problems.

Tubular aluminium snow stakes and *deadmen* were used as snow anchors. A considerable quantity was used in the Ice Fall, for fixing ropes, bridges and ladders and because of this we had to manufacture a further supply of deadmen for use on the mountain. We could have used 200 snow stakes and 50 deadmen. The tubular aluminium stakes were also invaluable for anchoring tents in soft snow. Stakes were taken in 18″, 24″ and 30″ lengths and the longest ones were easily the best. We could well have taken the whole lot in that length.

Ice pitons were used more for anchoring ladders and bridges in the Ice Fall than on the Face itself and we had more than enough. Very few rock pitons were needed though if we had gone on to the Rock Band undoubtedly more would have been used.

The *Hiebler Prussickers* were taken in case we experienced problems with Jumars on iced-up ropes but were not needed. The *Parba bolt kit, Etrier steps* and the *avalanche probe* were not used.

Our *Snowtread* snow-shoes were used after heavy snowfalls on the journeys between Camps 1 and 2 up the Western Cwm. They certainly speeded the progress of the person wearing them but were not very satisfactory in compacting a trail.

Aluminium ladders are essential for bridging and surmounting ice cliffs in the Ice Fall. They must be very strong as they are subjected to considerable pressures due to the changing nature of the Ice Fall. They must fit together easily and should have only a minimal sag when made up into twenty-five-foot lengths. The ones we took were excellent in every respect.

The small triangular nylon *marker flags* we took were excellent but we did not have anything like enough and had to improvise by sticking tape on top of the canes. A marker cane on its own is not easily seen. A flag is essential and we should have had three hundred.

Tentage, etc.

2	Black's Safari Regent tents	Black & Edgington Ltd
3	Black's Stormhaven tents	Black & Edgington Ltd
5	Black's Scott Tunnel tents	Black & Edgington Ltd
2	Black's Itisa Senior tents	Black & Edgington Ltd
6	Karrimor Whillans Boxes	Karrimor Weathertite Products
8	Ultimate Everest Boxes	Ultimate Equipment Ltd
1	Ultimate Assault tent	Ultimate Equipment Ltd
4	North Face tents	The North Face
1	Powderhorn tent	Powderhorn Mountaineering
6	Vango Force 10 Mark 5 tents	Vango (Scotland) Ltd
56	Open Cell foam mats	Kay Metzler
100	Karrimats	Expanded Rubber and Plastic
100	Aluminium tent pegs	Aalco (Glasgow) Ltd
20	Snow brushes	Myles Brothers

Notes on tentage

Good tentage on a long expedition is essential as morale must suffer if a group of people are living in cramped unsatisfactory conditions.

We found the large *Black's Safari Regent* family camping tents ideal for our communal living tent at Base Camp and Camp 2. They both comfortably withstood the foulest weather the mountain threw at them except when one was pitched at Camp 1 with only two climbers in residence. This tent collapsed due to the weight of snow on it as the occupants could not shovel it off fast enough. It was soon re-erected and continued to perform perfectly both at Camp 1 and later at Camp 2. The main zips on the doors of both tents eventually failed allowing spindrift to enter during storms. Spindrift also came in through gaps round the edges of the windows but these were easily sealed with adhesive tape. The tents were quite remarkably stable and we experienced no other problems with them whatsoever.

The *Black's Stormhaven* tents were used as cook tents at Camps 1 and 2, the Camp 1 tent surviving the whole of the expedition in spite of the tremendous weight of snow which accumulated at this camp. The Camp 2 tent survived most of the time but eventually succumbed to the final storm. It was buried right up to ridge height.

Black's special double-skin nylon *Tunnel tents* designed by Doug Scott eventually proved to be the strongest, most reliable tents we had. The layer of air trapped between the two skins gave welcome insulation when it got really cold and more than compensated for the consequent lack of space inside the tent as compared to our boxes. The joints on the fibre-glass wands which more than doubled the diameter of the wand for a short length made it difficult to pitch and strike the tents. Once they were up they could withstand the most severe weather.

Black's *Itisa Senior Tents* were used on the walk-in and at Base Camp. They were perfectly satisfactory until a heavy snowfall weighed down the flysheet to such an extent that the pole poked its way through the top. This would appear to be a failing in this single pole design of tent as the *Powderhorn Tent* which is of similar design also suffered in this way.

The *Karrimor Whillans Boxes* which have previously performed so well in the most adverse weather conditions were just not capable of withstanding autumnal Everest weather. The principal fault was that the framework bent and broke. The poles were different from those used on tents supplied to previous expeditions but Karrimor understood from the manufacturer that they were of equal strength. We proved to our cost that this was not the case and Karrimor are now reverting to poles which are to the original specification.

A less serious failing was that the Ventile material used on the sides and ends of the boxes was insufficiently strong. We had arranged for this material to be supplied by the manufacturers, Ashton Brothers, and had unwittingly used medium-weight Ventile instead of heavy-weight. We proved that a really strong material is needed to withstand the inevitable nicks and gashes it gets from axes, crampons and other sharp objects.

A minor but niggling fault was that the zipped door started to open from the bottom which was a nuisance when snow was piled high against it. It would be much better if a double-ended slider zip were used so that one could open the door from the top under these conditions and clear the snow away to prevent it all falling into the tent.

We found the boxes to be rather short, so short that the tallest members could not comfortably stretch out in them. We think the body of the box should be not less than seven feet and a storage bay should be built in so that rucksacks can be taken inside rather than left out to get buried in the snow.

We chose to take some *Ultimate Everest Boxes* as they were considerably lighter than the Whillans Box. We carefully checked design and construction with the manufacturer before deciding to use them but unfortunately did not realize a number of their failings. The box is lower than the Whillans and the lack of head-room made them most uncomfortable to live in. We also felt that they should be substantially longer to give room for kit storage.

Condensation was also a problem with these boxes. The ends, unlike the Whillans, are made from waterproof nylon and we found that heavy condensation occurred here causing consider-able problems.

In an attempt to strengthen the framework we added an up-right halfway along the longitudinal members. This upright had conventional tent pole spikes at each end and located into holes in the top and bottom longitudinal poles. Elementary physics would have told us that this pole served practically no useful function without a complementary pole between the two upper longitudinal members at roof height. Boxes tend to collapse due to the weight of snow piling up on the roof. The Ultimate Boxes did have fibre glass wands tensioned between these two upright members forming an arch but after a small amount of snow had landed on the roof, they soon flipped and served no purpose what-soever. The holes drilled in the longitudinal members to take the upright brace in fact formed weak spots in these poles and they often bent or broke at this point. We felt that these additional bracing members halfway along longitudinal poles were basically a good idea but they should be fixed with clips so as not to weaken the framework.

An interesting lightweight design of three-way corner piece was evolved for the Ultimate Boxes but this involved the use of a high tensile steel screw which became very brittle at low temperatures. They snapped with very little provocation. The zips on the door of the Ultimate Box suffered from the same failing as those on the Whillans Box.

It can be very cold inside a single-skin tent when the temperature outside drops to −35°C. Karrimor and Ultimate Equipment Boxes are both single skin, take a lot of warming up and lose heat quickly. Some form of double-skin boxes would undoubtedly be much more comfortable to live in when it is really cold.

Whereas the Whillans Box is erected by first assembling the framework and then throwing the tent fabric over it, the Ultimate Box is designed to be erected by one or two people sitting in the tent fabric itself. This seemed to be a very good idea as the people erecting the box were protected from the elements. It works well on a peaceful Scottish lawn on a summer's afternoon but in an autumnal blizzard in the dark, 25,000 feet up Everest it proved an almost insuperable problem. The Whillans Box was definitely found to be much easier to erect under adverse conditions.

The *Ultimate Assault tent* was a special lightweight design A-frame tent intended to be used at our projected Camp 7. In fact it never went above Base Camp but the basic concept seemed to be very good as Edward Whymper proved many years ago.

We had no particular function in mind for the little nylon *North Face tents* which are conventional A-frame tents with an American pattern (i.e. not down to earth and not bell-ended) flysheet. Due to our problems with tentage they were used both at Base Camp and Camp 2 for the whole of the expedition and stood up fantastically well. Although the flysheets eventually were torn to shreds up at Camp 2 and a few poles got broken, the tents were most useful to us.

The *Vango Force Ten Mark 5 tents* were exactly as supplied on the domestic market except that for lightness we took nylon flysheets and had a snow valance fitted. Their ease of pitching and roominess when up was much appreciated and they performed extremely well right up to Camp 2 for the whole length of the expedition. The nylon flysheets tended to get nicked when being dug out after a snow storm and the nicks gradually worked themselves into tears which finally destroyed most of the flysheets. The tents however were still in use right at the very end.

We think that it would have been worth having the heavier more robust cotton flysheets.

All our troubles seemed to centre on our tents. This was partly our fault in placing too great an emphasis on weight and giving insufficient thought to design and partly because we met far more inclement weather on the mountain than we envisaged.

We realize now that it is much better to take one tent which may be a full porter load but will last for the duration rather than try to economize by taking a tent which may be only three-quarters of a porter load and have to replace it as it has failed to withstand the conditions. Tent failure probably caused more changes of plan than any other single factor and had it not been for the fortunate fact that we were able to purchase four French box tents from the Pumori expedition it is questionable whether we would have had sufficient tentage to get as high as we did. Undoubtedly, the rule is to take tents which will stand up to the conditions, which are easy to erect in atrocious weather, which are comfortable to live in for prolonged spells and pay little heed to the weight factor.

We took comfortable open cell *foam mats* for use on the walk-in and at Base Camp and closed cell *Karrimats* for use higher up the mountain. Although we took a considerable number of both types we still did not have enough. This is partly because we suspect the Sherpas tended to 'acquire' them but also because we found that one Karrimat was just not thick enough to give adequate insulation in the very cold conditions. Two were acceptable and three definitely more comfortable. It is important to match the number of mats taken to the tent space available, not to members of the expedition. Members do not want to carry mats around with them; they should belong to the tent.

Comfort is important, the open cell mats were very popular even though they did get rather damp due to condensation building up on the underside.

We took V-section *aluminium tent pegs* about 12″ long but found these were of little use in the deep soft snow. The snow stakes referred to under Climbing Equipment and marker canes were used whenever possible to anchor tents.

Snow brushes, ordinary little hand brushes, are invaluable for sweeping the snow under the groundsheet or out of the tent, and every tent above Base Camp should be equipped with one.

Cooking Equipment

2	Primus gas double burner stoves	Bahco Tools Ltd
12	Primus gas single burner stoves	Bahco Tools Ltd
252	Primus 2202 gas cartridges	Calor Gas Ltd
8	Optimus paraffin pressure stoves	AB Optimus Ltd
14	Nester sets cooking pans	I. & M. Steiner (1950) Ltd
50	Knife, fork and spoon sets	I. & M. Steiner (1950) Ltd
50	Spare spoons	I. & M. Steiner (1950) Ltd
100	Plastic plates	Scot Thomas & Co. Ltd
100	Large plastic mugs	Sea Span
2	Large pressure cookers	Myles Brothers
4	Standard pressure cookers	Prestige Group Ltd
60	Baby can openers	Black & Edgington Ltd
60	Meta bar 20s	Black & Edgington Ltd
50	Pot scourers	Myles Brothers
2 sets	Kitchen knives	Swiss Cutlery (London) Ltd
300	Kitchen towels	Strentex Fabrics Ltd
1,000	Kitchen wipes	Strentex Fabrics Ltd
2	Trigano 6 tables	Black & Edgington Ltd
12	Trigano folding chairs	Black & Edgington Ltd
2	Cooking shelters 27′ × 20′	Tulloch Mountaincraft
	Other kitchen equipment	Kathmandu Bazaar

Heating and Lighting

8	Primus gas lanterns	Bahco Tools Ltd
2	Primus gas heaters	Bahco Tools Ltd
4	Optimus paraffin pressure lanterns	AB Optimus Ltd
1,000	Coolite chemical lights	Baxter Fell Products Ltd
	Candles	Kathmandu Bazaar
96	Ever Ready batteries	Brown Brothers
4	Hurricane lamps	Black & Edgington Ltd

Notes on cooking equipment, heating and lighting

Although cooking up to and including Camp 2 was done by Sherpas we found it useful to have a gas stove in each of the communal living tents for quick brews and snacks. The *Primus gas double burner stove* working off disposable cartridges proved ideal for this purpose. The Sherpas cooked on wood up to Base Camp and thereafter used *Optimus paraffin pressure stoves*.

The Sherpas are not economical in their use of paraffin, heat or hot water. The stoves we had stood up to Sherpa-abuse remarkably well but a good supply of spare parts is needed and double the quantity of stoves would undoubtedly have been useful. The Sherpas burn the stoves for twelve to eighteen hours per day usually melting water for a multitude of purposes. Furnaces, paraffin pressure stoves with four, six or eight burner heads, would certainly have speeded up the process of reducing enormous dixies of snow to boiling water.

For cooking above Camp 2 single burner *Primus gas stoves* were used and by and large these worked extremely well. A little difficulty was encountered with the regulating valve on the burners at and above 25,000 feet and occasionally the self-sealing device on the cartridge failed to work when a partly used can of gas was removed from the stove for some reason. These failings have been brought to the notice of the manufacturers and are now almost certainly eliminated.

Knives, forks, spoons, plates and *mugs* tend to get lost and we found that two or three of each per person on the expedition was about the right quantity to take.

Pressure cookers are invaluable for cooking rice and meat. Amazingly the Sherpas know how to use them.

Tables and chairs are important trappings of civilization which must be taken. Another two tables of the type we took would have been useful. No trouble was experienced with them but the chairs all collapsed in one way or another on the walk-in and we would have been better taking a stronger model.

The Sherpas use the *cooking shelters*, large heavyweight waterproof nylon sheets 27′ × 20′, to form small huts by building walls to fill the gap between the eaves and the ground. Although two were adequate another one could well have been useful.

The *Optimus paraffin pressure lamps* were used to light the kitchen shelters and communal tents. On occasion they objected to local impure paraffin but generally worked well. A large supply of spare mantles is needed, something approaching two per lamp per week.

The *Primus gas lanterns* working on disposable cartridges were used in the sleeping compartments of the communal tents and also for lighting individual members' tents up to Camp 4. They worked extremely well and though the mantles seemed more durable than the ones on the paraffin lamps a good supply of spares is necessary.

Coolite is a device comprising of a phial approximately 6″ long and 1″ in diameter containing a chemical, inside which is a small capsule with another chemical. While the inner capsule is unbroken the chemicals are inert but when the inner capsule is discharged by bending the outer phial almost in half the two chemicals can mix and give off a greenish glow. At normal temperatures this glow is just sufficient to read by and gives quite good lighting in a tent, but at low temperatures the chemical reaction slows down and light intensity diminishes. At normal temperatures the light intensity is fairly constant for about three hours whilst at low temperatures it continues at a much lower level for a considerably longer period. Coolites would be useful on some expeditions but not under the conditions we encountered on Everest.

Miscellaneous Equipment

4	Lightweight tarpaulins 12′×12′	Tulloch Mountaincraft
4	Heavyweight tarpaulins 12′×12′	Tulloch Mountaincraft
12	Large aluminium shovels	George Wolfe & Son Ltd
25	Kit bags	Laurence Corner
1,500	Polythene bags	British Visqueen Ltd
500	Polythene sheets 6′×6′	British Visqueen Ltd
12 tins	Suppletect	Stephens Belting Co. Ltd
100 prs.	Miraclaces	Stephens Belting Co. Ltd
24 tins	Dubbin	Caswell & Co. Ltd
12 tins	Boot polish	Caswell & Co. Ltd
12	Boot brushes	Myles Brothers
1	Sony TC 95 cassette recorder	Sony (U.K.) Ltd
4	Sony TC 40 cassette recorders	Sony (U.K.) Ltd
96	Mallory MN 1400 batteries	Mallory Batteries Ltd

300	Mallory RM 502 batteries	Mallory Batteries Ltd
300	Mallory MN 1500 batteries	Mallory Batteries Ltd
100	T.D.K. blank cassettes	Peter Bowthorpe & Associates Ltd
30	Pre-recorded cassettes	E.M.I. Ltd
30	Penguin paperbacks	Penguin Books Ltd
5	Silva No. 3 compasses	B. J. Ward Ltd
2	110 lb. spring balances	Salter Industrial Measurement Ltd
6	40 lb. spring balances	Salter Industrial Measurement Ltd
100	Aluminium tube containers	Metal Box Co. Ltd
3	Alarm clocks	Andrew & Co.
2 prs.	Binoculars	Butterworth (Edinburgh) Ltd
200	Waterproof cardboard boxes	Ashton Containers Ltd
26	Personal boxes	W.C.B. Containers Ltd
	Waterproof Vinyl tape	Samuel Jones & Co. Ltd
	2″ self-adhesive fabric tape	T. J. Smith & Nephew Ltd
100	Yale locks	Eaton Corporation
2	Thermometers	James Scientific Instruments
2	Altimeters	Royal Geographical Society
1	Anemometer	Royal Geographical Society
60,000	Rothmans 'Pall Mall' cigarettes	Rothmans of Pall Mall
6	Boxes for repair kit, stationery etc.	W.C.B. Containers Ltd
	Stationery requirements	Alna Press
	Comprehensive repair kit	
	Games	

Note: The nylon for cooking shelters, tarpaulins and stuff bags was supplied by Crepe Weavers and was Neoprene coated by British Vita Ltd.

Notes on miscellaneous

Tarpaulins are most useful, not only for keeping rain and snow off the loads stacked at camps but also for locating the bottom of loads buried in snow. The heavyweight tarpaulins gave great service up to and including Camp 2 and the lighter-weight versions made from two-ounce ripstop nylon were used higher up the mountain.

The small *avalanche shovels* manufactured by climbing gear manufacturers are quite inadequate to cope with the immense volume of snow encountered on a large Himalayan mountain. We used full-sized shovels with blades made of high-strength aluminium alloy and with 21" shafts. They all survived the whole expedition and were invaluable.

Kit bags and large polythene waste bags are most useful for assembling and keeping together porter loads. We had three hundred of the polythene waste bags amongst our fifteen hundred assorted polythene bags. Of the other size, the larger ones were found to be more than useful than the small ones.

The *six-foot square polythene sheets* were used to protect our porters and their loads from the monsoon rain on the walk-in. They performed very well after we had persuaded the porters to use them and were eventually useful for protecting the undersides of tents and for a variety of other purposes at Base Camp.

We found that because conditions were so dry on the mountain very little boot dressing was required though most of our high-altitude boots had a good coating of '*Suppletect*' before they left Britain and a further one or two coats during the course of the expedition. No trouble due to the leather of boot uppers freezing was experienced. The Ice Fall porters diligently *dubbined* their boots with considerable regularity. It seems wise to issue each Sherpa with his own tin of Dubbin; they are most reluctant to share!

The *Sony TC 95 cassette recorder* was used as a source of music during the whole of the expedition and performed faultlessly. The smaller *TC 40 recorders* were used as personal recorders and served not only as a music source higher up the mountain but also as an excellent means of keeping a diary. Some trouble was encountered with these in getting the batteries to connect properly, but this was the fault of the batteries and not the tape recorders. For some unknown reason, *Mallory cells* apparently differ very slightly in size from conventional batteries and it is often difficult to get them to make contact. When the batteries do work, they last for a very considerable time provided that one takes the trouble to keep them warm.

We were concerned that we might have trouble with the tape

in the blank *cassettes* getting brittle and breaking. In spite of the intense cold no trouble of any kind was experienced and very high quality recordings were made. A good selection of *pre-recorded cassettes* and a good library is essential to while away the time one is stuck in camp in storm conditions. It is interesting to record that the 'pop' music fanatics became more and more interested in classical music the higher they went up the mountain !

Fortunately we were never out in white-out conditions and did not have to use our *compasses*. Fortunately, because it is almost certain that the compasses would not have worked. The needle points to magnetic north ignoring the curvature of the earth. This means that in the southern hemisphere and regions close to the Equator the needle dips so as to point in a direct straight line to the north pole and the other end of the needle has to be weighted for use in these areas to compensate.

Spring balances are required to check the weight of porter and Sherpa loads and although the Sherpas never argued about the weight they were asked to carry, it is as well to ensure that one is not overloading them. The smaller forty-pound spring balances were used higher up the mountain; the larger ones were kept at Base Camp.

The problem of finding something in which to pack our equipment proved more of a problem than getting the equipment itself. A porter will carry sixty-five pounds and obviously it is important to have loads weighing as close to that figure as is possible. We decided to have really good boxes for our own personal kit and for the high-altitude Sherpas' kit. These were made from a fibre-board material with metal strengthening, and had a removable lid which could be locked by straps and padlocks. They worked very well, lasting the whole expedition and they were eventually used to crate our remaining kit for the return to Britain. The only disadvantage was weight; they weighed eighteen pounds which is a severe weight penalty when a porter will only carry sixty-five pounds.

For our other equipment we felt that a lighter box was essential and set a maximum weight for the box on its own of eight pounds. The box had to be waterproof as it would have to withstand up to twenty-one days monsoon rain without disintegrating and had to be adjustable for size as obviously not every sixty-five pound load was going to occupy the same volume. Eventually we discovered Ashton Containers who produced a cardboard with a layer of polythene bonded to both sides. As this material was used for making fish boxes we reckoned that it would be satisfactory for our purpose. In practice, although some deterioration occurred on corners where the polythene rubbed off, our loads made it to Base Camp without any mishaps.

A very comprehensive *repair kit* was taken and as well as the usual spare parts for stoves and crampons we took a full range of hand tools. Grips, pliers, hand-wrenches and hacksaws were probably the most used tools and a good quantity of malleable wire and bootlace nylon was also found useful.

Liar dice, packs of cards and 'Scrabble' proved very popular, but we probably could have done with a wider variety of games.

APPENDIX D

Oxygen:
Hamish MacInnes

On the 1922 British Everest Expedition, George Finch and Geoffrey Bruce used the first oxygen cylinders on the world's highest mountain. Porters had taken the cylinders to their camp on the North West Ridge, at a height of 25,000 feet. Here they spent two nights before a summit bid. They reached a height of 27,300 feet before giving up.

Since 1922 there have been great advances in oxygen equipment for high-altitude climbing and the Diluter-Demand system has emerged as the best all-round equipment, though even this, due to the extreme conditions experienced on the 1972 British Everest South West Face expedition, gave trouble.

In the intervening years several other systems were tried. The Closed-Circuit set had been used both on Mount Everest in 1953 and an improved version later on Kangchenjunga. Though this system gives the best possible utilization of a given supply of oxygen, the equipment is bulky and is also complex mechanically. A carbon dioxide absorbant is used, which must be renewed as well as the oxygen supply, thus the logistic problems are doubled. There is the further difficulty in that should the oxygen supply fail when the equipment is in use, the percentage of oxygen in the circulating gas can fall below that in the ambient air, without the wearer being aware of it. The set, with mask and tubing and with one soda lime canister weighs approximately 19 lbs. The canister would last as long as an 800-litre oxygen cylinder, which is an additional 11 lbs., filled (French cylinder).

Obviously, such a system is heavy as well as complicated, and it is seldom considered now for high-altitude work on mountains, though it has proved both reliable and good for lunar astronauts.

Thomas Hornbein designed a system which was very successful on the 1963 American Mount Everest expedition. It comprises a face mask, designed so that a variable quantity of manually regulated oxygen is delivered to the oro-nasal region of the mask at each breath. There is a manual regulation of the flow rate from 1–4 litres per minute. One of the disadvantages of the system is the restriction imposed by this regulation, for the system tends to be wasteful of oxygen at the lower respiratory rates and deficient at the high rates. The regulator is set prior to the day's climbing, but can be adjusted at any time by moving the regulator. On the other hand, the equipment is relatively simple and does not give a great deal of trouble.

The White Mountain Research Station of the University of California, Berkeley, were asked in 1969 to help design oxygen breathing apparatus for use on the 1971 international expedition which was going to attempt the South West Face of Everest. Dr F. Duane Blume was appointed Oxygen Officer of this expedition and he was mainly responsible for the development of the Diluter-Demand oxygen system for mountaineering.

This system is widely used in aviation and works on the principle that when the individual inspires he also draws ambient air into his mask through an orifice in the regulator, as well as pure oxygen from a cylinder through a demand valve in the regulator. The regulator as used for aviation purposes was altered to give four clip-stop ambient-air orifices in place of the original aneroid valve as this was not sensitive enough for mountaineering purposes. The four settings correspond to approximately 2,000 feet increments from 22,000 feet to 30,000 feet.

We used two types of oxygen clinders with the Diluter-Demand equipment. The first was a British cylinder, specially made for the expedition by Luxfer Ltd, Colwick Industrial Estate, Nottingham, and this weighed 12·3 lbs. empty and had a capacity of 1,000 litres. It was painted blue, as this colour stands out clearly and it also absorbs relatively little heat by radiation. It was fitted with the standard American valve for the Diluter-Demand system. These proved excellent.

The other cylinders used were French, also made from aluminium alloy, painted yellow, with a capacity of 800 litres and weighing 9 lbs. when empty. As these were fitted with the standard French valves, adaptors were made for us by Sabre Safety Ltd., Ash Road, Aldershot, who also supplied British face masks which we used for medical purposes. Some leakage occurred with the French valves.

The cylinders were filled by the British Oxygen Company with an American Specification Aviation Oxygen, with a dew point of 6 v.p.m. The complete oxygen system comprised the oxygen cylinder, a pressure reducer with pressure gauge attached, a length of high-pressure tubing, the Diluter-Demand regulator and a length of flexible, corrugated tubing integral with the face mask. A further orifice on the pressure reducer is used for the connection to the plastic sleeping mask, which supplies oxygen at a rate of one litre per minute, which was found to be adequate by all members of the expedition.

Our normal, every-day pack-frames were adapted to carry one British bottle inside, or two French. This was done by having each frame fitted with two straps inside the pack container for holding the cylinder(s) in a rigid upright position. Other equipment could be carried with the cylinder(s) inside the pack.

The cylinders were charged at a pressure of 3,000 p.s.i., and the modified Robertshaw on-off reducer gave a gas pressure reduction to 60–70 p.s.i. at its outlet. The mask for this equipment is the standard military A-14 oxygen mask assembly, which weighs 14 oz. (Sierra Engineering Co.) It is made of silicone rubber and has a reliable performance in cold conditions. The mask is readily crushable in place with a gloved hand, to free ice from the exhaust valve and ports. However, on our expedition, the build-up of ice in the mask on occasions was so great that this was not always successful. The total weight of the system when using a filled French bottle, with adaptor, was 13·8 lbs.

Despite the success of this equipment on the 1971 international expedition, we did experience major drawbacks during the post-monsoon attempt, which may be attributed to the severe conditions encountered. Trouble was experienced mainly at the demand valve, and though we made a point of having this enclosed within our eiderdown suits, freezing still occurred in certain instances. Two of these were replaced by spares during the expedition, and several changes of components were made between various sets to obtain better results. At the end of the expedition it was found that only one set gave what we felt to be a satisfactory performance. There were at least three occasions when complete blockage was experienced and the masks had to be removed. To combat spindrift, a further small 'mask' was made to fit over the inlet of the demand valve, and this proved to be quite successful. We also experienced leakage from the adaptors for the French cylinders and had to utilize 'home-made' rubber seals to prevent this.

APPENDIX E

Communications:
Major Kelvin Kent

On an expedition such as Everest a failure to communicate would be disastrous. A great deal more thought therefore went into the planning requirement and selection of equipment than in certain other spheres. In our case the requirements were broken down into four categories: –

1. A main supply route or line of communication from Kathmandu to Base Camp.
2. A radio rear link from Base Camp to the Sherpa town of Namche Bazar where limited facilities existed.
3. A solid communication link up the Ice Fall to Advance Base.
4. A good working radio net from Advance Base up the Face using very light-weight small walkie-talkies.

The Line of Communication

The main supply route was fairly obvious; a small airstrip exists at Lukla in the Dudh Kosi valley about a day's walk down from Namche Bazar. This was the key to fast physical carrying of mail, T.V. film and vital supplies from Kathmandu to Base Camp. Aircraft came in every day except for very bad weather, and we hired a local man to act as agent on the airfield. He held incoming mail for us and received outgoing film and mail from the mail-runner for putting on the next plane. Similarly in Kathmandu, we used the kind services of Miss Elizabeth Hawley (Tiger Tops Office) for mail and film and Mr Mike Cheney (Mountain Travel Office) for supplies and press reports. This arrangement worked very well as both parties did the same for us on Annapurna in 1970 and really knew the form – especially on the aircraft movements as they control much of the available space themselves!

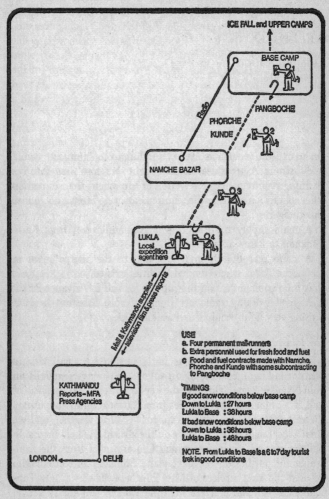

Mail-running system and main supply route

ICE FALL and UPPER CAMPS

BASE CAMP

PANGBOCHE

PHORCHE
KUNDE

Radio

NAMCHE BAZAR

LUKLA
Local
expedition
agent here

Mail & Kathmandu supplies —
television film & press reports

KATHMANDU
Reports – MFA
Press Agencies

LONDON ◄——— ● DELHI

USE
a. Four permanent mail-runners
b. Extra personnel used for fresh food and fuel
c. Food and fuel contracts made with Namche,
   Phorche and Kunde with some subcontracting
   to Pangboche

TIMINGS
If good snow conditions below base camp
Down to Lukla : 27 hours
Lukla to Base : 38 hours
If bad snow conditions below base camp
Down to Lukla : 36 hours
Lukla to Base : 48 hours

NOTE. From Lukla to Base is a 6 to 7 day tourist
trek in good conditions

From Lukla to Base Camp the only effective way to ensure prompt up and down delivery of mail, film and press reports etc., is to engage mail-runners. We decided on four men whose sole task was to run between these two places carrying the absolute minimum of personal equipment. We had to kit them out for the job and paid them a flat rate (50p. per day) plus a small road allowance whilst actually running. Each man had a torch and a spare set of batteries for night work.

Fuel (firewood and kerosene) and fresh food was contracted out to people in Sherpa villages round Namche, and the contractors sent up their own Sherpas and Sherpanis to carry the produce up. Sometimes yaks were used. These could carry the equivalent of three loads right through to Base if conditions were good: otherwise the yaks got as far as they could, and the herdsmen ferried the goods on to Base.

Radio

The plan catered for fourteen radios including one to be set up en route at Namche Bazar. My own tasks involved rather more than just the communications, and therefore I requested the Gurkha Signal Regiment in Hong Kong to release a capable operator to help me establish the various links. They readily agreed to this and sent Sgt Bartaman Limbu, a tough hardworking N.C.O. with whom I had served previously, to assist in the packing, testing and setting up phases. He met the expedition in Kathmandu and left about five weeks later having completed his job methodically and expertly.

The communication diagram shows in detail the relative locations and types of sets, and below are listed the actual models.

1. *Rear Link (Base to Namche Bazar)*
   Racal Squadcal–HF
   Mode: SSB
   Frequency: 4.1 MHz
   Antenna: Half Wave Dipole
   Output: 5 watts
   Power Supply: 14 'D' cells or 18v. supply
   Weight: 18 lb. complete with case, ancillaries and
     batteries.

2. *Ice Fall Net (Base–Camp 1–Advance Base)*
   Racal Telecal–VHF
   Mode: Narrow Band FM
   Frequency: 40–50 MHz
   Antenna: Telescopic Rod
   Output: 1 watt
   Power Supply: 8 'C' cells or 12v. supply
   Weight: 3.7 lbs. with batteries.
3. *Upper Camp Net (Advance Base to Camp 6)*
   Philips Handy Talkie–VHF
   Mode: Phase modulation
   Frequency: 47–57 MHz
   Antenna: Folding springblade
   Output: 400 MW
   Power Supply: 6 Penlight batteries or 9v. supply
   Weight: 2.2 lbs. including batteries.
4. *Radio Receivers (All India Weather Forecasts and World News)*
   Hacker Helmsman
   Bush VTR 178.
5. *Batteries*
   All radios were powered by MN 1300, 1400 and 1500 cold weather
   cells specially prepared by Mallory Batteries Ltd.

Conclusion

At no time was the operational or administrative planning held up through lack of communications forwards or rearwards. Unlike some of the previous Everest expeditions good communications, using the powerful Racal Telecals, were obtained through the Ice Fall and Western Cwm especially between Base Camp and Camp 2 (Advance Base) which were by no means in line of sight and separated by at least 4¼ miles. Further up, also, excellent, clear communications were possible with the very light, easy to operate, Philips Handy Talkie which also provided a listen-in facility at Base Camp. Rearwards the well-proven Racal Squadcal produced a good voice signal over the difficult 18-mile distance with a group of 23,000-foot mountains in between. It is significant that all sets, including the two excellent Hacker and Bush receivers, worked well on normal size Mallory batteries. No recharging facilities or engine were therefore necessary.

This time we chose the right sets for the right job. The overall

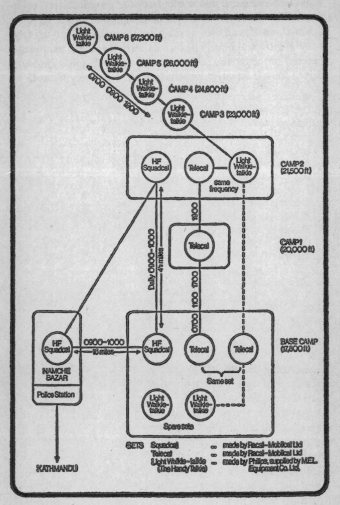

Communication diagram

result was successful and a tribute to the manufacturers' equipment. To withstand the rough handling of a 3-week monsoon approach march and then be subjected to conditions varying from scorching tropical heat (which could warp the side of hard plastic casings) to the intense cold of −40°C with gale force winds and driven snow is an advertisement in itself. I was very pleased.

APPENDIX F

Food:
Major Kelvin Kent

Time Problems

Pre-packed food in cardboard boxes formed half of the total expedition airfreight to Kathmandu. With local purchased supplements in Nepal something over eight tons was consumed altogether. It's not surprising therefore that food is the most talked about topic of conversation on a large expedition. It becomes an outlet for grumbling and a natural source of discontent under conditions of stress. Everyone knews what he wants, but I don't think any ration yet designed has been able to please all of the people all of the time.

The job of organizing the food was passed to me seven weeks before we were due to leave. This was nobody's fault, but it did mean that the majority of the items had to be obtained off the shelf and paid for. Normally, with any six months' preparation time, it would have been feasible to get eighty per cent of all contents supplied on a free basis by the larger catering concerns. As it was, we were extremely pushed to reach our deadline date for sorting and packing using Sainsbury and Tesco items of immediate availability. With helpful suggestions from Chris, Hamish, Nick, and my wife we set about producing the menu lists. We had about ten frantic days.

For packaging I went straight to Andrew Lusk & Co. Ltd, whose experience, helpful advice, and friendly co-operation made the whole thing a realistic proposition. To achieve this they had to work overtime for nearly three weeks including weekends in order to get everything to BOAC Air Cargo at Heathrow by the beginning of August – the deadline date for airfreight.

The Requirement

First we had to agree on the menu. An endless chain of visits

to supermarkets, testing, tabulating, and weight calculations
followed. The idea was to produce three different rations each
with four menus based on predetermined figures for man-day
intakes. These were to include the total Sherpa and Nepali strength
(over sixty in all). Various other factors, too, had to be taken
into account in the light of previous experience and based on
Chris's instructions and preliminary calculations. It is easier to
tabulate these:

1. Each food ration pack to be made up into strong, well-sealed
   full approach porter load. (Ideal maximum, 70 pounds.)
2. Breakdown ration packs (inside the main porter load) to be
   packed in strong, double-layer water resistant containers,
   suitable for Ice Fall carrying. (Ideal maximum, 38 pounds.)
3. Approach March and Base Camp rations to be designed in 12
   man-day packs, ideally at 1 lb. per man-day (to be supplemented by 2 lbs. per man-day of local food).
4. Advance Base ration to be 8 man-day packs, ideally at 2 lbs.
   per man-day (to be supplemented by 1 lb. per man-day of
   local food).
5. H.A. (Mountain Ration) to be 2½ lbs. per man in 2 man-
   day packs, not to weigh more than 5 lbs. in separate sealed
   water resistant bags. This ration to be a fully self-contained
   unit.
6. Weight to be kept to a minimum.
7. Budget to be watched carefully.
8. Items to be available now.
9. Menus to be interesting and easy to prepare.

Always Questionable?

For composition I examined the Annapurna ration, the British
Trans-Americas expedition ration, Mike Thompson's valuable
original homework on the subject, and various other guides. Out-
weighing all of this is basic common sense. The ideal theoretical
food ration is far removed from practical circumstance where
palatability, combined with an intense dislike for certain strong-
smelling items at altitude is more important than the stereotype
medical 3,000 calories-per-man-day approach. However good or
appetizing something looks on paper, it's no use if no-one will eat

it. Indeed, many of the mouthwatering luxuries end up being thrown away.

To achieve the bulk required within the weight allocated to food, it was necessary to rely heavily on dehydrated items in the packs and known availability of local rice, potatoes, *dhal*, onions, maize, *ghi, sempi, tsampa, maida* (flour) and cooking oil obtainable above Namche Bazar. Never will dehydrated meat or vegetables be as good as tinned items, but there is little alternative in the circumstances. Luckily our Batchelor's items were acceptable to most people despite inevitable monotony after a few weeks. The Cadbury's 'Appletree' fruit flake desserts were especially good value. But the tinned fruit, salmon, corned beef, good old digestive biscuits, and shortbread won the most praise. Tinned pears provide virtually no nutritious energy, but the sacrifice of weight for something popular and easily digestible is worth it.

Having got out the provisional menu lists, Andrew Lusks worked flat out on procurement and breakdown. Much was fairly straightforward, but the breakdown from bulk catering containers to one and two ounce packets was niggly and time consuming. A few headaches occurred over the procurement of margarine in one-ounce metal tubes. Stuffing it all up those painted toothpaste tubes must have been a devil of a job!

Other odds and ends which we included were cough sweets, candles, loo paper, good matches, and Kleenex tissues. But everything added to weight, and when a basic pack was weighed prior to packing, it was discovered that the combined weight was as much as twenty per cent more than previously worked out. This is partly because a 1 lb. cake does not take into account the tin; likewise everything else that is in a tin, jar, or wrapping

Containers

Another problem was that of outer containers suitable for porterage. Perhaps this is not so important in the dry season, but our loads were to be heaved, dropped, dragged, and humped across half of Nepal in monsoon conditions. We thought of plastic or fibreglass containers and even light plywood boxes, but the cheapest of these would have put another thousand pounds on the bill (both ways). The solution arrived at was good solid cardboard with waterproof paper covering and really strong binding. As it turned out only a minute percentage of food was spoilt or lost through bad or undurable packing, despite the approach-march man- and yak-handling.

Whilst Lusks were clearing their factory floor at Barking, I was hunting around for other 'goodies' which we thought would be advantageous to the main ration, provided we could get the items out as separate airfreight to Kathmandu. The following was obtained in addition to the ordinary rations:

One container of Lemonade Powder Two containers of medical throat tablets/ left-overs Two containers of Coburg Ham One container of kitchen cloths (like J cloths)	Expedition purchase. Expedition airfreight.
Three containers of Bauschpeck Bacon	Supplied free. Expedition airfreight.
Four containers of Kelloggs' Rise and Shine fruit drinks (mixed flavours). Eight containers of Pattersons Scottish Shortbread and Griddle Oat Cake biscuits. Four containers of Fortnum & Mason luxury hampers. Two containers of Chivers Jams, marmalades and honey in Minipots.	Supplied and airfreighted to Kathmandu by the firms concerned.

The above items proved essential and extremely popular with everyone. The meat was specially smoked and cured and lasted well.

Altogether the U.K. food despatched cost £4000 and required 158 porters to get it to Base Camp. In addition a further 350 loads of local purchase supplement was purchased at the beginning and throughout the expedition at a further cost of £1500. Most of this was consumed by the Sherpas who wouldn't touch the dehydrated food unless absolutely necessary. They were nevertheless quick to raid the packs for tinned meats, fish, and biscuits.

Here are the Menus:

Approach March and Base Camp Ration

12 man-day, 1 lb. per man-day with 2 lbs. local supplement. Four Packs (Menus A, B, C and D) to one approach-march porter-load.

Menu A (60):

1 × 13 oz. carton	Alpen Swiss Cereal
1 × 1 lb. tin	Nestlés Full Cream Milk Powder
2 packs	Flat Toilet Tissue
1 × 14½ oz. pack	Batchelor's Scotch Broth
1 × 9 oz. pack	Batchelor's Dried Cabbage
1 × 15 oz. pack	Batchelor's Farmhouse Stew
1 × 8 oz. tin	Egg Powder
1 × 8 oz. tin	Blue Band Margarine
12 bars	Mars Bars
2 × 7 oz. pkts	Garibaldi Biscuits
1 × 4 oz. pkt	Tea
1 × 8 oz. tin	Nescafé
2 × 1 lb. tins	Fruit Salad
1 packet	Kleenex
6 boxes	Brymay Safety Matches
2	Can Openers
2	Jiffy Lemons

Menu B (60):

1 × 8 oz. pkt	'Redibrek' Instant Porridge
1 × 1 lb. tin	Nestlés Full Cream Milk Powder
2 packs	Flat Toilet Tissue
1 × 1 lb. jar	Strawberry Jam
1 × 11½ oz. pack	Batchelor's Minestrone Soup Powder
1 × 16½ oz. pack	Batchelor's Savoury Mince
1 × 11½ oz. pack	Batchelor's Carrot Strips
4 packs	Cadbury's Smash Potato
1 × 1½ lb. tin	Dundee Cake
1 × 8 oz. tin	Blue Band Margarine
12 strips	Dextrosol
12 small bars	Cadbury's Fruit & Nut
2 × 7 oz. pkts	Garibaldi Biscuits
3 pkts	Cadbury's 'Appletree' Blackberry & Apple
1 pkt	Kleenex

6 boxes	Brymay Safety Matches
2	Can Openers
2	Jiffy Lemons

Menu C (60):

1×13 oz. pkt	Alpen Swiss Cereal
1×1 lb. tin	Nestlés Full Cream Milk Powder
2 packs	Flat Toilet Tissue
1×13 oz. pack	Batchelor's Beef and Tomato Soup
1×8 oz. tin	Egg Powder
1×14 oz. pack	Batchelor's Chicken Oriental
3 packs	Cadbury's Smash Potato
2×4 oz. packs	Batchelor's Peas
1×8 oz. tin	Blue Band Margarine
1×1½ lb. tin	Dundee Cake
12 strips	Dextrasol
12 bars	Crunchie
2×7 oz. pkts	Garibaldi Biscuits
1×1 lb. tube	Austrian Smoked Cheese
3 pkts	Cadbury's 'Appletree' Apple
5×4 oz. tins	Nestlés Cream
1 pkt	Kleenex
6 boxes	Brymay Safety Matches
2	Can Openers
2	Jiffy Lemons

Menu D (60):

1×8 oz. pkt	'Redibrek' Instant Porridge
3×3 oz. pkts	Cadbury's Smash
1×1 lb. tin	Nestlés Full Cream Milk Powder
1×1 lb. jar	Apricot Jam
2 packs	Flat Toilet Tissue
1×10 oz. pack	Batchelor's Clear Vegetable Soup
4×3½ oz. packs	Kraft Dairylea Cheese
1×16½ oz. pack	Batchelor's Minced Beef
1×13½ oz. pack	Batchelor's Mixed Vegetables
1×8 oz. tin	Blue Band Margarine
1×4 oz. pkt	Tea
1×8 oz. tin	Nescafé
2×8 oz. pkts	Chocolate Biscuits
12 strips	Dextrasol

12 bars	Mars Bars
3 packets	Cadbury's 'Appletree' Orange
5×4 oz. tins	Nestlés Cream
1 pkt	Kleenex
6 boxes	Brymay Safety Matches
2	Can Openers
2	Jiffy Lemons

Advance Base Ration

Eight man-days, 2 lbs. per man-day with 1 lb. local supplement. Four packs (Menus A, B, C and D) to one approach march porter load.

Menu A (36):

4×2½ oz. pkts	Alpen Swiss Cereal
1×1 lb. pkt	Granulated Sugar
1 pack	Flat Toilet Tissues
4 boxes	Brymay Safety Matches
4×1 pint pkts	Maggi Tomato Soup
2×7 oz. pkts	Digestive Biscuits
8 small bars	Cadbury's Dairy Milk Chocolate
8 bars	Mars Bars
8 strips	Dextrasol
8 pkts	Spangles
4×4 oz. ctns	Smarties
12 cubes	Oxo
2×8 oz. tins	Sardines in Oil
1×8 oz. pkt	Raisins
1×8 oz. pkt	Sultanas
4×2½ oz. pkts	Batchelor's Beef Granules
4×2 oz. pkts	Batchelor's Mixed Vegetables
2×1 oz. pkts	Knorr Onion Sauce Mix
1×8 oz. tin	Ovaltine
1×4 oz. bag	Orangeade Crystals
1×8 oz. tin	Nescafé
1×1 pint pkt	Jelly Crystals
1×1 lb. tube	Austrian Smoked Cheese
2×8 oz. tins	Red Salmon
2×8 oz. tins	Milac Milk Powder
3 pkts	Cadbury's 'Appletree' Blackberry & Apple

4×1 oz. tubes	Margarine
2	Can Openers
4 pkts	Mac Cough Sweets
2	Jiffy Lemons

Menu B (36):

1×8 oz. pkt	'Redibrek' Instant Porridge
1×1 lb. bag	Granulated Sugar
1 pack	Flat Toilet Tissues
4 boxes	Brymay Safety Matches
4×1 pint pkts	Maggi Minestrone Soup
2×7 oz. pkts	Digestive Biscuits
16 tubes	Polo Mints
1×6 oz. pkt	Kendal Mint Cake
8 small bars	Cadbury's Fruit & Nut
8 bars	Crunchie
1×8 oz. pkt	Sultanas
1×8 oz. pkt	Raisins
8 strips	Dextrasol
4×2½ oz. pkts	Batchelor's Beef Granules
4×2 oz. pkts	Batchelor's Surprise Peas
3 pkts	Cadbury's Smash Potato
1×11 oz. jar	Branston Pickle
1×8 oz. tin	Nescafé
1×4 oz. pkt	Cocoa
1×4 oz. bag	Orangeade Crystals
2×1 lb. tins	Fruit Salad
2×4 oz. tins	Nestlés Cream
1×1 lb.	Fruit Cake
1×8 oz. tin	Milac Milk Powder
3×3½ oz. boxes	Kraft Dairylea Cheese
4×1 oz. tubes	Margarine
2	Can Openers
4 pkts	Mac Cough Sweets
2	Jiffy Lemons

Menu C (36):

4×2½ oz. pkts	Alpen Swiss Cereal
1×1 lb. pkt	Granulated Sugar
1 pack	Flat Toilet Tissues
4 boxes	Brymay Safety Matches
4×1 pint pkts	Maggi Asparagus Soup

2×7 oz. pkts	Digestive Biscuits
8 bars	Kit Kat
8 bars	Bounty
8 pkts	Spangles
16 tubes	Polo
12 cubes	Oxo
2×7 oz. tins	Tuna
2×8 oz. tins	Sardines in Olive Oil
1×1 lb. tin	Heinz Vegetable Salad
8 strips	Dextrosol
4×2½ oz. pkts	Batchelor's Curry Granules
4×2 oz. pkts	Batchelor's Surprise French Beans
1×1 lb.	Fruit Cake
1×8 oz. tin	Milac Milk Powder
2×11 oz. tins	Mandarin Oranges
1×8 oz. tin	Nescafé
1×4 oz.	Horlicks
1×4 oz. bag	Lemonade Crystals
4×1 oz. tubes	Margarine
2	Can Openers
2	Jiffy Lemons

Menu D (36):

1×10 oz. pkt	Shredded Wheat
1×1 lb. pkt	Granulated Sugar
4 boxes	Brymay Safety Matches
4×1 pint pkts	Maggi Vegetable Soup
2×7 oz. pkts	Digestive Biscuits
8 small bars	Cadbury's Fruit & Nut
2×7 oz. pkts	Glacier Mints
4×4 oz. ctns	Smarties
4×2 oz. pkts	Nuts & Raisins
12 cubes	Oxo
2×1 pint pkts	Jelly Crystals
2×4 oz. tins	Nestlés Cream
8 strips	Dextrosol
1×1 lb.	Fruit Cake
2×7 oz. tins	Roy Roy Kipper Fillets
2 pkts	Cadbury Smash Potato
1×1 lb. tin	Heinz Baked Beans
4×2 oz. pkts	Surprise Peas
2×1 oz. pkts	Knorr Savoury White Sauce Mix

1×8 oz. tin	Nescafé
8×½ oz. sachets	Suchard Drinking Chocolate
1×4 oz. bag	Lemonade Crystals
1×16 oz. tube	Austrian Smoked Cheese
3 pkts	Cadbury's 'Appletree' Apple
4×1 oz. tubes	Margarine
2	Can Openers
4 pkts	Mac Cough Sweets
2	Jiffy Lemons

H.A. (Mountain Ration)

2 man-days, 2½ lbs. per man-day. Self-contained. Six packs to each sub-container with two sub-containers making up one approach march porter load.

Menu A (111):

3×2½ oz. pkts	Alpen Swiss Cereal
1×6 oz. bag	Granulated Sugar
30 sachets	Marvel Milk Powder
2×¼ oz. tubes	Salt
1×2 oz. bag	Dried Egg
4 sachets	Nescafé
4	Tea Bags
4 sachets	Suchard Drinking Chocolate
6 cubes	Oxo
1×2 oz.	Orangeade Crystals
2 strips	Dextrasol
1×1 pint pkt	Maggi Vegetable Soup
1×3 oz. pkt	Kendal Mint Cake
2 bars	Mars
2×1¼ oz. bars	Mapleton Fruit & Nut Bar
2 pkts	Spangles
1	White Candle
2 boxes	Brymay Safety Matches
2×10's pkts	Flat Toilet Tissues (Kleenex Pocket)
2×10's pkts	Kleenex Pocket Tissues
1×1 oz. tube	Margarine
1×1 lb. tin	Steak & Kidney Pudding
1×2 oz. pkt	Surprise Peas
1×3 oz.	Austrian Smoked Cheese

8 oz. k. pack (6 slices)	Sliced Fruit Cake
2	Can Openers
2 pkts	Mac Cough Sweets
1	Jiffy Lemon

Menu B (111):

1×3 oz. bag	'Redibrek' Instant Porridge
1×6 oz. bag	Granulated Sugar
30 sachets	Marvel Milk Powder
2×¼ oz. tubes	Salt
1×2 oz. bag	Dried Egg
4 sachets	Nescafé
4	Tea Bags
4 sachets	Ovaltine
6 cubes	Oxo
1×2 oz. bag	Lemonade
2 strips	Dextrasol
1×1 pint pkt	Maggi Chicken Soup
1×3 oz. bag	Fudge Pieces
2 small bars	Cadbury's Fruit & Nut Chocolate
2×1¼ oz. bars	Mapleton Fruit & Nut Bar
2 tubes	Polo Mints
1	White Candle
2 boxes	Brymay Safety Matches
2×10's pkts	Flat Toilet Tissue (Kleenex Pocket)
2×10's pkts	Kleenex Pocket Tissues
1	Jiffy Lemon
1×1 lb. tin	Ye Olde Oak Ham
1×2 oz. pkt	Surprise French Beans
1 pkt	Cadbury's Smash
1×4 oz. tin	Red Salmon
1×3 oz. pkt	Ration Biscuits
1×2¼ oz. jar	Meat Paste
1×3½ oz. pkt	Kraft Dairylea Cheese
2	Can Openers
2 pkts	Mac Cough Sweets

Menu C (111):

3×2½ oz. pkts	Alpen Swiss Cereal
1×6 oz. bag	Granulated Sugar
30 sachets	Marvel Milk Powder
2×¼ oz. tubes	Salt

1×2 oz. bag	Egg Powder
4 sachets	Nescafé
4	Tea Bags
4 sachets	Ovaltine
6	Oxo Cubes
1×2 oz. bag	Orangeade Crystals
2 strips	Dextrasol
1×1 pint pkt	Maggi Mushroom Soup
1×3 oz. pkt	Kendal Mint Cake
2 bars	Kit Kat
2×1¼ oz. bars	Mapleton Fruit & Nut Bars
2 pkts	Spangles
2 bars	Fry's Chocolate Cream
1	White Candle
2 boxes	Brymay Safety Matches
2×10's pkts	Flat Toilet Tissues (Kleenex Pocket)
2×10's pkts	Kleenex Pocket Tissues
1×1 oz. tube	Margarine
1×12 oz. tin	Armour Corned Beef
1×2 oz. pkt	Batchelor's Dried Mixed Vegetables
1 pkt	Cadbury's Smash
1 pkt	Cadbury's 'Appletree' Blackberry & Apple
1×4 oz. tin	Nestlés Cream
2	Can Openers
2 pkts	Mac Cough Sweets
1	Jiffy Lemon

Menu D (111):

1×3 oz. bag	'Redibrek' Instant Porridge
1×6 oz. bag	Granulated Sugar
30 sachets	Marvel Dried Milk
2×¼ oz. tubes	Salt
1×2 oz. bag	Egg Powder
4 sachets	Nescafé
4	Tea Bags
4 sachets	Suchard Drinking Chocolate
6 cubes	Oxo
1×2 oz. bag	Lemonade Crystals
2 strips	Dextrasol
1×1 pint pkt	Maggi Minestrone Soup
2 bars	Mars Bars
2×1¼ oz. bars	Mapleton Fruit & Nut Bars

2 pkts	Spangles
6×10 gram pkts	Brazil Nuts
2 tubes	Polo Mints
1	White Candle
2 boxes	Brymay Safety Matches
2×10's pkts	Flat Toilet Tissues (Kleenex Pocket)
2×10's pkts	Kleenex Pocket Tissues
1×1 oz. tube	Margarine
4×3¼ oz. tin	Chicken Breasts/jelly
1 pkt	Cadbury's Smash
1×2 oz. pkt	Surprise Peas
6 oz. k. pack (4 slices)	Sliced Fruit Cake
1 pkt	Cadbury's 'Appletree' Apple
1	Jiffy Lemon
1×4 oz. tin.	Nestlés Cream
2	Can Openers
2 pkts	Mac Cough Sweets

In the light of (further) experience

Not enough tinned meat foods. Too many sweets and chocolates. Cut out most of the Dextrasols. Include more powdered milk, sugar, and digestive biscuits – especially chocolate ones. Make sure that things can be heated sufficiently at high altitude. For example the steak and kidney pudding was taking over an hour to get warm and edible. Put in a few Army-type Irish stews.

The Coburg Ham and Bauschpeck Bacon was great in the higher camps as well as further down. Well worth the effort of getting it.

Alpen was an excellent cereal, but shredded wheat was also popular as a change. Porridge, too, would not have gone amiss. Tinned fruit is worth its weight. Put in more.

One last fairly obvious observation. Dehydrated foods require water, and melted snow and ice require more utensils and a lot more fuel.

Conclusion

The basic idea of food rations packed in containers to cater for different conditions, local produce availability and cooking methods on a defined man-day pack basis, is a good one. However, the pre-packed ration pack, even if supplemented with local fresh produce, will inevitably become monotonous however good its contents. It is therefore vital to include beforehand or pre-arrange locally (not possible in most cases) an adequate stock of protein-giving extras. These, plus a few luxury items, can be successfully made up into 'goodie parcels' and their distribution to camps reasonably controlled.

The general reaction to our rations with their twelve different menus was 'quite good'. Everyone got to Base Camp with no weight loss, and I didn't see any cases of malnutrition after twelve weeks. Of course it could have been better. In fact, given unlimited weight, bulk and financial budget I suppose we could have designed an excellent ration in fifteen seconds: 500 Fortnum and Mason hampers! Even so, a lot would still depend on the resourcefulness, ingenuity, and dogged determination of the unfortunate cook. Above Advance Base it is not what you feel like eating so much as whether you feel like getting the cooker going and producing more than a brew – if that.

APPENDIX G

Medical Notes
Dr Barney Rosedale

Preparations

The expedition members were widely scattered before we started, so most of the medical preparations were made by letter. All members were asked to have their haemoglobin estimated, their urine fully tested and their chests X-rayed. Tuberculosis is a severe risk in Nepal, and everyone was advised to ensure that they had some resistance to this disease by means of Mantoux testing and to accept BCG vaccination if the test showed it to be necessary. A dental check, treatment of piles, and attention to athlete's foot or troublesome toenails were recommended.

Lastly, a record was compiled for each member of his blood group, and serious diseases, operations or injuries he had had, any sensitivity to drugs and whether his appendix was still in.

Vaccination was carried out against smallpox and cholera (for both of which valid international certificates are required) and against polio, tetanus and typhoid (TAB). Infectious hepatitis is an appreciable risk to visitors to Nepal: injections of gamma-globulin give excellent levels of protection for about three months and were given to everyone soon after our arrival in Kathmandu. Although malaria is now very well controlled throughout most of Nepal, weekly Daraprim tablets were used to protect the team during the monsoon approach march.

Drugs and equipment were gathered together in U.K., mostly through the generosity of the firms listed below, and these were then repacked into personal kits, which accompanied each team member both on the approach march and on the mountain, rather larger camp kits, my medical box and emergency resuscitation kit and reserve stores of dressing and drugs.

The Approach March

This 200-mile amble runs through fairly well populated hills between 4,000 and 12,000 feet and was completed in monsoon conditions of high temperatures and very high humidity. The main hazards of this period were gut and skin infections, and the vital rules were to treat (clean, dry and dress) all skin lesions, however trivial, and to regard all water, however limpid its source, as infected. All drinking water was treated with Halazone tablets, but tea, boiled milk or water and yoghurt (dhai) needed no treatment.

Leeches were a considerable nuisance since the bites tend to become infected. Liberal use of ordinary insect repellent cream (e.g. Sketofax) will effectively deter them, but in such sweaty conditions the cream needs to be reapplied two or three times a day, and to boots and socks as well as exposed skin.

Sunburn is a problem on this route at other times of the year, but not in the monsoon. However, exertion in these hot, damp, conditions can produce enough sweating to deplete the body's salt resources, so salt tablets should be available. It is probably simpler though to encourage expedition members to take extra salt with their meals, and to ensure an adequate fluid intake it is similarly simpler to ask each member to ensure that they are drinking enough fluid to pass dilute urine, rather than insist on an arbitrary number of pints a day.

Porters were treated at the end of the day's march and the commonest problems were infected skin conditions, joint pains, dysentery, intestinal parasites and chest infections. A good deal of simple dentistry was done. The few cases of tuberculosis encountered were encouraged to go to their nearest hospital. In general we declined to treat the villagers in the areas we went through: transient treatment by passing trekkers does far more harm than good and can destroy confidence in their own developing medical services.

Throughout the approach march the only troublesome problems among the members were two cases of infected heel blisters and one of moderately severe diarrhoea.

Acclimatization

In the context of mountain expeditions this process really means becoming physically adapted to living at high altitudes and failure to adapt entails the risk of some degree of acute mountain sickness. This disease affects some people and not others, and youth or fitness are no protection against it. It may affect people at any altitude over 10,000 feet but the symptoms may not develop for one to four days after reaching the critical altitude.

The first sign, often not noticed, is passage of reduced amounts of urine: in fact susceptible climbers are retaining fluid in their bodies, and this excess fluid can affect the function of the lungs (high altitude pulmonary oedema) or the brain (high altitude cerebral oedema), or occasionally both.

Early symptoms are headache, nausea, loss of appetite and vomiting. Where pulmonary oedema predominates, breathlessness, cyanosis (seen as a blue discolouration of the lips, tongue and mucous membranes due to the low oxygen content of the blood) and chest pains occur. With cerebral oedema, giddiness, insomnia or nightmares, increasing confusion and personality changes are seen and the vision may be blurred. Both forms may proceed to coma and death, sometimes within hours.

Failure to recognize this syndrome, or confusing it with pneumonia, migraine or heart attack has in recent years led to many unnecessary deaths in the Himalayas among trekkers and mountaineers.

It is caused by going too high too fast. It is now possible to fly from Kathmandu to high air strips at the edge of the Himalayas, and a fit mountaineer going fast from such a landing strip to a Base Camp on the glaciers at 16,000 to 18,000 feet is in mortal danger. The crux of prevention is to avoid a fast ascent over 10,000 feet, ideally allowing about a week for each 3,000 feet above this height.

It is just as important that anyone suffering from any of the early symptoms should not be induced to go higher until he is feeling well again and is passing at least a litre of urine a day, and if things are not improving within two days he should waste no time in going down.

Diuretic drugs, which increase the output of urine have been shown to have some protective effect. Acetazolamide (Diamox 250 mg. three times daily) appears to be the best drug for this purpose, but it should not be used without good reason or for more than a week without medical advice, and extra drinking water and salt may be required during periods of exertion while on treatment. The more rapid acting Frusemide (Lasix) is probably best kept for treatment of the established disease. These severe cases also require oxygen by mask, injections of morphine and sometimes corticosteroids in the form of hydrocortisone or betamethazone, but above all the definitive treatment of acute mountain sickness is the valleys: arrangements must be started to get the patient down without delay.

This expedition had little trouble from this problem: although several members had headaches or poor appetites early on above 16,000 feet, the long walk in had given us a chance to acclimatize gently and we found that rest for a day or two allowed us to go on to further camps without any trouble.

A few points about this problem: very few climbers seem to meet an altitude barrier above which they cannot go however slowly they acclimatize. This is rare, and climbers going to the Himalayas for the first time and concerned about how well they will go at altitude may need reassurance in the early stages of the expedition. Women climbers can be affected by mountain sickness just as well as men. They should be advised not to take the Pill while at altitude and may require diuretic treatment in the premenstrual period. Sherpas are not immune, but the altitude at which symptoms start is much higher than for Westerners.

Medical Problems on the Mountain

The main hazards at Base Camp and above were intense cold, very low humidity, and injury. Some attention to hygiene is still required: neglected wounds heal poorly at altitude and it is important to ensure that the drinking water sources whether snow banks or, at Base Camp, glacier streams, are well away, up stream, and down wind, from the 'shitting areas' which must be both defined and enforced. All climbers should be encouraged to maintain a good fluid intake and to ensure that they are passing dilute urine. We found a screw-top plastic urine bottle an invaluable piece of equipment for everyone above Base Camp.

Food: the importance of a really palatable diet with a high proportion of fresh food cannot be too highly stressed. Iron and vitamin tablets were available to all members both on the approach march and on the mountain, the former to prevent depletion of body iron stores by the increase in blood cells formed at altitude, the latter mainly for psychological reasons.

Rescue arrangements: when climbing was in progress on the Face inflatable fracture splints were kept at a Camp on the Face, resuscitation and minor surgical equipment with me at Camp 2, with a sledge stretcher for evacuation down the Cwm and Ice Fall. Evacuation from Base Camp would be by helicopter to Kathmandu or by stretcher to Kunde Hospital depending on the nature of the emergency. In addition each pair of lead climbers carried morphine and Dexedrine, the latter to be employed only in an emergency to get down to safety and in fact never used. Each climber's personal kit also included a local anaesthetic eye drop for use in case of acute snow blindness to enable him to see well enough to reach camp for further treatment.

Two climbers required stitching for deep cuts of the face cause by falling stones: both were done at Camp 2 and healed well. Fortunately no emergency evacuation was called for on this expedition.

Frostbite: deep frostbite must be distinguished from two other conditions, frostnip (superficial frostbite) and frostnumb. In frostnip, exposed patches of skin become white and doughy, commonly on the cheeks, nose or ears and without the climber noticing it. It is thus important for the climber to keep an eye on his companion and warn him of early changes (the 'buddy' system). Frostnip will recover if the part is gently warmed by the heat from a hand, and then covered up. Like frostbite, it should never be rubbed.

Frostnumb is a loss of sensation commonly in the toes and fingers, occurring in those living continuously in conditions of extreme cold for prolonged periods. There is no blistering or loss of tissue and the condition recovers slowly within three months of return to warmer conditions.

True frostbite occurs when body heat loss is excessive and the core temperature is threatened: the problem is not just a cold hand or foot, but a generally chilled body losing heat faster than it is forming it. This is why an injured climber, who cannot maintain his heat production by active movements, and one who is shocked or panicking and thus losing excess heat, is at particular risk of frostbite. To reduce the heat loss from the most exposed parts (generally the hands and feet), spasm of small arteries cuts off the blood supply and the affected tissues freeze: the toes or fingers go numb, white and hard.

Left as it is, this frozen tissue may remain capable of some recovery for several days. But pressure, injury or rubbing will mechanically grind up the cells and destroy any possibility of their recovery. This established frostbite is best left cold and untreated, apart from measures to prevent any pressure or injury, until the climber can be brought to a centre where his body heat can be raised, the hands or feet be thawed out, and continued warmth be supplied.

This initial treatment was carried out at Camp 2: the climber was first warmed up with hot drinks and extra sleeping bags. Oxygen was given (it would be advantageous to warm and humidify the oxygen by bubbling it through very hot water on its way to the mask), and when the patient felt better, the hands or feet were suspended for half an hour in a large can of water kept at 42°C. After that he was kept warm, treated with an antibiotic, and evacuated down the mountain as soon as possible. Even in a mild case some blistering and blackening will occur, but of the four people frostbitten during the expedition only one suffered any residual tissue loss. When the frostbite is very extensive or severe, the use of low molecular weight dextran or rapid evacuation for treatment with hyperbaric oxygen should be considered after initial rethawing.

The use of vasodilator drugs such as Ronicol remains controversial. It seems likely that they have no place in prevention of frostbite, and are only justified during the thawing process once the core temperature is restored, when whisky is a more satisfactory alternative anyway.

Other problems: Cough and sore throat, caused by cold, dry air, seem to be an inescapable part of Himalayan climbing. Vast amounts of cough sweets and lozenges are required to help, but not overcome, this problem. Two climbers suffered from cough fractures. An old fashioned steam inhaler was found well worth taking. There is scope for developing a light heat exchange system for prewarming and humidifying inhaled air or oxygen and conserving heat loss from the lungs.

Diarrhoea was not a common problem on the mountain but an urgent one when it occurred. The 'Everest cocktail' of 2 teaspoons kaolin powder, 3 Lomotil tablets, 30 mg. codeine phosphate and 4–5 drops of tincture of morphine taken at night was justified under these circumstances and nearly always successful. Piles have been a source of much trouble and disablement on Himalayan expeditions, and all members were equipped with Anusol suppositories though only one needed them. Early attention to constipation will reduce the danger.

Snow blindness affected two Sherpas who went into the Ice Fall without goggles: this acute conjunctivitis responds to treatment with homatropine eye drops twice daily, antibiotic eye ointment, and avoidance of bright light for two or three days.

A few climbers found difficulty in sleeping at altitude, but fewer than might have been expected considering the cold and wind. Nitrazepam (Mogadon) seemed adequate and reliable, certainly superior to barbiturates whose action and side-effects at altitude are unpredictable.

Personal and Camp Kits

Personal medical kits were packed in Tupperware boxes which fit into a rucksack side pocket. They contained Fortral tablets (strong painkillers), codeine tablets, Lomotil tablets, sleeping pills (usually Mogadon), and suppositories for piles, each in a sealing plastic bag with instructions for use. There was also a selection of small wound dressings, antiseptic skin cream, lip salve, insect repellent and Lorexane shampoo (useful for lice), throat tablets, a tube of water-sterilizing tablets, local anaesthetic eye drops (for snow blindness first aid), sunburn cream, and a bandage with safety pin. In addition, tins of footpowder were issued to each climber, and morphine and tablets of Dexedrine were carried by lead climbers on the Face.

The camp kits, packed in rather larger Tupperware boxes, contained replacement stocks of most of the personal kit items but also small stocks of antibiotics (Amoxil and Septrin), Lasix, salt, vitamin and iron tablets, antibiotic eye ointments, homatropine and local anaesthetic eye drops, ear drops, an anti-congestant nasal spray, Valium tablets and aluminium hydroxide tablets, various dressings, bandages, elastoplast, scissors and a scalpel.

Health can make or break any expedition. Medical preparedness and proper drugs and equipment are clearly essential, but it is as well to remember that an expedition's health is related fairly closely to its morale which in turn depends on factors like the leadership, equipment, weather and the compatibility of its members under stress. The team member responsible for medical arrangements, whether a doctor or not, can contribute to morale by considering these principles:

1. Employ a maximum of preventive medicine beforehand, and a minimum of interference on the mountain.
2. Keep the hygiene rules to a simple minimum: a few basic rules are more likely to be observed than lists of complex and marginal instructions.
3. Make sure the medical packs contain only what is likely to be needed, that they are well understood by those who use them, and that they are in the right place at the right time.
4. Avoid unnecessary research procedures and long discussions of potential medical hazards: in fact maintain a low medical profile.

I should like to thank Dr Peter Steele who not only helped me with preparations but also gave a great deal of valuable advice about all aspects of mountain medicine from his experiences on the 1971 international expedition; Dr John Dickenson of the Shanta Bhawan Hospital, Kathmandu who advised on acute mountain sickness and more; and Dr Lindsay Strang, a staunch back-up to the expedition from his hospital in Kunde.

References

O. G. Edholme and A. L. Bacharach (editors), *Exploration Medicine* (John Wright, 1965).

Peter Steele, 'Medicine on Mount Everest', 1971 (*Lancet*, 3 July 1971, p. 32).

Bradford Washburn, 'Frostbite' (*New England Journal of Medicine*, 1962. Vol. 266, p. 974).

James Wilkerson, *Medicine for Mountaineering* (Vail-Ballon, Washington, D.C.).

Medical Equipment and Drugs

Bayer Pharmaceuticals Ltd
Beecham Products
Boots Company Ltd
Burroughs Wellcome & Co
CIBA Laboratories
Dista Products Ltd
Eli Lilly & Company Ltd
Evans Medical Ltd
Hoescht Pharmaceuticals
Imperial Chemical Industries
Lederle Laboratories
Lloyd Group of Companies
Merck, Sharp and Dohme Ltd
Parke Davis & Co. (Laboratories)
Roche Products Ltd
G. D. Searle & Co. Ltd
Smith Kline & French Laboratories Ltd
Smith & Nephew Ltd
Chas. F. Thackray Ltd
Vickers Ltd
WB Pharmaceuticals Ltd
Winthrop Laboratories

APPENDIX H

I Film
Mick Burke

Following the successful Annapurna filming we decided to follow basically the same format for Everest, namely, that we would try to sell newsreel and film rights in one package.

I.T.N., blackmailed by Don Horobin and David Nicholas, bought the newsreel rights. They in turn persuaded Jeremy Isaacs and John Edwards to buy the film rights for Thames Television.

Hopefully we would return film to Britain whilst we were on the mountain. I.T.N. sent Alan Hankinson out to Kathmandu to fix up arrangements there so that the film would pass through quickly and safely.

We would be using Ektachrome EF 7242 having a daylight ASA rating of 80. It isn't the ideal film for mountains but it did have the advantage that it could be processed at I.T.N. within an hour of arriving in London. We had the film in 50' 8mm. cassettes, 50' cassettes for the 16mm. Autoload cameras, 100' daylight spools for the Bell & Howell 70DR camera and 400' rolls for the Arriflex.

In total we had eight cine cameras. For interviews we had an Arriflex ST. It was used on either an Arriflex slip head tripod or on a special I.T.N. shoulder mount. The Arriflex went as far as Camp 2. It was left in Camp 2 with the Telestigmat lens so that Barney could film people working on the face. Above Camp 2 I used a Bell & Howell 70DR. We also had four Bell & Howell Autoload cameras and then a Bell & Howell 442 Filmosound camera and a Kodak XL33 camera.

The Arriflex had a 12–120mm. Angenieux zoom lens plus a set of Taylor Hobson lenses. The Bell & Howell 70DR had 1" and 2" Taylor Hobson lenses and an Angenieux 10mm. lens. The Autoloads all had Angenieux 10mm. lenses and one of them which was a twin turret Autoload also had a Taylor Hobson 1″ lens. The Bell & Howell had a 11–35mm. zoom and the Kodak XL33 had a 9mm. fixed lens. I also had a 300mm. Telestigmat lens for use on the Arriflex.

The Arriflex was used with a Bell & Howell Filmosound Cassette Recorder which had been modified to record a pulse from the Arriflex. Camp 2 was the highest we used this channel but the Bell & Howell 8mm. used with its own Filmosound Recorder was used at Camp 5 at 26,000 feet. We also had two Nagra SN Recorders. As we were unable to sync. them up to any of the cameras they were used purely to record wild track. They also were used up to Camp 5.

I had a lot of problems with filters due to the extreme cold. Luckily the Tiffen filters held up on the zoom and B.D.B. were able to make some of their Filtran filters up at short notice. For light meters I used my own Gossen Luna Six. For the Arriflex I had six nickel cadmium batteries. These were sent back in rotation to Kathmandu for re-charging. I had no trouble with them apart from them losing power sooner than they would at sea level. All the tape recorders were powered by Mallory cells and gave very little trouble. Our contacts for shipping our film back to Britain were built on our experiences from Annapurna. In practice we were able to get film from the mountain to London within four days.

Fortunately the only problems we had were minor ones. A battery shorting out, a battery cable with a loose connection and a main spring breaking on one of the Autoloads. The first two mendable, the third, well, we had a spare. Apart from these minor problems, the only other problem was persuading tall climbers not to put cameras outside at nights to give a little more room. I did spend quite a lot of the time at the higher camps with some piece or other of filming equipment inside my sleeping bag. It was my experience that in these very cold temperatures anything that was left outside at night was unlikely to work until it had had forty-eight hours inside a sleeping bag. I tried wherever possible not to take equipment, especially lenses, outside until the sun had made an appearance. This way I didn't have too many problems with lenses getting condensation between the elements. If I had to go outside whilst it was still very cold, I would try to introduce the lenses gradually to the cold. On the occasion when I did get condensation inside the lens, five or ten minutes holding a chamois leather to the front element would usually shift it. The light as we expected was very bright. Even with an 85 ND o6 filter, the aperture under bright sunlight was usually f8–11. Even when it was cloudy it normally opened up only one stop. To try to cut out some of the camera shake one normally gets on mountains I used wherever possible a shoulder mount which camera maintenance department at I.T.N. made.

Using the Lunasix exposure meter I generally relied on incident light readings. In mountains one constantly gets misleading readings from either the snow or the sky. To get accurate readings one has to use a little bit of commonsense. If one takes a general incident light reading faces and objects will tend to be underexposed, due to the greater influence that the snow and sky have on the meter. It is as well to slightly overexpose the snow. (I used to overexpose $\frac{1}{4}$–$\frac{1}{3}$ of a stop, generally.) However, on landscapes the snow and sky very quickly go wishy-washy, so one has to be very careful.

Back in London the film was viewed and edited by I.T.N. and they made up their news items as soon as they received the film. It was then passed on to Thames where John Edwards and Trevor Waite started to knock it into shape for the 'This Week' programme. The idea was that it would be transmitted as soon as possible after we had either succeeded or failed on the mountain. In actual fact it was transmitted one week after we had turned back from Camp 6.

In total we shot about 18,000 ft. of film and recorded about fifteen hours of tape. This has now been edited into approximately twenty news items of around three minutes each, a half-hour film for Thames, a second half-hour film for Rothmans, one of our sponsors and a six-minute film which Rothmans hope to release to cinemas in their Great Achievements series.

II Still Photography
Doug Scott

There are two lessons that the high-altitude climber learns; one, to conserve his strength by an economy of movement and the other, to compose his mind by avoiding complicated technicalities. Old hands, like Dougal Haston and Hamish MacInnes, know better than to fiddle with filters, light meters and camera lenses high on the South West Face of Mount Everest. Dougal, especially, has never had that compulsion to use his camera in the mountains. In this age of intense visual communication it is in some ways refreshing to find climbers who are not consumed with the burning need to capture on film every passing moment of a climb, and one can respect their point of view.

In Victorian times such 'vulgarities' as illustrations were usually left to the 'gutter press' as they were thought to 'encourage mental laziness which could lead to moral collapse'. In order to put over a message, there is no doubt that photographs do not demand the same intellectual effort as does the written word. This combination of Victorian snobbery and puritanism, as well as simple economics, was a feature of mountaineering publications, books and journals, up until the last war. Now, however, they become even more pictorial and glossy, and magazine editors in particular have an insatiable appetite for photographs to portray climbing events graphically.

Expedition leaders must badger their teams to use their cameras constantly, so that their sponsors are provided with adequate material. This is essential, since without the sponsors, the expedition would probably not be possible.

Apart from having the opportunity of seeing one's photographs 'in print' there was for all of us a natural wish to keep a personal photographic record of our visit to Everest. There was no holding back from taking photographs, fearing we might run short of film, since Kodak had supplied copious amounts to meet all our needs. They generously supplied:

300 rolls Kodachrome II	(A.S.A./25)
20 rolls High Speed Ektachrome	(A.S.A./160)
100 rolls Panatomic X	(A.S.A./30)
20 rolls TRI X	(A.S.A./400)

It was reassuring to know that all our pooled, exposed film was going back to the Expedition Secretary, Betty Prentice, and Wendy Bonington who between them sent the film for processing and then stamped every transparency with the photographer's name. This tedious job was only relieved for them by the opportunity to 'have a look' at our progress from the picture content. Wendy was also meticulous in sending out reports to each of us as to the quality of each slide. From her remarks we were able to make belated adjustments when necessary. The black and white material was extremely well processed by the *Observer* and all our printing was carried out by Marshall & Company of Nottingham. They produced high-standard prints at very short notice and gave us an excellent service.

Kodachrome II was far and away the most popular and effective colour film used on the expedition. It was fast enough to help produce sharp, lively results in the bright light prevailing on the mountain. Some highspeed Ektachrome was used on the approach march, to help with the dull monsoon conditions through the foothills. This was also a useful film at Base Camp whenever we wished to indulge in moonlit or fireside photography.

Exposure

Most of the team used inbuilt exposure meters. On the mountain we tended to shoot at 250 at f8–f11–f16, depending on whether the foreground was rock or snow or mixed ground. The relatively fast speed helped to compensate for camera shake, due to rapid breathing and strong winds – always a feature of this expedition. One problem on the mountain was in trying to preserve something of the texture of the snow, at the same time, attempting to show subject detail. If the faces of one's companions were in shadow then their features were usually lost. In this respect, the dark-skinned Sherpas gave noticeably poorer results, photographically, than the pale faces of the European members.

It was always a wise precaution to bracket exposures. With plenty of film available, it only required personal discipline to do this.

Camera Equipment

The majority of the expedition members used Pentax equipment, generously supplied by Rank Photographic, through the kind offices of Peter Railton their Marketing Manager. Kelvin Kent, Mick Burke and Nick Estcourt had all used Pentax equipment on the Annapurna South Face expedition. The author of this section had also used Pentax equipment on the European Mount Everest expedition.

For the actual climbing, a good combination of lenses was the interchangeable 28mm. and 85mm. Takuma lenses on two Spotmatic bodies. Providing the coloured filter is removed at the appropriate time, this equipment allows for both a full range of colour and black and white photography.

Useful extras were the 400mm. lens for long-range photographs from Base Camp into the Ice Fall, and from Camp 2 on to the Face. A 135mm. lens was found to be best for picking out detail from a range of subject matter, whilst the 85mm. was a useful lens for portraiture.

In the Western Cwm a 17mm. lens was used occasionally for special effects although, as Nick Estcourt suggested, a full panoramic view might best be achieved with a fish-eye lens placed on the floor of the Cwm.

Although none of the Pentax equipment had been winterized, none of it failed in the sub-zero temperatures. Chris Bonington used two Leica M2 cameras and two Nikon cameras. They all functioned perfectly well throughout the expedition. Ken Wilson, when he visited the expedition, used a 2¼ square camera. His Mamiyaflex Professional achieved good results throughout his short stay. His second camera was a Leica M2.

As a precaution against the S.L.R. mechanism freezing, Bonington and myself used Rollei 35 cameras from Camp 5 to Camp 6 at 27,300 feet. Whilst using two Rollei 35s at the site of Camp 6,

one of the author's cameras froze up. This was in temperatures of
—40°C and in winds of over 100 m.p.h. Unfortunately, that
particular camera had been left out of its leather case and outside
the duvet suit, for over five minutes. The film was removed back
in Britain after our return.

The Rollei 35 is, nevertheless, a very useful expedition camera,
being so compact and simple to operate and with the excellent
40mm. Zeiss lens gives very crisp definition.

One problem with changing from through-the-lens viewing to
a camera with side viewing, is that it is so easy to let thick
woollen mitts partly or wholly obscure the lens. Several potentially good photographs were lost at Camp 6 because of this.
Those members who used only Rollei 35 cameras took good care
not to allow this to happen – Graham Tiso and Dougal Haston
both achieved good results below Camp 4.

The expedition coincided with the launching by Kodak of their
new, revolutionary Pocket Instamatic range of cameras. On some
expeditions climbers have been reluctant to carry camera equipment when the combination of bad weather and altitude has
caused them to abandon all but the barest essentials in their
carrying loads. The tiny, lightweight, easy to use Pocket Instamatic was an obvious choice for the lead climbers who would be
making a summit bid. Kodak, therefore, generously supplied the
expedition with this range of cameras and Hamish MacInnes used
one all the way up the Face, to an altitude of approximately
26,500 feet. The results were excellent and since they are so
small and compact could be carried in our inside pockets and, as
a result, did not freeze up.

Results

The best results, as one might expect from the law of averages,
were produced by those photographers who ran most film through
their cameras. On the approach march several subjects were left
for someone else to cover who, in turn, also left them for someone else, with the result that leeches, for instance, were not very
well covered; neither was the full range of wild flowers covered.

In the Ice Fall, which lends itself to spectacular climbing photography, good results were obtained by all the team – even Dougal

distinguishing himself by having an excellent Ice Fall picture appear on the front page of the *Observer* newspaper!

Although results while lead climbing on the Face itself were comparatively few, they were probably better than those from previous expeditions. Because we were able to judge from previous photographs where the best camera positions were likely to be, we were able to improve on previous photographic performance.

Twice our efforts nearly ended in disaster – when Chris stepped back into a hidden crevasse in the Western Cwm when photographing his Sherpas, and when I stepped off the Face whilst photographing Mick Burke at Camp 5; I slipped down thirty feet before luckily stopping myself. Both times we were able to extricate ourselves from the misadventure.

We all had days off from photography, when it seemed inappropriate to let the camera interfere with the climbing experience. Thus few photographs were taken by actual lead climbers whilst pushing the fixed ropes up the mountain side. When there are only one or two days' lead climbing for each member, out of a three-month expedition, then perhaps he may be forgiven for wanting to climb rather than to mix it with photography.

APPENDIX I

Acknowledgements

Principal Sponsors

Members of the 1972 Everest South West Face expedition wish to express their gratitude to the following sponsors without whose support the climb could not have taken place:

British Mountaineering Council
Hodder & Stoughton
I.T.N. – Thames
Kodak

Mount Everest Foundation
Rothmans of Pall Mall
Stein and Day
The Observer

We should also like to thank the firms and individuals who contributed generously to the expedition.

We could never have organized the expedition in the short space of ten weeks and then carried it out without the help of many friends and organizations. We owe our special thanks to Pat Pirie Gordon of Williams Deacon our bankers; to Sir Jack Longland who helped us get a grant from the Sports Council; to Tony Moulam and Peter Ledeboer of the British Mountaineering Council and Tom Blakeney of the Mount Everest Foundation; to Terence O'Brien, British Ambassador in Kathmandu and Desmond Wilson, First Secretary, who both helped us get permission for the climb and assisted in so many other spheres; to the Government of Nepal; and especially to the Ministry of Foreign Affairs and the helpful officials in the department devoted to mountaineering expeditioning; to Lindsay Strang, doctor at the Kunde Hospital and Genevieve his wife, who helped us with supplies and agreed to supply us with medical back-up; to Lord Hunt who consented to be our Patron and gave me much valuable advice and support.

There are many others I may have missed. I should like to apologize if I have not thanked them personally and do so now.

INDEX